UNITED IRI

ÉMIGRÉS OF

ERIN

"Thank God I have lived to die in a free country."
Rev. Ledlie Birch

Springfarm Publishing

© 2021 S McCracken

& C Ó Ruairc

ISBN 978-1-9162576-9-6

Acknowledgements

Stephen McCracken

Firstly, I would like to acknowledge my family for their patience and help when compiling this book. I would like to dedicate this book to Katelynn and Callum McCracken.

Any who had contributed or helped are mentioned within the individual exile biographies. General contribution thanks to Kate Connolly of Ballymoney and Fiona Pegrum of Limavady.

A special thanks to Colum Ó Ruairc for suggesting and initiating this project.

Colum Ó Ruairc

On my behalf I would like to dedicate this book to Kayla, Sophia, and Ollie Dillon and baby Saorlaith O'Rourke.

I would like to acknowledge the help, support and advice from the following people during the composition of this project: Alannah Dillon, Co. Wicklow; The O'Rourke Family, Co. Wicklow; Owen J. Dunbar, Co. Wexford; Liam O'Sullivan, Co. Kilkenny; Conchobhar Ó Suilleabháin, Co. Limerick; Michael Fortune, Co. Wexford; Micheal Ó Doibhilin, Dublin; Shane Doyle, South Korea; Stephen McGarry; Turtle Bunbury, Co. Carlow; Damien Brazzil, Newfoundland; Larry Furlong, Florida; John Martin, Co. Down; Liam O'Rourke, Dublin; John Breslin (NUIG), Dr. Michael O'Connor, Co. Mayo; Peter Keenan, Co. Wicklow; Jim Conway, Co. Armagh; Eileen Coady, Nova Scotia; Stephen Coyle, Scotland; The Dillon Family, Co. Wicklow and everyone who follows and has supported the *1798 Rebellion Casualty Database* on Facebook since its conception in July 2017.

Many thanks to Stephen McCracken for co-writing this project with me. The man has tireless energy for research and a sincere passion for the period.

I am also grossly indebted for the help we received from Nicholas Dunne-Lynch, regarding the exiles who served in the Irish Legion during the Napoleonic Wars. I highly recommend that you keep an eye out for Nicholas' future work.

Go méadaí Dia thú

Timeline of Events

1690 -	The Battle of the Boyne
1697-	Penal Laws fully restored
1775-83	The wars of American Independence
1789 -	(July 14th) Beginning of the French Revolution
1791-	United Irish Society founded
1792-	(Jan 1st) *Northern Star* newspaper is born, backed by the United Irishmen
1793-	War breaks out between Britain and France
1794-	May, Proscription of the United Irishmen
1795-	Orange Order founded, encompassing the previous Orange societies. Clashes against the Defenders.
June -	The Cave Hill Oath
1796-	The formation of Yeomanry units across Ireland
December -	A French Expedition under Lazare Hoche fails to land at Bantry Bay
1797	
March 13th -	General Lake issues surrender of arms proclamation.
April -	The '*Dragooning of Ulster*' begins
May –	The Monaghan Militia destroys the *Northern Star*
Sept 18th -	Trial of William Orr of Farranshane
Oct -	William Orr is hanged at Carrickfergus.
1798-	Outbreaks of hostilities across parts of Ireland
March 12th -	The mass arrest of United Irish leaders at Oliver Bond's
May-	Martial law proclaimed across Ireland.
May 19th -	The arrest and wounding of Lord Edward Fitzgerald
May 21st -	The arrest of John & Henry Sheares leaves plans in doubt
May 23rd -	The Mail Coach signals orders mass mobilisation. The Rebellion begins
May 24th -	Kildare rises up. Mobilisations in Dublin fail. The Massacre of Dunlavin Green.
May 25th –	The Battle of Carlow fails. An attack at Hacketstown also fails.
May 26th -	The Battle of Tara fails. Wexford rises up.
May 27th -	The Wexford insurgents claim victory at Oulart Hill
May 28th -	Enniscorthy falls to the insurgents
May 29th -	The Battle of Three Rocks allows for the Wexford insurgency to take command of the county town. The Massacre at Gibbet Rath.
May 30th -	The Republic of Wexford is inaugurated.
June 1st -	Wexford insurgents are beaten at Newtowbarry (Bunclody).

4

	The garrison at nearby Carnew panic and order the massacre of prisoners in the ball alley of Carnew.
June 4th -	Government forces under Colonel Walpole obliterated at Tubberneering. Lord Edward Fitzgerald dies from his wounds.
June 5th -	The insurgents suffered horrific casualties at New Ross. The Massacre at Scullabogue.
June 7th -	The Battle of Antrim fails
June 9th -	Down rises up. The insurgents claim victory at Saintfield. The Wexford insurgents suffer heavy casualties at the Battle of Arklow.
June 10th -	Pike Sunday. County Down mobilises.
June 12th / 13th -	The Battle of Ballynahinch ends with failure for the Down insurgents.
June 14th -	Lord Cornwallis takes over the Lord-Lieutenancy of Ireland
June 19th -	The insurgents at Clonakilty, County Cork are dispersed by the Westmeath Militia during the Battle of Big Cross. The north Kildare insurgents under William Aylmer suffer defeat at Ovidstown.
June 20th -	Mjr-Gen. John Moore succeeds at destroying the South Wexford Division at the Battle of Goff's Bridge. The Wexford Bridge Massacre sees c.90 prisoners executed by rogue elements in the Wexford insurgency. General Lake's forces begin the encirclement of Enniscorthy.
June 21st -	The Battle of Vinegar Hill. The Wexford insurgents suffer dramatic losses. They divide into two groups.
June 24th -	The Battle of Castlecomer
June 25th -	The Battle of Hacketstown
June 30th -	The insurgents score a successful victory at Ballyellis, County Wexford.
July 2nd -	The insurgents defeat a strong yeomanry force at Ballyrahan, County Wicklow, but suffer loss of insurgents and resources in a wasteful siege. Father John Murphy is executed at Tullow, Co. Carlow. Rev. James Porter is executed at Greyabbey, Co. Down.
July 9th – July 12th -	The march into the midlands ends the Leinster Rebellion after the insurgents suffered harrowing and constant attacks across Counties Meath, Louth and north Dublin.
July 17th -	Henry Joy McCracken is executed in Belfast
July 21st -	The remaining leaders of the Wexford and Kildare insurgency surrender at Sallins, County Kildare. This includes William Aylmer, Hugh Ware, Edward Fitzgerald and George Lube.
Aug 22nd -	The French, under General Jean Humbert lands at Killala, Co. Mayo

Aug 23rd -	The French take Ballina, Co. Mayo
Aug 27th -	'*The Castlebar Races*' sees General Lake beaten by Humbert.
September 4th –	Humbert leaves Castlebar during a rainstorm and heads north.
September 5th –	The Battle of Carrignacat (Collooney) in County Sligo. The battle was won by the French but it hampered any time advantage it had against General Lake who was following Humbert. Insurgents of Granard in County Longford mobilise under the Denniston Brothers and is immediately quashed.
September 7th -	General Lake's cavalry under '*Black Bob*' Crauford harass the Franco-Irish rearguard as they proceed through County Leitrim. Exhaustion, hunger and mutiny befall upon the Franco-Irish forces.
September 8th -	The Battle of Ballinamuck. Humbert surrenders. Hundreds of Irish insurgents slaughtered on Edenmore Bog and at Shanmullagh.
September 16th –	James Napper Tandy and William Corbett arrive aboard '*Anacreon*' at Donegal's Rutland Island. Upon learning of Humbert's failure, they sail back to France.
September 23rd -	The Fall of Killala. The French outpost under Captain Truc surrenders. The Irish insurgents face brutality. The Downpatrick Head tragedy sees dozens of terrified locals killed by the hide tide whilst hiding in a blowhole.
October 12th -	The French fleet, under Bompard, arrive along the western coast of Donegal. They are engaged by John Borlase Warren's British flotilla resulting in a major sea-battle known as the Battle of Tory Island or the Battle of Donegal. Bompard surrenders and Theobald Wolfe Tone is captured as a result.
November 19th –	Upon being tried and awaiting execution, Wolfe Tone commits suicide at Dublin's Provost Prison.

1799

January 12th -	United Irishmen in Co. Clare assemble in Ennistymon, under Francis Lysaght and Hugh Kildea. It is brutally crushed.
February 15th –	The Siege of Derrynamuck, Co. Wicklow. Michael Dwyer escapes.
March 19th -	The State Prisoners are sent from Dublin to Fort George in Scotland, via Belfast.
August 24th –	The *Friendship* and the *Minerva* sail from Cork to New South Wales bringing the first batch of United Irish prisoners.
September 24th -	Billy Byrne of Ballymanus is executed in Wicklow

1800

April 24th -   The Newfoundland United Irish uprising is immediately put down

1801

January 1st -   The Act of Union comes into force. Ireland would not have its own parliament again for 118 years. The United Kingdom of Great Britain and Ireland commences as an entity.

March 4th -   Thomas Jefferson becomes the 3rd President of the United States. His tenure in power would prove beneficial to exiled United Irishmen.

April 27th -   Lord Cornwallis leaves office as Lord Lieutenant of Ireland. He is replaced by Earl Hardwicke.

1802

March 27th -   The Treaty of Amiens ends hostilities between France and Great Britain. It is reputed that Napoleon would not sign it until Napper Tandy was released.

July -   The State Prisoners are released from Fort George. They sail to the continent. Samuel Neilson sails to Ireland undercover and prepares to settle his affairs to go to the U.S.

1803

May 18th -   Britain declares war on France.

July 23rd -   The Emmet uprising fails in Dublin

August 24th -   James Napper Tandy dies at Bordeaux

August 29th -   Samuel Neilson dies from fever at Poughkeepsie, New York

August 31st -   The Irish Legion is commissioned by decree of Napoleon.

September 20th –   Robert Emmet is executed on Dublin's Thomas Street

December -   The end of the Wicklow Insurgency. Michael Dwyer surrenders.

1804

March 4th -   The Castle Hill uprising takes place in New South Wales. The ringleaders, who were predominantly United Irishmen, are executed.

September 20th -   Thomas Corbett & John Swiney partake in a duel at Lesneven. Corbett dies from his wounds later that evening. The event is a low point for the Irish Legion.

1809

December -   The Legion's First Battalion suffers defeat during the

Walcheren Campaign in the Lowlands. William Lawless and Terence O'Reilly escape with their Imperial Eagle and receive the Legion d'honneur in reward.

1810

April 21ˢᵗ - The Irish Legion storms the city of Astorga in Spain

April – July - The Legion partakes in the Siege of Ciudad Rodrigo

September 27ᵗʰ - The Legion's Second Battalion fight against the Connaught Rangers at the Battle of Bussaco.

1812

June 18ᵗʰ - The United States declares war on the United Kingdom. The War of 1812 officially begins. Many Irish exiles serve with distinction in the U.S. Arrmy.

1813

May 21ˢᵗ – The Irish Legion fights at the Battle of Bautzen

May 26ᵗʰ – They fight with distinction at the Battle of Hanau

August 19ᵗʰ – 21ˢᵗ – The Legion suffers tremendously to Russian cannon at the Battle of Löwenburg. John Tennant is instantly killed by a cannon-ball. William Lawless is viciously wounded. After the Saxon Campaign, Hugh Ware takes command and marches the decimated Irish Legion back to the Netherlands.

1814

April 6ᵗʰ - Napoleon Bonaparte abdicates the throne of France

August 24ᵗʰ - The British enters Washington D.C. and burns the Presidential Mansion (The White House) and the Capitol.

December 24ᵗʰ - The Treaty of Ghent ends the War of 1812 between the U.S. and the U.K.

1815

March 20ᵗʰ - Napoleon returns to Paris and resumes control.

June 15ᵗʰ - The Battle of Waterloo results in the end of the Napoleonic Wars and Napoleon is sent to St. Helena as a permanent exile.

Introduction

This project came about over a course of conversations that took place during the multiple Covid-19 lockdowns of 2020, regarding some Irish exiles of the 1798 Rebellion. We both felt that a book needed to be compiled which would feature as many of those who exiled from Ireland during the late 1790s and early 1800s. Due to the unfortunate island-wide closures of non-essential entities, we were hampered by not having archival support. Our methodology of compiling this work, in such a short space of time, involved searching through available materials and sources, personal collections, online newspapers and obituaries, online journals, family-lore and consulting several historians to find as many exiles as possible. We often read that around 30,000 people of Ireland, of all faiths and backgrounds, died as a result of violence in 1798; the majority being rebel insurgents or innocent civilians. What is rarely attached to these horrific figures is that an estimated 2000 exiles settled in the United States of America or across several European cities; c.2000 were sent to serve in His Majesty's forces in the West Indies or the Royal Navy; 318 insurgent prisoners were sent as a gift by Westminster to the King of Prussia and c.500 United Irishmen were bound to the harsh environments in the infant penal colony of New South Wales. Apart from the Great Hungers of 1718, 1740-42 and 1845-52, the seismic effect of such dramatic and violent depopulation had not been seen in Ireland since the mid-seventeenth century.

Over the course of our research, we uncovered some very interesting anecdotes about some of the exiles as well as finding many more Presbyterian church leaders, who were deeply involved in the United Irish movement, than what has been previously anticipated. The majority of those covered in this work are of northern Presbyterian background. During the American Revolution, King George III, famously called it the Presbyterian Rebellion, due to the substantial Ulster Presbyterian support towards the Colonials. Looking at what we have provided within this book, this period in our history could certainly be called the Presbyterian migration. We were struck by just how many Ministers and Probationers left from the Presbyterian Churches. As can be assumed, this book is an attempt to list those who had to leave as a result of the political and social instability during the turbulent period of 1798-1803. A letter from the Marquis of Downshire, writing to Dublin Castle in November 1796 summed up the encouragement of the Presbyterian clergy:

"the Presbyterian ministers are unquestionably the great encouragers and promoters of sedition, though as yet they have been cunning enough to keep their necks out of the halter. I think it hard that the rascals should enjoy the King's bounty to enable them to distress and destroy his government. It would be a good

time to reduce the regium donum to what it was in King William's time if not to take it away entirely."

This publication is not just a partial examination of the Presbyterian involvement during the Rebellion, although it does appear, as mentioned, that many exiles did in fact originate from the north of Ireland. It is unfortunate that the closure of the National Archives of Ireland forbids us to further clarify this point with more evidence from the remittals of court-martial sentences, held in the Rebellion Papers. In many cases, sentences were remitted to exile to America and unfortunately many of these names have not been entered here.

Further aspects of interest that we noted was some considerable ideological transitions or political hypocrisies from some United Irish exiles. The Society of United Irishmen pledged support for the abolition of slavery, universal suffrage and self-determination. What we find is some United Irishmen, in fact, became slavers or profited as a result of slavery in the southern states of America. Some of the exiles who fled to the French Republic clearly ignored the anti-democratic processes which resulted in the dismantling of the revered Republic and the creation of what would become a totalitarian empire, simply because of the promises of further French expeditions to Ireland, which never materialised. Exiles such as Thomas Addis Emmet, W.J. MacNeven, Robert Swanton and Valentine Derry would become disillusioned with France and eventually settle in America. What is fascinating is the interlapping relationships manufactured between United Irishmen in Hamburg, Paris, Philadelphia and New York. Insurgents who survived the battles of Vinegar Hill, Antrim and Ballinamuck would serve together, sit on benevolent immigrant committees or interact in business circles with the surviving former United Irish leaders like Addis Emmet, Arthur O'Connor, William Putnam McCabe and William Sampson. In some rare cases, relationships soured, resulting in fatality or wounded honour. We also designed our project to incorporate some family history to highlight the impact that many of the exiles had on the political and social aspects of their adopted countries.

Another aspect we considered was the categorisation of an Irish exile of 1798. After discussions, we agreed that we would only focus on those who were banished on terms of relocating to a country not at war with Great Britain; emigrated as a result of the turbulent period and those who fled as fugitives and who remained in their place of harbour. We decided not to include those judicially sentenced to convict or military impressed transportation. Also deducted are the banished exiles such as Michael Dwyer, Joseph Holt and the State Prisoners (Burke, Mernagh, Byrne & Devlin) who were sent, against their wishes, to New South Wales, even though they went as free settlers. They had originally anticipated being allowed to go to America but their choice was refused. We have also decided to not include post-1798 temporary exiles such as

Robert Emmet, Thomas Russell and Michael Quigley, who only resided on the European continent for a short period of time. Their intentions were for them to return to Ireland for what became the failed Emmet uprising of 1803. The same has been applied to Bartholomew Teeling, Theobald Wolfe Tone and Matthew Tone, who unfortunately never returned to France after the failed French expeditions of late 1798, therefore they were not exiles as a result of the Rebellion itself.

We hope you thoroughly enjoy this publication and the stories contained within. If you have any queries or additional information, please don't hesitate to contact us. You can find us on leading social media outlets under our respective pages.

Colum Ó Ruairc
1798 Rebellion Casualty Database
Email: 1798rcd@gmail.com

Stephen McCracken
Email: stmccracken@hotmail.com

The Émigrés

The Émigrés

ADAIR, Rev. William — Rev. William Adair was born in Co. Antrim in 1756. He was a Presbyterian Minister, based at Ballygraffan, Co. Down, and participated in the Rebellion of 1798, with references to state that he was second-in-command at Battle of Saintfield on 9 June 1798, on horseback with a green sash around his waist. An associated story related to his exile states that he escaped to America by hiding in a barrel. Other records indicate that he was captured and encouraged to exile to America. He is listed in a newspaper article as a passenger aboard the *Peggy*, in 1799. In Philadelphia, he became a minister of the Associate Reformed Presbyterian Church and was later sent to Monroe County (formed from portions of Greenbrier County, Virginia in 1799). On 10 August 1809, he married Ellen (Eleanor) Davis and they had no issue. They both died in December 1848, within days of each other, at their residence, *'Happy Retreat'*. In his will, Rev. Adair left his entire estate to his nephew William, son of James Adair. The Adair's are buried together at the Old Mount Lebanon Cemetery, Monroe County in West Virginia.

Inscription on Grave (*Pictured*)

"Sacred to the Memory of the Rev. William Adair and Ellen his wife. The former of Whome (sic) departed this life on the 11th day of December 1848 and the latter on the 8th day of Decr 1848 Each aged 90 years. Born in the same year and after living together as man and wife for more than 40 years, they died in the same week. Lovely and pleasant in their lives and in their death, they were not divided."

ADRAIN, Hugh — Hugh Adrain, a Belfast based printer, was arrested in July 1798, on charges of treasonable offences. He was subsequently sent to New Geneva, a transit camp in Co. Waterford. Having requested that he be subject to banishment, the authorities considered his case, however, it unknown where he exiled to.

ADRAIN, Robert - *The Rebel Mathematician.*

Robert Adrain was born on 30 September 1775 at Carrickfergus, Co. Antrim. Adrian was a learning the ropes at the Newtownards Presbyterian Church and held school classes. He got involved as one of the Co. Down United Irish leaders and he was elected to lead a company of United Irishmen leading a company of insurgents. Evidence conflicts on how he received a serious back wound at the Battle of Saintfield in Co. Down, on 9 June 1798. Some sources state he was piked in the back by his own followers. Adrain and his wife, **Nancy Pollock**, emigrated to the United States after the birth of a daughter in 1799. They settled at Princeton, New Jersey, and Adrain briefly became a schoolmaster at Princeton Academy before moving to York in Pennsylvania. Here, he became Principal of York County Academy. Whilst in this position, Adrain contributed to the mathematical journal, the '*Mathematical Correspondent.*' By 1828, Adrain had become vice-Provost of the University of Pennsylvania, and one of the influential figures to work in the field of mathematics in the United States. His most significant work, the method of least squares, was first published in 1809, to help reduce errors in observation. Robert Adrain died at his farm in New Brunswick, New Jersey, USA, on 19 August 1843.

Adrain had a large family. One of his sons, Garnett Adrain, a Democrat, was elected to represent New Jersey's Third Congressional District in the United States House of Representatives, serving from 4 March 1857 to 3 March 1861. After serving two terms, and being a vocal opponent of secession, he declined to run for a third term.

ALEXANDER, Samuel – Alexander was born at Ballyboe in Co. Donegal. He was appointed Sheriff's Deputy and joined the United Irishmen as a captain. He would drill 150 men at a place named **"Laird's Lea"** (field at the Castle farm in Newtowncunningham). After the Rebellion, Alexander went into hiding and sailed from the city port of Londonderry to Philadelphia. Once in the

United States Alexander succumbed to the rampant yellow fever epidemic, within eighteen months of arriving.

ALLEN, John – Allen was born in 1777 in Dublin City to Christopher Allen and Johanna Shaw. Allen worked as a woollen-draper from his residence at 80 Francis Street in Dublin. He appears to have been a militant United Irishman and was accused of killing a loyalist outside Astley's Theatre on Kevin Street, for having demanded that "***God Save the King***," be played after a performance. Allen was persuaded to leave Ireland by Lord Edward Fitzgerald and joined Arthur O'Connor and Fr. James Coigly in England to join in their mission to sail from Margate to France. This mission failed and Allen was held in the Tower of London to await trial for treason. He was eventually acquitted during the Maidstone trial which saw Fr. Coigly sentenced to death.

His whereabouts are unknown during the period of the Rebellion, however, he was back in Dublin in early 1799 working at his profession at 36 College Green. During this period, Allen helped reconstruct the shattered United Irish organisation in Dublin and eventually became a close associate of Robert Emmet. During the summer of 1802, Allen, under the alias of 'Captain Brown,' joined young Emmet on an unsuccessful mission to press the Spanish Government to support an Irish insurrection. After the failure of the Emmet uprising on 23 July 1803, Allen, one of its chief-organisers, fled Ireland and settled in France. Upon arrival, he joined the Irish Legion, having been commissioned as Lieutenant. In March 1810, Allen, by then a Captain of a company of *voltiguer* sharpshooters in the Legion's Second Battalion, was attached to Junot's 8th Corps of the Army of Portugal. A siege befell upon the walled city of Astorga. On 21 April 1810, Allen led a forlorn hope against the breach with his company suffering many casualties, including his drummer boy, who kept beating his drum after losing both legs. The Spanish defenders surrendered on the following day. Allen was hailed as a hero of France and was awarded the *Légion d'honneur* and would eventually receive further promotion to Colonel. In March 1811, Allen was captured by Spanish guerrilla fighters and brought to Cadiz, suffering sabre wounds from his Spanish captors in the process. He, William Dowdall and Sandy Devereux eventually escaped in 1812. At the end of

The walls of Astorga in Spain, upon which John Allen led a successful forlorn hope on 21 April 1810.

the Napoleonic Wars, Allen retired to Tours on half-pay before eventually settling at Caen where he died on 10 February 1855.

ALLEN, Robert – Robert Allen of Latimerstown, Co. Wexford, married

Mary Carty on 12 September 1794. The story of the Allen family emigrating to the United States was told by their grandson in the 1941 publication, *"The Hall Family of West River and kindred families."* He stated that they emigrated to the United States just prior to the 1798 Rebellion due to their liberal principles. They would become wealthy shipowners and merchants who settled primarily in Maryland.

ALLEN, Samuel – (1776-1862) Samuel Allen was

born on 12 January 1776 at Templepatrick, Co. Antrim. He was implicated in the Rebellion of 1798 and had been captured and charged for treason. The following year, he married **Jane Brown**, daughter of Stafford Brown of Ballybay in Antrim. In 1821, they decided to emigrate to the United States, travelling via Montreal and Lake Champlain. Within a year, they bought a farm at Ryegate, Vermont. Once they had settled, Samuel sent word for the remaining family members in Ireland to travel over. In the *History of Ryegate*, it states that Samuel had been a great reader and a self-taught mathematician. Samuel Allen died on 12 February 1862 and was interred at Hillside Cemetery in South Ryegate.

ANDERSON, Archibald – Anderson was tried at Maghera, Co. Derry,

on 16 June 1798, on charges of carrying arms during the mobilisation of insurgents in that town on 8 June 1798. Anderson pled guilty and was sentenced to be hanged and decapitated, however, this was remitted to voluntary banishment.

ANDERSON, John – It is recorded within, "*Forgetful Remembrance – Social Forgetting and Vernacular Histiography of a Rebellion in Ulster*" that John Anderson had escaped to America and settled in Cincinnati, Ohio. Anderson died in 1853 at the age of 101 years. Anderson had served as schoolmaster at Broughshane in Co. Antrim when he participated in the 1798 Rebellion.

ARMSTRONG, Walter – Walter Armstrong is briefly mentioned in a short biography about Thomas Armstrong, was a farmer in York Township in the State of Indiana in the United States. The family history claims that the Armstrong's had been driven out of Scotland by Mary, Queen of Scots, and later came to America on account of their participation in the Irish Rebellion of 1798. Armstrong, who was born in Enniskillen, Co. Fermanagh in September 1783, was a cooper by profession and a Presbyterian in faith, who first settled in Pittsburgh, Pennsylvania, before moving to Franklin County in Indiana. He was the son of William Armstrong and Margaret Stainer Latimore (1742-1826). Armstrong married Hanna Kautz who gave birth to four boys and a girl. One of Walter's sons was First-Lieutenant, William Armstrong, a student of West Point Academy, who was killed in September 1847 at Molino, near Mexico City during the Mexican-American War. Walter Armstrong died on 19 December 1849 at Vevay, Switzerland County, Indiana.

ARNOLD, Rev. John – Arnold was pastor of the First Ballybay Presbyterian Church in Co. Monaghan. He fought alongside the insurgents at the Battle of Rebel Hill, near Bailieborough, Co. Cavan, in late August 1798, in the aim of cutting off Crown forces who were travelling from Louth to face Humbert. Arnold eventually fled to America and whilst his property was being sold, the seal of the local United Irishmen branch was found to have been in his possession.

AYLMER, William – Aylmer was born in 1778 to Charles Aylmer and Esmay Piers of Painstown, Co. Kildare. Aylmer, a United Irishman and former officer of the Kildare Militia, took command of the north Kildare insurgency, basing their location in the bogs of Timahoe. He led the insurgents on sorties to Kilcock and Maynooth and commanded the insurgents during the Battle of Ovidstown (19 June 1798). After the Wexford and Wicklow insurgents failed in their march to the midlands, Aylmer, Edward Fitzgerald, Hugh Ware, Bryan McDermott and other insurgent commanders entered into negotiations with Dublin Castle to finally end the rebellion in Leinster. On 21 July 1798, the leadership formally surrendered and were conveyed to Dublin Castle. After his release in 1799, Aylmer,

originally listed on the Banishment Act, left Ireland for the continent and landed at Hamburg and made his way to Vienna, the capital of the Kingdom of Austria. Here he enlisted in the Austrian Army and would serve with distinction during the Napoleonic Wars against the French. Being a competent horseman, Aylmer (*pictured*) was attached as a cadet in the 5th Light Dragoons. He was awarded a lieutenancy in 1804 in the 10th Cuirassiers. On 22 April 1809, during the great Battle of Eckmühl, Aylmer was wounded and left on the battlefield. He was captured by the French and later exchanged, gaining the rank of Captain.

As Europe descended into peace in 1814, Aylmer was attached to the Austrian delegation team under Klemens von Metternich, who travelled to London to participate in the peace talks. Lord Castlereagh, the British Secretary of State for Foreign Affairs, would have recognised Aylmer, or at least remembered his name from Castle correspondence during the 1798 Rebellion, when he was Chief-

Secretary of Ireland. Despite his banishment, Aylmer would meet the Prince Regent and also engage in the sport of fencing with British officers.

Aylmer returned home to Ireland, having visited his childhood friend and fellow insurgent leader, Hugh Ware, in France. Interestingly, both had fought on opposite sides during the Napoleonic Wars, but their shared oppression during the 1798 Rebellion had solidified their friendship. Having been officially discharged from the Austrian service in 1816, Aylmer would reside at Painstown on his brother's land. In 1818-1819, he answered the call from John Devereux to participate in an Irish Legion to support Simon Bolivar's independence wars in South America with promises of gaining large wealth in the process. Aylmer enlisted after purchasing a commission in the Legion, alongside Francis Burdett O'Connor, the son of United Irishman, Roger O'Connor, and Morgan O'Connell, the son of the '*Emancipator.*' On 25 September 1819, this Irish Legion landed at Margarita, off the Venezuelan coast. The biggest task that Aylmer faced as the de-facto commander was to maintain discipline. The Legion suffered from poor drinking water, mutiny, disease and boredom, caused by the lack of use from Bolivar, which caused many volunteers to return to Ireland. In March 1820, he led what was left of the Irish Legion at the Battle of Riohacha and received wounds which failed to heal in the humid climate. Aylmer was transported to Jamaica and died there from his wounds on 20 June 1820.

BAILEY, William – William Bailey, a native of Co. Down, was a captain in the East India Company throughout the 1790s. Bailey was a member of the London Corresponding Society, which had entered into an alliance with the United Irishmen in early 1798, through the valuable labours of Benjamin Binns and Fr. James Coigly. Bailey travelled to Dublin in the spring of 1798 and liaised with the various United Irish leaders. Having remained in Ireland throughout the 1798 Rebellion, Bailey fled to France before travelling to New York, where he started to practice Law.

The BARBER Family – After the Battle of Antrim members of the Muckamore / Killead Presbyterian Barber family had to flee to America. Most notable was, **Henry Barber,** who was the son of John Barber and Hannah Read. Other Barber exiles are noted to have settled in Pennsylvania also, **John** and **Samuel.** It is unproven if these three were brothers. A notable member of this family worth mentioning is Rev. Samuel Barber of Rathfriland, Co. Down, who hailed from Killead, Co. Antrim. Samuel Barber was educated at the University of Glasgow and was licensed to preach in 1763. Rev. Barber, although not a United Irishman was a fervent supporter of emancipation, abolition and liberal reforming. He was arrested in 1798 on suspicion of being involved in the Rebellion but no evidence could convict him. Rev. Barber died in September 1811, aged 74 years.

BARKER, William – A brewer and merchant who hailed from Enniscorthy, Co. Wexford, Barker's story is somewhat confusing as a result of several mixed accounts. He was born c.1759 to Arthur Barker and Sarah Sherlock. Miles Byrne briefly described Barker in his memoirs.

"Another gentleman, one of the purest Irish patriots that ever lived, joined the people's camp at Enniscorthy on the 29th of May (1798). William Barker was a wealthy resident of the town, connected not only with all the Catholic aristocracy of the county, but nearly allied to the first Protestant families of the town and county; not belonging to any political society whatever, he did not hesitate to take a command, when a chance offered to set Ireland independent and free. He had, in my mind, more merit than almost any-one who took part in this war."

Barker had military experience, having served in Walsh's Regiment in the French Army in the 1780s. This valuable experience was strangely not embraced by the insurgents. Barker recommended an immediate attack upon what was then a poorly defended New Ross instead of Wexford Town. His recommendation was not heeded and of course the insurgents paid dearly for it on 5 June 1798 with mass casualties during the Battle of Ross. During the insurgent occupation of Co. Wexford, Barker held a position on the Committee of Public Safety in the scorched and ruined remains of Enniscorthy. As the sun rose on the morning of 21 June 1798, Barker and Fr. Mogue Kearns commanded the insurgent positions at Duffry Gate in Enniscorthy. They faced heavy attacks from Major-General Henry Johnson's forces until they were forced to fall back on the main bridge, where they organised a redoubt which saw some of the bloodiest moments of the Battle of Vinegar Hill. The insurgent leader, Thomas Cloney, later wrote of Barker, describing this defence: *"Mr. William Barker, a gentleman who had seen service on the continent, exhibited prodigies of valour, and lost an arm by holding his post to the last on the bridge; but the resistance was altogether unavailing against so powerful a force of regular troops, supplied with numerous artillery, and commanded by able generals."*

The seriously wounded Barker was relieved of his command by Fr. Kearns, who in turn also received a wound. Barker's shattered arm was later amputated by an English surgeon during house arrest. Without much time to heal, Barker was cast into the damp and overcrowded Wexford Gaol. Barker was tried by court-martial in January 1799 but was acquitted of all charges. Fearing the authorities would pin more charges on him, his brother, Arthur, immediately organised a ship to take the family to the continent. Upon arriving at Hamburg, the Barker Family set off for Paris where William was interviewed by the French Minister of Foreign Affairs regarding facts that could suit a renewed French expedition. They resided at St. Germain-en-Laye for a short period before settling in Morlaix, near the port of Brest. Barker would join the Irish Legion and hold the rank of Captain. Suffering dearly from wounds and the fever during the Walcheren Campaign of 1809, William Barker died in 1811 at Bois-le-Duc in Holland.

The Bridge at Enniscorthy, Co. Wexford, now known as William Barker Bridge. Note Vinegar Hill in the distance

BARR, John – Barr, born c.1766, was a participant at the Battle of Antrim, on June 7th 1798, which resulted in him fleeing to America. Barr is also recorded to have been a member of a Masonic Lodge, situated on Farranshane Road, the home area of William Orr, who was executed at Carrickfergus in October 1797. Notes claim that the Antrim Lodge paid for Barr's voyage and looked after him in the United States. He is remembered today by Antrim Masonic Lodge which is now situated in Antrim Town. Barr settled at Sugar Grove Township, Warren County in Pennsylvania, erecting a house upon a summit of a hill, living with his wife, Sarah McFall. The *History of Warren County* contains a small anecdote about Barr: ***"Among his personal possessions was an old-fashioned 'bulls-eye' watch, more weighty than accurate. He was, for some reason, perpetually annoyed by questions as to the time of day, to which he invariably replied: 'Six past nine, and be damned to ye."*** Barr died on 9 January 1839 and was interred at Cherry Hill Cemetery.

BARRET, Edward – Barret had been an insurgent who was tried and sentenced to death for his role of leading insurgents during the 1798 Rebellion. The *Gazette of the United States* (5 August 1800) recorded the following advertisement: ***"Capt. Delano, late of the brig, Bellona from Sligo, Ireland, thinks it a duty he owes to the public to inform, that a person by the name of Edward Barret, embarked on board his vessel amongst a number of other passengers for this country. Sometime after he failed, he found out that this Barret had escaped prison, where he had been confined, and was under sentence of Death, for leading a party of United Irishmen; and that there was a reward of 100 guineas offered by Government for his apprehension. This knowledge would not probably have come to the ears of Capt. Delano, had not Barret's infamous conduct while on board the Belona, led to an inquiry who he was – While some of the passengers***

on board, as well as the captain, were treated in the most villainous manner, he had the address, with some other, almost to persuade them to put the captain in irons, and take charge of the vessel without any provocation. Captain Delano is induced to believe, that this dangerous fellow is now in this city (New York City)."

BARRY, William – William Barry was a Presbyterian from Magherafelt, Co. Derry, or a scion of the Barry family of Killyfaddy. Barry was arrested in June 1798 and tried as a United Irishman and for participating in the Rebellion. He was sentenced to banishment. In October 1798, he sailed aboard the *Pallas*, however it had to turn back to Ireland due to storms. It is unknown if he succeeded in his banishment to the United States of America.

BASHFORD, Thomas Gunning – Bashford was a Protestant shopkeeper from Belfast. After Robert Simms resigned his commission before the outbreak of the Antrim Rebellion, Bashford denounced him and the Ulster Executive for their poor performance in preparations to rise up. Bashford called for an immediate outbreak of Rebellion in early June 1798. He was proclaimed in the Fugitive Act of 1798 and was able to escape to Massachusetts. He became a merchant and successfully traded with southern state ports and the West Indies.

BEATTIE, James – James Beattie was born on 12 January 1776, at Kells in Beaton Wall in Co. Antrim, the son of a farmer and member of the reformed Presbyterian Church. He emigrated to America in 1801. In 1804, he settled at Ryegate in Caledonia County, Vermont. He married Margaret Gillespie, who had ancestral connections to the Siege of Derry. They were hard working, God-fearing Reformed Presbyterian members of the community. James Beattie died on 30 December 1866 and was buried in Blue Mountain Cemetery in Ryegate Corner.

Alexander Mitchell Beattie (1828-1907 *pictured*) was a son of James Beattie and Margaret Gillespie. He served in the Union Army during the American Civil War as Captain and commander of Company F, 3rd Vermont Volunteer Infantry. He was awarded the Congressional Medal of Honor for his bravery at the Battle of Cold Harbor, Virginia on 5 June 1864. His citation reads: ***"Removed, under a hot fire, a wounded member of his command to a place of safety".***

CAPT ALEXANDER M. BEATTIE

BEATTIE, William – William Beattie of Knockbracken, near Belfast, settled in Vermont County, New York. He along with other Beattie family members fled from Ireland for having participated in the rebellion of 1798.

BEATTY, Rev. James – Although sympathetic to the cause of the United Irishmen, Beatty was actually accosted twice during the Wexford Rebellion by insurgents and at one point was sentenced to be executed. He was a brother-in-law of Rev. Gurley, who also left Wexford after the Rebellion. With Co. Wexford in ruin, Beatty sold his possessions in Ireland and settled with the Gurley's in Liverpool before emigrating to New York. He lived for ten years in Connecticut.

BELL, Thomas – Thomas Bell was a United Irishmen from Co. Tyrone, who emigrated to America immediately after the 1798 Rebellion. He settled in Amelia County in Virginia. In 1800, he married a young local lady who unfortunately passed away within months. After a brief business trip, Bell returned home and also died from the fever, at the youthful age of twenty-two years.

BINNS, Benjamin Pemberton – The oldest of the Binns brothers, Benjamin Binns was born on 18 January 1771 to ironmonger, John Binns and Mary Pemberton. After the death of his father in 1774, Benjamin and his younger brother, John Binns, had a sour relationship with their mother's new husband, George McEntegarte, and they decided to finish their education under the guidance of their grandfather. Benjamin completed his apprenticeship as a plumber. In April 1794, Benjamin travelled to London with John to advance their careers, but instead entered radical underground politics in London, similar to those of the United Irishmen. Benjamin Binns would become the Under-Secretary of the London Corresponding Society and one of its chief couriers. Binns was arrested in June 1798 and was held at Newgate Prison in London and later Dorchester Prison. After his release, Binns returned to Ireland and attempted to establish a business at Bray, Co. Wicklow, which eventually failed. In March 1817, suffering from agoraphobia

For the Pennsylvania Enquirer.
APPEAL TO NATURALIZED IRISHMEN.
You have assisted others often at the polls. No prove true to him who never deserted you. Suppo one of the few surviving men of '98. A Revolutio ary Officer, and a brother soldier of LORD EDWARD the faithful companion and friend of the Rev. Fa ther Coigley; the admirer of DANIEL O'CONNELL and the devoted Son of Erin. I have been
"Persecuted, but not forsaken;
"Thrown down, but not destroyed."
I have risked all for my country, and glory in th sacrifice; and would again, (though advanced in years should the opportunity present itself.
AMERICANS, IRISH, ENGLISH, DEMOCRATS, I have some claims upon you all. Five-and-thirty years faithful services and loss of property; three tedious years of solitary confinement in England, in '9 without TRIAL BY JURY, for advocating those princi ples that are now supported by the BRITISH MINIS TER himself—The Rights of Man my aim; the l dependence of my country the object. I love my cou try—or, more justly speaking, "THE LIBERTY o MANKIND;" and no American will think the less me for such avowal.
Then to the Polls, fellow-citizens. I call on yo for your suffrages, and you may be assured No tr Irishman was ever wanting in Gratitude.
Your faithful friend,
BENJAMIN PEMBERTON BINNS.

23

as a result of his tenure in prison, Binns eventually joined his younger brother in the United States and continue to work as a plumber.

Although he did not participate in American politics, it is interesting to note that some American newspapers contain various inputs from Benjamin P. Binns, where he is particularly defensive of the ideals and values of the United Irishmen and especially those who died for their cause, an example being Fr. James Coigly. Binns, an emotive and rallying writer, also wrote the poem, '*The Burning of Scullabogue Barn*,' which was later included on R.R. Madden's '*Literary Remains of the United Irishmen*.' Binns died on 27 January 1844, at his residence on North Eighth Street in Philadelphia. He was firstly interred at the Moravian Burial Plot, then Monument Cemetery and now rest at Lawnview Cemetery in Montgomery County, Pennsylvania.

BINNS, John – Binns was born in Dublin on 22 December 1772 to John Binns and Mary Pemberton. He grew up in affluent circumstances due to his father's successful ironmonger business. He was also closely related to '***Long John***' Binns, a radical merchant who was close friends with James Napper Tandy. Binns' father would perish whilst crossing the Irish Sea in 1774 and his mother's remarriage to George McEntegarte, saw young Binns move to Drogheda, Co. Louth. Suffering from mistreatment from their step-father, John and Benjamin Binns fled from Drogheda in 1782 and were taken into care by their grandfather in Dublin. Having received excellent education, Benjamin Binns entered an apprenticeship as a plumber whilst John became a chandler and soap manufacturer. In 1793, both brothers had joined the Society of United Irishmen, most probably influenced by their uncle,
George Binns. In April 1794, the Binns brothers travelled to London to work in their respective trades and eventually joined the London Corresponding Society, a liberal relative club that was politically similar to the United Irishmen. John Binns rose within the society's ranks with his oratory skills and agitating Paineite politics. On 11 March 1796, Binns was arrested on charges of sedition, however, he would eventually be acquitted. In 1796, he was one of the founding members of the London branch of the United Irishmen, which eventually morphed into the United Britons or United Englishmen. Binns' radicalism saw him enter into the conspiracies of 1798. He promised the Dublin Executive of the United Irishmen that he would rally support towards insurrection in Ireland. On 28 February 1798, Binns was arrested on charges of treason at Margate in southern England, along with John Allen, Arthur O'Connor and Fr. James Coigly. The group had planned to sail to France to communicate to the French Directory

regarding support for their insurrections and to encourage a French expedition to Britain. The trial at Maidstone exposed much connections between liberal Whig MPs and these radicals; Binns being close friends with Francis Burdett MP.

All, but Fr. Coigly, were acquitted, with Coigly being sacrificed to the gallows. When the United Irish suffered greatly during and after the 1798 Rebellion, Westminster cracked down hard on the societies based in England. On 16 March 1799, whilst in the process of rebuilding the societies, John Binns was arrested at Clerkenwell and incarcerated. In March 1801, Binns was released and on 1 July 1801, sailed from Liverpool to Baltimore in the United States aboard the *Orion*. John Binns settled in New York and joined the Society of Theophilanthropists, which advocated for free-thinking, radical republican politics. Binns was an avid and outspoken supporter of Thomas Jefferson and faced much attack from President John Adams' Federalist faction, who espoused nativist rhetoric and were outspoken against the troublesome United Irish emigrés settling in the United States. In March 1802, Binns moved to Northumberland in Pennsylvania, where radical thinkers like Joseph Priestley resided. He established a newspaper, the *Republican Argus*, which was pro-

Jefferson and became a successful paper amongst the Democratic Party. In 1806, Binns was married to Mary Anne Bagster by his friend and associate, Dr. James Priestley, and he later joined the Church of the United Brethren. Between 1807 and 1829, Binns edited the *Democratic Press*, the leading paper of Pennsylvania that supported the Democratic Party.

However, Binns used his influence to denounce Andrew Jackson in his strive to become President in 1824 and openly supported President John Quincy Adams during the election. The vicious verbal attacks against Jackson saw Binns suffering physical attacks and death threats in return. Binns would hold office as alderman in the city of Philadelphia for nearly two decades. Interestingly, whilst owning black slaves, Binns advocated that the US Federal Government should encourage legislation which would compensate slavers and allow the slaves to return to Africa. From America, Binns continued to hold views on the issues of Ireland, later claiming that national independence via physical force revolution was counterproductive and welcomed the Catholic Emancipation of 1829. In the later years of his participation in Philadelphian politics, Binns severely opposed the conservative

'Know Nothing Party' and their nativist attacks on Irish immigrants who were escaping from the starvations and diseases of the 1845-52 period as an entity similar to the Orange Order. John Binns retired and completed his autobiography in 1854. He died on 16 June 1860 in Philadelphia and was interred at Monument Cemetery. Today, his remains lie amongst those of his large family and his brother, Benjamin, at Lawnview Cemetery, Montgomery County in Pennsylvania.

BIRCH, George, Dr. – Dr. George Birch was a loyalist yeoman, from near Saintfield, Co. Down. Interestingly, his two eldest sons were members of the United Irishmen. In 1798 these sons fought with the insurgents at the Battle of Saintfield, on 9 June 1798. During the battle, one son was shot and the other, George Birch Jr, escaped when the Down Rebellion ended. When the authorities found him, he was dressed as a lady in a dressing gown, with his mother claiming him to be a daughter. Dr. Birch used his influence with Dublin Castle to get his son clear of the charges, however as a result he was compelled to go to the East Indies where he became a Lieutenant in the Bengal Infantry. He passed away in 1808 unmarried.

BIRCH, Rev. Thomas Ledlie – Thomas Birch, was born at Gilford in Co. Down in 1754. He was the Presbyterian minister of Saintfield, Co. Down. He graduated from the University of Glasgow and was ordained at Saintfield in 1776. He had been a prominent Freemason and a chaplain to the local Volunteer unit. His liberal politics had been public since he published his support for the American Revolution, something which would hamper any promotion in his profession. Birch called his manse *'Liberty Hill'* and the Society of United Irishmen in Co. Down first met under his chairmanship in January 1792. In

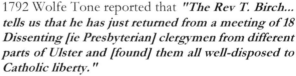

1792 Wolfe Tone reported that ***"The Rev T. Birch... tells us that he has just returned from a meeting of 18 Dissenting [ie Presbyterian] clergymen from different parts of Ulster and [found] them all well-disposed to Catholic liberty."***

In 1796, he struggled with many of his congregation over his support for Catholic Emancipation. In 1797, Birch, who was distrusted by local conservatives and loyalists, was arrested on evidence from an informer, Nicholas Price, but was eventually acquitted, on the conditions that he swear to an oath of allegiance, which did not conflict with his conscience in doing so. In April 1798, Birch was once again facing trouble for attempting to bribe Joseph Harper into not prosecuting a United Irishman. The charge was dropped when Harper was assassinated on a journey to Belfast. On the morning of 9 June 1798, a warrant came for the arrest of Rev. Birch, thus sparking the Battle of Saintfield. On Pike Sunday, as the insurgents amassed at Creevy Rocks, Birch preached from Ezekiel – *"Let every man come forth with his slaying weapon in his hand"*.

He also gave a stirring speech to the large congregation, which contained the following excerpt: *"We have grasped the pike and musket and fight for the right against might: to drive the bloodhounds of King George the German King beyond the seas. This is Ireland, we are Irish and we shall be free"*

After the insurgency were defeated at the Battle of Ballynahinch, Birch was arrested and was brought to Downpatrick and charged with treason at a military court. Rev. Birch's brother, George Birch, having remained a loyal yeoman throughout the Rebellion, encouraged the local magistrate to consider his brother for self-exile. Upon sentencing, Birch exclaimed,

"I cannot be any longer either happy or useful in this country."

Birch emigrated to Philadelphia, with many of his congregation. Suffering with homesickness for quite a while. His preaching would evolve into evangelical fervor, which caused some consternation with his congregation. Accused and eventually acquitted for adultery, Birch suffered from rejection by the General Assembly of the Presbyterian Church in Philadelphia and also the Ohio Presbytery. Birch firmly believed this was due to his public support for Jeffersonian politics. He would relocate to Washington County in western Pennsylvania. In his later years, he composed his memoirs, which were published posthumously in 1834. On his death-bed, on 12 April 1828, his last noted words to the Killrea born Rev. Lamont were:

"Thank God I have lived to die in a free country."

BISHOP, Thomas & William - Thomas and William
Bishop of Ballymorran, Killinchy, Co. Down, were court-martialled on 10 July 1798 at Downpatrick, charged with treasonable and seditious activities. Having both pled guilty, they were allowed to enter into recognisances to transport themselves to a country not subject to the Crown. A report from November 1798 stated that the

"FOSTERED UNDER THY WING, WE DIE IN THY DEFENCE."

brothers were on bail. It is unknown where in America they went to.

BLACK, Rev John – John Black (1768 - 1849) was born in 1768 in Ahogill, Co. Antrim, to John Black and Margaret McKibben. After graduating with a theology degree from the University of Glasgow, he returned to Ireland under the guardianship of the Rev. Gibson to prepare for his own ministry. In October 1797, after the death of William Orr, Black, like many others left Ireland for the United States, having been suspected of being a member of the United Irishmen. A recent arrival to Philadelphia in 1798, he immediately joined the radial scene and joined the fledgling Society of United Irishmen in the city. He taught the classics and aligned himself with the college in Philadelphia. In 179,9 he was licenced to preach by the Reformed Presbytery and was ordained in 1800 to the Ohio congregation. He was also  engaged as a classical teacher, and, in 1820, was elected Professor of Latin and Greek in the Western University of Pennsylvania. He resigned in 1832, allowing him to visit Europe. He was President of Duquesne College for one year. Rev. Black died at his Pittsburgh residence, on 25 October 1849.

BLACK, Thomas – Black was born in July 1766 in the Catholic Parish of Donoughmore, Co. Down and was a veteran of the 1798 Rebellion who attempted to flee to Cuba. He transferred mid-journey aboard a ship that travelled to St. John in New Brunswick, Canada, arriving there in November 1799. There he became involved as a drysalter and converted to the Anglican faith. Black died in Old Town on 22 February 1879, at the advanced age of 113 years.

BLACKBURN, Joseph – Blackburn was described as a young farmer who led the Carnmoney insurgents during the Battle of Antrim on 7 June 1798. He escaped to America and was active with other United Irishmen in New York.

BLENNERHASSETT, Harman -

Harman Blennerhassett was born on 8 October 1765 to Conway Blennerhassett and Elizabeth Lacy in Hampshire, England, and was reputedly a cousin of the renowned Emmet Family. He was raised and educated in Co. Kerry, on his family's 7,000-acre Castle Conway estate. Blennerhassett studied law at Trinity College, Dublin and was admitted to the Irish bar in 1790. After the death of his father in 1792, he inherited the vast estate. Politically liberal, he became a United Irishman and in 1794 he controversially married his niece, Margaret Agnew. After a number of political engagements, family disputes and attacks for his marriage, Blennerhassett felt the need to self-exile in 1797 to a land where as a newspaper later recorded:

"breath the air of freedom and enjoy the sweets of liberty undisturbed by spies and unmolested by informers".

Harman Blennerhassett, having sold his Kerry estate to Baron Ventry, he used the funds to purchase a plantation on an island on the Ohio River in the State of Virginia. Not only was he respected by the community as a charitable individual, he was also quite studious with a love of chemistry, music and astronomy. In 1798, he built the Blennerhassett mansion which was considered the largest and most beautiful home in what was then the frontier. His charity to his neighbours was well renowned. He once loaned money to a neighbour who then lost his possessions to a fire. Harman invited him to attend a dinner and once the meal was over, he cleared his visitor's debts. Of course, his humanity and former liberal views did not extend to abolitionism, as he was a noted owner of black slaves.

He befriended and became a business partner with former U.S. Vice President, Colonel Aaron Burr. One such business initiative undertaken between the partnership was ship building for an expedition. This expedition did not materialise and the angered and unpaid men that had been recruited ransacked the Blennerhassett homestead which was totally destroyed.

Blennerhassett and Burr were arrested and faced charges of conspiracy to annex Texas from Mexico or to create a new nation in the West. Having become disillusioned with America, the Blennerhassetts relocated firstly to Montreal then onto Bath, England to stay with relations. On 2 February 1831 Harman Blennerhassett died on the Isle of Guernsey.

BLENNERHASSETT, Margaret *neé Agnew*

Margaret Agnew was born in 1771 in Bishop Auckland in England. Her father, Robert Agnew, had served as Lieutenant-Governor of the Isle of Man. After her marriage to her uncle, Harman Blennerhassett, Margaret followed him into political exile to the United States. After the Blennerhassett's left America in financial ruin, they resided in England until Harman's death in 1831. In 1842, the widow Blennerhassett returned to America and unsuccessfully attempted to receive compensation from the U.S. Government for the damage incurred at Blennerhassett Island. She was left desolate and relying on the charity of the family of Thomas Addis Emmet for the rest of her remaining life. In 1842, she died in New York City and was interred within the Emmet vault at Marble Cemetery in New York. The famed Blennerhassett mansion was reconstructed in 1981 by the State of West Virginia and now operates as a State Park on Blennerhassett Island (*pictured*).

BOLTON, Lyndon

Bolton, who originated from Monkstown Castle in south Dublin, was born in 1760 to William '*Black Billy*' Bolton and Mary Lyndon. Having become a United Irishman, he was forced to flee to Hamburg in 1798. Bolton, who was recorded by Samuel Turner, as a "***most infamous*** *blackguard*," would remain in Hamburg until at least 1803, having helped direct United affairs on the continent, yet financially struggling in the meantime. His large family with **Jane Carpenter** included: Richard Bolton, Rev. Lyndon Henry Bolton (born in 1801), Elinor Bolton, Jemima Maria Bolton, Abraham Bolton, Jane Bolton, Charlotte Bolton, Emily Bolton, William Gordon Bolton, Belinda Bolton and Edward Bolton. His children Mary Bolton, Lyndon Bolton, Eliza Bolton, died within weeks of each other in Hamburg in 1799. The Bolton's eventually returned to Ireland after the Emmet uprising. Lyndon Bolton died in Dublin on 29 January 1852, having built a successful career as a woollen-draper.

The BOND Family *of Bridge Street, Dublin*

The Bond Family of Bridge Street in Dublin were ripped apart on 12 March 1798, when Oliver Cromwell Bond was arrested alongside much of the Leinster Directory of the United Irishmen. Held prisoner, he was tried and sentenced to be executed, despite influences from wealthy family and friends. Bond died on 6 September 1798 from suspected poisoning and was buried at St. Michan's Churchyard in Dublin. His widow, Eleanor 'Lucy' Jackson, the daughter of iron-monger and United Irishman, Henry Jackson, eventually emigrated to the United States to join her father in exile in Baltimore, Maryland. She brought with her, the four Bond children.

BOND, Eleanor *neé Jackson* – Eleanor Jackson was born in 1772 to Henry Jackson and Elizabeth McGrath. On 10 June 1791, she married Oliver Bond, a Donegal native who would become one of the leading United Irishmen in Dublin. After the death of Oliver, Eleanor remained at their residence at 13 Bridge Street until 1809, before emigrating to the United States to join her father in Baltimore. Eleanor Bond died in Baltimore on 13 September 1843 and was interred at the Independent Church Cemetery at Terry Bar, Spring Gardens, Baltimore.

BOND, Eliza – The youngest of the Bond children, Eliza was but a baby when her father died in his cell in Kilmainham Gaol. She cared for her mother in her later years and died unmarried in Baltimore.

BOND, Harvey Margaret – Harvey was born c. 1796. She emigrated to Baltimore with her mother in 1810. In February 1820, she married Evan T. Ellicott, who became a commissioner of finance for the city of Baltimore. Harvey Ellicott died in Baltimore on 14 June 1881.

BOND, Henry Jackson – Henry Jackson Bond was born to Oliver Bond and Eleanor Jackson at their residence on Dublin's Bridge Street in 1795. Upon settling in the United States, Bond married Jane Lefferts Lloyd and they settled in Tallahassee in Florida, where Bond became a merchant. Bond died on 5 February 1858 at Tallahassee, Florida. His son, Walter Lloyd Bond

(1840-1914) served in the Confederate Army during the American Civil War; such a stark contrast to the political support that his paternal forefathers held towards abolitionism.

BOND, Thomas Jackson – The eldest child of Oliver Bond and Eleanor Jackson, Thomas was born in 1792. After the family arrived in America, Thomas J. Bond moved to New Orleans. He was married to Caroline Franklin. Thomas Bond died at West Derby in Liverpool in 1878 and was interred at Toxteth Park Cemetery in Liverpool.

The BONES Family *of Randalstown, County Antrim*

BONES, Elizabeth *née Scott* – Elizabeth Scott, the wife of John Bones (1733-1799) and the matriarch of the Bones family, left her native Duneane, Co. Antrim, after the death of her husband in 1799, travelling with her daughter **Jane Bones Crawford**. She died in South Carolina on 26 October 1817 and is buried at Sion Presbyterian Cemetery in Winnsboro, Fairfield County (SC).

BONES, James – James Bones was born in 1776, to Presbyterian farmers, John Bones and Elizabeth Scott, from Duneane, outside Randalstown, Co. Antrim. Bones was arrested for his part in the Battle at Ballymena however it is unknown to the authors if they had taken part in the battles of Randalstown and Antrim. Although he had been arrested, Bones managed to escape. After several years residing in Jamaica and the United States, Bones returned to Ireland to his wife, Mary Adams (1770-1835). They resided at Ballyportery in Loughguile, until the death of Mary's father, John Adams, in 1810, when they chose to take the family to Augusta, Georgia. The family landed at the port of Savannah, South Carolina, in July 1810, and one of the first acts the family partook in was to celebrate the Fourth of July. James Bones died on 17 December 1841 and is buried at Summerville Cemetery, Augusta.

BONES, Jane – Jane Bones, born c.1775, was the only recorded daughter of John Bones and Elizabeth Scott. Jane was married to **Andrew Crawford** (1770-1842) and with their children, they emigrated to the United States, settling in Fairfield County in South Carolina. Her son, **John Crawford** (1797-1876) would become Minister at the First Presbyterian Church at Columbia, Richland County in South Carolina. Jane Bones Crawford died on 29 October 1823 and is buried at Sion Presbyterian Cemetery in Fairfield County, close to her mother.

BONES, John - John Bones (*pictured*) was a teenager when his parents, James Bones and Mary Adams, chose to move to Augusta, Georgia. Here, John Bones became a successful merchant and built the first cotton factory in Augusta, using the Augusta Canal for power. He married Mary Fitzsimmons Eve, and after her death in 1833, he travelled back to Randalstown, where he married his cousin, Mary Brown. John Bones died in October 1870, having never retired from his business. The following excerpt is from obituary published in *Chronicle & Sentinel* on 26 October 1870:

"It is our painful duty to announce the death of this good and prominent citizen of Augusta….His father and family, being under the ban of power of the British government for participation in the Rebellion of Ireland, were forced to emigrate at the loss of a large property, and to seek an asylum in the hospitable shores of the New World choosing the South as their place of refuge."

An Interesting Bones Family Connection:

Samuel Bones (1807-1840) was born in Randalstown in 1807 to James Bones and Mary Adams, thus being only a child when his family emigrated to the State of Georgia. Samuel Bones married Maria McGran, who bore for Samuel, the following sons: Thomas, John and James Bones. James Bones married Marion Woodrow, whose sister, Jennie Woodrow, had married Rev. Joseph Wilson. Their son was U.S. President, Woodrow Wilson, who was President of the U.S. from 1913-1921. Helen Bones, the daughter of James and Marion (Wilson) Bones, became the private secretary to her cousin-in-law during his term in office. The President's paternal grandfather, James Wilson, had emigrated to the United States from Strabane, Co. Tyrone, in 1807. Wilson married Annie Adams, another Ulster immigrant.

"Miss Bones was the daughter of the late Mr. and Mrs. James W. Bones. The family home still stands on East Tenth Street. She left Rome when a child and much of her young ladyhood was spent in the home of her first cousin, Woodrow Wilson, in Princeton, N. J. During President Wilson's first administration, Miss Bones resided six years in the White House, and was the social secretary of Mrs. Eleanor [sic] Axson Wilson. She knew intimately many of those who figured prominently on the national scene during that era." Rome News-Tribune.

BONES, Samuel – Samuel Bones, born c.1770, was son of John Bones and Elizabeth Scott, and a brother of the above-mentioned James Bones. In 1798, Samuel Bones was arrested for his part in the Battle at Ballymena and exiled himself from Ireland at his own expense. Bones established himself at Wilcox County in Alabama, and married Elizabeth Milling (1786-1835). Their children included: Mary Jane Bones (1809-1835), Elizabeth Bones (b. 1812), Sarah Milling Bones (1814-1832), Samuel William Bones (1816-1858) and John Hugh Bones (b.1821). Samuel Bones died in May 1849.

BONES, William – William Bones, born on 3 January 1779, was the youngest child of John Bones and Elizabeth Scott. With his brothers, Samuel and James, he participated in the Antrim Rebellion of 1798, as an insurgent. In the years immediately after the Rebellion, Bones emigrated to America, alongside his mother and sister, Jane Bones Crawford. Having established himself in Augusta, Georgia, as a successful merchant, he retired to Charleston County, South Carolina and died on 1 March 1858. He was interred with an elaborate marble headstone, close to his mother's plot at Sion Presbyterian Churchyard in Fairfield County.

BOORMAN, John – John Boorman, a native of Rasharkin, Co. Antrim, was a member of the Defenders. After having participated in the 1798 Rebellion, Boorman was allowed to emigrate to America. It is unknown if he did exile or where he settled.

BOYD, Adam – Boyd, who hailed from Ballynahinch, Co. Down, was captured after having participated in the Battle of Ballynahinch. He was tried on 10 July 1798 at Downpatrick, charged with seditious treason and having taken a commanding role. Boyd was found guilty and sentenced to death, however this was cancelled when he offered to supply information on other ringleaders involved. Boyd was released and emigrated to America. It is unknown where he exiled to.

BOYD, James

– James Boyd, born c.1768, was a native of Dungall, near Ballymena, Co. Antrim, where he farmed and worked as a linen weaver. Having participated in the 1798 Rebellion he fled to the United States, but returned home to farm after several years. In 1818, his wife and five children followed him to America, and settled in Livingston County in New York. Boyd died in 1820.

BOYD, John

– Boyd was held in Carrickfergus Gaol for having participated in the Rebellion on 1798. He was considered to be in very bad health and released so he could emigrate to America.

BOYLE, John

– John Boyle was born c.1777, a native of Co. Antrim. He was engaged in the Rebellion of 1798 and left Ireland in 1801 to settle in the United States. Having landed in Philadelphia, lacking financial support, his former education procured him a professorship in a seminary for young women, but later removed to Washington D.C. where he would for the remainder of his career. Boyle became a friend and associate of U.S. President, Andrew Jackson. He worked as the chief clerk in the U.S. Navy and served for brief periods as Acting-Secretary of the Navy, however, he was removed from the position after an altercation with a midshipman. Boyle was married to Catherine Burke, having no fewer than five children, including future Confederate Provost-Marshal, General Cornelius Boyle. Boyle died on 23 March 1849 and was interred at Saint John the Evangelist Catholic Church Cemetery, in Maryland.

> **TWO FOREIGNERS OUT OF OFFICE.**
>
> Doctor T. P. Jones, born in Europe, has resigned his place during the pendency of charges against him as Examiner of Patents.
>
> Mr. John Boyle, an Irishman, Chief Clerk of the Navy Department, is removed from office; we understand in consequence of his outrage on the person of Midshipman Walsh.

BRADLEY, Robert – Bradley emigrated with his family to the United States in 1800, after having participated in the 1798 Rebellion. They settled in Beaver County, Pennsylvania. His son, **John Bradley**, would serve in the War of 1812 and received a land grant as a reward.

BRANNIGAN, Pat – A native of Irishtown, in Dublin, Brannigan was a United Irishman who had worked as a timber merchant. Miles Byrne gives some details about Brannigan's time in France in his memoirs:

"Captain (Irish Legion) in April 1804. He made the campaigns and sieges with the Irish regiment in Spain and Portugal till the summer of 1811, when from the effects of a wound, his health began to decline; he died at Bejar, a small town in Estramadura, Spain. Poor Branaghan had to abandon his wife and children and escape to Bordeaux after the failure of the attempt in Dublin, July 1803. His courage could not be surpassed. He gloried in being in dangerous situations; he never despaired of seeing his country one day independent."

BROWN, Alexander – Sir William Brown of Liverpool (*pictured*) stated in a letter that he refuted claims that his father, Alexander Brown, went into exile to America for his part in the 1798 Irish Rebellion. The allegation was published in the *London Post* in 1863 by correspondent, W.H. Russell. Was he claiming the truth or was he ashamed of his revolutionary past? William Brown was born at Ballymena, Co. Antrim, on 30 May 1784. He was the eldest son of Alexander Brown of Ballymena, and Grace Davison (1764–1834) of Drumnasole. His younger brothers were George Brown (1787–1859), John Brown (1788–1852), and James Brown (1791–1877). The Browns were wealthy and able to send their children to boarding school in Yorkshire. In 1801, the whole family emigrated to Baltimore, Maryland where Alexander established a linen business, partnering with his brother, George Brown, who had emigrated some years previously.

BROWN, Chichester – Chichester Brown (1783-1849) was a son of John Brown who exiled to Newburgh, New York in 1798 from Co. Monaghan, and who established the Universal Store. The Brown family followed John to America in 1800. Chichester is cited in the records of Newburgh as one of the best physicians in Newburgh. He married Catherine Graham of Shawangunk in

Ulster County (NY). Chichester had a liberal education, followed for a time the occupation of his teacher but soon after became Dr. Graham's student, graduating in 1808. Brown died on 8 August 1849. His obituary stated that:

"no hardship was too great for him to encounter and the voice of suffering always found his ready at his call."

One of his main endearing attributes was that it simply did not matter how rich or poor you were, Brown was always supportive. He was buried in the Old Town Presbyterian Cemetery. Gravestone photographed.

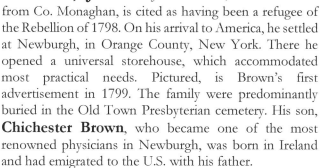

BROWN, John – John Brown,
from Co. Monaghan, is cited as having been a refugee of the Rebellion of 1798. On his arrival to America, he settled at Newburgh, in Orange County, New York. There he opened a universal storehouse, which accommodated most practical needs. Pictured, is Brown's first advertisement in 1799. The family were predominantly buried in the Old Town Presbyterian cemetery. His son, **Chichester Brown**, who became one of the most renowned physicians in Newburgh, was born in Ireland and had emigrated to the U.S. with his father.

BROWN, Robert – Robert Allen, originally from
Ulster, travelled to the U.S. at an advanced age with his daughter, **Mrs Allen**, to visit his daughters, **Jane** and **Agnes** and his son **Stafford Brown**, who were residing in Ryegate, Vermont. It was because of Stafford, who was implicated in the 1798 Rebellion, that the entire family had to flee to America.

BROWN, Stafford – Stafford Brown, having being involved in the
Rebellion emigrated to America in 1800, with his family. Having first resided in New Jersey, the family relocated to Ryegate, Vermont. Brown died in 1840.

BRUNTY, William – The Brunty family, it is believed, originally hailed
from Ballynaskeagh, Co. Down. William Brunty had served under Henry Munro and fought at the Battle of Ballynahinch in June 1798. Evidence is scarce but it seems that William's involvement may have turned the authorities focus upon the Brunty household. It is assumed that William exiled to America.

BRUNTY (BRONTË), Patrick -

William's brother, Patrick Brontë (1777-1861) (*pictured*), was born at Drumballyroney near Rathfriland, Co. Down, to Hugh Brunty and Alice McClory. In Patrick's early years, he trained in the blacksmith and linen trades, before becoming a teacher in 1798. He would've witnessed the 1798 Rebellion in Down, but we do not know to what extent. No evidence exists to highlight if Patrick Brunty was a member or even sympathetic towards the United Irishmen during that period, but their home was burned to the ground after the Battle of Ballynahinch. Patrick felt the need to leave Ireland and moved to Cambridgeshire in England in 1802, to study theology at St. John's College in Cambridge. Here, he changed the Brunty name to Brontë. Why? It is unknown. He was an admirer of the classics. He may have also wanted to cleanse his

Irish identity or family's rebellious relationship from his career. In 1812, he married Maria Branwell and the births of Maria, Elizabeth, Charlotte, Emily and Anne Brontë followed. Their lives would be dedicated to the literary world and their works are still respected to this day.

BRYSON Andrew '*Rebel Andy*' —

Andrew Bryson was born at Bangor, Co. Down, on 18 June 1767 to William Bryson and Jane Robb. This individual was a cousin of Andrew Bryson, a Co. Down United Irish colonel, who was sentenced to serve in His Majesty's forces for life but who eventually escaped from the West Indies to the United States. '*Rebel Andy*' Bryson left Bangor with his wife **Elizabeth Kennedy Bryson** (1770-1841) and their sons, **David Bryson** (1796-1867) and **William Bryson** (1796-1872). Nothing is recorded of his involvement in the 1798 Rebellion but family folklore claims that he was smuggled from a port within a water cask, which was not searched. Upon arriving in the United States, the Bryson family settled at Uniontown, Fayette County, in Pennsylvania (*pictured*), where they purchased 173 acres from Hugh Rankin, on 29 October 1799. '*Rebel Andy*' Bryson died on 16 May 1841, several months after the death of Elizabeth and was interred beside her at Associate Reformed Cemetery in Laurel Hill, Fayette County (painting).

BRYSON, Andrew – Andrew Bryson was a native of Ballysallagh, Co. Down. The son of Andrew Bryson and Isabella Barr, he was born in April 1779. Bryson rose through the ranks of the United Irishmen and would become Colonel by late March 1798, which initiated him into the Co. Down Committee of colonels. Bryson's role in the rebellion is not recorded in his narrative, but he was a wanted man with a £50 bounty on his head because of his rank. He was tried by court-martial in September 1798 alongside John Adams and James McCann and was sentenced to serve in His Majesty's forces abroad for life. His narrative, written in a large letter to his sister, Nelly Robb, from New York City on 28 May 1801, gives detail of his incarceration aboard the *'Postlethwaite'* prison tender in Belfast Lough in the winter of 1798 and the arduous march through Ireland to New Geneva prison camp in Co. Waterford in the spring of 1799. Bryson was sent to serve in the British military and journeyed to Martinique, in which he describes the ordeals and miseries in detail. He managed to escape to the United States with John Sibbet and established himself in New York City. Family correspondence records Bryson in 1806, but not afterwards

LE FORT ROYAL DANS L'ISLE DE LA MARTINIQUE Vu du Mouillage

which allows us to believe that he died. Historian, Michael Durey states his belief that Bryson possibly succumbed to the yellow fever that had gripped the United States during that period.

BRYSON, David – (1776-1845) A native of Ballysallagh, Co. Down, Bryson was the oldest son of Andrew Bryson and **Isabella Barr**. Bryson was brother of Andrew Bryson Jr, a colonel in Co. Down's United Irishmen, who was sent to serve His Majesty's forces abroad but who eventually escaped from Martinique to America. Due to his United Irish involvement, David sailed to America with his father in October 1798, settling in New York City. The Bryson's established a grocery, whilst David also worked as a currier and tanner at 48 Frankfort Street in the Swamp area. Bryson soon became established within

the Irish community, befriending Robert Swanton, a former Irish Legionnaire, who left France to reside in America.

When Swanton died in 1840, he left a considerable sum to his close friend, David Bryson, for his support throughout the years. He was noted for his benevolent nature and care for newly arrived Irish immigrants. He was a Chairman of the Democratic Republican General Committee, based at Tammany Hall. Bryson became involved in the Phoenix Bank alongside his son, Peter McCartee Bryson, securing a large share. He died on 15 November 1845. Another son, Andrew Bryson (1822-1892), would become a Rear-Admiral in the U.S. Navy, supporting the Union during the American Civil War.

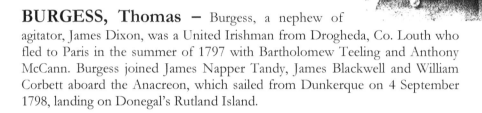

BURGESS, Thomas – Burgess, a nephew of agitator, James Dixon, was a United Irishman from Drogheda, Co. Louth who fled to Paris in the summer of 1797 with Bartholomew Teeling and Anthony McCann. Burgess joined James Napper Tandy, James Blackwell and William Corbett aboard the Anacreon, which sailed from Dunkerque on 4 September 1798, landing on Donegal's Rutland Island.

BURK, John Daly - John Daly was born c.1772 in Cork City. Having been educated at Trinity College in Dublin, Daly became a radical United Irishman. He was forced to flee Ireland and escaped from Dublin in 1796 disguised in petticoats, belonging to a woman named Burk. In honour of her assistance, Daly adopted her surname as his own in remembrance, thus becoming John Daly Burk. Upon arriving in the United States in October 1796, he briefly took refuge in Boston, becoming a journalist for the *Boston Daily Advertiser*. Burk viewed the United States as a bastion of true republicanism and viciously attacked those who threatened its existence. His bitingly partisan journalism in America brought a sedition indictment from Jefferson's rival, John Adams and the Federalist faction. Burk had accused Adams and members of the Federalists of attempting to subvert the American Revolution and publicly called for them to be tarred and feathered. Burk settled in Petersburg, Virginia, where he composed a *History of Virginia*, which he completed in 1804. He had also gained success with a play, which he composed on his journey to America in 1796, entitled, *Bunker Hill*. In 1808, whilst drinking in a tavern, he insulted a Frenchman, Felix Conquebert, who challenged Burk to a pistol duel. On 11 April 1808, Burk was killed instantly as a result of a bullet to the heart during this planned duel.

BUSHE, Rev. Fr. James - Bushe was a Dominican priest, based at Dublin's Denmark Street seminary, who was arrested and held in Kilmainham Gaol on 9 June 1798 on charges of treasonable practices. He was released in May 1800 on condition that he was to sail to Portugal, however, evidence shows that he sailed to America instead. Bushe ended up serving the Catholic community of Albany, New York and died from lung disease on 11 November 1808.

BYRNE, Garrett – Byrne hailed from Ballymanus, near Aughrim, Co. Wicklow. Born c.1762 to Garrett Byrne Sr and Christian Jans. The Byrne Family were prominent Catholic farmers in Wicklow and deeply connected to many families across Wicklow, due to their connections with the old Ó Bhroin clan. He was married to Mary Sparling of Hacketstown, Co. Carlow; a turbulent and controversial marriage and one without any issue. His first cousin was William Michael Byrne of Parkhill, Co. Wicklow, who was executed in Dublin in July 1798. Byrne would lead the south Wicklow men during the 1798 Rebellion; a unit called the *'Ballymanus Division,'* in honour of the Byrne homestead. This division supported the Wexford insurgents and fought gallantly at the Battle of Vinegar Hill on 21 June1798, where two of its principal leaders, Dan Kirwan of Kilpipe and another Byrne cousin, John Loftus of Annacurra, were killed. Byrne would become an influential commanding leader in the remnants of the Wicklow and Wexford insurgency during the retreat from Co. Wexford and the insurgents failed march to the midlands in early July 1798. After the collapse of the insurgent army in Meath and north Dublin, Byrne would eventually surrender to General Sir John Moore, on 20 July 1798 in the Glen of Imaal. One of the conditions of surrender was for Byrne to use his influence to encourage all insurgent groups to surrender. Miles Byrne mentions such a surrender notice to insurgent leader, Murtough Byrne of Little Aughrim in his memoirs, although the date he gives is incorrect.

"My dear Murtough,
I have this day surrendered myself to General Sir John Moore, who has engaged to obtain my pardon, and permission to quit Ireland and go to reside in a foreign country. It is at the General's request I now write: he promises to obtain the same terms for you or any of the other chiefs who will immediately avail themselves of this opportunity
Yours, Garrett Byrne"

Garrett Byrne's life after the Rebellion is somewhat confusing. He and a Wexford leader, Edward Fitzgerald of Newpark, were sent to Bristol in England, where they would remain until 22 March 1799, where they were removed to London and eventually the continent. The *Freeman's Journal* recorded this event:

"*They each appear to be between thirty and forty years of age; Fitzgerald, a remarkably ill-looking man, of rough manners; Burne (sic) with a rather pleasing countenance, and of manners apparently mild and gentle.*"

An April 1800 letter to his sister, Frances Byrne, states that he was residing in the free city of Hamburg. An 1806 lease of Ballymanus shows us that Garrett was resident of London and further correspondence pinpoints Garrett to Sidmouth in Devonshire, England. It is clear from papers within the Chief Secretary's Office, held in the National Archives of Ireland, that a Charlotte Byrne, wife of Garrett Byrne, petitioned Henry Goulburn in the Irish Office in London in early 1824. The letter states that Byrne was resident on the Isle of Jersey and they attempt to downplay Garrett's role in the 1798 Rebellion. A kinswoman, Miss Doyle, related that Garrett spent his final years at Caen in Normandy. This address is verified in a May 1827 petition from Garrett Byrne to King George IV, seeking a royal pardon, due to ill-health. Confusion continues to distort the memory and facts regarding Garrett, as one source claims that he was buried in 1832 in the cemetery of Vaugirard in Paris and another stating he was interred at Montparnasse in Paris, both having the year of death correct.

Garrett Byrne paid dearly for his participation in the 1798 Rebellion. He not only lost his lands and status; which Miles Byrne's descriptions of Garrett only allow us to understand the hurt pride felt by Garrett as he had been **"*brought up with high notions of what he owed to his ancestors.*"** His family mansion at Ballymanus had been burned by the Tinahely yeomanry on 8 May 1798. His brother, William, or Billy Byrne of Ballymanus as he is remembered today by the local GAA club, **'*The Billies of Ballymanus*'**, was executed outside Wicklow Town on 26 September 1799 for his involvement in the Rebellion and the family lands eventually were passed onto the Guinness Family, the renowned Dublin brewers.   *The Byrne Homestead, Ballymanus, Co. Wicklow*

BYRNE, John & Patrick –

The Byrne brothers, sons of wealthy merchant, Henry Byrne of Seatown and Mary Begg, were United Irish representatives of Co. Louth who fled to Paris in the summer of 1797 with Bartholomew Teeling and Anthony McCann. In late 1798, Patrick Byrne was residing in Töplitz Spa in Bohemia and died in 1812. John Byrne would reside in Worcester. In 1815, he married Caroline Byrn and died in the town of Bath in 1834.

BYRNE, Mrs Mary, *neé Harman* –

(1771-1860) Mary, a native of Killafeen, Laragh, in Co. Wicklow, was the sister of Lawrence and John Harman, who were prominent and notorious insurgents in Co. Wicklow during and after the 1798 Rebellion. It was not until 1817 that she made the decision to emigrate to the United States following in the footsteps of her brothers who had been exiled for their participation in the rebellion of 1798. Throughout her life she retained a strong Catholic faith. Having died on 4 July 1860, Mary received a detailed obituary and was buried at the Old Saint Thomas the Apostle Cemetery in Bedford, Pennsylvania.

BYRNE, Miles

The name Miles Byrne of Monaseed is universally recognised by all who study the turbulent times of the 1798-1803 period in Ireland, mostly because of his detailed memoirs. Miles Byrne was born at Ballylusk, Monaseed in north Co. Wexford, on 20 March 1780, to Patrick Byrne and Mary Graham. The family were reasonably well-to-do Catholic farmers, with Miles receiving an invested education, reared with Anglophobic tendencies as shown by his father's desire to never see his son wear a redcoat; having an understanding of his family's history and former social positions, but holding no religious animosity or sectarian attitudes.

MILES BYRNE
1840.
a drawing by Mrs Byrne
And by Mr Ed. Hedouin.

His memoirs contain much detailed and emotive writing. The loss of many childhood friends and relations during the 1798 Rebellion evidently affected Byrne as he wrote about them with deep reverence some five decades later. At only eighteen years of age, Byrne held an influential role in the Wexford United Irishmen and was a low-ranking officer with the Monaseed Corps of insurgents who fought at the First Battle of Enniscorthy (28 May 1798), Tubberneering (4 June 1798), Arklow (9 June 1798), Vinegar Hill (21 June 1798), Castlecomer (24 June 1798), Kilcumney (26 June 1798) and Ballygullen (5 July 1798). Byrne rose to become influential amongst the Wexford insurgent leadership and classed Fr. John Murphy of Boolavogue and Anthony Perry of Perrymount to be close associates.

When the Wexford Rebellion collapsed, Byrne chose to remain with the wounded and exhausted insurgents in the fastnesses of Glenmalure, within the Wicklow Mountains, whilst his comrades marched to near obliteration across Kildare, Meath, Louth and north Dublin. Working alongside Michael Dwyer and Joseph Holt, Byrne remained with the remnants of the Wicklow and Wexford insurgents until the autumn of 1798, when he chose to hide in Dublin, under the protection of his half-brother, Edward Kennedy. Being a fugitive, Byrne kept a low profile in Dublin, working as a clerk at Kennedy's timber-yard and maintaining links amongst the United Irish community also hiding out in Dublin's Liberties. In early 1803, Byrne was introduced to Robert Emmet, who was in the process of planning a takeover of Dublin City. Byrne's memoirs show devout loyalty towards Emmet. On the evening of 23 July 1803, Byrne, who was commanding the Wicklow and Wexford insurgents, were biding their time in the residence of Denis Lambert Redmond on Dublin's Coal Quay, were dismayed to find that Emmet's uprising had collapsed before it gained momentum. Byrne went into hiding in safe houses across Dublin in fear of the Castle authorities hunting him. Refusing to flee to France, Robert Emmet encouraged Byrne to go to Paris and explain the situation to his brother, Thomas Addis Emmet, who was residing in Paris at this stage. Wasting no time, Byrne met Captain O'Connor, a Wexford sailor, who agreed to smuggle Byrne to Bordeaux, France.

Upon arriving in France, Byrne immediately made his way to Paris where he engaged with Thomas Addis Emmet and William James MacNeven, having fulfilled his promise and informed them of the younger Emmet's failed rebellion. In December 1803, Byrne would join the newly initiated Irish Legion, holding the commission of sub-lieutenant, however, only on garrison duties. In 1808, Byrne was promoted to Captain and saw action in the Low Countries.

As the Napoleonic Wars progressed across the continent, Byrne would see action across the Iberian Peninsula, including the Battle of Fuentos d'Onoro. Other actions included counter-insurgency against the Spanish guerrillas, who were doing extensive damage to the French lines of communication. After years of bloody campaigns and the loss of many fellow Irish exiles to battle, Byrne would eventually be promoted to *Chevalier de la Légion d'honneur* on 18 June 1813, however, he would not be awarded the medal until 1832, from Louis Phillipe. With the Irish Legion officially disbanded upon the fall of Napoleon Bonaparte, Byrne entered a hiatus from war and did not participate in Napoleon's Hundred Days Campaign, which ended on the muddy fields of Waterloo in June 1815. A devout Bonapartist, Byrne faced banishment from France, under the restored monarchy, however, he successfully appealed the order and in November 1816, he swore allegiance to Royal Order of the *Légion d'honneur.* He would become a naturalised French citizen by decree on 20 August 1817 and would continue his time in France

as a captain on half-pay. In 1828, as a *Chevalier de St. Louis (pictured centre)*, Byrne was recalled to participate as a staff officer in the French Expeditionary Force in Morea, in support of Greek independence, a campaign which would see Byrne gain further promotion as **chef de bataillon** (Lieutenant-Colonel) of the 56th Infantry Regiment in 1830.

He retired in 1835 and on 24 December 1835, he married Fanny Horner at the British Embassy Chapel in Paris. They would produce no issue. and resided at 18, rue Montaigne (now rue Jean Mermoz, 8th arrondissement), close to the Champs-Élysées, where he entertained the Young Irelander, John Mitchell and other notable guests, whilst wearing his veteran medal, the **Médaille de Sainte Hélene** (pictured previous page) on his jacket, always showed immense interest in Ireland and its people, however, he would never set foot again on native soil.

Miles Byrne died on 24 January 1862, aged 81 years and was interred in the old Parisian cemetery of Montmartre, where a newly added Celtic cross stands, honouring his Irish and French military career. In 1863, his widow published his memoirs, which overwhelmingly sold in many editions since. Byrne's memoirs have been the base of research for many 1798 historians over time. Indeed, mistakes have been noticed but they are generally regarded as the best source from an insurgent's point of view.

(Image) Miles Byrne of Monaseed (1780-1862). Photographed in Paris in 1859. Aras an Uachtaran Collection. Colourised version permitted with many thanks by John Breslin (Old Ireland in Colour)

BYRNE, Patrick – Patrick Byrne was born ca.1740. He started a bookselling and publishing business at 35 College Green, Dublin in 1779. Further expansion of his business saw him move to nearby 108 Grafton Street, which he owned until his exile to America in 1800. Having joined the United Irishmen in its days of infancy, Byrne would become noticed by the authorities as a printer of radical literature, including Thomas Paine's '***Rights of Man***', which was a bestseller across Ireland. Having mistaken a Crown officer, who visited his bookshop, as a radical, Byrne's poor misjudgement saw the arrests of John and Henry Sheares. Byrne was also arrested on 21 May 1798 and his shop ransacked by the authorities. An eye-witness later wrote,

"It was a pitiful sight to behold the amount of property in beautifully bound books ruthlessly torn to pieces and tossed out of the windows into the street."

Byrne languished in Dublin's Newgate Gaol until June 1800, upon which he organised his exile to the United States. In November 1800, Byrne arrived at Philadelphia and within two years, had established himself as one of the city's principal booksellers and publishers, having taken on the contract to print the radical newspaper, *Aurora*. He established another bookshop in the city of Baltimore, which was managed by his son, William Byrne, until his untimely death in December 1805. Byrne's daughter would marry Edward Hudson, the Co. Wexford native, United Irishman and dentist, who arrived in America, having served several years at Fort George in Scotland. Patrick Byrne continued to print political literature until his death in February 1814.

BYRNE, William – A native of Dublin City and son of bookseller, Patrick Byrne. William Byrne established himself as a bookseller in the city of Baltimore, Maryland, however, he died on 20 December 1805.

CAHILL, Patrick – Patrick Cahill was a native of Bannow, Co. Wexford and a veteran insurgent of the 1798 Rebellion, who settled on Prince Edward Island in Canada, with his wife, Catherine Coady. Cahill died in December 1866 and his obituary highlighted that Cahill *"was actually engaged in the Rebellion of '98 in Ireland and was perhaps the last survivor of those of them who emigrated to America"*

CALDWELL – The Rev. William Wilson, from Moneymore, Co. Derry, (eldest son of William Wilson) was married to a Miss Caldwell of Glenkeen, and resided at her family farm. It seems that Miss Caldwell inherited the farm from her brother who had to flee Newtown Limavady in 1798. The forename of her brother is unknown.

The CALDWELL FAMILY *of Ballymoney, Co. Antrim*

The story of the Caldwell Family of Harmony Hill is one of the most recognised from any northern Presbyterian family who were exiled as a result of the 1798 Rebellion.

CALDWELL, Andrew – Andrew Caldwell, born in 1782, was son of John Caldwell and Elizabeth Calderwood of Harmony Hill, Co. Antrim. He emigrated with his family aboard the **Peggy** in May 1799 and settled in Salisbury Mills, in Orange County, New York. After the death of his older brother Richard in late 1812, Andrew became co-executor of his affairs. In August 1815, he married Harriet Brewster. Their children were: Catherine Banks Caldwell (b.1818), Elizabeth Freelove Caldwell (b.1819), Samuel Brewster Caldwell (1822-1822) and Richard Caldwell (1831-1901). Andrew Caldwell died on 9 January 1862 and was interred at the Caldwell Family Cemetery in Salisbury Mills (NY).

CALDWELL, Ann – Ann Caldwell hailed from Ballymoney, Co. Antrim. She was the niece of John Caldwell Sr of Harmony Hill and a cousin to the large collective of Caldwell's who were exiled after the 1798 Rebellion. A permit exists in the Public Record Office (NI) which details Ann travelling aboard the **Peggy** to the United States with her cousins and her sister, Flora Caldwell, in May 1799 (T3541/6/5; CMSIED 9406211). Ann settled in Baltimore in Maryland. Her sister Flora would later give a detailed account of their settling in America in which she described how Ann and her husband often cared for Francis Blackwell Mayer, one of America's notable artists, when he was a child. In 1855, it was Mayer who recorded Flora Caldwell's account.

CALDWELL, Catherine– Catherine Caldwell was born at Harmony Hill, near Ballymoney, Co. Antrim, on 12 August 1775. She was the daughter of John Caldwell Sr and Elizabeth Calderwood. When the Caldwell family were given no option but to exile themselves to America, Catherine helped organise the journey with her brother, John Caldwell Jr. They travelled aboard the *Peggy*, which left Belfast in early May 1799. After the family settled at Salisbury Mills, near Newburgh, New York, Catherine became engaged to a family friend, James Parks. They married in New York City on 3 April 1805. After James Park's untimely death in 1813, Catherine married the prominent United Irish exile, John Chambers. Catherine Parks Chambers died on 10 October 1856 and was buried at the Caldwell Family Cemetery, in Salisbury Mills (NY).

CALDWELL, Elizabeth – Elizabeth Caldwell was born at Harmony Hill in 1789, to John Caldwell and Elizabeth Calderwood. We can imagine the stressful childhood that Elizabeth suffered, having lost her mother at the age of seven and then being brought to the United States by her brother John in May 1799. Elizabeth married Joseph Tinkham and settled in New York City. She died on 12 April 1862 and was interred at the Caldwell Family Cemetery in Salisbury Mills (NY).

CALDWELL, Flora - Flora Caldwell was the niece of John Caldwell Sr of Harmony Hill and a cousin to the large collective of Caldwell's who were exiled after the 1798 Rebellion. She was the daughter of a merchant, who resided at Rosemary Lane, near the city of Londonderry. A permit exists in the Public Record Office (NI) which details Flora travelling aboard the *Peggy* to the United States with her cousins in May 1799 (T3541/6/5; CMSIED 9406211). Her personal account, recorded in 1854, gives a detailed account of her settling in Baltimore with her sister, Ann Caldwell, and meeting her cousin, Richard Caldwell, who had left Ireland in late 1798.

"In the spring of 1799 the brig Peggy was chartered and we sailed for America. There were nine clergymen aboard and our six weeks' voyage was the consequence the sailors said. We were boarded by a French Man of War but my cousin John's acquaintance with French saved us from capture and also his being a Mason. The bay of New York after a voyage, you can't think how delightful everything looked, beautiful. Oh but it was! The yellow fever prevailed and we landed at the Quarantine on Staten Island. And under the trees by a spring we milked the cows, our bread and milk was the greatest treat mortals ever had. Uncle settled in New York at Bayside (Long Island). We were two days in reaching Philadelphia by way of Newark and Elizabethtown and at Trenton bridge we crossed into Pennsylvania. We passed two days in reaching Baltimore stopping at Elkton, (Maryland) and arriving at the "Indian Queen" corner of Hanover and Baltimore Street."

CALDWELL, John Jr – John Caldwell Jr was born on 3 May 1769 to John Caldwell and Elizabeth Calderwood, at the family's prosperous home of Harmony Hill, outside Ballymoney, Co. Antrim. As a youth, Caldwell was

apprenticed to a Belfast shipowner, Samuel Brown, thus giving him maritime connections, which would later prove beneficial. Regarding his politics, Caldwell was openly liberal. He once recalled:

"In early childhood certain ideas of liberty were under various circumstances instilled on my mind, which, as I increased in years, increased with my age and strengthened my strength. Thus on the news of the Battle of Bunker Hill, my nurse Ann Orr led me to the top of a mount on a midsummer eve, where the young and the aged were assembled before a blazing bonfire to celebrate what they considered the triumph of America over British despotism when my nurse cried our – 'Look Johnny, dear, look yonder at the west. There is the land of liberty and there will be your country."

By the 1790s, he was a leading member of the United Irishmen in Co. Antrim, however before the Rebellion he declined to take part, letting his brother Richard take the lead. Richard was destined to command of the north Antrim insurgents, which would eventually result in the authorities cracking down on Harmony Hill. John was arrested in Dublin on 19 May 1798 however no incriminating evidence was found on his possession. At the height of the Rebellion, instead of participating in the fighting, John was helping to organise a lottery to help United Irish prisoners suffering from destitution. After the destruction of Harmony Hill, the Caldwell's were destined to exile to America. John first sailed on the *Pallas* in early October 1798 however it had to be abandoned at Cork after the ship got into storm difficulties. On 3 May 1799, he was successful in boarding the *Peggy* for New York, a ship which contained many of the North's prominent exiles; David Bailie Warden, Rev. Charles Wallace, Rev. John McNish, Rev. John Miles and Rev. William Sinclair. Some animosity was displayed against Caldwell during the early stages of the voyage. The prominent exiles had hoped to be brought to France however, Caldwell urged the ship's captain to strictly remain on the American route.

The Caldwell family settled in Salisbury in New York. They had of course been aware of ancestral relations who, having fought in the Williamite Wars, had emigrated to America in the early 1700s, establishing the town of Londonderry in New Hampshire. John spent most of his time with his new business interests in New York City and married the daughter of a Wexford minister. John went into partnership with his brother-in-law, James Parks, and started a wholesale liquor company, which allowed for further investment in a paper mill, a corn mill and a large general storehouse in the Salisbury area. Although he financially struggled at times, he was often noted as keeping on top of his debts, becoming known as '**Honest John**' Caldwell. He served as Treasurer of the New York's *Irish-American Society*, Vice-President of the New York's *Friendly Sons of St Patrick* and was a founding member of the Orange County Fair, which still exists. John Caldwell Jr passed away on 17 May 1850 and was buried at the Caldwell Family Cemetery in Salisbury Mills, Orange County (NY). A note of interest worth mentioning is that his obituary states that he was able to speak and write in the Irish language.

NEW YORK, June 14.

The brig Peggy, captain Watson, arrived at this port yesterday, in 39 days from Belfast. We hear she brings intelligence to the first of May, which we expect procure this morning. We have been favored with files of The Belfast News Letter, to the 26th April. They are filled principally with details of victory on the part of the combined powers over the republican armies; debates of the Irish parliament on the regency bill; and minutes trials for treasonable practices. The question of union is seldom mentioned in the papers; but we notice that in the English house of peers, on the 11th April lo Grenville introduced a motion, which was carried without a division, that " the resolutions agreed to, relative to an incorporated legislative union with Ireland, might presented to the king, in order that the same might be laid before the parliament Ireland at such convenient time as he should judge expedient.

CALDWELL, John Sr – The patriarch of the Caldwell Family during the 1798 period, John Caldwell, was born in 1742 to John Caldwell and Florence Ball. He was married to Elizabeth Calderwood and together they raised a family of twelve children. He held liberal views and was a captain in the Ballymoney Volunteers in the early 1780s, being one of the first officers to allow a Roman Catholic, Daniel Maxwell, into the ranks. On 9 June 1798, he was unaware of his son's involvement in the Battle of Ballymoney, and was naturally startled when the Crown Forces, under Major Bacon, arrived at Harmony Hill several days later, setting it alight. Caldwell, after securing his son, Richard, from execution, had to flee with his entire family to the U.S. The family predominantly sailed on the *Peggy* in May 1799 and made their home at Salisbury Mills, near Newburgh, (NY) and purchased a farm. John Caldwell Sr arrived aboard the *Prosperity* in August 1799. John Caldwell Sr died on 29 October 1803, at Salisbury Mills.

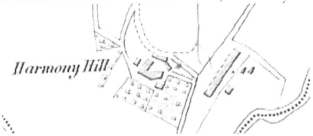

CALDWELL, Margaret – Margaret Caldwell was born in 1785 to John Caldwell and Elizabeth Calderwood. She was only a young teenager when the family were forced to emigrate to the United States in May 1799. On 18 September 1805, Margaret died at the Caldwell residence in Salisbury Mills, near Newburgh, New York.

CALDWELL, Mary – Mary Caldwell was born in 1772 to John Caldwell and Elizabeth Calderwood. Mary emigrated to the United States with her entire family aboard the *Peggy* in early May 1799. She died at Salisbury Mills, Orange County, New York in 1822.

CALDWELL, Richard – The story of the Caldwell family descends from the acts of Richard Caldwell, who commanded the United Irish insurgents at Ballymoney, on 7 June 1798. After the failure of the attack, Caldwell and an accomplice, John Gunning, fled to Scotland. Word had reached the authorities of Richard's leadership at Ballymoney. Lord Henry Murray arrived at the Caldwell residence at Harmony Hill, and ordered the burning of the house, outhouses and grist mill. The family were allowed only five minutes to get to safety before it was immersed in flames. On 22 June 1798, Richard was arrested at Kilcalmonell in Scotland and was sent to Coleraine, where he was tried and sentenced to hang.

John Caldwell Sr travelled to Dublin and appealed in person to the Lord Lieutenant, Cornwallis, in which he was successful in having his son's sentence reduced to voluntary banishment to America. Gunning's sentence was also commuted and he was ordered to be transported to New South Wales however he does not appear on any of the ship indent lists for that destination. Abiding by the demands and fearing further retribution, Richard sailed to the United States in the autumn of 1798, residing in Baltimore before joining his family when they arrived in the U.S. in mid-1799. Caldwell would marry Maria Chandler and raise their family at Salisbury Mills.

When the War of 1812 erupted between Great Britain and the United States, Caldwell was instrumental in organising a company within the 25th Infantry, U.S. Army. Whilst on campaign, Caldwell was leading his men across the frozen stretches of Lake Champlain and caring for their wellbeing, he divided his extra clothing amongst those more exposed to the harsh temperatures. He fell ill to pneumonia and died on 22 November 1812, aged 34 years, in the homestead of John Thurber. He was interred at Glenwood Cemetery in Clinton County (NY). Today, an exquisite memorial stands in Salisbury Mills, dedicated to the memory of Caldwell and the local men who died in the War of 1812 (*pictured*).

CALDWELL, William – William Alexander Caldwell was born on 16 February 1787 at Harmony Hill, near Ballymoney, Co. Antrim, the youngest son of John Caldwell and Elizabeth Calderwood. Having travelled to America with his older brother, John Caldwell, aboard the *Peggy*, in May 1799, William remained under his care until he reached the age of eighteen. He left New York to carve a career for himself as a merchant, based at Charleston, South Carolina. In June 1811, he married Dinah Williamson and together reared a large family. Their children were: John Williamson Caldwell (1812-1867), William Smith Caldwell (1813-1886), Richard Caldwell (1815-1879), Flora Caldwell (1817-1818), Andrew Parks Caldwell (1819-1883) and Joseph Triskham Caldwell (1823-1885). William Caldwell died on 1 October 1846.

The CALDWELL Family *of Limavady, County Derry*

CALDWELL, Robert & Elizabeth nee Snell – John Caldwell was only a child when he had to leave his home between Limavady and Coleraine in Co. Derry, with his parents. Robert had participated in the 1798 Rebellion in some capacity and was forced to flee to America, where he joined some of his family in Burke County, North Carolina. Robert Caldwell died on 10 December 1837, aged 88 years. Elizabeth Snell Caldwell predeceased her husband in April 1823. They are both buried at Oak Hill, Burke County, North Carolina.

CALDWELL, Elizabeth – Elizabeth Caldwell was daughter of Robert Caldwell and Elizabeth Snell. She was born on 12 July 1777. After the Caldwell family settled in Burke County, North Carolina, Elizabeth married Isaac Pearson, a son of Irish immigrants, who managed Silver Creek Plantation in Burke County. She died on 21 December 1857.

CALDWELL, John – John Caldwell was born in August 1779 to Robert Caldwell and Elizabeth Snell. It is unknown if he joined his father in the 1798 Rebellion, but he did emigrate with them to the United States. He married Hannah Pickett Robinson and settled close to his parents in Burke County, North Carolina. John Caldwell died on 26 May 1857 and was interred at Cherry Fields Farm Cemetery in Morganton, North Carolina.

His son, Tod Robinson Caldwell (1818-1874, *pictured*), was a State Governor for North Carolina. In 1840, having graduated in law from the University of North Carolina, he was admitted to the bar and established a legal career in Morganton, North Carolina. He was the principal solicitor of Burke County, a member of the North Carolina House of Commons, (1842-45, 48-49, 58-59) and served in the

North Carolina State Senate, (1850-51). He was elected the first Lieutenant Governor of North Carolina in 1868 and assumed the duties of the governorship when Governor William W. Holden was impeached, in 1870. In 1871, he was elected as a Republican the

41st Governor of North Carolina, serving until his death from cholera morbus at age 56.

CALDWELL, Mary – Mary Caldwell was born on 31 October 1791 to Robert Caldwell and Elizabeth Snell, at their residence near Limavady, Co. Derry. She went to the United States with her family after the 1798 Rebellion and settled in Burke County (NC). She would marry Alfred Perkins and raise a family. Mary Perkins died on 9 February 1854 and was interred closed to her parents at Oak Hill.

CAMPBELL Anthony – Not much is known about Anthony Campbell. He was briefly mentioned as an exile in a biography of Varina Howell, wife of Confederate President Jefferson Davis, in which it claimed that he was the last of the 1798 exiles from Ireland, and had been a close associate of James Kempe a Donegal United Irish exile. See *KEMPE*. Campbell placed an advertisement in a local newspaper seeking the return of a runaway slave, whom he described in detail as having **"been lately well whipped for theft and…the scars are not yet healed."**

CAMPBELL, Neal – Neal Campbell hailed from Coalisland, Co. Tyrone. As a result of the Rebellion, Campbell travelled to America and settled at Youngtown, Ohio. He purchased a farm and had a farm and settled down with his family.

CANNON, Timothy – On 25 November 1864, a 98-year-old man took his last breath in Clay Township, Butler County in Pennsylvania. This man carried his information which he passed onto John McDivitt before his death. It stated that he: "*was born on the 13th day of Dec A.D, 1765, in Roscommon county, Ireland. Came to this country in 1818 - was in the Irish Rebellion of 1798 and was taken prisoner by the Government.*"

We cannot ascertain if Cannon had gone to America as an outcast for his participation in the 1798 Rebellion, thus resulting in him having to self-exile but it is possible that this could have been the case.

CARLIN – The Carlin brothers are mentioned in the biography of William Carlin of Illinois in the book *Virginia Cousins* (1887). The brothers are cited as having been involved in the 1803 uprising fled Ireland as a result. One brother, Thomas Carlin, briefly settled in Virginia and the district, Carlin Springs, was named in his honour. He relocated to Missouri. The forename of Thomas' brother could not be sourced.

The CARROLL Family – The Carroll Family hailed from Co. Wexford and emigrated after the Rebellion to New York City, as a result of the patriarch's involvement in the insurgency and having fought at the Battle of Vinegar Hill. Having fled as a result, his wife and young children followed him soon after to America.

CHAMBERS, Charles – Charles Chambers was born in April 1784 to John Chambers and Christian Mary FitzSimon. After his father's incarceration in 1798, Charles became involved in the United Irishmen and had to flee Ireland after Emmet's failed uprising of July 1803, eventually joining his father in business in New York City. On 1 September 1817, Charles Chambers married Jane Mullanphy. As a wedding gift, her father purchased a tract of land in Missouri for the couple where they eventually went to reside. Chambers invested his time improving the land and establishing a working, profitable farm to sustain their  large family. Charles Chambers died on 1 February 1862 and was interred at Calvary Cemetery & Mausoleum in St. Louis, Missouri.

CHAMBERS, John – Chambers was born in Dublin in January 1754, the son of a Protestant wine merchant. In his youth, he was apprenticed in a printworks, resulting in the establishment of his own printworks in Dublin in 1775. In December 1780, Chambers married Christian Mary FitzSimon, however, she died in 1796. By 1781, Chambers ran his business from 5 Abbey Street. As a representative of the St Luke's stationers' Guild, he secured full rights for Catholic members. Chambers' business suffered greatly when his premises were burnt down on 7 January 1792, at an expense of £3000. In 1797, having become a director of the Bank of Ireland, he opened a warehouse for the sale of merchants' and traders' account books.

Chambers was a supporter of Catholic emancipation and had reprinted **"An argument on behalf of the Catholics,"** a popular pamphlet composed by Wolfe Tone. Chambers would become a member of the Dublin Society of United Irishmen in late 1792 and advocated for parliamentary reform. Chambers would rise to become one of the influential members of the United Irishmen. In March 1798, as Dublin Castle cracked down on the United Irishmen, Chambers' premises were severely ransacked. With a bounty of £300 on his head, Chambers surrendered to the authorities and was placed in Kilmainham Gaol in late August 1798. In 1799, he and the other leading United Irishmen were sent to Fort George in Scotland, where they were held in comfort until the Treaty of Amiens ended the war with France and Britain in 1802. Upon being released, Chambers travelled to France. In August 1805, Chambers travelled to the United States and established a new stationary business on New York's Wall Street in Manhattan. His son, Charles Chambers joined as a business partner in 1808 and married Catherine Caldwell Parks, sister of the Antrim exiles, John and Richard Caldwell. In 1816, with his friends, Thomas Addis Emmet, William James MacNeven and William Sampson, he helped establish the *New York Association for the Relief of Emigrant Irishmen*, with the aim of settling newly arrived Irish immigrants in the American interior. One bombastic idea was to petition Congress to given a large section

BROADWAY SHOWING TRINITY CHURCH   NEW YORK CITY   AND GRACE CHURCH CHAPEL
1820

of new land to the Irish people. This idea of course failed. During his retirement Chambers became President of the *Friendly Sons of St Patrick* in 1828. John Chambers died at his residence at 73 White Street in New York City on 8 February 1837, and was interred at the Caldwell Family Cemetery, in Salisbury Mills, Orange County (NY).

CHAMBERS, William – William Chambers was a United Irish Presbyterian from Co. Down. In 1797, he was arrested and incarcerated in Stewartstown. Having managed to escape, he fled to the United States with his wife, **Mary Hazlet**. Family folklore later claimed that whilst on their journey, William had to hide under cabbages when their ship was searched. They settled at Beaver Township in Lawrence County, Pennsylvania, where they had several children. They have been described as a family who **"are fond of religion and whiskey and a bit of a fight"**. William Chambers died on 21 February 1855 and was interred at Mount Jackson United Presbyterian Cemetery in Lawrence County, Pennsylvania. Their son, **John Chambers**, was sent to Baltimore to be educated in theology, thus becoming a pastor. Rev. Chambers would become a close friend of the unpopular U.S. President, James Buchanan. His theology eventually went from the Reformed to the mainstream Presbyterian Church. His church, the Chambers-Wylie Presbyterian Church is still evident today.

CHARLESS, Joseph – Joseph Charless was born on 16 July 1772 in Killucan, Co. Westmeath. After the failure of the 1798 Rebellion, Charless fled Westmeath to France and from there, he relocated to America where he settled firstly in Philadelphia and then to the frontier State of Kentucky. Upon arrival in Philadelphia, Charless married Mrs. Sarah Jourdan McCloud. Charless was a printer by trade and joined with another Irish exile, Matthew Carey, a notable publisher. He formed the acquaintances of men such as Henry Clay and Alexander Hamilton, among others. He was encouraged by Henry Clay to move to Kentucky, where he resided for several years before settling in St. Louis, where he founded and established the notable *Missouri Gazette* newspaper. This was the first paper to be published to the west of the Mississippi River. One of their children, Joseph Charless Jr. (1804-1859), became

MISSOURI GAZETTE.

VOL. IV.   ST. LOUIS, SATURDAY, JULY 18, 1812.   No. 201.

a banker and financier. Joseph Charless died in St. Louis on 28 July 1834 and was interred at Bellefontaine Cemetery in St. Louis, Missouri.

CLANDENNIN, Alexander – Alexander Clandennin was a chandler from Newtownards, Co. Down. He was tried at Newtownards on 26-27 June 1798, on charges of leading a group of insurgents; ordering James Lowry to take up arms and for ordering the requisition of lead, cattle and meal from Lord Londonderry's estate at Mount Stewart. He was sentenced to be transported for life, however, he later entered into recognisances to emigrate away from Ireland. Clandennin was formally released in 1799 on security that he would go to America.

CLARK, Margaret *neé Mullen* – Margaret Clark was wife to William Clark, a casualty of the 1798 Rebellion. Mrs. Clark decided to leave Ireland and emigrated with her family to America as exiles at the close of the Eighteenth Century. Margaret first settled in Philadelphia then relocated to Pittsburgh, Pennsylvania, where she lived to the advanced age of 103 years.

CLARK, William – William Clark was son of William Clark, a casualty of the 1798 Rebellion and the above-mentioned Margaret Mullen. He emigrated to the United States after the end of the Rebellion and married Lucy Sanders, a daughter of a covenanting preacher. Clark would become engaged in the War of 1812 and left Pennsylvania to reside with his family at Jeffersonville in Indiana. Their son, Lewis A. Clarke was born in Pittsburgh on 15 October 1824 and was associated with the press of St Louis for many years. After a good schooling Lewis travelled west and founded the newspapers, *The Arena* and *Dramatic Mirror* in Cincinnati, Ohio.

CLOKEY, Andrew - Andrew Clokey was imprisoned in July 1798 for participation in a robbery. Having been court-martialled on 24 July 1798, he was sentenced to transportation, however this was reduced to exile to America. It's unknown if Clokey had been a United Irishman, however, his sentence was commuted to voluntary banishment.

CLOKEY, Joseph Sr. –

Joseph Clokey was born on 7 March 1754 in the vicinity of Ballynahinch in Co. Down. Described as a Presbyterian, who rose from being a shoemaker to a successful leather merchant in Co. Down. Clokey married Elizabeth Mitchel in October 1774 and together they had a number of children including, Joseph Clokey Jr, who is cited in the *"Compendium of American Genealogy Vol. V"*, as being the 18-year-old aide-de-camp to the Co. Down General Monroe. Clokey was tried and executed for his role in the Battle of Ballynahinch. Clokey Jr had refused under interrogation to reveal the hiding place of his father, who like his son, was a United Irishman and had supposedly turned his cellar into a United Irish armoury. After the execution of his son, Joseph Clokey, now a widower, managed to flee to America and settled at Dauphin County in Pennsylvania, arriving in March 1799. Dauphin County was the homeplace of his brother, James Clokey, who later moved to Washington D.C. Within two months of arriving, Joseph married widow Mary Sawyer on 30 April 1799. Together, they had five children. Their first child, Jane Clokey, married the Unitarian Rev. Alexander Wilson, (*headstone pictured*).

Their second child Joseph, named in honour of both his father and late brother, became the Rev. Joseph Clokey D.D. of the Presbyterian Church - see attached Biography from the minutes of the General Assembly

JOSEPH CLOKEY, D. D., of the Presbytery of Xenia, was born in Dauphin county, Pa., December, 25, 1801, and was the son of Joseph and —— (Sawyers) Clokey. The place of his first confessing Christ was Peters Creek Church, Washington county, Pa., but the exact date of it has not been ascertained. He graduated at Jefferson College, Canonsburg, Pa., in 1823. He attended the Associate Theological Seminary at Canonsburg four terms, and was licensed by the Associate Presbytery of Chartiers, July 4, 1826. He was ordained by the Associate Presbytery of Muskingum, September 18, 1827. He was pastor of the Associate congregations of Belmont and Mt. Pleasant, Ohio, from 1827 till 1834, and of the Associate congregations of Mt. Pleasant and Piney Fork from 1834 till 1840. At this time, passing with the congregation of Piney Fork into the Associate Reformed Church, he was pastor of Piney Fork and Warrenton congregations from 1840 till 1848. He was pastor of St. Clair congregation, Pa., from 1848 till 1855, and of the congregation of Springfield, Ohio, from 1855 till 1875. He was Professor of Pastoral Theology and Homiletics in the United Presbyterian Theological Seminary at Xenia, Ohio, from 1859 till 1874. He was Moderator of the United Presbyterian General Assembly in 1860, the third meeting of the Assembly. He was twice married, to Miss Jane Patterson, of

In later years, Rev. Joseph Clokey had three sons, one of whom became the Presbyterian minister, Rev. Alexander Wilson Clokey and the other a Colonel Josiah Michael Clokey. Both sons had extremely respectable careers. The Rev. Alexander W. Clokey was the father of the Rev. J. F. Clokey, assistant pastor of the First Presbyterian Church in Pittsburgh, and one of the most widely, known ministers in the country. Old Joseph Clokey died in Dauphin County on 31 January 1826.

CONNELL, "Rev". James – Connell was a Presbyterian probationer, based at Garvagh in Co. Derry. In Presbyterian Churches, one who, after examination and approval by the Presbytery, receives a licence to preach. He may assist the minister but must not administer the sacraments until he is ordained to a charge of his own. Details are scarce regarding Connell's participation with the United Irishmen and the 1798 Rebellion but he did flee to America as a result. It's unknown what happened after or where in America he settled.

CONNOLLY, Michael – Michael Connolly was a Galway United Irishman who fled Ireland in 1798 and settled in Halle, in the Prussian Province of Saxony. In April 1821, Sir George Henry Rose, the Envoy to Munich and Berlin corresponded with the Office of the Chief Secretary of Ireland, stating that Connolly, also known as **Karmelli** regarding his claims to an inheritance. The file concludes that Connolly has been misinformed and that his remaining family in Co. Galway are **"all miserably poor."**

COOK, Duncan – Cook, a native Scotsman, was recorded in the *"History of Fair Haven, Vermont,"* as having been taken prisoner by General Burgoyne during the Irish Rebellion and came to America in 1798 as a result of the insurrection and settled at Fair Haven in Vermont.

CORBETT, Thomas – Corbett was born at Ballythomas, Co. Cork in 1773 to Frederick Corbett and Amy Purcell, thus being the oldest of the Corbett brothers. Corbett entered Trinity College in Dublin in 1787 and graduated with a Bachelor of Arts in 1791. He was a member of the College's yeomanry corps and joined the Society of United Irishmen. In 1797, when the authorities threatened to suppress *The Northern Star* newspaper, it was Thomas Corbett who managed its production in its dying days, before the Monaghan Militia smashed its printing press in May 1797. Corbett was accused of politically influencing his brother, William Corbett, and other students at Trinity, and suffered expulsion from the 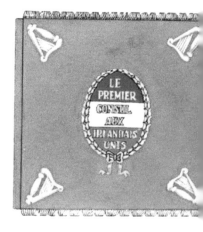 College Yeomanry for his membership in the United Irishmen. As the Rebellion erupted in May 1798, the Corbett Brothers fled to France via Trondheim,

Copenhagen and Hamburg and joined the French Army. Under the alias of *'Cowan,'* Thomas participated in the Hardy Expedition, which failed off the western coast of Donegal in October 1798. Corbett's ship escaped from the horrific sea battle and Thomas returned to France, where he survived by teaching English at Pyrtanée and involving himself in French politics, which included support towards Zionism, urging that all the Jews of the world should organise a new homeland in Palestine.

When the Irish Legion was formed by decree of Napoleon, Thomas Corbett was commissioned as Captain. The Legion had been formed in a divided state; divisions inherited from ideological and personal clashes within the United Irish leadership. Corbett sided with the Arthur O'Connor faction. On 3 June 1804, he refused to sign a document which confirmed that the entire regiment had sworn allegiance to Bonaparte, claiming that Captain John Swiney, who was a member of the Addis Emmet faction, had not done so. The next day, Swiney struck Corbett on the parade ground of Morlaix and a fight ensued. After a period of detention, the quarrel was far from over. After his release, Corbett challenged Swiney to a duel of pistols. On 20 September 1804, Corbet and Swiney met at Lesneven and attempted the duel was attempted several times dues to misfires and Corbett receiving wounds, which did not deter him from surrendering. The paces were decreased from ten to six and Swiney's sixth bullet ended the duel. Thomas Corbett suffered from multiple wounds and succumbed that evening. The feud caused much consternation within the Legion, resulted in several resignations and damaged its honour with France during the period.

CORBETT, William – William Corbett was born on 17 August 1779 at Ballythomas, Co. Cork to Frederick Corbett and Amy Purcell. Corbett was educated firstly by his father before entering Trinity College in 1792, thus graduating with a BA. Whilst a student, Corbett was Secretary of Trinity's Historical Society and had befriended Robert Emmet and the poet, Thomas Moore. Although a Protestant, Corbett deeply supported Catholic Emancipation and eventually joined the Society of United Irishmen. During the Visitation of Lord Clare to Trinity, Corbett, his brother Thomas, Robert Emmet and others were expelled from the college and marked from the rolls.

In May 1798, knowing the authorities had them marked, Thomas and William Corbett left Ireland for France, travelling through Norway, Zealand and Hamburg. Upon arriving in Paris in August 1798, William joined the French military and was assigned as a captain in Napper Tandy's expedition to Ireland. The expedition, which consisted of one ship, the *Anacreon*, was given the mission to replenish Humbert's forces, but upon arriving at the desolate and rocky Rutland Island in Co. Donegal, on 16 September 1798, they learned that they were a week too late and decided to sail back to France. The ship, damaged by storms, was forced to dock at the Norwegian port of Bergen, causing a difficult journey for the officers of the expedition. Upon arriving at Hamburg on 3 November, Corbett applied for a passport but was refused. With fellow officers, James Blackwell and Hervey Morres, they waited for Tandy's arrival, as he had taken another route to the rendezvous.

On 24 November 1798, the group, including Tandy were arrested by the British consulate. Corbett's imprisonment conditions were harsh. His cell would often flood and the harsh continental winter was one of the coldest they had experienced. Corbett's determination saw him petition the Hamburg senate, even going as far as to write a pamphlet entitled, "**The Conduct of the Senate at Hamburg Revealed**," which he published nearly a decade later. He clearly held a grudge. Corbett's health started to decline rapidly due to the freezing and damp conditions, however, he was transferred to Dublin's Kilmainham Gaol, arriving there on 17 November 1799, to stand trial for the treasonable expedition. It is worth noting that his alias name of George Peters was entered on the prison log alongside his real name. The incarceration of Corbett, Blackwell and Tandy had caught the ear of Napoleon, who demanded their return to France, but to no avail. Sharing a cell with Thomas Trenor, Corbett's health started to deteriorate once again. Trenor organised and planned an escape, procuring a ladder, manufactured from knotted silk fabric. On 23 February 1801, the escape plan was initiated as it was a stormy night. Corbett climbed over the high walls of Kilmainham and injured himself from a vicious fall, however, the plan was a success and he eventually made it to France. Between 1801 and 1803, Corbett taught English at the College of St Cyr, until he received papers that he was to be commissioned as a captain in the newly formed Irish Legion, alongside his brother.

In September 1804, William would naturally side with his brother Thomas during the controversial dispute with John Swiney, which resulted in a pistol duel and Thomas' eventual death. On 2 December 1804, Corbett, being a senior captain in the Irish Legion, represented the regiment in his attendance of the coronation of Napoleon Bonaparte at Notre Dame, alongside John Tennant. Corbett's grief over his brother's loss, combined with him being side-lined in a promotion issue over seniority, resulted in him becoming disillusioned with the

Irish Legion and he was eventually moved to Division Staff. He left the army in 1806 and became reemployed as a teacher at St. Cyr. When the Irish Legion marched to fight in the Iberian Peninsula, Corbett felt the itch to re-join the army, but was attached to the 70th Regiment, instead of joining his old friends, and enemies, in the Irish Legion. Corbett would serve with great distinction and valour under Marshal Masséna and Marshal Marmont during the Peninsular War. Corbett would experience the horrors of the battles at Dresden, Leipzig and Bautzen and was awarded the honourable position as a commander of the *Légion d'honneur*. Corbett would eventually reach the rank of colonel, however, after the fall of the Bonaparte regime, Corbett was placed on half-pay.

In 1828, Corbett was given a place on the staff of Marshal Maison for the expedition to Greece. By 1831, he had been promoted to the rank of Brigadier-General and eventually the honourable position as commander-in-chief of the French forces in Greece. Upon returning to France, Corbett was again promoted to Major-General and was awarded a Knighthood of St. Louis. Corbett died at Saint-Denis, near Paris, on 12 August 1842 and was interred at Montmartre.

CORCORAN, John, Tom & Patrick – The Corcoran brothers hailed from Castlebar, Co. Mayo. Having fought with the Franco-Irish forces during Humbert's expedition, they escaped and fled to Canada.

CORCORAN, Peter - Peter Corcoran, having been arrested for his part in the 1798 Rebellion, was incarcerated at Kilmainham Gaol in Dublin. In his notes it states that he was willing to go to America if he is allowed to prepare.

CORMICK, John – Cormick, born c.1762, was a feather-merchant, based in Dublin, who was sworn into the United Irishmen in early 1797. In April 1798, William Lawless brought Lord Edward Fitzgerald to Cormick's residence, to use as a safehouse. During a house raid, Cormick fled to London and finally to Guernsey, where he was eventually arrested. He confessed his involvement to General Sir Hugh Dalrymple and offered his services to the Government in order to secure a full pardon. Upon sailing to Ireland to give evidence against former accomplices, Cormick again fled. During the summer of 1798, as the Rebellion submerged much of Ireland into ruin, Cormick sailed to the United States and settled in the southern States where he purchased an estate and its associated slaves, an act which would have disgusted many of his United Irish friends and associates and obviously an act which went against his own political ideals when resident in Ireland. In 1806, his marriage collapsed into a formal separation as his wife had not travelled to join her husband in the United States. Cormick's sister was married Mr. John Lube of Summerhill, a brother of George

Lube, a Kildare insurgent leader during the 1798 Rebellion. Miles Byrne simply records Cormick in his memoirs:

"John Cormick, at whose house in Thomas Street, Dublin, Lord Edward Fitzgerald frequently met his numerous friends. Mr. Cormick escaped to the United States, where he settled, and never was allowed to return, though he was led to expect that a permission would be given him, in 1822 to go to Ireland for a few days on family affairs; I met him at Paris in company at that period with General (William) Lawless and Edward Lewins, both these gentlemen seemed satisfied with the account Mr. Cormick gave them about the way he effected his escape to America, etc."

Cormick returned to his plantation in Georgia, eventually marrying Mrs. Catherine Butler Beach, in 1823. He died on 3 June 1826 and was interred at Magnolia Cemetery in Augusta, Georgia. His obituary stated:

"Captain Cormick…possessed of the purest Republican principles, and most firmly attached to a Religion, whose faith has descended unchanged from the Apostles; he entered warmly into the patriotic defence of that Liberty and Religion, which by the British Government was falsely denounced as rebellious."

CORMICK, Joseph – Joseph Cormick, a brother of John Cormick and a relation by marriage to the Lube Family of Corcoranstown, Co. Kildare, had fought in the north Kildare insurrection, under William Aylmer and Hugh Ware. Cormick was listed as one of the insurgent commanders, who surrendered at Odlum's Mills, near Sallins, Co. Kildare, on 21 July 1798. After the 1798 Rebellion, Cormick fled to the United States and settled in Augusta, Georgia. Having suffered from ill-health after his years of incarceration, Cormack died on 19 August 1806 and was interred at St. Paul's Episcopal Church Cemetery in Augusta. His ornate tombstone reads:

"This tomb encloses the mortal remains of Joseph G. Cormick. He was a Native of Ireland and in Common with the Majority of his Countrymen, felt the varied wrongs which afflict that devoted land. In an attempt prompted by Patriotism, guided by Honour, and supported by courage, failing to redress these wrongs, he turned from the enslaved shores of Europe to America, the only asylum of Liberty."

CORR, ? – Corr was a United Irishman from Co. Meath who fled to Hamburg in 1798.

COSTIGAN, Vincent – Costigan, a schoolteacher, was a United Irishman, who fled to Newfoundland after the failure of the 1798 Rebellion. His descendants settled at Harbour Main in Newfoundland.

COULTER, John

COULTER, John – John Coulter was born on 24 July 1777 in Co. Antrim. Having fought as an insurgent during the 1798 Rebellion, he eventually decided in 1803 to emigrate to America, settling in New York. Having relocated to Cincinnati in Ohio, Coulter purchased land at Mill Creek, which he improved. In 1807, he married Margaret Gibson, a native of Fermanagh. Coulter died on 13 February 1857 and was interred at Sabina Cemetery, Clinton County, Ohio.

COX, John – This individual was held in Carrickfergus Gaol in Co. Antrim in late 1799 alongside Robert Henry. Without being tried, it is recorded on a trial list from March 1800 that they were *"liberated some months ago, under recognisance to transport themselves, but not having done so in the limited time apprehended again."* It is unknown if Henry and Cox became exiles.

COX, Dr. John Coates – Dr. John C. Cox emigrated to America as a result of his participation in the 1798 Rebellion. His legacy would be determined by an event which had happened previously in 1781. Cox had served as a naval surgeon. On one maritime adventure, his ship docked on the western coast of Africa. Upon trekking with some acquaintances, they became lost and had to rely on local tribesmen to lead them to a secure location.

When Cox left Ireland, the ship upon which he was travelling was wrecked off the American coast and he was able to save the lives of his wife and son. Having briefly settled and practiced in North Carolina, the Cox family relocated to Natchez, Mississippi. Here he was astounded to discover that his neighbour's slave was the son of King Sori of Guinea, who had preserved his life and sent him back to civilisation when lost in Africa all those years before. Cox attempted to purchase the slave Ibrahima in order to liberate him, even offering a large sum of $1,000 but was refused. Cox died on 15 December 1816, however his son, William Rousseau Cox, continued his father's wishes to see Ibrahima (*pictured*) set free. Ibrahima was referred to as **"*Prince*"**, a title he kept until his final days. After spending forty years in slavery, he was eventually freed in 1828 by order of U.S. President, John Quincy Adams and the

Secretary of State, Henry Clay, after the Sultan of Morocco requested his release.

COX, Dr. William Rousseau – William R. Cox was the son of Dr. John Cox and was a young boy when he went to the United States with his parents. William graduated from the University of Pennsylvania in 1817 and practiced in Natchez, Mississippi. He died on 25 September 1831.

CRAIG, Rev. John - Rev. John Craig of Corroneary, Co. Monaghan fled to the United States in 1793 for his support of republicanism. It is noted that he took some of his flock with him and it can be assumed that he continued to minister to them. One of his former service attendees, Gamble of Knockalosset, was hanged in 1798.

CROMBIE, Joseph – (1776 – 1806) Crombie, a United Irish son of Rev. Dr. James Crombie of Belfast, who faced execution, was helped by Martha McTier's letter in which she begged General Nugent to remit Crombie's sentence and to allow him to emigrate to the United States. It is unknown to the authors if Nugent had given a reply to Mrs. McTier, but during a prisoner transfer at Donaghadee, Co. Down, Crombie made his escape, and fled to the United States. He settled with his brother who had already made his home in America.

CRONLY, John – John Cronly emigrated after the Rebellion in 1798 and settled in Utica, New York. In 1842, his cousin, William Carroll, placed an advertisement in New York's *Freeman's Journal*, seeking information about Cronly and his whereabouts.

CRUSE, Thomas – (1762-1832) Thomas Cruse was a successful wine merchant from Belfast. He was arrested after the 1798 Rebellion and imprisoned in Dublin. He accepted the terms of three months release to get his affairs in order to exile himself to America. He settled in Alexandria, Virginia. Cruse established himself as a merchant and in 1802 partnered with William Billingham to start the Potomac Brewing Company. He also used his fortune in later life to try and purchase female slaved to set them free. He was a stringent campaigner for abolition.

CUMACK, William - William Cumack was a United Irishman who was implicated in the 1798 Rebellion. He, like many, exiled to New York. In 1812 he joined the *"The Irish Blues"* which was a regiment were raised by the Ballymoney native Caldwell Family of Salisbury County (NY). Cumack was given a captaincy in the regiment. Interestingly, this unit was comprised mostly of United Irish exiles from the Ballymena/Ballymoney area of Co. Antrim.

CUMMINGS, Dr. George – (1768 – 1830) George Cummings was born c.1768 to a Scotch-Irish family in South Carolina. Around 1788, he travelled to Ireland having inherited land in his ancestral Co. Down. Having graduated in medicine from the University of Edinburgh, he returned to Ireland to practice, settling in Co. Kildare, where he befriended Lord Edward Fitzgerald and Arthur O'Connor. Having significant influence within the United Irishmen, Cummings was present at Oliver Bond's house when it was raided by Dublin Castle officers on 12 March 1798. This arrest saw Cummings spend the summer of 1798 in Kilmainham Gaol. In March 1799, he was conveyed to Fort George in Scotland, along with the other prominent United Irish prisoners. After his release from Fort George, Cummings returned to his property in Newry, Co. Down, and began organising his return to his native United States. In 1802, Cummings left Ireland and settled in New York City, where he became a devout Jeffersonian Republican and immersed himself in various Irish-American societies and exile committees including the *Friendly Sons of St Patrick*. He continued to practice medicine and died in New York.

CUMMINS, Dr. John B. – John Cummins, or Cumming, was a native of Co. Galway. Having studied medicine at the University of Edinburgh, Cummins returned to Ireland and practiced in Co. Carlow. Holding an influential role in the United Irishmen, his obituary claims he fought at the Battle of Carlow (25 May 1798). After his arrest, he was tried for treason and placed into Kilmainham Gaol on 22 June 1799, where he would remain until 9 April 1802. Upon release, Cummins fled to the continent, settling for a short period in Cadiz, Spain. Having passed into France, he was given a lieutenancy commission in the Irish Legion, however, he retired in 1806, in which Miles Byrne states he went back to Cadiz. Cummins emigrated to the United States, where he practiced for several years in Williamsburg, South Carolina before relocating to Augusta, Georgia. His obituary in the *Charleston Courier* (25 July 1842) describes how Cummins had joined General Andrew Jackson as a field-surgeon during his brutal challenges with the Seminote Indians. John Cummins retired to Savannah, Georgia, and passed away on 19 July 1842.

CURRY, William – William Curry was one of the leaders of the United Irishmen from Islandmagee, near Larne, Co. Antrim. After the Rising, a bounty of £50 was placed upon the head of William by the Government, therefore he would be categorised as a "***Fifty Pounder***". Curry is reported to have escaped to New York. After several years in the United States, Curry returned to Ireland to reside at Islandmagee.

CUST, John – John Cust, a Presbyterian United Irishman was banished to America along with many others from the Limavady area of north Co. Derry.

His family had worked with the local landlord for many years as rent collectors, court leet officers and held their own lease of land. In 1807, the landlord, Marcus Gage of Bellarena wrote to the Government on behalf of Cust hoping to seek a pardon. It's unknown if he returned from America however there was a John Cust leasing land to Magilligan's Rev. Samuel Butler in the 1810s.

CUTHBERT, Joseph - Joseph Cuthbert, a master tailor, was born in Belfast c.1762. He played a significant and leading role in the Belfast United Irishmen from its inception. Cuthbert was appointed to forge alliances between the United Irishmen and the Defenders Movement. Having been arrested, he was brought to Kilmainham Gaol on 1 May 1797, alongside Robert Redfern and Israel Milliken, where he would remain until he was sent to Fort George in Scotland in March 1799. After his release in 1802, Cuthbert sailed to New York City with his family and recommenced his profession of tailoring. He died at his residence at 81 William Street in Lower Manhattan on 1 February 1805.

DALY, Richard – Daly was arrested for his part in the 1798 Rebellion and was imprisoned at Kilmainham gaol. Daly is recorded on the National Archives of Ireland Irish-Australian Transportation Database, in which it states that he was willing to go to America if he was allowed to prepare.

DALZELL, John – Dalzell, a scion of an old Scot Covenanter family, had served with the insurgency in his native Co. Down during the 1798 Rebellion, which resulted in him fleeing to the United States. He settled in Oneida County in upstate New York. His children included: Mary Ann (1802-1869), Robert Dalzell (later resided in Rochester, NY) and James Dalzell (later settled in Columbus, Ohio).

DARRAGH, William & Family – William Darragh was a United Irishman who was captured in Newtownards in Co. Down, for participation in the 1798 Rebellion. Darragh was court-martialled and permitted to exile to the United States, taking his family with him. It's unknown what became of this family after arriving the United States.

DEMPSEY – In the 1930s, Tombrack N.S. Schools' Folklore (Co. Wexford), recorded the following story which was collected by Charlotte Redmond, regarding the apprehension of two north Wexford insurgents named Martin Rourke and Dempsey during the 1798 Rebellion. *"A woman named Nancy Gilchrist lived in the gate lodge of De Renzy's swore against Martin Rourke and Dempsey. She said they were there and left the children with her. They were taken to Bunclody and a summary trial held on them. They were found guilty and were to be hanged next day. At some time during the night Dempsey* *asked leave to go out in the yard for a few minutes. When he got out, he got over the gate, seven feet high and escaped into Ryland Wood. He got off safely and later escaped to America."*

The DENNISTON BROTHERS *of Clonbroney, County Longford*

The Denniston brothers, Alexander & Hans, are synonymous with the 1798 story in Co. Longford. They inspired the generations of Longford revolutionaries that followed, especially future political leader, Sean MacEoin, *"The Blacksmith of Ballinalee,"* who had a distant maternal relative, named Treacy, who was hanged by Crown Forces at the big tree of Bunlahy in 1798. The Denniston's descended from a respectable Presbyterian farming background and held leading positions in the Mostrim Yeomanry before the outbreak of the 1798 Rebellion. The Denniston's are associated with the Battle of Granard, which was fought on 4 September 1798. On that date, thousands of insurgents assembled across Co. Longford. A letter, scribed by Captain Cottingham of the Cavan and Ballyhaise Infantry, describes the events of the day in detail.

"Granard, 5th of September 1798
My Lord,
I have the honour to state to your Lordship that the rebels were yesterday defeated near this place with great slaughter. Having received orders from Major Porter of the Argyle regiment, who commanded at Cavan, to proceed without delay with detachments from the Cavan and Ballintemple corps of Yeomen infantry, consisting of eighty-five men, to the relief of Granard, which was threatened by the rebels - I marched from Cavan at three o'clock in the morning of the 5th instant with all possible expedition, and arrived between 7 and 8 at Granard - the rebel army was then in view of the town, in full march to it, armed with musquetry and pikes, amounting (as appeared by the testimony of several prisoners) to more than 6000 men, and commanded by Mr. Denniston, a lieutenant in the Mostrim cavalry, who, with others of that corps, and several respectable persons in that neighbourhood, had joined the rebel standard."

The Battle of Granard is one of the most understudied battles of the 1798 Rebellion and is sadly forgotten behind a long list of skirmishes, clashes and other events of the period. A field, in the townland of Rathbracken, near Granard, was locally known as *"The Farm of the Burnt House,"* in memory of the Denniston farmhouse, which was destroyed during the Rebellion. Local folklore, it seems, has amalgamated the brothers into one individual, as highlighted by Guy Beiner. The following account shows us one example:

"One of the leaders at the Battle of Granard in '98 was Denniston, a Presbyterian who lived in Lower Rathbracken, parish of Granard. When the French surrendered at Ballinamuck the Irish soldiers who escaped retreated to Granard and made a last stand there. Sept 8th '98. The principal leaders were Pat O'Farrell and Denniston. In the evening when the Irish forces were outnumbered Denniston escaped and made his way by "The Rocks" (beside Granard) through Clough and down near his old home. through Cranally. He told the people to go to his house and take whatever they could out of it because the Yeos, he said, would surely burn it. Denniston was a well-to-do gentleman farmer and his house had a great supply of meal, bacon, butter etc. The people around were afraid to go near the house so it was burned by the Yeos. The old people used to say that the smell of the burning bacon was carried miles. There were a large number of fine cows on the farm, and as they were in full milk they suffered dreadfully as no one would go near the place to milk them. Some of the cows sucked themselves and so saved their lives but the others died of milk fever. Denniston had many friends who used their influence so that his wife was spared and he was allowed to remain in Ireland, but he never came back to Rathbracken. His farm was given to a Protestant named Gosling who built cattle sheds with the stones of Denniston's house. He also built a hut for a herd and his wife but they could never sleep in it. One could sleep if the other remained up at night, but not otherwise."

DENNISTON, Alexander -

Alexander Denniston was born on 19 September 1766 to John Denniston and Ann Peebles. It is clear that they had been United Irishmen as they revealed their allegiances during the outbreak of the Longford Rising. His younger brother, Hans Denniston had been dispatched to Belfast to receive instructions. His return to his native county, on 3 September 1798, was the signal for the '*turn out*' to occur and to support the French, under General Jean Humbert. After the failure of the Rebellion, Alexander Denniston had relatively little option but to emigrate to the United States. It seems he had survived execution because of their family's respectable standing in Co. Longford and also their close family links to Governor George Clinton of New York, who would become the fourth Vice-President of the United States in 1805. This relationship, we can imagine, would prove beneficial to the Denniston brothers upon their settling in the United States.

Alexander Denniston's Commission, signed by U.S. President, James Madison

Alexander Denniston would become the appointed Lieutenant-Colonel of a Battalion of New York Volunteers on 1 February 1813, during the War of 1812.

On 15 April 1814, he took command of the US 47th Infantry, but he is mostly remembered for his command of the 27th Infantry, which was raised in New York City on 12 May 1814, and would contain many Irish veterans of the 1798 Rebellion, who fled their homeland in the years after the Rebellion.

The following is a letter of correspondence from an Irishman, Thomas Toole, to President Madison, urging him to commission a regiment of free black men to fight within the US Army, using Denniston as an example of leadership.

"No 6 Courtland St New York 2 Septr. 1814

Sir,

Feeling sensibly for the premature and unexpected destruction of the Capitol, as well as your personal Loss, and distress of mind, Occasioned by the Enemy I therefore beg your Excellency will permit me as an humble Irishman to address You for the purpose of Suggesting a matter of great Inportance for the defence of this City as well as for the use of the army in general, Viz, To raise two or three Thousand able Bodied free men of Colour Simply armed With a pike and case of pistols for close action, with such men the front of Strong advancing columns, as Well as artillery, and Cavalry, may be attacked with great Success, and ultimately Inspire the Malitia (sic) with great confidence to Stand their Ground.

Had one Thousand or fifteen hundred Stout pikemen been attached to the Baltimore Volunteers at Bledensburg, The rapid progress of the Enemy would have been Stopped, and the Capitol Saved, In Ireland in 1798, the Pesantry with pikes alone, with incompetent commanders in many places, as the officers appointed were either shot, hung, or confined in Prison, by order of the British Government, In many, many, Engagements, The pikemen charged and destroyed the flower of the British Troops, cut up their Cavalry, and took their Artillery. This is a matter of fact, and a Strong criterion to convince your Excellency, that Such acts of Valour can be performed by pikemen in this Country. For the authenticity of this, I beg leave to refer You to Col. Alexander Denniston, 27 U. S. Intfy, in or near this city, who had the honor to command a large Body of Pikemen in Ireland in the Year 1798. There are many others in this city to Whom I can refer if necessary, Should this Idea meet Your Excellencys Approbation, I would recommend Six pieces of flying Artillery attached to the pike Regimt, to cover their advance, at a criticle moment, to the Enemy's lines, or Overpowering Columns, to Measure a nine foot pole & pike, after deliberately dischargeing their pistols, with the British Bayonet, If the Secretary at War will honor me with a Captns. Commission in the Pike Regimt. I will enter the field with great Confidence, to fight for my adopted Country against an Enemy whose Government and acts, I so much detest, I beg to be honored with an Answr. of the result of Your Excellency's Consideration. I am, Respectfully Your Excellencys Obdt. Servt.

Thos. Toole"

Alexander Denniston married Maria Parker on 25 June 1814 and was honourably discharged on 15 June 1815. Their children included John Alexander Denniston (1815-1880), Hans Peebles Denniston (1818-1859), Anne Maria Denniston (1821-1884), George Bond Denniston, Harriet Sophia Denniston (1827-1902), William Fleming Denniston and Benjamin Denniston. Upon returning to visit his native Longford in 1830, Maria died on the journey. She is buried at Corboy Presbyterian Church in Co. Longford. Alexander would travel back to the United States a widower. The eldest Denniston eventually died on 4 April 1846 at Bethel, Sullivan County in New York State. No known headstone exists for such a paramount name of Longford's revolutionary past. His grandsons, Private George Andrew Denniston and Corporal John Alexander Denniston (*pictured together*) were both killed during the American Civil War.

DENNISTON, Hans Peebles – Hans

Denniston was born on 9 July 1769, at Leitrim, a townland close to Ballinalee, Co. Longford, to John Denniston and Ann Peebles. Hans Denniston appears to have been the leading United Irishman in Longford during 1798. He most probably avoided the severest penalty due to family or friendly influences. On 3 August 1803, Denniston was arrested by Colonel Thewlis on suspicion of having been involved. 1798 historian, Dr. Ruan O'Donnell believes that Denniston was a marked man thanks to the published books by Sir Richard Musgrave and John Jones, which described the infiltration of the Mostrim Yeomanry by the United Irishmen in 1798. The Kilmainham Gaol registers highlight that Hans was incarcerated there on 18 September 1803 on charges of treasonable practices. He was eventually discharged on 3 December 1803, most probably on an agreement of self-exile. Little evidence

exists to describe the American life of Hans Denniston. He married Maria Turkington and their children are listed as: Maria Anne Denniston (b.1814), Eliza Catherine Denniston, John Alexander Denniston, Hans Peebles Denniston Jr (b.1819), Richardson Denniston and Robert Falls Denniston (1824-1889). Hans Denniston died on 16 June 1837, in New York City. Today, his remains lie at Green Wood Cemetery, Kings County in Brooklyn, New York, with only his name simply inscribed.

Denniston's grandson, Hans Powell, was born in Dublin on 14 February 1844. His father, George Powell had served as Secretary of the Royal Board of Education. Hans Powell studied medicine and received his diploma from the Coombe Hospital in late 1860. He attended Mercer's Hospital and lectures at the Royal College of Surgeons. In January 1863, Powell sailed to the United States aboard the *Columbia*, and applied to the Governor of New York for a position to serve in the Union Army, which was engaged in the American Civil War. Powell was promoted as surgeon of the 3rd New York Volunteers for distinguished services at the capture of Fort Fisher.

DENVER: An American city named after the Grandson of a 98 exile.

DENVER, Patrick, Sr – Patrick Denver of Co. Down, born c.1747, had been an active member of the United Irishmen and participated to some degree in the 1798 Rebellion. Fearing arrest or retribution, he fled to the United States in 1799, taking his young son and namesake. The family arrived in New York City on 18 December 1799, the date in which President George Washington was laid to rest. After a brief period in New York, the Denver family relocated to Frederick County in Virginia. Patrick Denver Sr died there on 31 March 1831, aged 84 years.

DENVER, Patrick, Jr - Patrick Denver Jr was born in Co. Down in January 1787. He accompanied his father to the United States in late 1799 and spent his youth in Frederick County, Virginia. When the War of 1812 commenced, young Denver enlisted to serve his adopted country and became a sub-Lieutenant in the U.S. Army and would serve with distinction and gain promotion. He married Jane Campbell and in the 1830s, the family relocated to Wilmington, Ohio. Patrick Denver Jr died on 29 July 1858 and was

interred at Sugar Grove Cemetery in Wilmington, Ohio.

James William Denver (*pictured*) led a fascinating life, having served as a Union Brigadier-General during the American Civil War and also a U.S. Congressman. His career began during the Mexican-American War during which he had served as Captain in the 12th Regiment, U.S. Infantry. After cessation of hostilities, Denver moved to California in 1850, which was then experiencing a tremendous gold rush. He was elected to the State Senate in 1851 and appointed California's State Secretary in 1852. In 1855, he was elected as a Democrat to the Thirty-fourth Congress, serving until 1857. From 1857 to 1859, he served as Commissioner of Indian Affairs and as Governor of the Territory of Kansas. At the outbreak of the Civil War in 1861, President Abraham Lincoln commissioned him Brigadier-General in command of all Union troops in

the State of Kansas. Denver commanded the 3rd Brigade during the Siege of Corinth in 1862 and served as the Kansas Union garrison administrator until his resignation from the U.S. Army in March 1863. After the war ceased, he practiced law in Washington D.C. and was as a delegate to Democratic National Conventions in 1876, 1880, and 1884. The frontier town of Denver in Colorado was named after this great man as a way to gain popularity with the local Commissioners and the Governor, only for them to realise he had left office a week previous. James W. Denver died in Washington D.C. in August 1892.

His son, Matthew Rombach Denver (*pictured*), the great-grandson of Patrick Denver Sr, became a U.S. Congressman. Born in Wilmington, Ohio, he graduated from Georgetown University, Washington, D.C., in 1892 and became a successful banker. For many years he was a delegate to the Democratic National Conventions and was a member of the Democratic Ohio State committee. In 1907, he was elected as a Democrat to the Sixtieth, Sixty-first and Sixty-second Congresses, serving until 1913. Upon declining the candidacy for re-election, Denver returned to banking and served as president of the Ohio Bankers' Association. He was elected a member of the Democratic State committee, serving and was president of the Clinton County National Bank & Trust Company, until his death in 1954 in Wilmington, Ohio.

DERRY, Valentine – Derry was born c. 1761 at Donaghmore, Co. Down to John Derry and Rose Maseby. He is reported to have been a Lieutenant in the United Irishmen and was not only a relative but a close associate of Fr. James Coigly, who was executed in England in June 1798. Derry fled to Paris and became a teacher of the Classics at the College of La Fléche and helped the notable Miles Byrne with learning the French Language. He was commissioned a Lieutenant in the Irish Legion in December 1803, followed with a promotion to Captain in March 1804. In 1806, he resigned his commission upon realising there would be no French expedition to Ireland and emigrated to the United States. He established himself at the Academy of Erasmus Hall at Flatbush in Brooklyn, New York, where he held the title of principal teacher between 1808-1809. Derry, with the support from fellow exile, William Sampson, established his own academy at Newtown in Queens, which charged students $200 for annual tuition and board. On 3 October 1821, Valentine Derry died at his New York residence, 100 Greenwich Street, aged 60 years, and was interred in the old churchyard of the Basilica of St. Patrick's.

MR. DERRY'S ACADEMY, BLOOMINGDALE.

A FEW additional Boarders can be accommodated in this Academy; where young gentlemen, whether studying the Mathematics, preparing for the Counting-House, the Freshman, Sophomore, or Junior Class, have the advantage of learning to write and speak both the French and English Languages.

The second year after Mr. Derry's arrival in this country, Dr. Wilson favored him with the following Testimonial:

" At the instance of Mr. Valentine Derry, principal Teacher in the Academy of Erasmus-Hall, Flatbush, and of other gentlemen interested, I have examined some of the classes studying under the care of the former, and must, in justice, declare, that a number of young gentlemen, notwithstanding the difficulty of the undertaking, appear to have been instructed at once in three different languages, Latin, French and English, with great care and accuracy. They were at the same time well initiated in Latin Prosody: and, considering the time they had spent in acquiring the elements of the Greek language, they acquitted themselves in a manner that does credit to their instructor. Their translations from English into Latin, and their corrections of bad English, discovered an accurate acquaintance with the grammars of both languages.

"P. WILSON, L. L. D."

September 8, 1809.

TERMS: Board, Washing, and Tuition, including French, $200 per annum; Day Scholars, $50. Music, Dancing, and Drawing Masters, attend and instruct, on moderate terms.

Letters, communications, &c. for the Academy, are received by Mr Chambers, 48 Wall-street, and at counsellor Sampson's office, No. 6 Murray-street, New-York.   april 9—1in

DEVELIN, Charles – Charles Develin was imprisoned on the *Postlethwait* prison ship in Belfast Lough during the 1798 Rebellion. It's unknown what particular role he played during the rebellion. Develin was released in September 1798, having paid for his own transport to the United States.

DEVEREUX, Alexander, 'Sandy' – Born in 1777 at Cooladine, near Enniscorthy, Co. Wexford, to Alexander Devereux and Catherine Etchingham. Miles Byrne described the story of Sandy Devereux's background and arrival in France in September 1803.

"One day Mr. Thomas Addis Emmet read me a letter he had just received (at Paris) from William Dowdall, stating, that he, and John Allen, and a young man by the name of Sandy Devereux, had escaped safely to Cadiz (Spain) after many risks and perils. He asked me questions about Devereux. As to Allen and Dowdall, he said, I known them sufficiently enough myself, to answer for them. I told them that Devereux was one of our hurling associates at Donnybrook Green; that he was from the County of Wexford and employed at the mercantile firm of Cornelius McLoughlan and company in Dublin; that I did not think committed in our unfortunate affairs" Devereux joined the Irish Legion and was given a commission of sub-Lieutenant.

DEVEREUX, John – Devereux was born in 1778 to William Devereux and Mary Dixon, into a comfortable farming and distilling background at Taghmon, Co. Wexford. Devereux was a junior officer in the Southern Division of the Wexford insurgency during the 1798 Rebellion and fought at the Battle of New Ross, on 5 June 1798. After William Devereux was imprisoned in Wexford Gaol, young John Devereux was placed into safety by Francis L'Estrange, a Carmelite friar in Dublin. The news would reach him that his father would die from illness as a result of the incarceration. At the intercession of Lord Cornwallis, Devereux was pardoned and the lands secured from forfeiture on condition that he self-exiled himself. Devereux fled to France and joined the Irish Legion however, it seems that his term in France did not extend for more than a decade. By 1812, Devereux was residing in Baltimore, Maryland, in the USA, in voluntary exile and as a US Citizen. In 1812, at a time of increasing hostilities between Britain and the United States, he shipped a cargo of coffee through a British blockade from Baltimore to France. In 1815, upon arriving at Cartagena (Columbia) with a cargo of arms and ammunition, Devereux made a bombastic proposal to the patriots under Simon Bolivar that he would muster up an army of supporters from Britain and Ireland, claiming he had friends at Westminster and that he had commanded an Irish army in 1798. The patriots were intrigued by Devereux's proposals and offered him the reward of £175 per soldier that he recruited. It was an ambitious plan but not entirely fruitless. After visiting Buenos Aires, he untruthfully attempted to convince the authorities that he could try raise a loan of two million pesos, backed by the US Government. Upon arrival at Haiti, Devereux met Robert Sutherland, a British merchant in Port au Prince. In July 1817, Sutherland liaised with Bolivar about Devereux's offers of raising an Irish Legion. Bolivar agreed and Devereux, continuing his ambitions, landed in Ireland in 1818 and started a process of mustering a force. Devereux was in luck as mass-demobbing from the British Army saw Irish who had served in the Napoleonic Wars enlist in the project. There was much enthusiasm towards the venture, even so that Morgan O'Connell, son of Daniel O'Connell, enlisted as an officer, with a forged document offering the commission from Bolivar. Francis Burdett O'Connor, the son of United Irishman, Roger O'Connor and nephew of Arthur O'Connor also enlisted and created a legacy in South American independence history. A substantial amount of 1798 veterans from all sides enlisted. What was interesting about this venture was that former Irish pikemen were enlisting alongside former yeomen and Waterloo veterans. Over 1700 enlisted in Devereux's Legion, with a thousand sailing to Margarita, an island off the coast of Venezuela in the autumn of 1819. The excitement declined when the Legionnaires faced mutiny because of poor drinking water, tropical diseases and lack of military usage by the Bolivar leadership, whilst 'General' Devereux remained at home with his newly created wealth from selling commissions. Many returned disillusioned to Ireland and Britain.

On 27 April 1820, Devereux sailed from Liverpool to Jamaica, via Barbados and Riohacha, in search of the Legion. He quarrelled with fellow officers and was imprisoned for several months after an altercation with the Vice-President, General Narino. Devereux was pardoned by Bolivar for the poor conduct and mutinies within the Legion. Devereux was reimbursed for his expenses and appointed to the General Command at Bogota. In late 1823, Devereux was appointed as the Columbian emissary to the royal courts of Europe. Whilst in Italy, he was arrested and imprisoned in Venice on charges of potential agitation. Devereux's role in the independence struggles minimised afterwards, however, his arrogance and vanity allowed for exaggeration to prevail on written accounts. In his later years, his eyesight diminished to complete blindness as a result of tropical illnesses from his time in Latin America. John Devereux died on 25 February 1860 at his residence on Hertford Street in London's Mayfair.

THE DEVEREUX FAMILY *of The Leap, Enniscorthy, County Wexford*

The Devereux Family hailed from The Leap, a townland west of Enniscorthy, in the Adamstown district of County Wexford. The children of Thomas Devereux and Catherine Corish not only included the following recorded emigrants to the United States, but also James Devereux, who was killed at the Battle of Vinegar Hill, on 21 June 1798 and Catherine Devereux (Mother Mary Frances de Sales) who founded the Presentation Convent in Enniscorthy in 1826. The death of one brother in the Rebellion, another fleeing to the West Indies and the untimely death of their father as a result of the Rebellion had forced the Devereux Brothers to emigrate to the United States.

DEVEREUX, John Corish – John Devereux was born at The Leap in August 1774. Due to local agitation, John left home in 1796, going first to France and then the United States, where he resided for a short period in Connecticut, where he was employed as a dance tutor and where it is said he danced thousands out of the Americans. Having amassed a comfortable fortune, Devereux moved to Utica in upstate New York in 1802, where he established a dry goods merchant business. In 1806, he was joined by his brothers, Thomas, Luke and Nicholas Devereux, who left Ireland after the lease of their family lands was taken from them for the family's support of the insurgents during the 1798 Rebellion. Luke Devereux joined John in his enterprise until his death in late 1817.

In 1815, Devereux entered into a partnership with his youngest brother, Nicholas Devereux, a decision which would prove extremely fruitful. The construction of the Erie Canal brought tremendous employment to a once rural and depopulated area. The Devereux's flourished during this project, allowing them to invest in other businesses. In 1813, his wife, Ellen Barry, died. He later remarried Mary Colt but they had no family. Instead, he adopted his nephew, John C. Devereux, after the death of Thomas Devereux in Ireland. Noted for his benevolence, Devereux donated thousands of dollars to the development of Utica's Catholic and Presbyterian churches, gaining much

JOHN C. DEVEREUX & Co.
Have received a large aſſortment of faſhionabl
DRY GOODS,
calculated for the ſeaſon. ALso, a general aſſor
ment of Groceries, Leather, Iron, Crockery, &
which will be ſold low for Caſh or Country Pr
duce---and by wholeſale, at the uſual Credit.
Utica, May 26, 1807.   ['16

popularity. In 1840, he was elected the first Mayor of Utica. John C. Devereux died on 11 December 1848, leaving a vast fortune of $400,000 and was interred at the grounds of the Sisters of Charity, near St. John's Church in Utica.

DEVEREUX, Luke – Luke Devereux emigrated to New York with his younger brother Nicholas Devereux around 1806 and they joined their brother, John C. Devereux at Utica, New York. An advertisement from the *Columbian Gazette*, dated 31 March 1807, highlights that Luke had become a partner in his brother's growing business, however, this business was dissolved on 18 June 1810. Another venture dissolved in May 1814. Luke also either established or managed Utica Crown Glass, as shown on the advertisement pictured, dating from 1814. Luke Devereux suffered an untimely death from yellow fever at the frontier town of Natchez in the State of Mississippi on 20 October 1817. It is possible that Devereux was visiting Natchez on business or meeting fellow Wexfordian, Nicholas Gray, who was resident of Natchez as a land surveyor and who would die during the following year.

UTICA CROWN GLASS
Warehouse.

THE subscriber informs the public that he has on hand a general assortment of UTICA CROWN GLASS, and that all orders will be immediately attended to. The great attention paid to the packing of his Glass, the superiority of its quality, and the reduction of the price, must give it a decided preference.

LUKE DEVEREUX.

Utica, Feb. 14—70

DEVEREUX, Nicholas – The youngest of the Devereux brothers, Nicholas Devereux was born on 7 June 1791, so he would have remembered or witnessed the events of the 1798 Rebellion in his native Wexford. When he was a teenager, young Devereux travelled to the United States, with his brothers, Luke and Thomas Devereux. Having arrived in the United States, the trio made their way to Albany in New York before joining their brother, John Corish Devereux at Utica. With the Devereux's dry goods business having periods of success, young Nicholas was employed by his brother as a clerk, where he gained much business experience. Having partnered for a period with his brothers, John and Luke, young Nicholas established a partnership with George Tisdale, which proved successful upon the construction of the Erie Canal. In November 1817 he married Mary Dolbear Butler. Their daughter Hannah Devereux, who married Francis Kernan, a future U.S. Senator and son of a 1798 exile. In 1835, Devereux was a major part of a consortium who purchased the Holland Land Company, which had been formed as a result of the Holland Purchase in the 1790s, amounting to c.400,000 acres. He oversaw much development in Utica,

including the establishment of the United States Bank in the town (*pictured*), which benefitted many of the families of Irish labourers, working on the Erie Project. and profited from various railroad projects. As Devereux's wealth expanded, so did his philanthropy. Being an ardent Roman Catholic, Devereux reputedly read the Holy Bible seventeen times. Alongside his brother, John, he was a trustee of St. John's Orphan Asylum, and before he died, he founded the Assumption Academy, which was ran by the Christian Brothers. He donated 200 acres of land and oversaw the foundation of the St. Bonaventure University in Allegany, New York, and was a major conduit in the spread of Roman Catholicism in rural western New York. Amassing a fortune of over half a million dollars, he was an inspiration to immigrant Irish, who often sought financial advice from Devereux, in which he gladly gave. Nicholas Devereux died on

29 December 1855 and was interred at St. Agnes' Cemetery in Utica, New York, where his headstone still remains in relatively good condition. After his death, his widow carried out his wishes to see an American College founded in Rome, to educate American priests.

DEVEREUX, Thomas – Thomas Devereux travelled to the United States with his brothers, Nicholas and Luke, however, he returned to Ireland within several years, marrying Mary Redmond.

DEVEREUX, Walter – Walter Devereux was born in 1773. On 1 April 1798, he wrote to his brother, John C. Devereux, exclaiming in detail the turbulent occurrences across their native Wexford. He wrote:

"Dear John it is the greatest happiness to you that you left this unfortunate country, now the pray of Orange and Castle bloodhounds. Almost every county in poor old Ireland under Martial Law and the poor country peasants shot or hanged or Bastilled (imprisoned) without law or form of trial."

Walter Devereux became involved in the 1798 Rebellion and later fled to Martinique in the West Indies, disguised as a sailor. It is unknown what became of him.

DEVLIN, Patrick – Patrick Devlin, from Co. Tyrone, was patriarch of a Quaker family, who had to flee to the United States. Patrick and his son Richard Devlin were both implicated and arrested for their part in the 1798 Rebellion, and were encouraged to voluntary exile. Patrick chose to go to settle in Philadelphia.

DEVLIN, Richard '*Daredevil Dick*' – Richard Devlin, a native of Co. Tyrone was the son of the above-mentioned Patrick Devlin. Having being implicated for their part in the 1798 Rebellion, the Devlin's were arrested and were sentenced to voluntary banishment. Richard Devlin fled to France

The DEVLIN BROTHERS - According to Maghera (Co. Derry) Historian, Joseph McCoy, Paul Devlin, a blacksmith in the Maghera district during the 1798 Rebellion, had seven sons who fled to the United States. Paul Devlin was suspected by the authorities of making pike-heads for the local insurgency and matters came to a head when it became known that arms were being stored at the local rectory in Ballinascreen. A group of the Devlin family raided the rectory, seizing all the weapons that they found there. Of course, there was an outcry when the theft was discovered. Tradition has it that the seven Devlin sons managed to escape to America but their father was hanged between the shafts of his own farm cart.

DICKEY, John – John Dickey of Crumlin, Co. Antrim, was the older brother of James Dickey, an insurgent leader who was executed for his role in the Antrim Rebellion of 7-9 June 1798. John was arrested in September 1798, court-martialled and conveyed to a Dublin prison. Having been sentenced to transportation to the West Indies, he eventually managed to escape and made his way to America.

DIXON, Margaret '*Yalla Madge*' – Margaret Dixon, informally remembered as '*Yalla Madge*' Dixon, due to her apparent dark skin, was wife of Tom Dixon of Castlebridge. Various folklore stories portray Madge Dixon as a heroine whilst others state that she had been attacked by soldiers, which manifested into a ruthless desire for revenge. Her heritage is disputed. Some of the mentioned folklore categorises her as a sister of Wexford insurgent leader, Edward Roche of Garrylough, whilst others state that her maiden name was Brown of Kilcorral. It is indicated that she fled to America with her husband to avoid retribution for the Dixon's role in the Wexford Bridge Massacre.

Regarding the Wexford Bridge Massacre, Miles Byrne attacked the actions of the Dixons in his memoirs:

"...and the cowardly Dixon who got the prisoners put to death on the bridge of Wexford, was a seafaring 'cannibal' who took advantage of the chiefs being away at the camp, to commit this atrocious crime: these brave leaders would have saved liberty this lamentable disgrace; not one of them ever suffered or countenanced such reprisals."

DIXON, Tom –
Tom Dixon of Castlebridge, Co. Wexford, was born c.1742, a son of Nicholas Dixon, a miller and merchant. He was also a cousin to Fr. James Dixon, who was transported to New South Wales in 1799. A seafarer, Dixon would play a horrific part in the 1798 Rebellion in Wexford. He masterminded an intimidatory role over the Wexford leadership, Matthew Keough and Bagenal Harvey, even instigating plans to murder them. As General Lake was enveloping the north Co. Wexford, Dixon, who was influential over a group, ordered Wexford Gaol to be emptied of many of its prisoners; many of whom had been yeomen or zealous loyalists before the outbreak of rebellion in Wexford. We do not know for certain if Dixon's orders to execute the prisoners was wholesomely because of their religion or retaliation for their extremities against innocent people before the outbreak. Regardless of the reason, the nature of the killings would place Dixon as a notorious tyrant. Over ninety prisoners were individually piked to death on Wexford Bridge and their remains dumped into the harbour. It only ceased when Fr. Corrin arrived and demanded the bloodletting to quit. Dixon remained with the insurgents until the total collapse of the Leinster Rebellion. Folklore has indicated that he fled to the United States with his wife, Margaret Dixon.

DOBBIN, Anthony –
In 1823, Anthony Dobbin wrote an article in the *Washington Review and Examiner*. He stated that he knew a man called 'Gauger' Gregg in his native Co. Derry. Gauger, a noted loyalist, sent many United Irishmen into exile from Co. Derry. Anthony Dobbin was one of them. He gave further details that Gauger was a violent persecutor and that several of those who were exiled were in a very distressed constitution as a result of their dealings with Gregg. He records that Gregg eventually had to flee to England and then possibly to America for a reason unknown. Anthony settled in the town of Newry in Franktown township in the county of Huntingdon, Pennsylvania.

DOBBIN, George – George Dobbin (*pictured*) hailed from Co. Armagh and fled as a result of General Lake's crackdown in April 1797. Dobbin settled in Baltimore, Maryland. There he became a printer and became a co-proprietor of the *Baltimore American* newspaper. George Dobbin died unexpectantly on 17 December 1811 aged 38 years. He was buried in the Second Baltimore Presbyterian churchyard, which was established by fellow exile, Rev. Glendy.

The Dobbin Family *of Connagher, County Antrim*

DOBBIN, James – In June 1798, the Dobbin family had turned out to engage in the insurrection. Three brothers, James, John and William Dobbin, all played their part with their father. Having been captured James was put at the mercy of his capturers and was banished from Ireland and sent into exile.

DOBBIN, John Sr – John Dobbin Sr, having married Mary Miller and fathered three sons, travelled to America in the 1770s where he apparently participated in the American Revolutionary War, on the side of the colonists. Upon returning to Ireland, his wife died shortly afterwards. In 1798, the Dobbin family answered the call and as United Irishmen participated in the Rebellion. John fled with his youngest sons, David Miller Dobbin and Samuel Dobbin to America. They landed in Virginia and made the rest of the journey to Washington County, New York, by foot. John Dobbin Sr is buried in an unmarked grave at Christy Cemetery, New York.

DOBBIN, John Jr – During the Antrim Rebellion, John, having been captured was put at the mercy of his capturers and was banished from Ireland and sent into exile. He settled in Washington County in New York, at the close of 1798. He married Jane McKillop and died on 22 March 1860 and was interred at Old Shushan & Eagleville Cemetery in Eagleville (NY).

DOBBIN, William – William Dobbin was born on 22 February 1771. After the Rebellion failed, Dobbin had a bounty placed upon his head which resulted in him going into hiding, while his two brothers escaped to America. After a period of time, he married Jane Andrew and settled with his family in his native Connagher, Co. Antrim. In 1824, the family emigrated to Washington

County, New York. He became a leading elder in the United Presbyterian Church in Shushan. William Dobbin died on 24 June 1858 and was interred at South Argyle Church Cemetery in Washington County photographed.

DONAVIN, John – John Donavin was a Methodist from Co. Armagh. He fled to the United States in the months preceding the outbreak of the Rebellion across Ireland, however all sources about his life claim he fled as a result of the civil disturbances. Donavin settled in Lancaster County in Pennsylvania, marrying Jane McElroy, before moving to Shippensburg, in Cumberland County (PA). Donavin died in 1863, aged 91 years and was interred at Spring Hill Cemetery in Shippensburg.

DOUGAN, Peter – Peter Dougan was tried by court-martial at Newtownards, Co. Down. He was allowed to banish himself to the United States

DOUGHERTY, James – James Dougherty is recorded within the publication, *Fayette County, Pennsylvania Biographies*: **"*James was a native of Ireland and came to America at the close of the Irish Rebellion of 1798, in which he was a prominent actor.*"** Nothing else is known about Dougherty other than he settled in Fayette County, Pennsylvania. *Find A Grave* does display a number of Dougherty graves within this county.

DOUGLAS – Mentioned in the biography of the notable Judge Benjamin Pennebaker Douglas of Harrison County is a mention of his unnamed grandfather. He came to the Shenandoah Valley in Virginia, a native of the north of Ireland, as an exiled Captain from the Irish Rebellion of 1798. Douglas was compelled to flee his country.

The DOUGLAS FAMILY *of Killinchy, County Down*

DOUGLAS, Adam – Adam Douglas (1790-1849) was the son of William Douglas of Killinchy who fled to America after the 1798 Rebellion. He came to the United States with his immediate family and his uncle Adam Douglas, but returned to Ireland in 1812. There he joined an Irish regiment in the British Army and took part in the Battle of Waterloo (1815), where he was twice wounded and had his horse shot from under him. Soon afterwards, he returned America and settled at New Market, Virginia, where he became a teacher and carried surveying. On 27 April 1819, Adam Douglas married Nancy Pennebaker,

sister of Isaac Pennebaker, the U.S. Senator from Virginia. They moved to Laconia, Indiana. Douglas died on 28 June 1849 and was buried in the old Goshen Cemetery, close to Laconia. Benjamin Douglas (1829-1904), a son of Adam, became a judge. He was a teacher, merchant, attorney, and politician who made his home at Corydon, Harrison County, Indiana.

DOUGLAS, Adam – Adam Douglas, uncle of the above Adam Douglas, fled Ireland after the 1798 Rebellion to the State of Virginia with his brother William and family.

DOUGLAS, William – William Douglas, the patriarch of the Douglas family of Killinchy, fled Ireland and settled in the Shenandoah Valley in Virginia They were compelled to flee their country. He fled with his family and brother Adam Douglas. He later returned to Ireland and died in Brookfield, Belfast in 1849.

The DOUGLAS FAMILY *of Dungiven, County Derry*

DOUGLAS, James – (1733-1804) James Douglas was married to Margaret Clarke, who originated from Maghera, Co. Derry. Their sons, Jackson and James, were implicated in the 1798 Rebellion and the entire family all fled Ireland to Baltimore, Maryland.

DOUGLAS, Jackson – Jackson Douglas was born in 1760 to James Douglas and Margaret Clarke. After participating in some capacity in the 1798 Rebellion, Jackson Douglas fled to America with his parents and died soon after, in Baltimore, Maryland, leaving four children: James, Jacob Davies, Samuel, and Sarah Glen Douglas.

DOUGLAS, James Jr – Having participated as a United Irishman in the Limavady district, Douglas was forced to flee with his family to Baltimore. Nothing much is known about James, apart from being mentioned in the *Alexandria Gazette* (18 February 1895):

"Death of Mrs. Law. - Mrs. Louisa Douglas Law, widow of the late Major James O. Law, of Baltimore, and sister of Mr. James S. Douglass of this city, died yesterday at her residence in Baltimore, aged eighty-two years. Funeral will take place Tuesday from her late residence. Mrs. Law was the daughter of the late James Douglas, of this city and a granddaughter of Jackson Douglas, of Newton, Limavaddy, County Derry, Ireland, who was an IRISH REBEL against England in the REBELLION of 1798, in which *Robert Emmet fought and for which he was hanged. Mr. Douglas, with his family, had to FLEE to this country to escape, perhaps a similar fate. His granddaughter, Miss Louisa Douglas, was married to Major James Owen Law, [Mayor of Baltimore] HER COUSIN, on January 21, 1836, just fifty-nine years ago, and her husband died on June 6, 1847, forty-eight years ago, after eleven years of happily married life, so Mrs. Law has, therefore, rounded out a half-century of widowhood. For nearly a quarter of a century, Mrs. Law had resided with her eldest daughter, Mrs. SPEAR, the wife of James Otis Spear, living a quiet and devoted life surrounded by her two daughters, Mrs. Spear [Elizabeth Davies Law] and Miss Maggie Law, and her grandchildren."

DOUGLAS, Jacob Davies - Jacob Davies Douglas was born in Newtown-Limavady, Co. Derry on 11 June 1788 and was the second son of Jackson and Jane Davies. Only a boy during the 1798 Rebellion, he had to flee to the United States with his entire family. Jacob Davies Douglas served with distinction during the War of 1812, gaining the rank sergeant-major. He was for many years a prominent merchant based in Alexandria, Virginia. He died at his farm on 1 May 1873 and was interred at Zanesville, Ohio. Jacob's son, John Jackson Douglas, became a Colonel in the Union Army. He first joined the 10th Tennessee Infantry and held the rank of captain and made it higher through the ranks.

General Orders, No. 7.
Capt. John J. Douglas (10th Tenn. Inf. vols.) and aide-de-camp is hereby relieved from duty on the staff of the general commanding, by reason of the expiration of his term of service.

The general commanding cannot part with Capt. Douglas without acknowledging the valuable and efficient services he has rendered to his country and government in the capacity both of an enlisted man and as a staff officer. He has always proven himself to be energetic and faithful in the dis- charge of his official duties, and upon the battle field he has at all times displayed signal coolness and courage. The general commanding regrets that the injury received by Capt. Douglas while making a charge upon the enemy at Kingsport, Tenn., on 14 December 1864, should *"have resulted in a permanent disability, and can only commend him to the protection of that government he has so devotedly served."*

DOUGLAS, Paul –

Paul Douglas, from Parkgate, Co. Antrim, was a United Irishman who fought at the Battle of Antrim (7 June 1798). In the 1770s, Douglas was involved in the *"Hearts of Steel"* movement. He is said to have killed two dragoons at the Battle of Antrim and quickly made his escape to America. There is a known story that a Major Siddons took a liking to Douglas' wife, and blackmailed her that Paul would be free to return if he could use Mrs Douglas. Douglas did return home to Parkgate but later he took his wife with him to America. *Postcard photo of Parkgate circa 1910*

DOWDALL, William –

Dowdall was the illegitimate son of Hussey Burgh, who recognised his offspring. Dowdall was raised in Mullingar, Co. Westmeath and supported his natural father's liberal views. In the 1790's, Dowdall, a lawyer, became a United Irishman and supported the network when Arthur O'Connor, John Allen, John Binns and Fr. Coigly were arrested at Margate in February 1798. He edited the United Irish newspaper, *The Press*, throughout April and May 1798, before travelling to Maidstone in England to give support to Arthur O'Connor during his trial. Dowdall was arrested on the following week and held in Newgate Gaol in Dublin. When Dublin Castle offered opportunities to leading United Irish State Prisoners in August 1798, in return for information on the organisation, Dowdall refused to comply. He was conveyed to the comforts of Fort George in Scotland (*pictured right*), which saw many personality clashes between the United Irish prisoners. Dowdall and Wexford based United Irishman, Edward Hudson, suffered one such personality clash when Hudson accused Dowdall of attempting to bully him into accepting further

conspiracy. In January 1802, Dowdall returned to Dublin and set about reorganising the United Irish movement in Dublin.

He also played a significant role in recruiting Colonel Edward Despard into the movement, however, Despard would later suffer death for plans to attempt regicide. Dowdell often travelled between London and Dublin on United business, acting as a clerk for Philip Long and was instrumental in establishing hurling clubs across Dublin to allow insurgents to publicly drill. When Emmet's Rising failed on 23 July 1803, Dowdall fled Ireland for Cadiz in Spain, and there awaited on correspondence from Thomas Addis Emmet to enter France. With permission granted, Dowdall settled in France, and was awarded a commission as sub-Lieutenant in the Irish Legion, quickly rising to full Lieutenant and Captain within months. Dowdall quickly grew impatient with the Irish Legion's lack of military participation and requested a transfer to a French regiment, but this was refused. On 1 August 1809, Dowdall was badly wounded during the Siege of Flushing (*pictured*) and died of his

wounds several days later at a hospital in Ghent.

DOWLING, Matthew - Matt Dowling, a native of King's County (Co. Offaly) was born in 1756. Interestingly, as a Roman Catholic, he entered Trinity College in Dublin, where he studied law, however, he did not complete his

degree. In 1777, Dowling was admitted to the Irish bar, and practised from his office at No.4 Longford Street in Dublin. Dowling participated in the Patriot Movement and became involved in the Volunteer Movement, serving with the Goldsmith's Corps. Having become friends with James Napper Tandy, who shared Dowling's appetite for radical politics, they would become founding members of the Dublin Society of United Irishmen in November 1791. Dowling also held influence within the Catholic Committee. His temperament appears to have been spontaneous, judging from his organised duel with the private secretary of the Chief Secretary of Ireland and also his ordering out the Dublin based Volunteer units in December 1792 to commemorate a French victory. This action tormented the Government and it resulted in the eventual cessation of the Volunteer Movement in 1793. When Napper Tandy faced charges, Dowling served as his attorney, however, knowing Tandy stood no chance of acquittal, proposed that he flee Ireland for the United States. Dowling not only represented various United Irishmen in the courts but served officially in the movement and held various positions. In the summer of 1797, Dowling was instrumental in organising the north Wexford United Irishmen by swearing in Anthony Perry of Inch, who eventually became a commander of the insurgents during the 1798 Rebellion. In one instance, Dowling was referred to simply as "*the executive officer of sedition and rebellion.*"

In March 1798, Dowling was hired to represent ninety United Irish prisoners who had been rounded up in Co. Wicklow. His radical intensity was also reported to Dublin Castle by informers who claimed that Dowling was involved in a plot to kidnap the Lord Chancellor, Lord Clare. Dowling was arrested in May 1798 and was held as a State Prisoner until his official release in July 1802, upon which he tried to heal the dangerous rift between Thomas Addis Emmet and Arthur O'Connor. Upon arriving at Cuxhaven, Dowling proceeded to Rotterdam before settling in Paris.

Miles Byrne briefly recorded some moments of meeting Dowling in Paris.

"*Matt Dowling bore up with his misfortunes like a philosopher of olden times, retaining all his gaiety and amiable manners which used to endear him so much to the citizens of Dublin, who were in the habit of electing him King of the island of Dalkey. I spent one evening at his lodgings in company with Paul Murray and Arthur MacMahon and he nearly made us forget we were far away from our home; - he made us proud of being exiles in a good cause.*"

Matthew Dowling died in Paris in June 1805, after suffering from a two-day illness which was blamed on his love for French brandy.

DOYLE, Denis – Doyle was a native of Monaseed, in north Co. Wexford, who fought as an insurgent during the 1798 Rebellion. Miles Byrne recorded meeting Doyle after the Battle of Tubberneering (4 June 1798), which Byrne records this individual's excitement in his memoirs,

"Denis Doyle was one of them whom I knew from my childhood, as both he and his family were our neighbours and we were accustomed to meet every Sunday at the chapel of Monaseed. He had been a short time settled in Gorey as a timber merchant, and he expected every moment either to be dragged to prison, or shot. I was the first he recognised amongst our forces, and he ran to meet me with open arms: he could scarcely contain his wonder and joy when I told him about the battle we had just gained…Denis Doyle from that day became one of our brave active officers; he was young, handsome and spirited. When the war terminated, he had the good fortune and spirited. When the war terminated, he had the good fortune to escape to America and set up in the same business at New York, which he had been following at Gorey. His brother Davy had been practicing as a lawyer in America for two or three years previous to this, which no doubt induced him to go and join him there."

D'OYLEY, Capt. John –

1783

(1760-1850) John D'oyley was born in 1760 to James Monk D'Oyley and Eleanor Devereux, daughter of John Devereux of Kilrush, Co. Wexford. John was sent to France to get educated and became acquainted with the Marquis de Lafayette. In 1777, he accompanied Lafayette to America to aid the colonists under General George Washington in the American Revolution. D'oyley was appointed a Captain in the 1st Pennsylvania Regiment in 1783. After the 1783 Treaty of Paris and after receiving the Membership of the *'Order of Cincinnati'* (*crest pictured*), D'oyley returned to Ireland. He took an active part in the 1798 insurrection and later had all his property confiscated. He fled to France to visit his old friend, Lafayette, before arrangements could be organised to sail for the United States. Upon settling in Philadelphia, the penniless D'Oyley would succeed in obtaining a teaching role in an academy in Philadelphia. In 1799, he married Anna Maria Welch, daughter of a rich merchant in Philadelphia. D'Oyley died in Philadelphia on 12 May 1850 and was interred at the Old Cathedral Cemetery in Philadelphia (PA).

DOYLE, Johnny –

According to folklore and song in Newfoundland, Johnny Doyle was a native of Ballyshannon Lane, in Co. Wexford. When Crown soldiers were in search for him, he ambushed and killed three of them. Doyle fled to St. John's in Newfoundland and eventually to the coastal village of Placentia, where many Wexford men were employed by Pierce Sweetman, a successful fishing merchant, who was closely connected with the Sweetman Family of Newbawn, Co. Wexford. Thanks to Michael Fortune of folklore.ie who brought his to our attention

DOYLE, Matthew – Doyle was a native of Polahoney, Arklow, Co. Wicklow. Doyle was a wealthy cattle dealer who was instrumental in organising the south Wicklow United Irishmen. He was involved in the Battle of Arklow on 9 June 1798 and the subsequent guerrilla campaigns alongside Holt and Dwyer in Wicklow. After his capture, Doyle was sentenced to serve in His Majesty's Forces, where he saw action in Egypt against the French. After the Treaty of Amiens, he was demobbed and returned to Ireland. He was encouraged by Arthur Devlin to take part in the Emmet uprising of 1803, and worked in one of the secret arms depots, which resulted in him receiving a scalding burn. After the collapse of the Emmet uprising, Doyle, with £500 bounty on his head, fled to Liverpool and re-enlisted in the British Army and served throughout the Napoleonic Wars until 1815. Doyle returned to Arklow, Co. Wicklow, and died on 24 October 1841.

DOYLE Moses – Moses or Mogue Doyle, was born c.1764 in the Parish of Ferns, Co. Wexford, to James Doyle and Ann O'Brien. Having served with the insurgents, Doyle was captured and sentenced to death by the British. Legend remains, that on the morning of his set execution, when the guards came to prepare him for hanging, they discovered it was not Mogue in the cell but his very brave fiancée (and future wife), Judith O'Neill. Mogue had escaped the previous night, dressed as Judith, during their farewell visit. He escaped on a fishing vessel to Cape Breton, Nova Scotia, and a few years later, seeking pardon after the Act of Union in 1801, he returned to Ireland, where he spent many years as a tenant farmer on the land owned by Earl Fitzwilliam. In 1824, Mogue and Judith Doyle returned and settled at the Margarees, in Nova Scotia, with his children, James, Ann and Sarah Doyle. Many thanks to Eileen Coady of Margaree Forks, Inverness County, Nova Scotia, for this information

DRISCOLL, John – Driscoll was a native of Cloyne, Co. Cork. Having become a United Irishmen and receiving a wound during the 1798 Rebellion, Driscoll fled into exile to New London, Connecticut, with his wife and died in January 1817.

DUKE, John – John Duke served as an insurgent during the Down Rebellion in June 1798. He led the Hoggstown brigade into Donaghadee, Co. Down, during the insurrection. On 16 July 1798, Duke was court-martialled at Newtownards, Co. Down, on charges of being a traitor. Having being found guilty, Duke was sentenced to transportation for life, however, it was later downgraded to voluntary banishment to America.

DUNCAN, Innis – In a June 1892 article within Kentucky's *Evening Bulletin*, was an item advertised for sale; the item being a bust of Rev. John Wesley (*pictured*) which was brought over to Kentucky by Innis Duncan, who settled in America shortly after his participation in the 1798 Rebellion.

DUNN – During the turmoil of General Lake's Dragooning of Ulster in 1797, Dunn, a treasurer of the Belfast Society of United Irishmen, fled to America, taking over £1000 of the society's money

DWIGHT, Henry Edwin – Henry Dwight went to America in 1798 immediately the Rebellion, establishing himself and his family in New York City. A grandson, Albert Dwight became a Union Officer during the American Civil War, enrolling on 19 September 1862, and was mustered as a private soldier in Company E, 155th New York Volunteer Infantry on 18 November 1862. He was promoted to Corporal, and was wounded in action on 12 May 1864 at the Battle of Spotsylvania. He was eventually promoted to 2nd Lieutenant on 19 June 1864, but was killed in action three days later at the Battle of Petersburg, Virginia.

The Emmet Family *of St. Stephen's Green, Dublin*

EMMET, Christopher Temple – Christopher T. Emmet was born in September 1798, to Thomas Addis Emmet and Jane Patten. Named after his famed and long deceased uncle, young Christopher's youth saw many changes, including a period without seeing his exiled parents, as he was cared for by his aunt, Mary Anne Emmet, in Dublin, until he was reunited with his parents in New York in 1805. Christopher T. Emmet was not an exile of the 1798 Rebellion however, his emigration was indeed a result of it. After a period of receiving his education at Flushing in New York, Christopher Emmet joined the U.S. Navy, serving as Midshipman aboard the *United States*, during the War of 1812. Whilst on a naval tour in the Caribbean, Emmet's ship was infected with yellow fever. Christopher Temple Emmet died aboard the *Macedonian* on 23 July 1822 and was buried at sea.

EMMET, Elizabeth — Elizabeth Emmet was

born in Dublin on 4 December 1794 to Thomas
Addis Emmet and Jane Patten. Young Elizabeth
joined her mother when she resided at Fort George in
Scotland during her father's incarceration there
between 1799 and 1802. Elizabeth Emmet became a
renowned artist and resided at a stock farm in
Potsdam, New York, with her husband, William
Henry Le Roy. The distance was a melancholic
experience for the close-knit Emmet family, with her
father's letters highlighting reminisces to the distress
that her mother felt when they had to exile from
Ireland, knowing they would never see family and
friends again. Elizabeth Emmet Le Roy died at New
Rochelle, New York, on 31 December 1878.

EMMET, Jane, *neé* Patten — Jane Patten, the matriarch of the exiled

MRS. JANE PATTEN EMMET.

Emmet family, was born at Clonmel, Co. Tipperary, on
16 August 1771 to Rev. John Patten and Margaret
Colville. On 11 June 1791, Jane married Thomas Addis
Emmet at St. Mary's Church in Dublin. They would
purchase the residence next door to the Emmet Family
of Stephen's Green. Whilst Thomas Addis Emmet was
engaged between his legal profession and the activities of
the United Irishmen, they reared several children, Robert
Emmet (1792-1873), Margaret Emmet (1793-1883),
Elizabeth Emmet (1794-1878), John Patten Emmet
(1796-1842) and Thomas Addis Emmet Jr (1797-1863),
before their lives were disrupted in 1798. When Thomas
Addis Emmet was arrested in early 1798, Jane was
carrying Christopher Temple Emmet (1798-1822), giving
birth to him in September 1798. The Emmet family
suffered tremendously when Thomas Addis Emmet was
sent as a State Prisoner to Fort George in Scotland.
Having previously stayed by her husband's side at
Kilmainham Gaol, Jane Emmet was given permission to reside with Addis
Emmet at the Scottish fort, staying there until the summer of 1802, when the
prisoners were granted liberty. They had a new addition to the family, with the
birth of Jeanette Erin Emmet (1802-1890). Unable to return to Ireland, the
Emmets travelled to the continent, spending the winter of 1802 in Brussels. Jane
followed her husband to Paris, where he interacted with the French Directory
on behalf of the United Irishmen. Whilst in France, Jane gave birth to Catherine
Emmet in January 1804, whilst Thomas Addis Emmet had become engaged as

an officer with the Irish Legion. Becoming disillusioned with Bonapartist France, the Emmets sailed to New York City and where they became established in legal, political and exile circles. Their daughter, Mary Emmet, was born in New York in March 1804 and a son, William Colville Emmet was born in 1807. The widow Emmet, having shared a life of woes and wealth with her beloved husband, Thomas Addis Emmet, died in New York on 10 November 1846.

EMMET, John Patten

EMMET, John Patten – John Patten Emmet was born in Dublin on 8 April 1796 to Thomas Addis Emmet and Jane Patten. John was but a small child during his family's turbulent period of 1798-1802 and remained in the care of his grandparents and aunt, Mary-Anne Emmet, in Dublin. When the Emmets emigrated to the United States in late 1804, young John P. Emmet, Christopher T. Emmet and Thomas A. Emmet Jr, were sent to join their parents in New York. Having been educated at Flushing, John P. Emmet entered West Point Military Academy as a cadet. Within two years, his standard of mathematics excelled, resulting in him being awarded with the post of Acting-Assitant Professor, even before his graduation.
Suffering with ailing health, Emmet was encouraged to reside in warmer temperatures and established a medical practice in Charleston, South Carolina. With support from former U.S. President, Thomas Jefferson, Dr. J.P. Emmet was awarded the post of Professor of Natural History at Charottesville, Virginia. In 1827, he married Mary Byrd Tucker. Upon sailing to New York, their ship was caught in a hurricane, causing it to lose course for over a month. John's health seriously declined and upon arriving at New York, he died.

EMMET, Margaret – Margaret Emmet was born in Dublin on 21 September 1793 to Thomas Addis Emmet and Jane Patten. Margaret witnessed the turbulence of her father's incarceration between 1798 and 1802, although she was brought by her mother to reside at Fort George, where she was tutored by United Irish prisoners. After the Emmets settled in New York, it is Margaret who appears to cement a loving relationship between all of the siblings. Margaret remained single for her entire life and died on 1 March 1883. She was interred at New Rochelle, in New York.

EMMET, Robert – Robert Emmet was the eldest child of Thomas Addis Emmet and Jane Patten and named after his paternal grandfather and infamous uncle. Robert Emmet was born on 9 September 1792 and resided with his family in St. Stephen's Green. Young Robert's childhood was turbulent. House raids, his father's incarceration and settling at Scotland's Fort George, saw young

Robert being tutored by United Irish prisoners. After the Emmet's arrived in New York in November 1805, Robert Emmet was educated at Flushing, New York. He completed his education at the University of Columbia and entered his father's legal practice, taking it over after Thomas Addis Emmet's death in 1827. He led a distinguished career and served in the New York State Assembly and on the Supreme Court bench. Robert Emmet died at New Rochelle, in New York, on 15 February 1873.

EMMET, Thomas Addis –

Thomas Addis Emmet was born in Cork on 24 April 1764 to Robert Emmet and Elizabeth Mason. After studying at Trinity College in Dublin, he graduated with a BA, however, he continued his education at the University of Edinburgh to study medicine, graduating with an MD in 1784. Emmet found medical experience at Guy's Hospital in London for several years. After the sudden death of his older brother, Christopher Temple Emmet, in 1788, Thomas Addis Emmet changed careers from medicine to law, with encouragement from his father, who was at this period, Ireland's State Physician. After finishing his law degree, Addis Emmet was admitted to the Irish Bar in 1790. On 11 June 1791, he married Jane Patten and they eventually resided beside the Emmet Family beside the Royal College of Surgeons, overlooking Dublin's St. Stephen's Green. Having been exposed to liberal politics at university and home, Emmet joined the Dublin Society of United Irishmen on 14 December 1792.

Emmet strived for parliamentary reform and universal male suffrage, composing, "*Address to the Poorer Classes*," in February 1794. When the organisation was forced underground, Emmet became a rising figure, representing many United Irish and Defender members in courts across the country. He helped reorganise the organisation into secretive cellular units and appealed to the idea of revolution with French assistance. Emmet would disagree with the ultra-militancy of Lord Edward Fitzgerald and Arthur O'Connor, who encouraged open rebellion across Ireland, with or without French assistance. Emmet represented the more militarily cautious and constitutional reformist elements within the United Irishmen, alongside his lifelong friends, Dr. William James MacNeven and William Sampson. On 12 March 1798, when Dublin Castle descended upon the Leinster delegation meeting at Oliver Bond's residence, Emmet was arrested at his Stephen's Green home and brought to Newgate Gaol. When the Kilmainham Treaty was discussed in August 1798, between Dublin

Castle and the State Prisoners, Emmet was dismayed that the conditions of self-exile were not honoured by the authorities, considering he and the other State Prisoners had surrendered the information about the United Irish organisation. His incarceration would continue. On 18 March 1799, with only twenty-four hours' notice, the State Prisoners were sent to Fort George, near Inverness, Scotland. Here, they resided in relative comfort and solitude for several years. Emmet's wife and children would join him at Fort George, thus relieving him of some of his surrendered liberty. Whilst at Fort George, Emmet's poor relationship with the O'Connor Brothers, Arthur and Roger, intensified to a point that a duel was considered, however, it was not carried out.

On 30 June 1802, Emmet was released from Fort George and made his way to Cuxhaven on the continent. He would spend the winter of 1802 amongst his family and several exiles at Brussels, before settling in Paris, where he corresponded with the French War Department on behalf of his younger brother, Robert Emmet. After the failure of his brother's uprising and his subsequent execution, Thomas Addis Emmet still acted as a United Irish envoy, petitioning the French Government and Napoleon Bonaparte to establish a new French expedition to Ireland. Napoleon appeared interested in this idea and established the Irish Legion for this sole purpose. The Legion was conceived in late 1803 with the O'Connor and Emmet divisions rife amongst the officers. When Napoleon's enthusiasm for an Irish expedition declined, Emmet became disillusioned with France and Napoleon. On 4 October 1804, Emmet sailed from France to the United States, arriving in New York on 17 November.

Upon arrival in New York, Emmet attached his national political loyalties to the liberal Jeffersonians and within New York, he supported the Clinton and DeWitt Clinton faction. He was admitted by special appointment to the legal profession without the necessary examinations, a unique act considering he had been struck off from the bar in Ireland. Emmet and his family flourished in New York, to a point that his practice was earning $15,000 annually.

His successes were symbolically morphed by Irish Nationalists into the image that America was truly the land of opportunities for immigrants. Alongside

MacNeven and other Irish exiles, he became an advocate in establishing societies across the city, such as the **Shamrock Friendly Society**, that cared for Irish and other immigrants who arrived in America. His noted liberalism in New York politics saw him also advocate for abolition of slavery; representing fugitive slaves in the courtrooms. He befriended the iconic hero of the United Irishmen, Thomas Paine, and became executor of Paine's last will and testament. In 1812, Emmet was appointed Attorney-General of the State of New York for one year, as repayment for his loyalty to the Clintons. In his aged years, Emmet's portrait (*pictured*) was painted by the inventor, Samuel Morse. On 14 November 1827, after suffering a fit during a trial, Thomas Addis Emmet died and was interred at Vault 10 in the Churchyard of St. Mark's-in-the-Bowery, in East Village, New York (*pictured*). There are two cenotaphs, within the churchyard of St. Paul's in Lower Manhattan dedicated to both Thomas Addis Emmet and his close friend and fellow United Irishman, William James MacNeven.

Thomas Addis Emmet is possibly the most prolific Irish exile from the 1798-1803 period. What might interest historians today is that he never expressed his thoughts or grief about his brother's failed uprising of 1803 and claimed that he would never set foot on Irish soil as long as it belonged to Britain. His family continued to contribute to American and world society. His grandson, Richard Stockton Emmet also became Attorney-General of New York and his great-granddaughters, Rosina Emmet Sherwood, Lydia Field Emmet and Jane Emmet de Glehn each became renowned painters. His grandson, Dr. Thomas Addis Emmet, an Irish-American activist and the founder of plastic surgery, who financed a failed search operation to find the remains of his famous grand-uncle in the early 1900s, expressed his wishes that upon his death that he be buried in Ireland. Today, a large Celtic cross, designed by James and Willie Pearse, stands erect beside the O'Connell Tower in Glasnevin Cemetery, the grave of Dr. Emmet. Another descendent of Thomas Addis Emmet was Valentin Ribet, a French human rights lawyer, who was killed during the terror attacks at the Bataclan in Paris on 13 November 2015.

EMMET, Thomas Addis, Jr – Thomas

Addis Emmet Jr was born in Dublin on 29 May 1797 to Thomas Addis Emmet and Jane Patten. Only a baby during the turbulent period of the 1798-1803 period, Thomas would remain in the care of his paternal grandparents and his aunt, Mary-Anne Emmet, until he was reunited with his parents in New York in 1805. Young Thomas was educated at Flushing in New York before entering Columbia. In 1823, he married Anna Riker Tom and they resided at 'Mount Vernon' on Manhattan's Third Avenue (now 60th & 61st Streets). Having a distinguished law career, Tom Emmet died on 12 August 1863 and was interred at Marble Cemetery in New York.

ERRETT – The Errett's were a Protestant family, with paternal connections

to Arklow, Co. Wicklow. Isaac Errett was born in New York on 2 January 1820. His paternal grandfather was shot and killed in Arklow during the 1798 Rebellion. *The 1798 Rebellion Casualty Database* confirms that a William Errett, a private in the Castletown Yeomanry, was killed at the Battle of Arklow, on 9 June 1798. The remaining family exiled to New York, where they became notable Protestants in New York and his father became a preacher who published a book on *"Defence of the principles now advocated by the Disciples."*

ERWIN, Oliver – Oliver Erwin fled to the United States as an exile of

1798. His son, James Erwin married Ann Davis, the eldest daughter of U.S. Congressman, General John Davis (1788–1878) and sister of, William Watts Hart Davis, who became a Brigadier-General of the Union Army during the American Civil War.

EVANS, Hampden – Evans was a wealthy landowning United Irishman,

who hailed from Mount Evans, Portrane, Co. Dublin. In January 1769, Evans married **Margaret Davis**. Having been incarcerated at Kilmainham Gaol for treasonable practices, he petitioned the Lord Lieutenant, Charles Cornwallis, in August 1798, to be allowed leave Ireland, stating that he wished to go to Hamburg. Historian, Paul Weber, records that Evans had been listed on the Banishment Act and fled to Hamburg in early 1799, before settling in Paris. Evans' period in Paris is mentioned occasionally by Miles Byrne. He states:

"I paid few visits, only to some of Mr. Emmet's friends, and fellow prisoners, such as Matt Dowling, John Sweetman, John Swiney, Hugh Ware and Hampden

Evans: the latter having lost one of his daughters a short time before I arrived, lived retired, in a comfortable house on the boulevard des Invalides, opposite the rue Plumet. Mrs Tone, and other ladies such as Mrs (Pat) Gallagher, Mrs Hamilton, etc., wives of the exiles, were always well received by this excellent family, consisting of the father and mother, young Hampden and his three sisters, Mary, Nancy and Sidney. The first was afterwards married to William Lawless; the second was married to Mr. George Putland, and the third to her cousin, (Rev. Thomas) Acton."

Hampden Evans died on 22 April 1820, aged eighty years. His son, George Hampden Evans, became a Whig MP for Dublin County. An American article from 1867 details Evans in a romantic view:

"The princely gentleman, too, was Hampden Evans. He had a large family, numbering among them three beautiful girls; and he had a princely fortune to support them withal. Amongst the United Irishmen he was a foremost leader; and for Ireland he cheerfully risked property, and life, and the joys of his happy home. For he was a man who loved his home-life, and enjoyed its quiet pleasures intensely. It was his better fortune to escape to France and save the estate. But he was one of those Irish gentlemen whose names we cannot afford to forget."

EVANS, Hampden, Jr – The son of the above-mentioned Hampden Evans of Portrane, Co. Dublin, and brother of George Hampden Evans, who would become a liberal MP for Dublin County in Westminster. Evans went to France and served in the Irish Legion however, he was killed during the Battle of Goldberg on 19 August 1813.

FERGUSON, Henry – Henry Ferguson hailed from Ballyrogan, near Newtownards, Co. Down. He was tried by court-martial at Newtownards on 19 July 1798 for rebellious activities and sentenced to be transported for life to New South Wales. His sentence was remitted to allow him enter into recognisances to self-exile to America.

FINLAY, James – James Finlay died on 3 June 1811 at Cotton, near Bangor, Co. Down, aged 57 years. It is recorded that he participated in the 1798 Rebellion and had fled from Ireland to the United States where he resided for several years before returning home, which he became involved in Robert Emmet's planned uprising of 1803, in which he was to oversee the capture of two regiments for Emmet however his plans were not executed. Finlay was arrested and spent two years in prison before spending the remainder of his years on his Co. Down farm.

FINN, Laurence – Laurence Finn was the eldest brother of the renowned
Finn brothers of North Wexford, who fought during the 1798 Rebellion. Miles Byrne regaled many of their acts of bravery within his memoirs:

"Three brothers of the name of Finn, Laurence, Luke and Dan, rather small sized men, distinguished themselves by their bravery and by their brotherly attachment; they seldom separated, and frequently saved one another in the greatest danger. One day, when charged by cavalry on the high road, Luke fell under the horse's feet, whilst his brother Laurence escaped over a hedge or ditch; the latter turning round to ascertain what had become of Luke, perceived him lying on the ground and two horsemen in the act of firing their pistols at him; he instantly shot one of them; Luke, though knocked down, kept his fowling piece by his side, raised it up, shot the other horseman, escaped with his brother and gained the main body soon after. They were first in every action, and always the last to quit the field of battle."

Byrne states that Laurence Finn eventually fled to America.

FITZGERALD, Edward – Edward Fitzgerald was
born c.1770 into a Catholic middle-class farming family from Newpark, near Blackwater, Co. Wexford. Little is known about his early life apart from being a champion hound-hunter and steeplechaser. Accused of being a United Irishman, Fitzgerald was arrested and incarcerated at Wexford Gaol. On 29 May 1798, as the insurgents gathered in their thousands before Wexford Town, the authorities sent Fitzgerald and John Henry Colclough to meet the insurgents and encourage them to disband. Fitzgerald, being wise, did not pass on the demands but reluctantly accepted the insurgency's pleas for him to take command. Fitzgerald served in the Northern Division of the Wexford insurgency and took part in the Battles of Tubberneering, Arklow, Vinegar Hill, Hacketstown and Ballyellis. He participated in  the failed campaign of early July 1798, which saw the remnants of the Wexford and Wicklow insurgents joining with William Aylmer's Timahoe insurgents in north Kildare. The demise of so many leading Wexford leaders saw Fitzgerald elevated to one of the leading commanding ranks, however, his command of a depleted, fatigued, starving and ragged force, was short-lived. He received a vicious wound at the last stand of the Wexford pikemen at Knightstown Bog in north Co. Dublin on 14 July 1798. An insurgent veteran of the final stand of the

Wexford insurgents, who had endured for nearly seven weeks, gives a detailed account of its decimation:

*"**But the artillery came up and opened a shower of grape on us. I think our officers were wounded, although none of them seriously, but a great number of our men fell with that discharge. A great number of us jumped from our horses and put them between us and the enemy. General** (Garrett) **Byrne was in the midst of us. Fitzgerald was covered with blood. The enemy was rapidly extending their lines with superior numbers to surround us.** (Anthony) **Perry rode up to Fitzgerald at this time and the latter, pointing his sword to the high ground, that was convenient, said: 'Whelan! Lead for the road. Men! Follow him!' Perry and the other officers, at a short distance from Fitzgerald, directed their march for the same road. Here the cavalry closed on us to prevent our getting off. But General Byrne brought up the few pikemen we had and we forced our way through them, leaving many of our fine comrades behind us.**"*

After the fall of the Wexford insurgency, Fitzgerald clearly made his way back to northern Kildare, joining William Aylmer and Hugh Ware on the boglands of Timahoe. Negotiations had been underway between Aylmer's father and Dublin Castle through influential friends. Fitzgerald was the only remaining Wexford leader to return to the Timahoe camp. On 21 July 1798, the Kildare insurgents surrendered near Sallins. The conditions granted would allow the lowly pikemen to be given immediate pardons upon surrender whilst the officers were arrested and brought to interrogation at Dublin Castle. He and a south Wicklow leader, Garrett Byrne of Ballymanus, were sent to Bristol, England, where they would remain until 22 March 1799, when they were arrested. On 8 April 1799, both Byrne and Fitzgerald composed a letter to Dublin Castle, stating:

*"**We are certain we have not committed any act of deserving censure, and cautiously avoided the slightest appearance, that possibly could give offence except that of breathing the free air.**"*

They were eventually released but encouraged to go to the continent, leaving from Yarmouth on 30 April. We can tell from Byrne's correspondence that times were financially tough for them both in Altona. Edward Fitzgerald died in Hamburg in 1807, having never recuperated from the exhausting excursions of the 1798 Rebellion or the imprisonment afterwards.

FITZGERALD, Lady Pamela –

Stéphanie Caroline Anne Syms, or informally known as Pamela Syms, was born c.1773. Her background has been examined by many historians however, no certain lineage can be determined due to the prospect of illegitimacy. Having spent her infancy in the care of a washerwoman in Dorset, she was adopted by Félicité de Genlis, who is thought to have been her natural mother. It has been generally considered that her natural father was Louis Phillipe II, the Duke of Orléans. Her immense beauty was recognised across French circles. It caught the eye of an Irishman, Lord Edward Fitzgerald, who was in France to witness the events of the revolution. They immediately fell in love with each other and courted briefly before they agreed to wed.

On 27 December 1792, the loving couple married at Tournai. In January 1793, the newlyweds attended a ball to commemorate the guillotined King Louis XVI. To everyone's surprise, Lady Pamela entered the room dressed in black with a red ribbon tied in her hair. Edward entered, also dressed in black but sporting a red cravat; the red symbolising Jacobinism. The Fitzgerald's resided in France for a short period before returning to Ireland, where they resided between Kildare Lodge in Kildare Town, Frescati House in Blackrock, Leinster House in Dublin and Carton House in Co. Kildare. Lady Pamela gave birth to three children: Edward Fox Fitzgerald (1794-1863), Pamela Fitzgerald and Lucy Louisa Fitzgerald (1796-). Pamela stood by her husband's radical politics, as he immersed himself deeper into the United Irish conspiracy. After Martial Law was declared, Edward was forced to rely on the safehouse network whilst Pamela resided alone, apart from her children and a maid. After the arrest and fatal wounding of Edward on 19 May 1798, Pamela did not wait around for the authorities to question her. In late May 1798, whilst her husband languished in Newgate Gaol, Pamela fled Dublin for London, bringing the children. She would hear about the tragic and lonesome death of her beloved husband in the company of his family. After a period spent with Edward's mother and sister, Pamela left for Hamburg on account of a bill of attainder, which encouraged that she was no longer desirable in Britain.

On 13 August 1798, Lady Pamela arrived in Hamburg and resided with her step-sister, Henriette de Sercy Matthiessen. In 1800, having lost all hopes of regaining Edward's vast properties and possessions, and seeking financial security for her and the children, Pamela married Joseph Pitcairn, the U.S. Ambassador to Hamburg, however, it was an unhappy relationship which eventually foundered. In 1802, after the release of the Irish State Prisoners, Arthur O'Connor, a close friend of Lord Edward and who shared mutual political and military sentiments, arrived in Hamburg and met Lady Pamela. The author of Arthur O'Connor's biography, *Arthur O'Connor, United Irishman*, details the meeting.

*"**Arthur had last seen Pamela FitzGerald when he left Dublin in those frenzied days of January 1798. Her daughter was five years old now. The girl later recalled: 'I once saw Arthur O'Connor at Hamburgh, when I was a child, and just remember a very handsome man patting my head and crying over me'. It was a hard meeting for Arthur. How often had Pamela begged him not to encourage Edward, not to urge him further into conspiracy? Now Edward was dead and Pamela, with almost no income and keeping only one of her three children with her, had accepted an offer of marriage which brought her no joy. Still lovely, she was a sad figure.**"*

We cannot comprehend the misery felt by Lady Pamela Fitzgerald. She had been practically ostracised by the Fitzgerald family and Lady de Genlis and financially struggled for many years. She was without her eldest children, who remained in the custody of the Fitzgerald's in London. Eventually, Pamela left Hamburg for Paris, a widow who mourned her dear Edward for the remainder of life. On 7 November 1831, Lady Pamela Fitzgerald died, clutching Edward's handkerchief, which was buried alongside her at Montmartre in Paris. Pamela's headstone was destroyed during the Siege of Paris in 1870. Irish littérateur, J.P. Leonard, upon learning that her remains were to be discarded, retrieved them and re-interred them with those of her daughter, Pamela Campbell, at St. Nicholas' Churchyard in Thames Ditton in Surrey, England. It can be considered unfortunate that her remains were not brought to St. Werburgh's in Dublin to rest beside her beloved husband, Edward Fitzgerald.

FITZHENRY, Jeremiah

FITZHENRY, Jeremiah – Fitzhenry was born in 1774 at Borohill House, Ballymackesy, Co. Wexford to William Fitzhenry and Catherine Hegarty. Fitzhenry's father, William, had held the role of High Constable of the Barony of Bantry in the mid-Eighteenth Century, a position that gave the family a comfortable status.

Little is known about Jeremiah Fitzhenry's participation in the 1798 Rebellion however, historians agree that he was present during much of the Wexford Rebellion, including the Battles of New Ross and Vinegar Hill. After the Rebellion, Fitzhenry fled to France and was commissioned a captain of the Irish Legion's Carabineer Company in December 1803. Miles Byrne recorded meeting Fitzhenry in his memoirs:

"I met Jeremiah Fitzhenry at Paris in 1803. He had taken an active part in the County of Wexford insurrection of 1798, being with Bagenal Harvey at the Battle of New Ross, on the 5th of June – After the execution of his wife's brother, John Colclough, he feared he could no longer remain with safety in Ireland. He accordingly came over to France with his wife and his two little girls. He went to reside at Saint-Germain-en-Laye, where he met his friend and countryman, Mr. William Barker, who had been living there with his family."

After the birth of a third daughter, Fitzhenry sent his family back to Ireland whilst he remained with the Legion. Adjutant-General Alexandre Dalton, the ADC to the French Minister of War, wrote a simple note about Fitzhenry: *"Jeremiah Fitzhenry, aged 28. Came to France two years ago with a small part of his fortune, having left the rest in County Wexford, where he commanded, during the rebellion a considerable party of rebels, which often fought against the British forces. He was amnestied but did not wish to profit from the pardon, coming to France in the hope of continuing to serve his country. He is energetic and well-instructed."*

Whilst campaigning in Spain in late 1808, the commander of the Second Battalion defected, leaving Captain Fitzhenry to take command of the battalion. Noted for his leadership qualities, Fitzhenry was promoted to Lieutenant-Colonel of the Legion in the Peninsular War. With the arrival of Colonel Daniel O'Meara, a noted alcoholic and incompetent officer, Fitzhenry was side-lined, until O'Meara's recall by the War Department. Fitzhenry was placed back in command of the Second Battalion and provisional commander of the Irish Legion in Spain. Fitzhenry was taken prisoner on 22 April 1811 and in early May 1811, Fitzhenry defected to Lord Wellington's camp but did not divulge any information or join the British forces. The reason for this defection was simply down to two factors: homesickness and being made feel manipulated and sidelined by his superiors. With support from the Lord Wellington, Jeremiah Fitzhenry was allowed to return to Ireland in June 1811 and took over his father's land at Borohill House in Ballymackesy. He was tried in absentia in December 1811, on orders of Marshal Marmont, but was acquitted. In 1829, during a civil court hearing, Arthur Barker, the son of his old friend, William Barker, publicly attacked Fitzhenry for his actions of desertion. It was recorded in detail within a news article. "*To use his own expressions, 'My only offence against Napoleon consisted in a desire to die in Ireland. In indulging a desire so natural to the human heart, and that after many years of toil, of danger, and of sorrow, have given way to the instinctive wish, to spend the residue of their lives in that spot which was consecrated by the association of childhood and which had been endeared by separation.*" Jeremiah Fitzhenry died on 23 February 1845 and was interred at Ballybrennan Cemetery, Co. Wexford.

FITZHENRY, John – Fitzhenry was born in 1768 at Dungiven, Co. L. Derry to Hugh Fitzhenry and Mary Rankin. Fitzhenry had been an active United Irishman during the 1798 Rebellion and later fled to France, where he joined the Irish Legion as a sub-lieutenant. Fitzhenry died during an operation on a swollen knee at a hospital in Landernau in June 1806. Miles Byrne recalls his time with Fitzhenry, however, he wrongly recorded him as John McHenry.

"*He was an honest Presbyterian from the North of Ireland, and a true patriot. He and I one day in March 1804, taking a walk at Quimper, down the river. Thinking we might meet wolves we charged our muskets, with ball cartridges. Returning, he saw a wild duck dive in the river, and when it put its head up over the water, he fired and killed it; when we examined the duck, we found the ball had split the head in two. So enchanted was he with this musket that he determined to lay out two or three guineas in getting it newly stocked and polished, in the best style. I told him to try it again before going to any expense, so we went next day to the ruins of an old windmill, a league from the town, and we placed a sheet of paper on the wall. He said he would go about the same distance from the mill that he was from the duck. After firing three rounds, without once hitting the target, he flung the musket on the ground, swearing at it. He was very good humoured.*"

FORSYTH – Local folklore from the Limavady area in Co. Derry states that the Presbyterian Forsythe Family of Artikelly were implicated in the 1798 Rebellion resulting in their exile to the United States.

FOX, William – On 7 June 1798, William Fox, a Colonel in the Co. Down United Irishman climbed Scrabo Hill, near Newtownards, Co. Down, expecting to see local United Irishmen gathering there after hearing about the Antrim Rebellion. Fox found the hill deserted. When the Down insurgents rallied on 9

June 1798, Fox rode to Bangor and Donaghadee to encourage the people to rally. William Fox eventually fled to the United States.

The FRAME Family – The Frame Family, of Ulster Presbyterian stock, participated in the 1798 Rebellion and were forced to flee to the United States. One son, Rev. David Frame was born in 1805. After graduating from Princeton College, he was set to preach in Binghamton in Connecticut before moving to Morris County in New York. He was known for his sermon delivery and preparation. Ill health forced him to take up a position at Bloomfield Academy in Newark, New Jersey. He was much loved and held in high esteem by his pupils and fellow educators. He died in 1879 and was buried at Montclair, Essex County, New Jersey.

FRAZER, James – Frazer had been a United Irishman, who was forced to emigrate to the United States and settled in Savannah, Georgia, where he joined the city's militia.

FRAZER, Richard – Richard Frazer, a Colonel in the Co. Down United Irishmen, was apprehended for his involvement in the 1798 Rebellion, court-martialled and sentenced to serve the King of Prussia, however, this sentence was remitted to voluntary exile to the United States.

FREELAND, Robert – Robert Freeland, a native of Co. Armagh, fled to America as a result of his participation in the 1798 Rebellion.

FURLONG, John – John Furlong was

reputedly the son of Matthew Furlong, originally from Templescoby, Co. Wexford, the insurgent officer who rode to the barricades of Three Bullet Gate at New Ross, with the mission of delivering Bagenal Harvey's request for the garrison to surrender in the early hours of 5 June 1798. Although under a white flag of parley, Matthew Furlong was shot from his horse and killed. His death spurred rage and anger amongst the thousands of insurgents who were camped before the town, causing mass indiscipline, which played a prominent factor in the insurgents losing the battle with horrific casualties. Today, the prominent 1798 memorial in New Ross depicts Matthew Furlong and his flag of parley (*pictured*).

Furlong's son, John Furlong was captured and impressed into the Crown Forces. Whilst stationed with the British Army in Canada, Furlong, who had become acquainted with French settlers, was informed by them of Julian Dubuque and his excursions of searching for lead. Furlong escaped from the British Army and made his way along the Mississippi River. He eventually settled at Galena and successfully found lead ore. In 1818, when Illinois formally became a U.S. State, Furlong purchased large tracts of land. In 1824, he reached success when he uncovered a rich vein of lead ore at Cave Branch, which he named Vinegar Hill, in honour of the infamous battle of the 1798 Rebellion. As the mine flourished, so did the population of the township, which saw many Irish settlers arrive. Today, nothing remains of the town except the tour of the Vinegar Hill mine at Galena and an old burial ground, filled with headstones of those Irish settlers. Many thanks to Larry Furlong (Florida, USA), for bringing the story of John Furlong to our knowledge.

The GALBRAITH Family –

The Galbraith Family were Ulster Presbyterian exiles, possibly from Co. Antrim, who settled in Franklin County, Ohio, having left Ireland as a result of the 1798 Rebellion. Dr William Galbraith (1827-1899), who was born in the U.S., may have been first generation Irish-American. His son, John H. Galbraith, was a journalist who wrote for *United Press and the Columbus Dispatch*, as well as other publications. He had a particular interest in politics and history, and served for a time as Vice-President of The Legislative Correspondents Association.

GALLAGHER, Bernard –

Bernard Gallagher fled to the United States in 1803 after his participation in Robert Emmet's failed uprising. Upon arrival in America, he married Abigail Davis. Gallagher was father of four son however he died in 1814. His son, William Davis Gallagher (*pictured*) was born in Philadelphia in August 1808, and became a poet, journalist, author and a Government official. Whilst only a child of eight years, the Gallagher's moved west and settled at Mount Pleasant in Ohio, before eventually settling in Cincinnati. Among some of William D. Gallagher's writingsare:

"*A Journey Through Kentucky and Mississippi*" (1828); "*Fruit Culture in the Ohio Valley*" & "*Miami Woods*" c.1881, Gallagher died at Louisville, Kentucky in June 1894.

GALLAGHER, John –

In a biography of John Gallagher, a Philadelphian publisher, it mentions that his grandfather, John Gallagher and his family, fled Ireland to America from Co. Derry.

GALLAGHER, Pat -

On 13 July 1798, Pat Gallagher, a gunsmith's clerk, was tried on suspicion of acting traitorously against the Crown. The evidence against Gallagher was that, on 19 May 1798, he tried to lure William Cusack, a yeoman, into joining a riot, created by the arrest of Lord Edward Fitzgerald and the shock raids organised by Dublin Castle upon suspected United Irish houses. It was claimed in court that Gallagher apprehended Cusack on Dublin's Vicar Street, when he refused to join the rallying crowd as they made their way to create riots. Gallagher was later arrested for this action but somehow escaped custody before, what it appears, making his way to the insurgent hillside camp of Blackmoor Hill in north Co. Wicklow. The authorities combated Gallagher's attempts to claim innocence in court. Knowing that he was Lord Edward Fitzgerald's bodyguard, combined  with his actions against Cusack and at Blackmoor Hill, Pat Gallagher was sentenced to death by hanging. The sentence was remitted to transportation. Upon waiting on a prison ship in Dublin Bay, Gallagher organised a parting dance aboard the ship. With the party in full flow, he escaped from the boat and swam to an awaiting boat. He eventually fled to France. Gallagher remained active in the United Irish network and couriered a message from Robert Emmet to Thomas Addis Emmet and the Irish exiles in Paris in late May 1803, regarding the planned insurrection. Miles Byrne recorded Gallagher in his memoirs:

"His name will never be forgotten in Dublin, as the brave and faithful bodyguard to the ever-to-be-lamented Lord Edward Fitzgerald, who had been obliged to change frequently his hiding place, from house to house in the Liberty, in order to escape the police of the Castle hacks. Gallagher was always one of the most determined of Lord Edward's escort when changing his abode."

Gallagher was commissioned with a lieutenancy in the Irish Legion in late 1803, rising to Captain in 1804. In 1805, he was one of those who became disillusioned with the Legion, when it became clear that Bonaparte had no intention of launching an Irish expedition. Gallagher resigned his commission and settled with his family at Bordeaux, where he became a ship broker. According to the historian of the United Irishmen, R.R. Madden, Gallagher

"returned some years ago to Ireland, then went back to France, where he died in excellent circumstances and in good repute.

GANNON, Michael, Rev. Fr. – Father Gannon hailed Castlebar, Co. Mayo. He was educated in the Irish College in Paris and had served as chaplain to the Duke of Crillon, however, he had returned to Ireland at the height of the French Revolution, gaining service as curate in Louisburgh, Co. Mayo. When General Humbert and his expeditionary force landed at Killala Bay on 22 August 1798, Fr. Gannon acted as an interpreter and a commissary for the French. After the collapse of the Franco-Irish army at Ballinamuck, Gannon remained as a fugitive until he was arrested in November 1799. He was granted certain conditions and was allowed to depart the country. Having travelled to Lisbon in Portugal, Gannon wrote to Lucien Bonaparte, the younger brother of the infamous general that was becoming a rising star in France. The younger Bonaparte, who was an ambassador in Madrid, invited Gannon to the Spanish capital, securing for him a passport. Gannon returned to France and settled for a period close to Paris. He died at Lille c.1820, having served as a chaplain in the French Army.

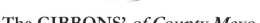

The **GIBBONS'** *of County Mayo*

GIBBONS, Austin – Gibbons was born in 1774 to Patrick Gibbons and Mary Davies. He was described by Richard Hayes, as *"a former sea captain, and was such was a frequent emissary between Ireland and France before the French landing."* Having served with the Franco-Irish forces during Humbert's Expedition, Gibbons survived the Battle of Ballinamuck and fled back to Mayo, where it seems he was apprehended. Held in Castlebar Gaol, Gibbons mounted a successful escape alongside his cousin, John Gibbons Jr and Fr. Myles Prendergast, resulting in the death of the sentinel. Having fled to France, Gibbons would become an officer in the Irish Legion. Whilst there, he composed a letter to an old neighbour.

"I take the liberty together with this opportunity, which is the first that offered since I came to France, of troubling you with a few lines, as I look upon you to be a man of principles and a man of honour. I expect you'll be so kind to acquaint my father (if he lives), Oliver Knight, Roger Toole or any man whom you may depend upon, that I am well in this town since I came to France; and so are those that left Ireland along with me. We are allowed a pension of four shillings a day from the Government. We expect to see Erin once more – and in such a manner that perhaps no man in that kingdom could suppose or imagine."

In June 1806, Gibbons resigned his commission in the Legion, citing that he could not support his family on the pay of a lieutenant and was facing mounting debt. Having resigned, Gibbons remained in France.

GIBBONS, Edmund – Edmund 'Ned' Gibbons was the eldest son of John Gibbons and Honora Monaghan of Drummin, near Westport, Co. Mayo. Having participated in the Connacht Rebellion, Gibbons was captured upon returning from Ballinamuck. He was tried and sentenced to death on 18 October 1798. Whilst awaiting execution, an order arrived claiming that the sentence had been remitted to transportation. Hayes claims that whilst aboard a transportation ship, they were intercepted by a French man-of-war and rescued, however, there is no evidence of any transportation ships being boarded or captured by France during this time. Gaining a commission in the Irish Legion, Miles Byrne records Ned Gibbons in his memoirs: "*He fought bravely at Flushing in 1809, in the Irish battalion, commanded by Colonel Lawless; the latter being badly wounded there, could not tell if Ned Gibbons was killed or made prisoner by the English troops when they entered Flushing.*"

GIBBONS, John – '*Johnny Eamuinn*' – John Gibbons of Drummin, Co. Mayo, was born c.1741 to Edmund Gibbons and Honora Hynes. He served as land agent to Lord Altamont for two decades and also held a considerable small estate in the Westport area, worth £2000 annually. His marriage to Honora Monaghan bore two recorded sons, Edmund (Ned) and John Jr (Johnny). Gibbons was an enthusiastic United Irishman who played a significant role in building the organisation across Mayo with James Joseph MacDonnell, serving as County Treasurer and County Secretary, and carrying out the role as organiser of pike production. On 27 August 1798, when Humbert took Castlebar, John Gibbons led a detachment of Westport men, alongside his brother, Thomas Gibbons, to join the Franco-Irish forces. After the collapse of the Rebellion, Gibbons remained as a fugitive until his capture in November 1799. Gibbons was referred to by Lord Sligo, as "*a shrewd old man.*" Upon settling in France, Gibbons, with support from Arthur O'Connor, joined the Irish Legion as a sub-lieutenant and was the oldest recruit, at the age of sixty-three years. His age of course would not help in any career advancement. Miles Byrne recorded old Gibbons in his memoirs:

"*Mr. John Gibbons, a wealthy gentleman of the County of Mayo, and upwards of seventy years of age, had to fly from his home, although he took no part in the general rising of the people to aid the French on their landing. His son Ned, being taken prisoner after General Humbert's capitulation, was condemned to be hung, and the rope was about his neck, when some humane person interfacing, his sentence was commuted, and he was transported to Botany Bay for life. But the father, who was hiding in the mountains for some time, and learning that all his property had been plundered and destroyed, escaped to Paris, and at the formation of the Irish Legion in 1803, being told it would be necessary to hold some rank in order to be allowed to embark in the expedition for Ireland, replied, that he was ready to accept that of corporal sooner than remain behind.*"

Byrne further mentions that Gibbons would be reunited with his son, Edmund, who apparently escaped from New South Wales. When the Legion was inspected in late 1804, it was noted by a French official that Gibbons was **"an old man who is respectable and recommendable because of his age, his conduct and his past suffering; he is not fit for military service."**

The Legion's commander, Petrezolli, commented that Gibbons was incapable and often drunk. In 1807, Gibbons died at Antwerp. His remaining son, Johnny *'the Outlaw'* Gibbons, remained at large as a fugitive insurgent until his capture and execution in 1806.

> *"Oh Johnny Gibbons, my five hundred healths to you,*
> *You are long away from me in Germany;*
> *Your heart without guile was always joyous,*
> *And now on the hills we are weak to help."*

GIBBONS, Peter — A native of Newport, Co. Mayo, Gibbons, a son of Thomas Gibbons of Inver in Erris, was noted to have been enthusiastic when news of the French landing at Killala occurred on 22 August 1798. Gibbons, a former yeoman, had planted a Tree of Liberty in Newport before a French detachment arrived at the village, under Captain Boudet. In April 1799, Gibbons was tried by court-martial at Castlebar and sentenced to death. He escaped and fled to America.

GIBBONS, Richard — Richard Gibbons was brother of Peter Gibbons of Westport and a son of Thomas Gibbons of Inver in Erris, Co. Mayo. For his support of the United Irishmen, Gibbons was arrested in October 1798 and tried in the following month. He had been sentenced to be executed, however, Lord Cornwallis remitted the sentence to that of banishment. Richard Hayes states that Richard Gibbons went to England and eventually died there in poverty.

GIBBONS, Thomas — Thomas Gibbons, the brother of old John Gibbons, was the son of Edmund Gibbons and Honora Hynes. At the time of the French Expedition in August 1798, Gibbons was resident at Crotts, near Westport, Co. Mayo. Gibbons was a noted insurgent leader and was recorded as having carried the flag of the insurgency into Castlebar, on the day of battle, at the head of a large group of insurgents. Historian, Richard Hayes, wrote that Thomas Gibbons remained at large for over a year, before being captured and sent to Germany. Hayes further states that Gibbons later returned to Ireland, causing annoyance to the local authorities.

THE GIBSON FAMILY *of Ballymena, County Antrim*

GIBSON, Rev. John –

John Gibson was born in 1791 to Rev. William Gibson and Rebecca Mitchell in Ballymena, Co. Antrim. John went to Ryegate, Vermont with his father, Rev. William Gibson. Young John was educated by his father and attended Vermont University before becoming a Covenanting Minister. Gibson settled in Baltimore in Maryland and married Elizabeth Gates, daughter of the American Revolution hero, Horatio Gates. Rev. John Gibson died on 3 June 1869 and was interred at Hollidaysburg Presbyterian Cemetery in Blair County, Pennsylvania. His son, William Gibson entered the U.S. Navy and rose to the rank of Commander. His youngest child, Robert Gibson had served as a lawyer before serving as a captain in the Confederate Army during the American Civil War.

GIBSON, Rev. Robert –

(1793-1837) Robert Gibson was born on 1 October 1793 to Rev. William Gibson and Rebecca Mitchell, at Ballymena, Co. Antrim. Young Gibson was but a child when his parents fled to America in 1797. Whilst at Ryegate, Gibson studied firstly under his father and became noted as an excellent scholar, before entering the seminary in Philadelphia and was licensed by the Middle Presbytery on 5 June 1818. He was ordained the pastor of Little Beaver, Pennsylvania, on 6 September 1819. Gibson eventually resigned this charge on 16 October 1830, and moved to take the charge of Second Reformed Presbyterian, in New York City. At the division of 1833, Gibson chronicled the departing and declining course of the New Light party. Despite failing health, he stood for the old Covenanter testimony until his death, in New York City on 22 December 1837. He wrote several pamphlets defending the Old Light position of the Reformed Presbyterian Church.

GIBSON, Rev. William — Rev.

William Gibson was born in 1753 to Robert Gibson and Joanna McWhirr. 1753-1838) In 1775, William Gibson graduated in theology from the University of Glasgow before continuing his studies at Edinburgh. He was a member of Rev Steveley's Knockbracken Reformed Presbyterian Church however his parents were members of the Presbyterian Church. Gibson was ordained and took over the Covenanting Churches of Kellswater and Cullybackey. Due to the subjects upon

FLAG OF THE COVENANTERS.

which he preached from the pulpit, Gibson came to the notice of Dublin Castle and was suspected of countenancing rebellion as a member of the United Irishmen. As a Covenanter, he refused to take the oath of allegiance required during the civil upheaval. Under this threat of arrest and execution, Rev. Gibson fled to New York at the end of 1797. In America he was joined by his brother-in-law Rev. James McKinney. In America, Rev. Gibson settled at Ryegate in Vermont and ministered to the Covenanting families in the area, many of whom had also fled persecution from the Ireland. In 1798, a call was sent out by eight communicants to the Rev. Gibson to the Reformed Presbyterian congregation of Vermont. He was installed on 10 July 1799 as pastor. The Rev. Gibson settled in the outback settlement and farmed during the week. He was described as a muscular man who excelled in logic and public speaking, he also published two books on the Reformed Presbyterian Church. He died in 1838.

GILLON, Andrew — Gillon was an Antrim Roman Catholic who had served the Crown Forces during the Battle of Antrim. He emigrated to Canada, settling in Saint John, New Brunswick. On 13 March 1839, he stumbled from a loft, breaking his neck and died, aged 67 years. Gillon was interred in the local Catholic graveyard.

GILMORE, Peter — Peter Gilmore, a labourer hailed from Ballyhurley, Co. Down. For participating in the insurrection, Gilmore was arrested and court-martialled on 3 September 1798, at Newtownards, Co. Down. He was found guilty of having acted like a traitor and sentenced to fourteen years in His Majesty's service. In November 1798, Gilmore was reported to have entered into recognisances and was prepared to sail to the United States.

GILLESPIE, David & Sarah –

David Gillespie and his wife, **Sarah**, were Presbyterian United Irish supporters from Co. Monaghan. The "*History of Madison County, Illinois*" supplies details to the Gillespie story in America. It also details that Sarah's brother (name unknown) also fled to America for his part in the United Irishmen. The Gillespie family and moved west from New York to Madison County, Illinois. They had two sons Mathew and "Judge" Joseph Gillespie (1809-1885). Sarah Gillespie died in 1831. David, desiring change, moved to Grant County in Wisconsin and died

JUDGE JOSEPH GILLESPIE.

there in 1855. In his youth, Joseph Gillespie worked at the lead mines of Galena before pursuing a career in law, eventually becoming a judge. Joseph Gillespie would become one of the most respected citizens of his time in of Illinois, was a friend and colleague of Abraham Lincoln, having served with him in the House of Representatives, representing their home state. It is recorded that Lincoln often sought the trusted confidence of Gillespie during times of stress. In 1858, Lincoln visited Edwardsville and the residence of Judge Gillespie. They remained firm friends until Lincoln's death by an assassin in 1865.

GLENDY, Rev. John –

(1755-1832) John Glendy was born on 24 June 1755 in Londonderry. Having studied theology at the University of Glasgow, Glendy started his ministry at Maghera. In 1778, he baptised a young boy called Henry Cook who would make his own impression of the Presbyterian Church. For his participation in the 1798 Rebellion, Glendy was issued with an arrest warrant. What followed is subject to contradictions:

1) After hiding out for several days Glendy gave himself up to the authorities. He always declared that he had taken no part in the 1798 Rebellion but nevertheless he was convicted and sentenced to perpetual banishment from Ireland. It was stated to the Presbyterian Synod that he was permitted to leave for America by Colonel Leith.

JOHN GLENDY,
(1755-1832)
Presbyterian Minister of Maghera, Co. Der
Patriot, 1798.

the Revd John Glendy, being charged with Seditious Practices, was permitted by Col. Leith to transport himself & Property to America;

2) Glendy hid out for two weeks after the rebellion in a place called the Grove. With Sarah MacQuirken, who dressed him as a lady, they made flight to Londonderry and then into exile where Mrs Glendy was waiting.

Rev. & Mrs. Glendy landed at Norfolk, Virginia, in 1799. There, Glendy started to preach in Norfolk which attracted a lot of attention for his oratory display. The maritime climate of Norfolk was unsuitable to Mrs. Glendy, so on the advice of a physician, they relocated to Staunton Lower, Virginia. Whilst temporarily based at Bethel, Glendy preached a printed sermon on the "*eulogy of Washington*" which grabbed the attention of the U.S. President Jefferson. On the President's invitation, Glendy visited Washington D.C. and delivered an oration which gained him much admiration. Soon afterwards, he became a minister at Baltimore and in 1806 he was chosen as chaplain to the Lower House of Congress and to the Senate in 1815. In 1822, the University of Maryland made him a Doctor of Divinity. John Glendy died on 4 October 1832 and was interred at the Second Presbyterian Church Burial Ground in Baltimore, Maryland.

"On Thursday night, 4th inst. after a lingering and painful illness, the Rev. JOHN GLENDY, aged 77 years, formerly Pastor of the 2d Presbyterian Church, of Baltimore, where he will be long remembered with affectionate regard for his many virtues".

Glendy's son, William Marshall Glendy (1800-1873), became a Commodore in the U.S. Navy during the American Civil War.

GORDON, Frances Henry – Frances H. Gordon was a member of the United Irishmen based at Saintfield in Co. Down. He was also a member of Rev. Thomas Ledlie Birch's Saintfield Presbyterian congregation. It is noted that he was in charge of the insurgent artillery pieces at the Battle of Ballynahinch and an interesting relationship worth noting was that he was a nephew of Rev. Arthur McMahon, a fellow United Irishman, who fled to France and served in the Irish Legion. After the collapse of the Rebellion, Gordon was allowed to emigrate at his own cost to America. Gordon died by accidental drowning in Lake Ontario.

GORDON, George – George Gordon was a native of Antrim Town and was implicated in the 1798 Rebellion. He fled to New York as a result. During

the War of 1812, he joined the "*The Irish Blues*" which was a regiment raised by the Caldwells of Salisbury County, fellow '98 exiles originally from Ballymoney, Co. Antrim, a unit in which Gordon gained the rank of ensign.

GOUDY, Rev. Alexander P.

REV. ALEXANDER P. GOUDY, D.D.

GOUDY, Rev. Alexander P. – Alexander Goudy was ordained at Donaghadee in Co. Down on 14 March 1780. He resigned in June 1791 and was disposed in August 1804. From 1791 to his exile in 1804, he was under the care of the Bangor Presbytery. As a supporter of the United Irishmen, he was forced to self-exile to America. It is unknown if he was connected to Rev. Robert Goudy of Dunover, who was executed in June 1798 for his part in the Rebellion. It is unknown what became of Goudy in America. The history of Donaghadee Church states that he left his church in 1791, fleeing to America.

GOWAN, Jonathan – Jonathan Gowan, a malster from Ballyquintin, Co. Down, participated in the Down Rebellion in June 1798. On 3 September 1798, he was court-martialled at Newtownards on charges of acting like a rebel and exciting treason and rebellion. Gowan was found guilty and was sentenced to fourteen years in His Majesty's service abroad. In November 1798, it was stated that Gowan had entered into recognisances to sail to the United States.

GRACEY, William – A devoted Presbyterian and a United Irishman, Gracey fled Ireland as a result of the 1798 Rebellion. He married Pricilla Graham and together they had a son, Rev Robert Gracey (1811-1871), pastor of Chambersburg, 1837; Pittsburgh, 1853; released 1867. William Gracey died in 1845 ages 63 years. His family remained in Pennsylvania and flourished. It is unknown exactly where in Ireland Gracey or but originated from but we suspect it was either Antrim or Down.

GRAY, Rev. Dr. James – Was born in 1770 and his story was told by his step son who penned a great biography of his father. James was the son of Captain John Gray of Co. Monaghan and mother`s maiden name was Niblock. He went to Glasgow University and studied theology and graduated in 1793, came home and was licenced by the Presbytery of Monaghan. The bio states that he was opposed to the civil and ecclesiastical condition of things in the British Isles and sailed for the United States in June 1797. It has suggested that he was a member of the United Irishmen. In the United States he attached himself to the Presbytery of Washington and the Associate Reformed Presbyterian Church and settled in Hebron New York. In 1803 he received a calling from Spruce Street in Philadelphia and removed to that city, Old Scots or First Presbyterian Church. In 1808 he received an honorary doctorate from the University of Pennsylvania and started teaching, Gray served as a manager of the Bible Society in partnership with United Irishman Samuel Brown Wylie from 1808-1817. In 1817 he resigned as he felt the college was taking away from his pastoral duties. He then removed Baltimore where he took a break from pastoral duties and started writing and publishing church material. He wrote for the Presbytery and at own cost his own ecclesial books. In 1823 he left Baltimore and made Gettysburg his last home. The following year this great servant of Christ fell asleep-

Gray, Rev. James
Died at the residence of the Reverend Charles G. McLean, in Cumberland township, on the 20th instant, after 16 days illness of bilious fever, the Rev. James Gray, D.D. in the 54th year of his age, 1824.

GRAY, Nicholas –
Gray was born c.1774 at Whitefort House, near Oilgate, Co. Wexford, to Nicholas Gray and Joyce Sophia White. Having studied law, Gray became an attorney, settling at Whitefort. In 1795, he married Elinor

Hughes of Ballytrent House, a sister of Henry Hughes, who would also play a significant role in both the 1798 Rebellion and Emmet's uprising of 1803. On 30 May 1798, Gray, a leading United Irishman, became Secretary to the Wexford Senate. He was chosen, not only for his professional skills or his social background, but for his Presbyterianism. The Senate was designed to incorporate religious equality. Gray would also serve as aide-de-camp to Beauchamp Bagenal Harvey, who held the rank of Wexford's commander-in-chief, until his resignation after the Battle of New Ross and the Massacre of Scullabogue. After the quashing of the Wexford Rebellion, little is known of Gray's whereabouts, however, he was arrested in 1799 and held at Wexford Gaol for administering an unlawful oath.

Gray was released, most likely due to influential connections. He purchased Rockfield House farm, on the borderlands of Counties Kildare and Laois, and resided with his two unmarried sisters-in-law. Maintaining his links to the United Irishmen, Gray was given command of the Kildare insurgency by Robert Emmet in 1803. Gray was to lead the Kildare insurgency into Dublin after Emmet's hopeful takeover of the capital. Gray remained cautious and Ruan O'Donnell's research of the Emmet uprising gives one theory that Gray was unimpressed with the soakage of insurgents from north Kildare to support Emmet's uprising. Having reached Naas, Gray decided to pull out of the uprising and returned to Rockfield. After the collapse of the Emmet uprising, Gray was arrested and conveyed firstly to Athy Gaol before being sent to Kilmainham Gaol, charged with treasonable practices. Twice he had been held by the Government for serious acts of treachery, however, his influences again served him and he was eventually released, most likely on the conditions of exile. Around 1807-1808, whilst financially insecure, Gray left Ireland for the United States. His family would follow him afterwards and received support from Thomas Addis Emmet. The following letter is from Gray to John Patton, brother-in-law to Thomas Addis Emmet:

"My Dear Mr Patten, I must first tell you that my poor wife, children arrived here safe after some narrow chances for their lives, and when they arrived, I was gallivanting about two hundred miles from New York and knew nothing of their arrival until by chance I happened to come to Town when your dear sister wished me joy of their safe arrival. I nearly had a cent when I met them. The great and good Mr Emmet released me out of my difficulties and has been a father to us since and the situation I have now obtained is through his interest. We lived in the city of Hudson about 130 miles from New York for some time on his bounty for I almost cut my foot off splitting a junk of wood with a damned axe, and was laid up for three months. I separated the great toe of my left foot smack off together with the ball of the foot but as soon as I got the boot off I bound it again together and when it could bleed no more, then I was three months near lame, then when I recovered we got the existence I now have. I support tolerably my family upon 400 dollars yearly or 90 British that I earn by walking four miles each day to Town, for I live in the summer house of a friend, not as yet being able to afford to rent one mile from the City of Albany; there at nine in the morning, home at one dine, and back at two, stay there till five quill driving, and then home. I have not the best furnished house in the neighbourhood, I unquestionably have the most elevated, for I am more than one thousand yards above the highest steeple in the city of Albany among the larks, sometimes basking in a well-aired cloud. We once complained of receiving 1s/11d a day from Government when in Kilmainham, but unfortunate man you never know when you are well off, where in this free country a large family can be supported upon 81/2d per day each, how could you grumble you ingrate at 1s/11d nearly three times as much, and had nothing to do but eat beef, drink whisky and make songs! But if I live till Spring, I shall have my salary doubled. Give my best respects to all our old acquaintances - Hicks, Cassin, Ridway, Tandy, Long, my good old friend Coile. I have not heard

anything of poor Harvey (Henry?) Hughes since my family arrived. May every happiness that visits the abode of mortals be yours is the prayer of me and my family, your and my dear friends the beloved Emmets are all well. Did you know Mr. Thomas Traynor who once made an extraordinary escape out of the Castle? He is now here and is well, all of his family are well also, they live about 10 miles from here. I am an Officer of the State and hold my situation under the supreme Court. Yours, Nicholas Gray."

Gray became personal secretary to Governor, Daniel D. Tompkins, who later became a U.S. Vice President, and served briefly as engineer in the New York Militia and Inspector General of New York 3rd District. At the outbreak of the War of 1812, Gray offered

his services to his adopted country. He oversaw the construction of artillery batteries on the New York border of Niagara, one of which was named in his honour; Fort Gray. Gray, a Lieutenant-Colonel, commanded the artillery during the Battle of Queenston Heights on 13 October 1812 (*pictured*). On 30 March 1814, Gray was appointed Registrar of the Land Office in the state of Mississippi, overseeing the district west of Pearl River, near Natchez. Having served as Inspector-General for the United States and overseen the mapping of the Canadian frontiers, Gray was honourably discharged from the U.S. Army in December 1814. Having suffered from years of ill-health as a result of his incarcerations in Ireland, Nicholas Gray died in 1819.

Gray's son, Nicholas Gray Jr, also worked as a land surveyor and in 1837, he

purchased land at Vicksburg, Mississippi. Here he constructed '*Wexford Lodge*' (*pictured*) to commemorate his father's native county. During the Siege of Vicksburg, the *Wexford Lodge* was the only building to survive the severe bombardment. Today, it is protected on the battlefield memorial park.

GREEN/NUGENT – The 1895 publication, *Memoirs of Georgia*, give detail to the Green Family who settled firstly in Beaufort, near Charleston, South Carolina. Green, a young educated and liberal minded individual became a teacher alongside his wife, whose maiden name was Fitzgerald. They became respected teachers at an academy in Beaufort, before later relocating to Savannah, Georgia. Green would become a lecturer at Athens  University in Georgia. On Christmas Day 1804, their son, Thomas Fitzgerald Green, was born in Beaufort, South Carolina. In 1850 he became the superintendent of the Georgia Lunatic Asylum and died in February 1879 and is interred at Memory Hill Cemetery in Baldwin County, Georgia.

GREEN/NUGENT – Green's wife, simply recorded as formerly a Fitzgerald, is recorded as the first cousin of Lord Edward Fitzgerald. It has been speculated that their name was changed when they arrived in America, adopting the name Green. On his death bed, upon being asked about this speculation, old Green whispered the surname Nugent. He was possibly the son-in-law of Sir Thomas Nugent.

GREER, William - A native of Wellbrook, Cookstown, Co. Tyrone. Greer was tried by court-martial at Cookstown on 29 June 1798 on charges of seditious language and for attending unlawful meetings. Greer was noted for having stated:

"*Down with the Orange and up with the Green and to Hell with anyone who Dare Say against the Roman Catholicks* (sic) *Getting what they Want.*"

Wealthy and influential friends intervened and Greer was sentenced to be transported to a country not at war with Britain or the United States, however, Greer went to the United States.

GREGG, Gauger – Gauger was from the City of Londonderry. He is described as by Anthony Dobbin (a United Irish exile) as a violent persecutor of the United Irish. For certain crimes, he was forced to exile to England and then may have went to the America.

GREY, George – Grey was a Dublin United Irishman who fled to Hamburg in 1798.

GURLEY, Susanna, *née Beatty* – Susanna Gurley was born in Ballycanew, Co. Wexford, on September 30 1778. She married Rev. William Gurley in 1795 and would emigrate to the United States with him after the Rebellion. Susanna Gurley died on 28 September 1848 and was interred at Perkins Cemetery, Erie County (OH).

GURLEY, Rev. William – William Gurley was born on 12 March 1757 in Co. Wexford, to John Gurley and Sarah Chamberlain. At the age of sixteen, he became an apprentice silversmith and acquired a large library of books for his age. Desiring to serve God, Gurley became a Methodist minister, and was reputedly ordained by John Wesley. By the late 1780s, Gurley was making a very good living in Wexford as both merchant and minister. In 1795, he married Susanna Beatty of Ballycanew, and together, they would raise twelve children. He had initially been sympathetic to United Irish politics, however, he remained somewhat loyal during the Rebellion. He was imprisoned for several weeks during the period and at one point was sentenced to be executed by insurgents. On 20 June 1798, Gurley's brother, Jonas Gurley, was piked to death on Wexford Bridge by Tom Dixon's rabble. With Wexford in a state of destruction and many of his inhabitants killed or having

emigrated, Gurley sold his possessions and moved his family in Liverpool, before eventually deciding to settle in the United States. In 1801, he emigrated with his family to New York City, before moving to Connecticut, where he worked as a silversmith for several years. In late 1811, Gurley purchased a large farm at Bloomingvale in Ohio and continued silversmithing, which saw him accept a contract to make the silver eagles worn on the caps of the U.S. Zanesville troops during the War of 1812. As the war progressed, it threatened his existence and in fear of attacks from Native Indians, the family relocated to Milan, Ohio. Gurley continued to preach throughout his life. He organised the first Methodist Society, west of Cleveland, Ohio and preached many sermons at Bloomingville, Ohio. Rev. William Gurley died on 15 January 1848. The graves of William & Susannah Gurley are next to each other in Perkins Cemetery near Sandusky, Ohio, previously called the "*Stone House Burial Ground*" and was

the private cemetery of the Beatty Family of Ballycanew, who had also settled there.

GUY, Robert – Robert Guy, a United Irishman, was brother in-law of the Rev. John Glendy, who also emigrated as a result of the 1798 Rebellion. In 1804, Guy settled in Augusta County, Virginia.

HAMILL, John – John Hamill was a United Irish leader based in the Newbliss area of Co. Monaghan. He was responsible for the recruiting of many Presbyterians into the United Irish movement. After the Rebellion failed, Hamill made a dramatic escape whilst being chased through a bog and eventually reached the port at Londonderry, making his way to America.

HAMILTON, James – James Hamilton of Belfast was involved in the 1798 Rebellion and eventually fled to New York after being released in September 1798. During the War of 1812, Hamilton, like many exiles to New York joined the *"The Irish Blues,"* a regiment commissioned by the Caldwells of Sailsbury County, who were also exiles. Hamilton was awarded a lieutenancy in this unit.

HAMILTON, William Henry – Hamilton, a native of Enniskillen, Co. Fermanagh, was born c.1771, a son to Johnston Hamilton. He was a United Irishman and a close associate of his uncle-in-law, Thomas Russell, who helped him establish a branch of the United Irishmen in Fermanagh in October 1793. Whilst studying law in England, Hamilton was a prime motivator in forming a coalition between the United Irishmen, the United Britons and the London Corresponding Society. In April 1798, he sailed to Hamburg and proceeded to the Hague, where he engaged with Charles-François Delacroix, the French Foreign Minister, informing him of the proposed United Irish military plans. Hamilton proceeded to Paris and would join the Hardy Expedition of October 1798, which was intercepted off the coast of Donegal by the Royal Navy. Unlike Tone, Hamilton escaped being recognised and eventually got back to France. In 1802, Hamilton was assigned by Robert Emmet to become an adjutant to Thomas Russell during his failed attempt to rally the North in July 1803. With a considerable bounty on his head, Hamilton went into hiding at Ballybay in Co. Monaghan, the homeplace of the Jackson families. In October 1803, Hamilton was arrested and held in Kilmainham Gaol until the restoration of habeas corpus in March 1806. Interestingly, Miles Byrne recorded that Hamilton had fled to the United States and had become a councillor. Conflicting history states that Hamilton remained in Dublin and contributed to the *Dublin Evening Post* and composed a play, *The Portrait of Cervantes*. In 1819, being an editor of the *Evening Post*, Hamilton was instrumental in promoting John Devereux's Irish

Legion to support Simon Bolivar's struggles for independence in South America. Hamilton endorsed the Legion to a point that he sailed to South America to personally support Bolivar. Having been commissioned as Colonel, he travelled to Philadelphia to negotiate the purchasing of a ship. Upon returning to Bogota, William Hamilton died of fever at Santa Anna in Colombia on 26 December 1825.

HARDY, Christopher – Christopher Hardy was a United Irishman, an inventor, saddler and a prestigious freeman of the City of Londonderry. In 1797 Hardy was implicated in the administering of the United Irishmen oath to a Tipperary Militiaman. He is imprisoned at the request of the MP for Derry George Hill. In 1798 his name was wiped from the freemen's list and it's assumed that he self-exiled to the United States under the recommendation of George Hill.

HARMAN, John – The youngest of the Harman brothers of Killafeen, Co. Wicklow, John Harman was noted to have been the most notorious of the family and involved in particularly gruesome ambushes and murders during the 1798 Rebellion and the period of guerrilla activity in Co. Wicklow afterwards. In March 1801, John and Laurence Harman left Wicklow for Dublin, believing they were to sail aboard the *Lydia* for Baltimore in America. This of course did not happen and Laurence Harman was arrested and sent as a convict to Australia. Bro. Luke Cullen, who recorded many stories from veterans of the 1798 period took note that John Harman had returned from New South Wales to settle his affairs in Ireland before going to Canada. No convict indents or trial transcripts exist to say that John was transported along with Laurence. It is plausible that the story confused Laurence for John. *The Bedford Gazette* (13 July 1860) recorded the obituary of Mary Byrne *neé* Harman, a sister of John and Laurence Harman, who settled in Pennsylvania in 1817 and indicates that both her brothers also settled in America.

HARMAN, Laurence – Laurence Harman, born c.1766, hailed from Killafeen, Laragh, Co. Wicklow. He was a brother of the notoriously violent Wicklow insurgents, John & Nicholas Harman. In March 1801, John and Laurence Harman left Wicklow for Dublin, believing they were to sail aboard the *Lydia* for Baltimore in America. This of course did not happen and Laurence Harman was arrested. Harman was tried in Dublin City in July 1803 and sentenced to transportation for life in New South Wales. Harman sailed as a convict aboard the *Tellicherry*, from Cork, on 31 August 1805, which arrived in Sydney, Australia, on 15 February 1806. Little is known of the later lives of the Harman Brothers. If a convict abided by the colony's laws and received an absolute pardon, then he was free to leave the colony and return home if he had the financial means. Bro. Luke Cullen, who recorded many stories from veterans of the 1798 period took note that John Harman had returned from New South Wales to settle his affairs in Ireland before going to Canada. No convict indents or trial transcripts exist to say that John was transported along with Laurence. It is plausible that the story confused Laurence for John. *The Bedford Gazette* (13 July 1860) recorded the obituary of Mary Byrne *neé* Harman, a sister of John and Laurence Harman, who settled in Pennsylvania in 1817 and indicates that both her brothers also settled in America.

HARPER, Rev. James – James Harper was a native of Mallusk, Co. Antrim. In 1771, he had been ordained as minister of Knockcloughrim Secession Presbyterian Church. He was arrested and charged with having sympathies towards the United Irishmen during the 1798 Rebellion. His service proximity to Tobermore and Maghera indicates that he could have been a participant in the insurrection. Not long after his arrest, Harper fled to the United States. He continued preaching for several years in Virginia and passed away in September 1802.

HARPER, Nicholas – Harper was a Wexford native and insurgent who fought at the Battle of Vinegar Hill on 21 June 1798. During the battle, Harper was injured yet escaped, however, he lost two brothers during the eventful morning battle. When his wound healed, Harper fled to America. Harper served as a clerk in the U.S. Treasury Department for thirty years and served for many years in the U.S. Navy. The Navy enabled Nicholas to travel worldwide. Nicholas Harper died on 29 January 1843, at the age of 73 years, in New Jersey.

HARPER, William – William Harper, the son of Rev. James Harper, was a United Irishman who fled to the United States, after participating in a leadership role during the assembly of insurgents on Crewe Hill before the failure to takeover Maghera, Co. Derry. His family property was confiscated and Harper lost any claims to inheritance.

HARRISON – Harrison was a United Irish exile who was based in Paris. Upon many of the Irish exiles joining the Irish Legion, he hosted a dinner event in their honour, which included Miles Byrne, Thomas Addis Emmet, William Lawless, John Tennant and Pat Gallagher as guests. His humour was noted by Miles Byrne, who described Harrison's seating arrangements, which saw some French guests receiving a filling Irish meal whilst many of the Irish guests received a French selection of soup, causing Pat Gallagher to jokingly remark about dining on frogs. Harrison's home was decorated with the flags of France, the United States and a green flag with a harp and '***Erin go Bragh***' emblazoned in gold, to represent the United Irishmen. After the Bourbon Restoration, Byrne occasionally met Harrison in Paris and often met him for lunch at the Café de la Rotunde at Palais Royal. In 1841, Miles Byrne and his wife, whilst strolling in Paris, met Harrison, who appeared in good spirits, exclaiming in jest that his cousin, by the name of Harrison, had won the U.S. Presidential election. Byrne

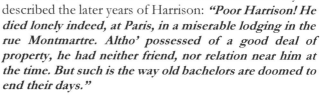

described the later years of Harrison: *"Poor Harrison! He died lonely indeed, at Paris, in a miserable lodging in the rue Montmartre. Altho' possessed of a good deal of property, he had neither friend, nor relation near him at the time. But such is the way old bachelors are doomed to end their days."*

HAYS, Elizabeth, *née Fulton* – Elizabeth Fulton of Ballykelly, Co. Derry, married Samuel Hays, in 1770. Some of their known recorded children include: **Elizabeth Hays** (1790-1873), **Jeanette Hays** (1781-1855) and Thomas Fulton Hays (1794-1872). Elizabeth died in 1824 and was interred beside her husband at Rocky Glen Cemetery in Crawford County, Pennsylvania. **HAYS, Samuel** – Hays was born in Co. Donegal in 1757 to Thomas Hays and Jane Buchanan and would become involved in the linen business at Ballykelly, Co. Derry. After his involvement in the 1798 insurrection, he fled from Ireland to the United States with his wife, Elizabeth Fulton. Hays died on 13 October 1822 and was interred at Rocky Glen Cemetery, Crawford County, Pennsylvania.

HAYS, Thomas Fulton – Thomas Fulton Hays (*pictured*) was born at Ballykelly, Co. Derry, in February 1794 to Samuel Hays and Elizabeth Fulton. Having settled with his family in Pennsylvania, Hays would serve the U.S. Army during the War of 1812. He would relocate to Dodge County in Wisconsin with his wife, Sarah Dunlap, There, he died on 22 September 1872. He was interred at Saint Paul's Episcopal Cemetery in Dodge County. His son, Samuel Hays would serve the Union Army during the American Civil War and died in Tennessee on 21 January 1863.

HENRY, Robert – This individual was held in Carrickfergus Gaol in Co. Antrim in late 1799 alongside John Cox. Without being tried, it is recorded on a trial list from March 1800 that they **were "*liberated some months ago, under recognisance to transport themselves, but not having done so in the limited time apprehended again.*"** It is unknown if Henry and Cox became exiles.

HERON, William – William Heron, a Co. Down clockmaker had participated in the Down Rebellion and was later arrested. He was sentenced to transportation but this was later remitted to voluntary banishment. Heron sailed with John Caldwell aboard the *Pallas* on route to America however due to bad weather it had to land at Cork. On his arrival back to the North he was re-arrested. He was permitted again in 1799 to exile to America.

HOGE, Rev. Thomas – Hoge was born on 3 May 1775 in either Tyrone or Derry. Having been educated at the University of Edinburgh, he was appointed as a probationer in the Presbyterian Church in Tyrone. Having been implicated as United Irishman, Hoge may have been pressurised to leave considering Tyrone saw a substantial crackdown throughout the summer of 1797. Hoge left Ireland in 1797 bound for the United States. Having arrived he was welcomed as a probationer by the Presbyterian Church in Pennsylvania and settled at Carlisle in rural Pennsylvania. On 18 October 1798, he married Betsey Holmes. By 1799, he left the church and became a successful merchant based at Greensburg and also

served as Treasurer of Westmoreland County. In 1816, he decided again to become a minister and was taken under the care of the Ohio Presbytery, being officially ordained as an evangelist in January 1817. He was presented before the Synod of Pittsburgh as a Licensee from the Presbytery of Tyrone Ireland.

Hoge focused primarily with missionary work and was noted for his evangelical zeal. In 1818, he was elected to succeed the Rev. Francis

Herron as Clerk of the Pittsburgh Synod. In 1821 he was installed as pastor of the United Congregations of Claysville and East Buffalo. He left a legacy of increasing attendance and baptisms. Thomas Hoge passed away on 23 January 1846, aged 70 years, and was interred at Woodlands Cemetery in Philadelphia.

HORE, George – Hore was a Spanish General in the Bolivian War of Independence. It is stated within an announcement regarding a battle that he was a native of Co. Wexford who had left Ireland after the 1798 Rebellion. It unknown if he was a United Irishman or had actually participated in some capacity.

HORNER, James – James Horner, the son of Thomas Horner and Jane McCracken of Innisconager, hailed from the Moyes/Bovevagh townland close to Limavady, Co. Derry. His brother was John Lyle Horner. They were possibly related to Rev. James Horner of Dublin and our next subject John Horner. Horner, a Presbyterian United Irishman became involved in the 1798 Rebellion, thus forcing him to flee to Philadelphia. In letters that he composed, he claimed that he left his father at the "Clare River" before departing. His letters are a great window into this period and can be found on the '*Documenting Ireland: Parliament, People & Migration*' website. In one such letter, written to his family, Horner mentioned the following listed name, John Horner. The authors firmly believe that James Horner was a relative to Andrew Long Horner, Liberal Unionist M.P. for South Tyrone, who in 1904 was appointed to King's Counsel and became Crown Prosecutor for Co. Cavan. Andrew L. Horner died on 26 January 1916, aged 53 years. Thanks to Muriel Stringer for additional information.

HORNER, John – John Horner was a brother of Rev. Dr James Horner of Dublin, Presbyterian natives of Carnet near Limavady, Co. Derry. In 1798, the Horner family had taken an active part in the United Irish movement. Horner was particularly active in the production of pikes. In June 1798, the Horner homestead was raided by the military and a quantity of weaponry was discovered. Horner managed to evade the authorities and escaped to the United States.

HOY – According to local tradition in the Donegore/Kilbride area of Co. Antrim, a member of the Hoy family fought at the Battle of Antrim on 7 June 1798. Hoy subsequently fled to Hamburg, where there was a thriving Irish exile community. From Hamburg we have no further information.

HUDSON, Edward – Edward Hudson was born in October 1772 to Captain Henry Hudson and Jane de Tracy in Co. Wexford. Having become orphaned as a child, Hudson was adopted by his cousin, the renowned Dr. Edward Hudson, who owned a clinic at 38 Grafton Street and The Hermitage demesne in Rathfarnham, now recognised as St. Enda's (Pearse Museum). In 1797, he became close friends with Robert Emmet and the poet, Thomas Moore, who later penned, *"The Origin of the Harp"*, in dedication to Hudson. Their friendship was based on their common interest in old Irish traditional airs and poetry. Although Moore  claims not to have been a United Irishman, he was aware of Hudson and Emmet's involvement. Hudson was present at the Leinster Directory meeting, held at Oliver Bond's residence, which was raided by Castle authorities on 12 March 1798. Hudson was held in Kilmainham Gaol until the State Prisoners were sent to Fort George in Scotland on 19 March 1799. Whilst at Fort George, Hudson was hired by the local gentry to perform his dentistry skills that he had learned from his cousin. When the Treaty of Amiens brought peace between France and Britain, the State Prisoners were released, on terms of not returning to Ireland. Hudson sailed to the United States and settled in Philadelphia, where he married Maria Bridget Byrne, the daughter of exiled United Irish bookseller, Patrick Byrne. Hudson would become a pioneer in American dentistry and was associated with the replacement of dental pulp with gold foil, and for modernising primitive dental practices. Hudson died in Philadelphia on 3 January 1833.

+HUDSON, Maria Bridget *neé Byrne* –

Maria Bridget Byrne, born c.1792, was the daughter of Patrick Byrne, a renowned Dublin bookseller and United Irishman. When Byrne accidentally implicated John and Henry Sheares in a United Irish conspiracy, he was arrested and his Grafton Street bookshop was smashed by soldiers. After his release, Byrne fled to the United States with his son, William Byrne and daughter, Maria Bridget Byrne. The family prospered once again upon establishing a bookshop in Philadelphia and engaging in the printing of liberal compositions. In 1805, Maria married the United Irish exile, Edward Hudson. On 14 August 1812, Maria Hudson died as a result of an abscess in the lungs, aged 20 years.

HUEY, James – Huey, a United Irish woollen draper, was a relation of

the renowned Caldwell family of Ballymoney, Co. Antrim. It is unknown if he participated in the Rebellion, but he did act as a prosecution witness against many United Irishmen whom he knew from north Antrim. The Huey's left Ireland and settled in Maryland before relocating closer to the Caldwell family, who were based near Albany, New York. Whilst on the journey the ship capsized and Huey was drowned.

HUGHES, Henry – Henry Hughes was born c.1768, at Ballytrent House

(*pictured*), Co. Wexford to Henry Hughes and Jane Mary Goodall. Hughes' sister, Elinor married Nicholas Gray, an attorney from Whitefort. Both Hughes and Gray would play significant roles in both the 1798 Rebellion and the Emmet uprising of 1803. Hughes, a United Irishman, most likely sworn in by Beauchamp Bagenal Harvey, served on the staff of the Southern Wexford

Division during the insurrection and particularly during the devastating Battle of New Ross (5 June 1798). Little is known about what occurred to Hughes after the collapse of the Wexford Rebellion in late June 1798. His family's influence may have protected him from the fate of other local Protestant United Irish leaders like Harvey, Cornelius Grogan and John Henry Colclough, who were all executed by the British on Wexford Bridge.

On 24 July 1803, Hughes, on orders from Robert Emmet, made his way to his native Barony of Forth in south Wexford, hoping to rally old insurgent acquaintances. Having called to Quigley's residence at Donard, near New Ross, Hughes met Thomas Cloney, a former accomplice. The following day, they received news of the failed Emmet uprising of 23 July. Hughes, who had injured

his arms in a bad horse fall, rested his arms in slings to give support, however, the local population began to gossip, claiming that Hughes had received his injuries in the commotions in Dublin. Fearful of his brother-in-law's safety, Hughes set forth to ride from New Ross to Rockfield House, the homestead of Nicholas Gray, near the Kildare town of Athy. On 14 September 1803, Hughes was arrested with Gray and held in Athy Gaol before being conveyed to Kilmainham Gaol on 3 December 1803. He was spared from execution because of his influential family. The bicentennial memorial at Ballytrent highlights that Hughes was officially disowned by the Hughes Family and lost his claims to the Ballytrent lands. Ruan O'Donnell claims that Hughes emigrated to the United States. This is verified by Burke's Peerage, which highlights Hughes selling Ballytrent House and went to America. There is indications that Hughes later returned to reside in Co. Wexford. Ballytrent House would become the family home of the Redmond Family, which bore John and Willie Redmond, leaders of the Irish Parliamentary Party in the late-1800s.

HUGHES, John - John Hughes, a Presbyterian bookseller from Bridge Street, Belfast, had been an early member of the Co. Down United Irishmen. At a young age, Hughes had served an apprenticeship under Henry Joy who had taken over from his father as editor and owner of the *Belfast Newsletter*. Regarding his political activities, Hughes was particularly active and spent much time in Dublin, forging links and friendships amongst the east coast United Irish, especially with Bartholomew Teeling and Lord Edward Fitzgerald. In October 1797, Hughes was arrested in Newry, Co. Down and charged with treason. He chose the path to become an informer in the pay of Dublin Castle. In March 1798, John Hughes attended a meeting with the Northern United Irish Directory at Hays Tavern (not the mistranslated Keys, probably at Brown's Square in Belfast). It was from here that he had access to the provincial commander, Adjutant-General Robert Simms and most probably influenced Simms to be cautious and wait for the expected French assistance. This action led to divisions in the organisation in Ulster, resulting in Simms resigning from his position when he refused to call out the Army of Ulster in late May 1798.

On the eve of the Antrim Rebellion, James Hope of Templepatrick travelled to Belfast to find Rev. Steel Dickson, who had been arrested only several days previously. Hope was commissioned to give Dickson the order to rise the Army of Down on 7 June, whilst the Army of Antrim was attacking Antrim Town. Hughes was arrested on 7 June 1798 as the Battle of Antrim raged. For the price of £200, he supplied evidence against former friends and fellow United Irishmen at a secret committee of the Irish House of Lords. For his actions he could not reside in Ireland any longer and emigrated to South Carolina in early 1802. Writing in the 1850s, the renowned historian of the United Irishmen, R.R. Madden stated that Hughes had *"bought slave property in the southern states and died there a few years ago"*.

HULL, Rev. James Foster – James F. Hull was the son of the Rev. James Hull of Limavady, Co. Derry, who had been a much-respected minister who had preached in Tyrone and later at Ballyvaron, near Bangor in Co. Down. He had also served as Moderator of the 1769 Synod. James Hull Jr was born in Bangor in 1776 and eventually attended the University of Glasgow, following his father's footsteps in theology. Upon returning to Ireland, Hull was licenced by the Presbytery to preach. From its conception, Rev. Hull had been associated with the United Irish movement and was a close associate of Presbyterian probationer, David Bailie Warden. On 7 June 1798, when Henry Joy McCracken called out the Army of Ulster, Hull and Warden made their way to the summit of Scrabo Mountain, outside Newtownards. This was where the United Irishmen of north Down were to assemble and prepare for insurgency. When the turn out did not manifest, Hull attempted to rally those associated with the United Irish cause. After the Down Rebellion was crushed, a bounty of £50 was placed upon the apprehension of Rev. James Hull. He escaped both shackle and informer and immediately fled to the United States.

3 to America — Bangor Presb. report, That Mess.rs Ja. Hull, John Miles & David Warden, lately Licentiates of their Presbytery, having been charged with being concerned in the Insurrection of June 1798 & not having stood their Tryals, but as they understand having sailed for America, are not to be considered as Probationers under their care. They further Report, That the Rev.d D.r W.m Steel Dickson, hath been from the beginning of June 1798, a State Prisoner, & is now such at Fort George, in the Highlands of Scotland. They also report, that they ordained the

One in confinement

Two Ordained

132

Hull settled in Baltimore, where the Rev. John Glendy of Maghera had established himself after also fleeing from Ireland. After a short period, Hull and his family relocated to the southern states, embracing new paths in the towns of Augusta and New Orleans. Having settled in New Orleans, Hull officiated as a Presbyterian Minister and his popularity saw him being pressed by the Episcopalian Church to also preach to them. In January 1815, the British and American armies clashed in the Battle of New Orleans, a battle which interestingly saw former French General, Jean Humbert serve with the U.S. Army, having left France during the rise of Bonaparte. Hull had also volunteered his services upon greeting General Andrew Jackson who apparently stated:

"I don't presume you will go with us to fight the enemy?" Jackson said
"Why not, General, if you will take me with you?." Hull Replied
"How could you help us dear Black Coat?" said Jackson
"Why you know I have had some encounters with the red coats, and perhaps I could be of some use to you"

Hull was ordained in New Orleans a year later and ministered until his death 1833, carving out a career of bonding some of the various churches of New Orleans together.

The JACKSON Family *of Ballybay, County Monaghan*

The Jackson Family were one of the wealthiest Presbyterian linen merchants in Co. Monaghan. The patriarch, Hugh Jackson (1710-1777) of Creeve, founded the town of Ballybay in Co. Monaghan, bringing much employment to the linen trade. With his wife, Eleanor Gault, they would have five sons out of which, James, Henry, Hugh and John Jackson, would become prominent United Irishmen. The extended Jackson family would become involved in the United movement, resulting in many fleeing to the United States of America.

JACKSON, Alexander - Alexander Jackson was the son of Hugh Jackson Jr of Ballybay. He emigrated to the United States alongside his brother, Humphrey Jackson, settling for a short period in Louisiana, but they eventually

133

grounded in the Texas area, becoming pioneer settlers in the Houston and Galveston areas.

JACKSON, Henry-

Henry Jackson was born c.1750. was a member of the United Irishmen, and iron founder and son of Hugh Jackson and Eleanor Gault of Creeve in Co. Monaghan. Hugh had become wealthy and introduced the Linen trade to Ballybay in Monaghan. In 1766, Jackson established an iron-mongers at Pill Lane in Dublin, making him considerably wealthy by the time he joined the Society of United Irishmen. His interest in reforming politics began with his interactions with James Napper Tandy, whilst a member of the merchant's guild. In late 1791, Jackson became a member of the United Irishmen and honourably named his home in Dublin, *Fort Paine*. He acted as secretary and treasurer on multiple occasions and was present in 1794 when its final meeting was raided by the authorities.

When the United Irishmen were driven underground, it was known that Jackson's foundries were enthusiastically producing cannon balls to suit French specifications. On 12 March 1798, as the authorities raided the residence of Oliver Bond, his son-in-law, Jackson was arrested elsewhere and conveyed to Kilmainham Gaol. Mostly due to his influential friends, Jackson was effectively allowed to self-exile to the United States, thus avoiding the fate of many other State Prisoners, who were either executed or sent to Fort George. Jackson was released from Kilmainham Gaol on 28 September 1799. He settled at first in Pennsylvania before establishing himself in Baltimore. Henry died in New York on 4 July 1819. For reference to Jackson's daughter's family, please see the *BOND* family within this book.

JACKSON, Hugh Jr –

In 1792, when the *Northern Star* newspaper was inaugurated, Hugh Jackson of Ballybay, was one of its main subscribers and distributors in Co. Monaghan, making it one of the County's most popular papers. Co. Monaghan had already strong radical elements within its society. In July 1796, a cart of weapons, manufactured in the pits of Hugh Jackson's mill at Creeve, was uncovered at Drumconrath turnpike. Unknowing to the authorities, they were destined for Henry Jackson's foundry in Dublin's Pill Lane. Monaghan's United Irishmen grew rapidly throughout 1796, but faced decline in the summer of 1797 as a result of two principal factors: the failure of the anticipated French landing and General Lake's harsh crackdown across Ulster. Hugh Jackson was arrested in May 1798 for his deep involvement in the United Irishmen. He seems to have evaded being banished like his father and was able to stay in Dublin managing his father large business interests. He exiled to the United States in 1803 after Emmets last United Irishmen rebellion. Jackson's daughter, Ellen Jackson, married William Tennant, a Belfast United Irishman and brother of William Tennant, who was killed serving in the Irish Legion. Hugh Jackson died in 1810.

JACKSON, Humphrey – Humphrey Jackson, born on 24 November 1784, was the son of Hugh Jackson Jr and Letitia Thompson. Around 1800-01, he emigrated to the United States alongside his brother, Alexander Jackson. They settled for a short period in Louisiana, but they were eventually grounded in the Texas area, becoming pioér settlers in the Houston and Galveston areas, as part of Stephen Austin's '*Old 300*' Colony. On 13 October 1814, he married Sarah Merriman, settling in Crosby, Texas. Jackson died on 18 January 1833 and was interred at Warren Family Cemetery in Harris County, Texas.

JACKSON, James Jr- James Jackson was born on 25 October 1782 to James Jackson and Mary Steel. After his uncle Henry's release and subsequent exile to Philadelphia, James Jackson, sailed to the United States and settled in Nashville, Tennessee, where he was operating a store by 1807, alongside his American wife, Sarah Moore McCulloch. Jackson, being a director of the Bank of Nashville, helped finance General Andrew Jackson's army during the War of 1812, including supplying the General with personal loans. Jackson's equestrian interests followed him to the United States. At his plantation, the Forks of Cypress, he established a renowned racing stable, often visited by the above-
mentioned, General Andrew Jackson, the future President of the United States, who was also a noted admirer of horse-racing. Jackson would become de-facto financier and money-lender to General Jackson on multiple occasions. Their personal and working relationship would eventually end when Andrew Jackson proposed a duel with James Jackson, believing James would use information against him during his presidential race.

The duel threats did not manifest into anything. In 1818, James Jackson moved to Florence in Alabama and developed a new plantation, using the old name, the Forks of Cypress, and continued to breed and care for successful race-horses. His unique mansion (*pictured*) would incorporate a neo-Greco style, being the only example of its kind in Alabama. The house would eventually burn down in 1966 and the brick pillar colonnade, which surrounded the mansion remains today, and is somewhat reminiscent of the

ruined Parthenon in Athens. In 1830, Jackson became President of the Alabama Senate. James Jackson died on 17 August 1840 and was interred at the Jackson Cemetery in Lauderdale County, Alabama

JACKSON, John – John Jackson was born in 1773 to James Jackson and Mary Steel. After his uncle Henry's release and subsequent exile to Philadelphia, young John Jackson and his bride, Elizabeth McCrae, sailed to the United States and settled in Philadelphia. Jackson immediately established himself as a merchant and resident at 231 Market Street. In 1823, having moved to Alabama, he purchased a tavern, the Florence Hotel. John Jackson died on 28 April 1832 and was interred at the Jackson Cemetery in Lauderdale County, Alabama.

JACKSON, Washington

– Washington Jackson, the youngest son of James Jackson and Mary Steel of Ballybay, was born on 21 January 1784. His flamboyant forename was evidently given in honour of America's George Washington, showing the Jackson family's deep interest in the revolutionary tidings of America. Young Jackson sailed to the United States and settled with his brother, James, in Nashville, Tennessee. Washington Jackson soon established his own merchant store, with connections to Natchez in Mississippi and Philadelphia. Alongside his brother James Jackson, Washington became Director of the Nashville Bank, thus becoming acquainted with many of the elite settlers in the Nashville area, including 'Old Hickory' Andrew Jackson. During the War of 1812, he was noted for supplying the shoes of General Andrew Jackson's army, a favour which would not be forgotten. Jackson married Anna M. Dawson. After 1813, Jackson invested into a sugar plantation in Louisiana and also advertised the first steam-powered cotton press in the Natchez district. His wealth expanded and within a few years, Jackson was a cotton broker in New Orleans. In 1850, at an advanced age, Washington Jackson retired to Liverpool, England, having accumulated a vast fortune and died in London on 14 July 1865.

JACKSON, James – It was suggested that this individual might have been an exile who died after his arrival to New York City. Jackson's headstone in Washington Square Park, Manhattan, clearly states that he was a native of Co. Kildare. He died on 22 September 1799, aged 28 years.

JOHNSTON, Samuel – Samuel Johnston was from Ballymacbrenan in Co. Down, outside Saintfield. He was imprisoned in Downpatrick Goal for his part in 1798. He petitioned the authorities to be able to emigrated to America in 1799.

JORDAN, Edward, *The White-Toothed Pirate from Carlow* – Jordan was born into a farming background in Co. Carlow in 1771. He fought with the Wexford insurgency during the 1798 Rebellion and upon being arrested, he became an informer and received a pardon. Jordan married Margaret Croke and they attempted to settle in Co. Wexford. After several years, they left for New York City and travelled north to Nova Scotia. Having become disillusioned with farming, Jordan attempted to make good with fishing, but he became disillusioned with this trade also. Having constructed a schooner named the *Three Daughters,*' Jordan fell into debt and was incarcerated upon visiting Halifax. Upon being bailed, he was warned by the debtors to sort his finances or face losing his schooner. Jordan engaged in light piracy. On 13 September 1809, as an officer's crew arrived to take the *Three Daughters,*' Jordan requested one final journey on it to sail his family to a new destination near Halifax. It was agreed. Upon sailing to Halifax, Jordan, his wife and an accomplice, John Kelly overtook

the officer's crew and retook the schooner. Captain Stairs was flung overboard into the icy waters near Halifax, but survived. Jordan, hiding in Newfoundland and hoping to sail to Ireland, had a bounty of £100 placed on his head. The group were eventually intercepted and arrested. On 23 November 1809, Jordan was executed near Freshwater Beach, Halifax. His remains were painted in hot tar and gibbeted within an iron cage and hung at Point Pleasant for over thirty years. Jordan's skull is within the care of the Maritime Museum of Halifax.

KEAN, Thomas – Thomas Kean was mentioned in a letter from John Caldwell, an exile who was a resident of New York to former United Irish commander, Robert Simms.

KEAN, William, *The Star Man* - William has been immortalised in the past few years in the book *The Star Man*. He was a clerk employee of the radical United Irish newspaper, the *Northern Star*. Kean was also an early member of the United Irishmen and in 1797 was imprisoned in Kilmainham Gaol along with Henry Joy McCracken. He was later released and fought at the Battle of Ballynahinch as an aide-de-camp to Henry Munro. Subsequently, William was arrested and imprisoned, however he managed to escape by jumping from a third-story window of a provost prison and eventually fled to Philadelphia. When his old employer, Samuel Neilson arrived in the United States, Kean engaged with him for advice of setting up an evening newspaper. Historian, Michael Durey records this individual as Thomas Kane in *Transatlantic Radicals*, so it is possible the above-mentioned Thomas Kean was this individual.

KEEGAN, Thomas – (c.1781-1889) Thomas Keegan, a native of Ridges, near Newry, Co. Down, died at the grand age of 108 years on 28 March 1889. He went to America in the year 1814, so we cannot determine if he went to America as an exile but his age is worthy of mention. His obituary states that he had fought in the Irish Rebellion of 1798 and had been resident in the town of Hollidaysburg, Pennsylvania for his final years. At the time of his death, it was said that he was unquestionably the oldest man in the U.S. He was a keen smoker and never missed Presidential elections; his first vote was for Andrew Jackson in 1828. Unusually, having no children, it is unique that such investment was given to Thomas' remains, which were brought back to Ireland where he was interred at St Patrick's Cemetery in Newry, Co. Down.

> **Thomas Keegan, Aged 108.**
>
> Thomas Keegan, who resided in th[e] "Ridges," six miles west of Newry, died sud denly at 10 o'clock on Monday night, at th[e] remarkable age of 108 years. He was a na tive of Ireland, and had a very distinct re collection of the "rebellion of '98," havin[g] been 17 years old and having carried a pik[e] in that bloody episode in the history of h[is] unhappy country.
>
> Mr. Keegan emigrated to the Unite[d] States seventy-five years ago and was f[or] many years a residen[t] of this county, [of] which he was unquestionably the oldest i[n]habitant at the time of his death. He w[as] quite well preserved for a man of his ag[e] and presented himself at the polls last N[o]vember, where he deposited a democrat[ic] ballot as had been his habit ever since [he] became a citizen.
>
> His wife died several years ago, and as [he] was never the father of any children, [he]

KELLY, Bob – Bob Kelly of Coronary, Co. Monaghan was an important figure amongst the Monaghan Presbyterian community, and played a significant role in the Battle of Rebel Hill, in late August 1798. After the Rebellion he escaped to America, having spent a period of time hiding withiin a secret chamber in *"The Rock House"*. This was located near Derrynure, between Bailieborough and Shercock.

KELLY, Lawrence - Kelly hailed from Mountmellick, Queen's County (Co. Laois). Having been listed on the Banishment Act, Kelly established himself in London as a malster.

KEMPE, James – James Kempe was born into a Church of Ireland family, at Castlefinn, near Lifford, Co. Donegal in 1760 (died in 1819). Having been associated with the United Irishmen Kempe was forced to flee to the United States, settling in moved to Natchez, Mississippi, where he acquired a large plantation. When the War of 1812 began, Kempe was commissioned as a captain in the Natchez Troop of Horse seeing action at Pensacola in Florida and then fighting at New Orleans, eventually rising to Colonel in the Mississippi Cavalry. James Kempe died in 1819.

KENNEDY, Arthur – Kennedy fought at the Battle of Antrim and managed to escape to Belfast after its failure. He made his way to his uncle's residence on James Street and hid within a coal cellar for three weeks, eluding capture and organising to smuggle himself to New York. Kennedy died at the age of 25 years.

KENNEDY, Samuel – Kennedy, a Belfast native had originally been secretary in the minute but radical Jacobin Club in Belfast, before it was absorbed into the Society of United Irishmen. Kennedy would become a compositor on the *Northern Star* newspaper. In September 1796, with the suspension of habeus-corpus, Kennedy was targeted by Dublin Castle and an arrest warrant was issued for his incarceration. In September 1798, Kennedy fled to the United States, where he established a newspaper in Baltimore, Maryland.

KEOUGH, Patrick – Keough had been only sixteen years of age when the Rebellion broke out in his native Wexford. Originally from Edermine, near Enniscorthy, Keough would settle in Newfoundland and married Ellen Phelan. Keough died on 22 July 1826 and was interred at St. Patrick's RC Cemetery in Carbonear (NL).

KERNAN, William –

William Kernan was born in Co. Cavan in February 1781 to John Kernan and Jane Brady. After participating in the 1798 Rebellion, Kernan fled to the United States, arriving in August 1800. Kernan briefly worked for William Weyman of Maiden Island, before going into partnership with Thomas O'Conor. This partnership saw the pair buy a large tract of land in Steuben County in rural New York. When O'Conor faced financial difficulties and returned to New York City, Kernan remained on the farm. Kernan offered his services to the U.S. Army during the War of 1812. On 31 May 1812, Kernan married Roseanna Stubbs, an Irish exile and daughter of the clothier, William Stubbs, who had supported several Dublin based United Irishmen before the outbreak of the 1798 Rebellion. Together they had a large family: Margaret Mary Kernan (1813-1844), Francis Kernan (1816-1892), Edward Kernan

(b.1818), Jane Kernan (b.1820), Winifred Kernan (b.1822), Alice Kernan (1824-1914), Roseanna Maria Kernan (b.1827), William Kernan (b.1831) and Michael John Kernan (b.1833). William Kernan died on 20 March 1870 and was interred at St. Agnes' Cemetery, Utica, in New York's Oneida County.

His son, Francis Kernan (1816-1892) (*pictured*), having been educated at Georgetown College, would become a successful attorney. In 1843, he married Hannah Devereux, the daughter of Wexford exile, Nicholas Devereux. Kernan entered politics, supporting the Democratic Party. Having served in the New York State Assembly, Kernan became a U.S. Representative before further progressing to a U.S. Senator in 1875. Francis' grandson, Bob Peebles Kernan, a renowned athlete and American Footballer, would become a consensus All-American in 1901.

The KERR Family–

Within the book *"History of Fayette County, Indiana"* is the story of James Kerr, who was born in Co. Antrim on 22 October 1791. He went to America when he was eight years old, as a result of his father being a political refugee on account of his participation in the Irish Rebellion of 1798. The family left their native town of Antrim with their two sons, James and Henry. On 12 December 1799, the Kerr family arrived at Charleston in South Carolina and by April 1800, they had established their home at Abbeville. They were members of the Methodist Episcopal Church and were active in local civil affairs, thus becoming very influential in Abbeville. In his later years, the family

relocated to Fayette County in Indiana. James Kerr died on 16 September 1873 and was interred at Mount Zion Cemetery in Everton, Indiana.

KIRWAN, Denis

KIRWAN, Denis – Little is known about Denis Kirwan of Kilpipe, Co. Wicklow, other than what is inscribed to his memory at a family plot at the old graveyard of Kilcashel, on the Wexford and Wicklow border. He was a brother of Dan Kirwan, the Wicklow United Irish captain, who was killed during the Battle of Vinegar Hill on 21 June 1798. Another brother, Laurence Kirwan, was one of those who was executed at the
ball-alley of Carnew, in the earliest days of the Rebellion. According to the headstone, Denis had been somewhat involved in the 1798 Rebellion, giving him cause to flee Ireland and to give service to France. The gravestone reads:

*"**Erected by the Very Reverend John Kirwan P. P., V. F. New Ross to the memory of his father Dermot Kirwan of Kilpipe, who died 24th of January 1824, of his mother Sarah, daughter of John Foley of Knickeen (Knockeen) near Kilenure (Killinure) Co. Wicklow and Bridget Doyle of Ballykeady (Ballykealy) Co. Carlow died 1851 of his grandfather Timothy Kirwan who died 1803 and his great grandfather Dermot Kirwan died 1760 and of his great-great grandfather Denis Kirwan of Kilpipe who died 1707; of his uncle Dan Kirwan killed at the Battle of Vinegar Hill leading the men of Wicklow; of his uncle Laurence Kirwan shot as a rebel in 1798; of his uncle Denis transported as a rebel 1798 and afterwards killed in the service of France."*

KNOX, Samuel, Rev. Dr.

KNOX, Samuel, Rev. Dr. - In the *History of Baltimore, Maryland*, Knox is briefly described. *"Rev. Samuel Knox, a descendent of John Knox, who was a thorn in the side of royalty in Britain three centuries ago. Samuel Knox was educated in the University of Dublin and began his ministry in Ireland. Espousing the cause of the oppressed in the Irish Rebellion in 1798, he found it expedient on the collapse of that movement to emigrate, which he did, coming to America and settling in Maryland."* It is further mentioned that Knox corresponded and formed a deep friendship with President Jefferson. Knox died at Frederick, on 31 August 1832, aged 76 years, and was interred at Mount Olivet Cemetery, in Frederick (MD).

LAWLESS, Luke –

Luke Lawless was born c.1781, one of twenty-one children of Philip Lawless and Bridget Savage. Lawless was a nephew of William Lawless. Little is known of Luke's participation in the United Irishmen or the 1798 Rebellion but having studied the classics, law and spent a period in the Royal Navy, he eventually emigrated to France in 1810. It is hard to determine if Lawless was in fact an exile or emigrant as a result of the 1798 Rebellion. He was commissioned as a lieutenant in the Irish Legion. In September 1811, he was requested to visit Ireland by the French Government and report on the conditions there as well as calculations of British military strength. He was assisted in his mission by Archibald Hamilton Rowan and Thomas Drumgoole. He returned to Paris and was awarded with a promotion to captain and became a staff officer. Interestingly, upon the dissolution of the regiment in 1815, Lawless was one of the few officers who did not experience any combat. Viewed with suspicion by the restored Bourbon authorities, he was expelled from France. Instead of returning to Ireland, he emigrated to the United States, becoming a lawyer at St. Louis in Missouri. Lawless rose to become a judge. He is best remembered controversially when he attempted to manipulate a jury's outcome in a case that had caused national scandal. On 28 April 1836, a free black man, Francis McIntosh, was brutally lynched and killed in St. Louis. On 16 May 1836, a grand jury was convened to investigate the occurrence, with Lawless presiding. Lawless encouraged no indictment for the crime and no one was ever charged for the murder of McIntosh. Lawless informed the jury that no judicial action could be taken for something that was a mass phenomenon. He incited that McIntosh had somewhat encouraged his own death and misinformed the jury that McIntosh had been a pawn to local abolitionists. Lawless was condemned for his actions during the trial. Luke Lawless died on 3 September 1846.

LAWLESS, William -

William Lawless, was born around 1765 to John Lawless and Mary Beauman of Shankill, Co. Dublin. Little is recorded about his early years, however, he was apprenticed to the surgeon, Michael Keogh of Meath Street in the early 1780s. He obtained letters testimonial from the Royal College of Surgeons in Ireland (RCSI) in June 1788 and was within a year appointed to the role of superintendent of dissections at the College's surgical school in Mercer Street. Having become an elected member of the College in March 1790, Lawless established his own practice in Meath Street. In September 1794, he was appointed professor of anatomy and physiology at the Royal

College of Surgeons, where his skills and progressive theories were embraced with much respect.

Régiment étranger (légion irlandaise) Porte-Aigle 1812

Being quite close to Thomas Addis Emmet via their mutual profession, Lawless became enticed by the liberal politics of the Society of United Irishmen. Having joined, Lawless would become a trusted friend to leading United men such as Lord Edward Fitzgerald and John Sheares. On 19 May 1798, as the wounded Lord Edward was being carried to Dublin Castle for interrogation, Lawless, along with an elected Dublin United Irish colonel, Edward Rattigan, collected some weapons from a watch house on Catherine Street and proceeded to rescue Fitzgerald. This rash move failed. Lawless, knowing that the Castle was after him with a £300 bounty on his whereabouts, decided to flee underground and we do not have a clear understanding of his location during the gruesome summer of 1798. Lawless eventually escaped to France in late 1798, and his legacy within his profession was to fall victim for his participation in the United Irishmen. He was stripped of his membership in the Royal Irish Academy and the Royal College of Surgeons. Upon arriving in Paris, Lawless enlisted in the French Army and served under General Brune during the campaign to expel the British expeditionary force in Holland and was awarded a temporary commission as *chef de bataillon*.

In August 1803, an Irish brigade was established with the purpose of training Irish exiles in the event of another Irish expedition, which of course never occurred. Lawless was given a full commission as Captain and moved with this new Irish Legion to Brittany, where they trained for war. In July 1809, Lawless and his subordinates were sent to Vlissingen in Holland to engage and halt a British held siege in what is now referred to as the Walcheren Campaign. The battle ensued and Lawless was badly wounded with a gunshot to his face: the musket ball having penetrated beneath his right eye and lodged under his ear. Whilst getting his wound treated by his friend Dr. Moke, the French positions at Flushing fell to the British. Lawless spared no time during the evacuation and with Terence O'Reilly, honourably saved the Imperial Eagle of the Irish Legion, by rowing in a small open boat whilst under fire, an act that would reach the ear of Napoleon Bonaparte. For this act, Bonaparte promoted Lawless to Major and awarded him the *Légion d'honneur*.

Lawless used his new commission to help reorganise the Irish Legion and refreshed its ranks with many prisoners-of-war. In February 1812, he was promoted to Lieutenant-Colonel of the Legion. In 1813, the Legion was sent to Silesia, where it suffered dreadful casualties at the First Battle of Löwenberg on 19 August 1813. During this brutal battle, the Irish Legion formed square against the harassing Russian cavalry. This allowed them to be heavily blasted by artillery, resulting in nearly 400 casualties in the Irish Legion. Two days later, during the opening stages of the Second Battle of Löwenberg, Lawless led the command of the Legion. During their march to the enemy positions, Lawless was hit by a cannon-ball, which severely shattered his leg. Napoleon, distraught upon hearing the news, ordered his prime battle surgeon, Baron Dominique Jean Larrey, to immediately operate on Lawless behind the lines. The leg was in a state beyond repair and had to be amputated. Lawless' battlefield career was effectively over. Upon convalescing at Leipzig, he was to be promoted to General of the Brigade, however, Napoleon's abdication in April 1814 prevented the award occurring. Lawless faded into obscurity and retired to his country house, Rochefouret, near Tours in France, where he entertained guests and old friends. He did not get involved in the Bourbon Restoration or the One Hundred Days Campaign of 1815. William Lawless, the respected surgeon, a United Irishman and a battlefield hero of Napoleon, died in Paris on 25 December 1824 and was interred in the Pére-Lachaise Cemetery, in a plot paid for by another United Irish exile and Irish Legion officer, Miles Byrne.

The Laughlin Family of *Ballygraffan, County Down*

LAUGHLIN, Andrew – Andrew Laughlin was born on 21 February 1797 to Hugh Laughlin and Elizabeth Clark, of Comber, Co. Down. He would later inherit his father's land in Ryegate, Vermont, and would become an elder in the United Presbyterian Church. His son, Andrew Scott Laughlin was a horologist until the American Civil War broke out. He joined the 5th Vermont Volunteers, serving under Captain Xerxes Stevens. In the summer of 1863, before the Battle of Gettysburg, Laughlin was struck with sun stroke and was sent home until the war's end, never properly healing. Andrew Laughlin Sr died on 12 July 1872 at Greensboro, Vermont.

LAUGHLIN, Elizabeth *née Clark* — Elizabeth Clark married Hugh Laughlin of Greyabbey, Co. Down on 14 February 1792. Having emigrated with her husband aboard the *Peggy*, the Laughlin family would settle in Ryegate, Vermont. Elizabeth Clark Laughlin died on 22 June 1852.

LAUGHLIN, Hugh — Hugh Laughlin was born in 1761 into a farming family at Ballygraffan, Comber, Co. Down. It is claimed that Laughlin served in the United Irishmen as a Lieutenant Colonel after which a bounty of £50 was placed on his head. His homestead and livestock fell victim to the Crown Forces. He went on the run and on one occasion of being chased he hid beneath a feather bed, the blades of a soldier's bayonets slicing between his arm and body. In early May 1799, the Laughlin family fled to the United States aboard the *Peggy*, using the alias of Hess to avoid capture from the authorities. They, like many Ulster Presbyterians who went via New York, made it to the thriving Reformed Presbyterian community, who were residing in Ryegate, Vermont. It is worth noting that the population of Ryegate doubled between 1800 to 1810, mostly as a result of Ulster immigration. In Ryegate, the Laughlin's settled and immersed themselves in the affairs of the town. Eventually, Hugh Laughlin was elected a Justice of the Peace and town Representative on a number of occasions. He became a prominent citizen, serving as Justice of the Peace and a deacon in the Congregational Church at Bath. Elizabeth Laughlin was a strict Covenantor and when a service was held in their new barn, she brought forward her daughter for baptism, for which she was censored for. Hugh Laughlin died on 29 January 1824.

LAUGHLIN, Mary Jane — Mary Jane Laughlin was born on 23 October 1794 to Hugh Laughlin and Elizabeth Clark, at Comber, Co. Down. Mary Jane would become a teacher and also composed poetry and sketches for the local press. She died on 24 March 1873.

LAUGHLIN, Dr. William — William Laughlin was born to Hugh Laughlin and Elizabeth Clark, near Comber, Co. Down, on 29 November 1792. William was only a mere boy during the turbulent period of the 1798 Rebellion and the family's subsequent exile to America. Having studied medicine at Fairfield Medical College, Laughlin became a doctor and later inherited his father's homeplace in Ireland, in which he briefly returned to the land of his birth. In December 1828, he married Amanda Barber of Connecticut. Laughlin died on 19 January 1862 and was interred at Oswego Bitter Cemetery, Onondaga County (NY).

LEARY, Jeremiah –

Leary was the manservant of the leading United Irishman, Arthur O'Connor, up until their arrest at Margate in February 1798, whilst attempting to sail to France. After their acquittal in the Maidstone trials, Leary fled to the United States and died in Philadelphia in 1806.

LEDLIE Joseph –

Joseph Ledlie was born c.1774 to George Ledlie and Margaret Crawford, at Carnan, outside Coagh, on the border of counties Tyrone and Derry. His father, a linen draper, had been politically active in the Volunteer movement in the 1780s and would publicly advocate for political union between Britain and Ireland after the 1798 Rebellion. In 1796, Joseph married **Margaret Ekin** (1777–1850) of Ballygonny. Throughout this period, Joseph Ledlie had been an active member of the United Irishmen and after the rebellion a warrant was issued for his arrest, in defiance in a letter he declared-

"no man that ever trod the earth should make a prisoner of him."

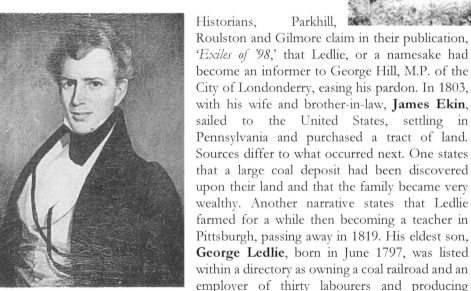

Historians, Parkhill, Roulston and Gilmore claim in their publication, *'Exiles of '98,'* that Ledlie, or a namesake had become an informer to George Hill, M.P. of the City of Londonderry, easing his pardon. In 1803, with his wife and brother-in-law, **James Ekin**, sailed to the United States, settling in Pennsylvania and purchased a tract of land. Sources differ to what occurred next. One states that a large coal deposit had been discovered upon their land and that the family became very wealthy. Another narrative states that Ledlie farmed for a while then becoming a teacher in Pittsburgh, passing away in 1819. His eldest son, **George Ledlie**, born in June 1797, was listed within a directory as owning a coal railroad and an employer of thirty labourers and producing 480,000 bushels annually. James Ledlie was born

James Ekin Ledlie (6) 1806-1891

146

in 1806 to Joseph and Margaret Ledlie in 1806. On 10 September 1832, he married Caroline M. Grace and converted to Roman Catholicism. By 1837, he was established as a commission merchant, dwelling at Hay Street, Pittsburgh. He was also upon the board of the Exchange Bank of Pittsburgh and had extensive interests in the glass industry, as shown by his association with firms such as '*Mulvany and Ledlie.*'

LEITH, William – Leith fought at the Battle of Antrim and escaped to Belfast, to a house on the Limestone Road in Belfast. When Mary Ann McCracken was searching for Henry Joy McCracken, Leith was one of the men who guided her to him whilst McCracken was hiding out in the Belfast Hills. Leith eventually fled to the United States.

LENNON, Edward – National papers across the United States recorded the death of Edward Lennon, who died in New York in March 1891, aged 105 years. The papers rejoiced that the Co. Derry native had **"*carried a pike in the great Irish Rebellion of 1798*,"** and had papers to prove his birth in 1785.

LETT, James Moore - '*The Boy Lett*'

– Young James Moore Lett was born at Newcastle, Co. Wexford, into a prominent Protestant farming background. He was but a boy of adolescent experience, yet he led a charge into the choking smoke of death at the Battle of New Ross and survived. History does not help us regarding the life of James Moore Lett. Some accounts state that Lett was captured after the Rebellion and upon facing the wrath of Lord Chief Justice Kilwarden, the innocent youth of Lett being lifted up by a guard at the dock resulted in Kilwarden quashing the trial and ordered him to be sent back to his mother. Accounts conflict about what occurred to Lett; some state he was pressed into service into the Royal Navy, whilst others said he decided to leave Wexford for adventure, however, he died of a disease at the age of 17 years.

The following is an account from the Schools' Folklore Collection. The story was told by Mrs. Banville of Shanowle, Co. Wexford, in the 1930s - Caroreigh N.S. Volume 0883, p.p. 072-77.

"On Sunday the 5th June was the anniversary of the battle of Ross, and of the many brave heroes who took part in that eventful fight in 1798, one young lad on account of his youth (for he was only 13 years of age,) deserves a place on the scroll of fame. His name was James Moore Lett, the second son of Stephen Lett of Newcastle, Wexford. His mother was a niece of Bagenal Harvey and it is interesting to recall that the tract of land called "The Commons of Wexford" was sold by public auction and bought by Stephen Lett for the sum of £650. The first notice we have of James Lett, the boy insurgent, is when a body of Insurgents visited the residence of Mrs. Ann Sealy of Bloomhill not far from Killinick. They were very hungry (provisions being scarce at the time) and they eagerly eat up a quantity of bread that Mrs Sealy had baked. They asked for more and while preparing it she discovered that the party were accompanied by young James Lett. Mrs Sealy who was sister of Charles Lett of Tinacurry claimed to be a blood relation to young Lett and for the service she had rendered he asked what return or favour he could make to her. She asked for tea and sugar (great luxuries in those days) to be sent to her from Wexford which was faithfully done. This Ann died in 1844 aged 86. After this young Lett accompanied the southern army, under the command of his grand-uncle (Bagenal Harvey) to the outskirts of New Ross on the memorable day of the 5th June. The insurgents were on the point of being finally repulsed when, a young gentleman of 13 years saw the disorder of the men and the incapacity of their leaders and with boyish impulse he snatched up a banner and calling out "Follow me who dare" rushed down the hill 10,000 pikemen followed uttering the same cry. In a moment he was at the Three Bullet Gate and rushing upon the yeomen he destroyed a great lot of them. There is also a song composed about the battle of Ross and here it is:

"At length with boyish ardour
The brave young hero, Lett
Pointed to the enemy
And waved a bannerette;
At headlong speed he rushed on
The foremost British square
And as he went he shouted
"Follow me who dare."

Ten thousand pikes are gleaming
With Kelly in the van
Shot and shell came screaming
Still young Lett led them on
Dwyer, Cloney and Byrne
Charge Skerrett's Grenadiers
And the scarlet line went down in death
Before the Shelmaliers

Oh! cried the youthful hero
"Follow me who dare"!

And the waving bannerette was seen
'Mid the cannons deadly glare;
Through leaping flame and hissing lead
Though bitter was their loss,
The pikemen swept o'er piles of dead
And swarmed into New Ross.

The Union Jack in blood and dust
Before the pike went down
And the Rebel Green is floating high
And bright o'er New Ross town
Johnson now in swift retreat
And sunk in deep despair
While the warcry of the Shelmaliers
Is "Follow Me Who Dare."

LEWINS, Edward – Edward Lewins was born c.1756 in Dublin. Having a deep interest in entering the seminary, Lewins was educated in France, but returned to Ireland and eventually became a barrister. Being a member of the United Irishmen and a commander of the French language, Lewins was tasked by the United Irish leadership to take part in a crucial mission to France, arriving in Hamburg in late March 1797. The mission was to continue to urge the French Directory and Spain for assistance and to gain a possible substantial loan. He engaged with Charles Reinhard, the French ambassador to Hamburg. At first, Reinhard suspected Lewins of being an informer, but his worries were later quashed when further communication with the United Irishmen substantiated Lewins' requests. On 20 May 1797, Lewins left Hamburg and joined Theobald Wolfe Tone in Paris, as part of the United Irish delegation. In June 1797, without time to settle in Paris, Lewins joined Tone in travelling to the Hague, where they were to be attached to the Dutch command under Jan de Winter of the Batavian Republic, an attachment which ended after the Battle of Camperdown. Upon their return to Paris in late 1797, Lewins and Tone faced friction from James Napper Tandy, solely over issues of emissary leadership, a division that would frustrate the French authorities in their organising of another expedition. Lewins' influence in France, as powerful as it was before the 1798 Rebellion, started to wane afterwards, mostly because of his moderate principles. Tandy and Tone were gone and the new exiles preferred to appoint William Putnam McCabe, who had established himself in Rouen, as the chief United Irish emissary to Paris. Miles Byrne recorded Lewins within his memoirs: **"*Some of the exiles of that period thought that Lewins did not exert himself sufficiently with the Directory, to obtain for them the aid they so much needed.*"** Lewins remained in France. During the reign of King Charles X, Lewins gained some influence when his close friend, the Abbé de Fraysinous, the Bishop of Hermopolis, became a French Government Minister. Lewins was appointed

Inspector of Studies at the University of Paris. He would remain in good relations with the Irish exiles who remained in France and they repaid his good faith by attending his funeral at Père-Lachaise. Edward Lewins died on 11 February 1828.

LINTON, John – Linton, a son of William Linton and Sarah Penquite, was born c.1773 in Co. Derry. He was educated at Magilligan and whilst immersed in his studies, Linton became involved in the 1798 Rebellion, which resulted in him fleeing to the United States. He settled in Cambria County in Pennsylvania. Linton married Ann Park and they set up a large family on their Johnstown farm. John Linton died on 25 July 1818 and was interred at Grandview Cemetery in Southmont, Pennsylvania. His son, John Linton Jr, would become a successful merchant of pig iron.

LOGAN, John – Logan fled from Ireland after participating in the 1798 Rebellion. He took up abode in South Carolina before permanently settling in Madison County in Alabama. Logan died on 18 May 1838, aged 65 years.

LOGAN, Thomas – Logan fought amongst the insurgents at the Battle of Ballynahinch on 12/13 June 1798. In November 1798, he emigrated along with his family, aboard a ship called the *"Brothers,"* captained by Thompson of the City of Londonderry, bound the United States. After 45 days they arrived within sight of the New York coastline. A British frigate that was lurking along the American coast boarded the *Brothers* and pressed the male passengers into service, including Logan. Actions like this would eventually cause the War of 1812 between the United States and Britain. In 1811, Logan jumped ship some three miles from Belize, swimming ashore and courageously made his way slowly back to New York City. Whilst traversing through America, he joined the Kentuckians under Colonel Decker, accepting the role as Sergeant-Major in their militia to engage and push back local Indian tribes. Having healed from a severe leg injury, he continued his journey for New York. After 110 miles, his horse died from exhaustion. Upon reaching New York, he found that his parents had relocated to Boston. Being a stranger in New York City, local benevolent societies took over his cause. In July 1812 the *Columbian* newspaper ran an article focused on helping Logan to reach Boston. His wound prevented him from walking the remainder of the journey and had he no financial means. The leading New York politician, DeWitt Clinton urged New Yorkers to support Logan. It is unknown to the authors if Logan ever made it to Boston. (Image - *Battle of Tippecanoe*, 1811).

LOGAN, Thomas Sr –

Thomas Logan Sr fought alongside his son at the Battle of Ballynahinch and fled with his family in November 1798. Unlike his son, who had been taken captive by the British off the New York coast, Logan Sr made it to New York and established a grocery. In 1812, he moved to Boston.

LONG, James - The Long family have been associated with the parish of Magilligan, Co. L Derry, since the plantation of Ulster. James became a member and parochial commander of the United Irishmen, eventually being tried at Limavady with other members of the United Irishmen from the Magilligan area such as John Cust. Long was originally sentenced to transportation, however this was reduced to banishment to the United States. In the U.S. a letter, composed by Long to President Thomas Jefferson, outlines his troubles which had beset him. He had left Ireland was 300 guineas and tried his hand at farming on the Ohio River. However, this initiative failed and he made his way to New Orleans where he seen an opportunity to produce whiskey as gin was so expensive. He purchased a still, however in the middle of making whiskey his still blew up and he was set alight, suffering severe burns. This business also failed and Long found himself bankrupt and not being able to work. In the letter, Long stressed his hopes that Jefferson would award him with a commission in the U.S. Army.

LOWRY, Alexander – Lowry, a Rathfriland merchant, was the treasurer of the Co. Down United Irishmen and a close friend of James Napper Tandy. He had previously been an office in the Volunteers. During the summer of 1797, Generals Lake's orchestrated and severe crackdown on Ulster's United Irishmen, saw many United Irish officials flee to the continent. Lowry fled to France where he eventually gained passage to America. In Paris, he met with the other United Irish exiles. In 1806, he was permitted by Lord Castlereagh to return to Ireland; however, his ship was blown of course and it docked in Norway. In Norway he

married a local girl and eventually brought her to Ireland. He died in his native Katesbridge in Co. Down in 1820.

LOWRY, William – William Lowry was imprisoned on the prison tender, *Postlethwaite*, which was moored in Belfast Lough during and after the 1798 Rebellion. Lowry was released after proving security to exile himself to the United States.

LUBE, George – George Lube hailed from a Catholic farming family, based at Corcoranstown House, near Kilcock, Co. Kildare. Little is known about George Lube's early life, although we can accept that he supported his brother, John Lube's liberal political thinking. John Lube of Summerhill had joined the Society of United Irishmen in February 1792. The family strengthened their United Irish connections when John married the sister of Joseph Cormick of Parliament Street and John Cormick of Thomas Street. Lube served in the north Kildare insurgency, which was based on the boglands of Timahoe, upon the border with King's County (Offaly). Lube would've been involved in the numerous raids and attacks in the Enfield and Kilcock districts during June and early July 1798 including the Battle of Ovidstown (19 June 1798). It is also worth noting that Sir Fenton Aylmer's 21 July 1798 list of surrendering insurgent leaders in Kildare ranks George Lube directly behind William Aylmer and Hugh Ware. They had surrendered on condition that they be permitted to leave Ireland forever. Upon surrendering, Lube was held in the Royal Exchange in Dublin before being incarcerated as a State Prisoner in Kilmainham Gaol (*entrance pictured*) in November 1798. Whilst Aylmer was allowed to leave Ireland, Ware and Lube remained imprisoned for several years, Lube petitioned Lord Cornwallis on two occasions to allow him to settle in Portugal, with the second memorial highlighting ailing health due to his incarceration. On 16 May 1801, Lube was transported from Kilmainham Gaol and conditions made for his banishment. Miles Byrne briefly described George Lube's whereabouts in his memoirs: "***George, who had to escape to America, had been the companion of William Aylmer and Hugh Ware in the insurrection of 1798.***"

Historians indicate that Lube died young whilst in America. Having searched the Lube Family in the Catholic Baptisms for the Parish of Kilcock, there shows the baptismal record of *Georgium Lube*, son of *Johannes Lube* and *Maria Egan*, who was christened on 29 July 1786. If this is the same family, that would have made Lube only 11 years of age during the time of the Rebellion, unless of course he was baptised when he was a boy or teenager. Ridiculous as it may sound but boy leaders, although rare in the insurgency during the 1798 Rebellion, were evident, especially if they came from a land or deep-rooted respectable background with status. With respect, it is also worth noting that Kilcock's parochial records began recording in 1771, indicating that George Lube could have been born beforehand and that the above-mentioned boy may have simply been a close relative.

LYLE Peter – Peter Lyle was an insurgent captain in the Dervock United Irishmen, in north Co. Antrim. He participated in the gruesome takeover of Ballymena on 7 June 1798. After that affair ended, Lyle and another insurgent, John Nevin, made their escape to Buckna, where, according to previous understanding, they took refuge in the house of a distant friend of Lyle's, named Moore. However, Moore informed the authorities. Surrounded by yeomen, the insurgents escaped and hid in a cornfield. The Yeomanry would eventually burn down the Lyle home at Orbie, outside Ballymoney, thus forcing him to flee to America. In the 1820s, Lyle was recorded in Philadelphia and had a "*reported unproven*" number of notable sons, Stewart Lyle, a merchant and shipowner; David Lyle, a Chief-Fireman and Colonel Peter Lyle. (This family connection has not been fully proven, as it was written down in the early 20th Century, thanks to Ian Hart & Lyn Lloyd-Smith)

One of Peter's "*unproven*" sons, Colonel Peter Lyle (*pictured*) of the 90th Pennsylvanian Infantry, was born in 1820. He was apprenticed as a cigar maker and later became a coal merchant. At the age of 39 he joined the Pennsylvania Militia unit, which was used to put down the nativist riots in 1844 and later became the commanding officer of that unit. He served as Colonel and commander of two different regiments - the 19th Pennsylvania Volunteer Infantry, and the 90th Pennsylvania Volunteer Infantry. He commanded the latter regiment at the Battle of Gettysburg, where it was in Henry Baxter's I Corps brigade (1st Corps, 2nd Division, Second Brigade). In the brutal and confused fighting of the first day of the battle, he temporarily commanded the First Brigade of his Division, when four previous commanders had been either wounded or captured. He was brevetted Brigadier-General, U.S. Volunteers on 13 March 1865 for "*faithful and gallant service in battle*".

COLONEL PETER LYLE

After the American Civil War, General Peter Lyle was elected Sheriff of Pennsylvania and went into business with his adjutant, David Weaver, in the carriage making business. He served as colonel of a Pennsylvania militia unit until 1877. He died in reduced circumstances having lost much of his money in the 1873 crash having invested in Maryland farmland.

LYLE William – William Lyle, a brother of the above-mentioned Peter Lyle of Dervock, apparently fled to America after the affair in Ballymena in June 1798. However, his American Naturalisation occurred in Philadelphia in February 1798, so this is evidence that he had arrived before the Rebellion. Lyle died on 24 January 1812 and was buried in the Third Presbyterian Church in Philadelphia.

LYNCH, John – Lynch and leading United Irishman, Henry Jackson, fled Ireland for the United States aboard a merchant ship belonging to Thomas Trenor.

LYNCH, Patrick – Lynch was born in Dublin c.1782. A United Irishman, he was arrested and held for several years in prison. In 1802, after the Treaty of Amiens brought peace between France and Britain, Lynch was released exiled himself from Ireland. He travelled to the United States and settled at Bennington, Vermont, where a fellow United Irish acquaintance, Thomas Trenor presided over an iron-works. Lynch established a dry-goods business at Bennington. In 1812, he married Charlotte Gray in Troy, New York, and they settled in Bennington to raise a family. Their children were Anne Charlotte Lynch (1820-1891) and Thomas Rawson Lynch. During the War of 1812, Lynch traded in buffalo skins and eventually served in the US Army. In want of expanding his business, Lynch began to work in trade with Caribbean ports. Patrick Lynch died in 1819 after the ship upon which he was travelling sank off the coast of Puerto Principe, in the West Indies. Anne Charlotte Lynch (*pictured*) became a respected poet and notable socialite within New York society and married an Italian professor, Vincenzo Botta. The renowned American author, Edgar Allen Poe said of her:

"She is chivalric, self-sacrificing, equal to any fate, capable even of martyrdom, in whatever should seem to her a holy cause. She has a hobby, and this is the idea of duty."

LYNN, James – James Lynn, an Antrim native, died in South Carolina in March 1856, aged 100 years. His obituary stated that he was a native of Ireland and had taken part in the 1798 Rebellion, although it is brought to our attention by Gilmore, Parkhill & Roulston, in their publication, '*Exiles of '98 – Ulster Presbyterians and the United States*' (2018), that it wrongly stated that he fought at '*the Battle of Wexford Bridge.*' Upon emigrating to the United States, Lynn settled in Jackson's Creek in Fairfield County, South Carolina.

MacDONNELL, James Joseph – MacDonnell was born into a
Catholic landowning family at Carnacon, near the northern shores of Lough Mask in Co. Mayo. In his youth, MacDonnell was educated in Austria and later studied law in London, where he befriended Theobald Wolfe Tone. Upon their return, both Tone and MacDonnell worked together on the Catholic Committee. MacDonnell joined the United Irishmen and was influential in establishing the society in his native Mayo, where he embraced the membership of Ulster exiles who fled from Orange persecution in the mid-1790s, establishing themselves in Mayo. When General Humbert landed in Mayo in August 1798, MacDonnell was commissioned with a leadership role and fought at the Battle of Castlebar and at Ballinamuck (8 September 1798). After the failure, knowing the magistrate Denis Browne would warrant his arrest, MacDonnell fled to Paris. The Mount Pleasant N.S. Schools' Folklore contains a story about MacDonnell:

"*James Joseph McDonnell of Carnacon house who was nicknamed "Séamus Ruadh" was colonel of the united Irish men. He marched to Ballina to meet General Humbert. He led his men to Castlebar and fought against the English at Stabawl hill in Castlebar town. He also fought at French hill outside Castlebar. He accompanied Humbert to Collooney hill in Co. Sligo. From there he went to Ballinamuck in Co. Longford. After Ballinamuck he hid in a field. He was discovered by an English officer who attempted to arrest him but McDonnell drew a purse from his pocket containing twenty gold coins and offered then to him. The officer said he would get no reward for arresting McDonnell so he released him and took the coins. McDonnell came again to Carnacon. The English were watching him and he had to remain hidden at last he got word that the English were coming to surround the place where he was. He went to Murrisk on Clew Bay about five miles from Westport. Here Ó Máile the well-known smuggler had a boat and he sailed with him to France. He lived for some time in Paris. It is supposed that he went to America and died in New York.*"

A family source claimed that MacDonnell fled from Aughris in a smuggling vessel belonging to the Coneyses, and commanded by a Captain Agnew. In 1803, whilst in Paris and having been commissioned as a Captain in the Irish Legion, MacDonnell married Scottish born Henrietta Mackie, who gave birth to a daughter, Josephine Mary, in 1805. Upon falling out with the Legion's commander, Bernard MacSheehy, MacDonnell resigned his commission and went to reside in Cadiz in Spain, where he engaged in commerce for a short period before they sailed to the United States. In 1809, whilst journeying to visit her parents, Henrietta died, leaving Josephine stranded at Plymouth, England. She was fostered by Lady Whitshed, a royal lady-in-waiting, who resided at Hampton Court Palace in London. When corresponding with Lady Whitshed regarding repatriation, MacDonnell addressed her only as '*Mrs. Whitshed,*' highlighting his republican courtesies. Both father and daughter were later reunited. James Joseph MacDonnell died in Jersey City (NJ) in 1848, having served as a Judge of the Inferior Court of Common Pleas of Hudson County, New Jersey.

MacMAHON, Arthur, Rev.

— MacMahon was a native of Co. Down and was an established Presbyterian minister at Kilrea. MacMahon also held a high rank in the United Irish organisation in Down, being a member of the Ulster Committee. When General Gerard Lake initiated the 'Dragooning of Ulster' in April and May 1797, Rev. MacMahon decided to flee to the continent. In June 1797, he arrived in London and interacted with Fr. James Coigly and members of the United Britons, organising republican structures there in advance of a proposed French expedition. His espionage and radical actions caught the attention of Westminster, courtesy of the informer, Samuel Turner. When the Rebellion failed in Ireland, MacMahon decided to settle in France, where, in poor health and suffering severe pains in his legs, he joined the Irish Legion after its conception in late 1803. MacMahon served with distinction with the Irish Legion, especially at Flushing in the Lowlands in September 1809. Having been captured, he was conveyed to Britain as a prisoner-of-war and would remain there until the collapse of Bonaparte's Empire in 1814. Upon release, MacMahon returned to France in May 1814 and was ordered to join his old friends in the Irish Legion, which had been transformed into the *3rd régiment étranger*. During the collapse of Napoleon's Empire, MacMahon had grown disillusioned with the regime and settled at Boulonge-sur-Mer, receiving a pension, but suffering from paralysis. He died not long afterwards.

Régiment étranger (irlandais), Voltigeur, 1812.

MacMAHON, Bartholomew, Rev. –

Father MacMahon was a Dominican priest, based at Dublin's Denmark Street seminary, who was involved in the Society of United Irishmen. He eventually fled to the United States, however, he succumbed to the yellow fever endemic in Philadelphia in 1800.

MacNEVEN, Dr. William James - William James MacNeven was

born on 21 March 1763 in Ballinahown, near Aughrim, Co. Galway. MacNeven was directly descended from the Mac Cnáimhín clan, who had lost their Loughrea and Portumna estates to the Earl of Clanrickard, in the early Seventeenth Century. For generations the scions of that family, like many from the old Gaelic clans, had fled to Europe to pursue careers in Imperial courts and armies. Young MacNeven, conscious of his position as a Roman Catholic and lawfully shackled from many civil liberties, might have felt frustration and some bitterness upon examining such a position. He adored the stories of his ancestors and used to traverse across the old battlefield of Aughrim, imagining what might have been if the Jacobites had won. At the age of eleven, MacNeven was sent to receive his education at his uncle's residence on the continent. This was, as mentioned above, partly due to him being a Roman Catholic, where career choices and advanced education were very limited to him in Ireland. His uncle, Baron William O'Kelly MacNeven (1713-1787), a physician to Empress Maria Theresa of Austria, played an influential role in MacNeven's career choices. Whilst there, young MacNeven would've crossed paths with Wolfgang Amadeus Mozart, who played concerts at their residence. It is worth pointing out that the progressive ideologies of the Enlightenment, which were discussed and debated amongst the elite and educated of Europe, may have overwhelmed MacNeven's thoughts, who as an Irish Catholic, at a time of penal restrictions, combined with his deep interest in Irish history, started to develop his own progressive views.

Having completed his undergraduate studies at Prague, MacNeven travelled to the University of Vienna to study medicine under Professor Pastel. Equipped with French, German and some Spanish, but most importantly, having secured a medical degree, William MacNeven returned to Ireland in 1784.

Having established himself in Dublin, Dr. McNeven created his own practice at Thomas Street and took up a position at Jervis Street Hospital and was appointed to a professorship at the Royal College of Surgeons, which would result in him forging a strong relationship with the Emmet Family. He became a member of the Royal Irish Academy and also translated many modern German medical texts with the hope of progressing the Irish medical environment to the standards seen in Vienna, Prague, Dresden, Berlin and Königsberg. Politics would soon interest MacNeven and he became deeply involved in the Catholic Committee, which introduced him to Theobald Wolfe Tone. He was introduced to the Society of the United Irishmen by Mary Moore, with whom, it is believed, he had a love affair with. MacNeven positively embraced the ideals of the United Irishmen and befriended

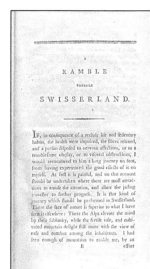

not only Tone and Thomas Addis Emmet, but also Lord Edward Fitzgerald, who he often visited at Frescati in Blackrock. His standing within the organisation was eventually noted by Dublin Castle and Secretary Cooke who stated,

"MacNeven is very eloquent and very clever. Calculated by his talents to taking a leading part in this treason. A frequent visitor to Lord Edward Fitzgerald. He must be watched."

On 27 June 1797, McNeven left Ireland, under the alias, "Williams," on an important mission to assist Edward Lewins, the United Irish plenipotentiary at Paris to help persuade the French to re-attempt an intervention. Having arrived at Hamburg, he faced passport issues but directed a detailed memo to be sent to the Directory in Paris. This memo fell into the hands of London agents, thus marking McNeven as a chief conspirator upon his return to Ireland. At 11am, on 12 March 1798, a gathering of Leinster's elite United Irishmen met at Oliver Bond's residence on Bridge Street. The secret password for entry went as follows,

"Where is McCann? Is Ivers from Carlow come?"

Little did the officials know that some particular people had gained entrance to the meeting, disguised in civilian clothing. They were from Dublin Castle and armed with pistols and warrants. Fourteen of Leinster's elite United Irish Delegates were immediately arrested and their seditious papers seized. Nearby at 5 King's Inn Quay, Lord Edward Fitzgerald and Dr. MacNeven waited patiently in the residence of William Stubbs (1757-1831), a wealthy clothier. Noting the commotion outside Bond's residence, Stubb's apprentice immediately warned Fitzgerald and MacNeven. The young apprentice noted that the two eminent gentlemen looked at each other in an earnest look, before MacNeven turned to him and said, "Very well boy, that will do." Fitzgerald and MacNeven remained in the house for a short while without displaying alert. The soldiers quickly made their way across Church Street Bridge and surrounded Stubb's residence. The boy again warned Fitzgerald and MacNeven, but again he was given a confusing yet calm reply from MacNeven, *"Let them come boy."* As the officials from

Dublin Castle stormed the building, Dr. MacNeven freely surrendered himself and openly admitted his identity to the arresting party. Fitzgerald, it seems, had somehow eluded the arresting party and made an escape. MacNeven had

selflessly gave himself up to allow Lord Edward time to escape. He had his name struck from the Royal College of Surgeons and he was officially banned from visiting inmates at the South Dublin Union, which he had done out of his own interests.

"Both MacNeven and Fitzgerald had a lifelong interest, and some training, in military science, but they differed widely about the tactics required to bring about independence. MacNeven felt strongly about a need for leadership, training and discipline, and argued that this could only be supplied by the command structure of a French revolutionary force....Fitzgerald argued for quick action in Dublin, followed by something more similar to what is now called guerrilla warfare."

It was noted that the two individuals used to discuss military strategy whilst visiting the Shakespeare Gallery in Dublin, pretending to admire the artwork. His patriotism was not only a passionate conviction but a deep-rooted principle. Upon being questioned by the Irish Parliament's Secret Committee on August 8th 1798, MacNeven was asked, *"What occasioned the Insurrection?"*. MacNeven firmly replied,

"It was occasioned by house burnings, whipping to extort confessions, tortures of various kinds, free quarters and murders by magistrates and the army."

After an uncertain period of languishing in Kilmainham Gaol, MacNeven and other incarcerated United Irish leaders were sent, in April 1799, to Fort George, near Inverness in Scotland. It was reported that their sedition did not cease during their incarceration, with MacNeven's inquisitive nature attempting to scale any possible public dissent in the locality and gathering intelligence on the military presence around Inverness. Whilst there he translated the Ossianic mythological cycle into English and drafted his notes on what he would eventually publish as *"Pieces of Irish History."* He would remain at Fort George until he was released after the 1802 Treaty of Amiens, between Britain and France. Upon being released, MacNeven clearly desired new pastures. He travelled to the continent and visited Prague and Vienna before deciding to walk across Switzerland en-route to Napoleon's France. From this adventure he later penned, *"A Ramble Through Swisserland,"* which has since been recognised as a classical tourist guide, filled with historical anecdotes and political points. Upon reaching France, MacNeven attempted to negotiate French assistance in securing independence for Ireland via Charles de Tallyrand-Périgord. He enlisted in Napoleon's Irish Legion, earning the commission of Captain. Upon seeing Napoleon's lacking in any investment towards Ireland, MacNeven grew disillusioned with the concept of a successful revolution and eventually sailed to the United States. On 4 July 1805, Dr. MacNeven landed in New York City. It is noted he chose New York City specifically and not the South, where many exiled United Irishmen had established themselves. This choice was apparently down to his progressive views on abolition.

"He brought to America a firm commitment to democratic social justice, combined with a scientific pragmatism. Among his many social welfare innovations was the very first unemployment agency, out of his own funds, with job advertisements placed in immigrant newspapers. He separately funded an employment agency for women, and got men jobs on projects like the Erie Canal."

In 1810 he married a widow, Jane Margaret Riker Thom. He also remained close to his old friend, Thomas Addis Emmet, who became Attorney-General of New York State in 1812-13. Such strength and bond was their friendship, that Thomas Addis Emmet Jr (1797-1863) married Anna Riker Thom, MacNeven's stepdaughter. MacNeven became somewhat influential in New York society and pressed Congress to help fund Irish immigrants in purchasing land in the West frontier as well as establishing a bank to assist immigrants. He championed radical reformers such as Thomas Paine, Fanny Wright and the socialist, Robert Owen. In 1812, as Britain and the USA went to war, MacNeven openly supported America and offered to establish an Irish Brigade, filled with Irish immigrants, to show their loyalty and to assist the American effort. In his later life, MacNeven made some political enemies after he vocally attacked some of President Andrew Jackson's actions of removing deposits from US banks. He died on 12 July 1841 and was buried at Riker Farm in Queens. A large obelisk memorial was dedicated to him at St. Paul's Episcopalian Church in Lower Manhattan, close to another similar structure that was deducted to his great friend, Thomas Addis Emmet. His funeral was the largest ever seen in New York City's history. His legacy in the United States; his encouragement of using modern medical techniques and his highly respected publication, ***"Exposition of the Atomic theory of Chemistry and the Doctrine or Definitive Proportions,"*** earned MacNeven, the affectionate title of ***"The Father of American Chemistry."*** An old United Irish acquaintance who had also settled in the USA, William Sampson, boldly stated of Dr. MacNeven that,

"If Ireland ever fails to cherish his memory she will prove utterly unworthy of him."

MacSHEEHY, Patrick – MacSheehy, a native of Killarney, Co. Kerry, was born in 1774 to Michael MacSheehy and Marie Anne Fagan. He was a scion of the renowned MacSheehy Family, which had gained many honours whilst in service in the Army of France during the Eighteenth Century. MacSheehy was educated at Sorbonne in Paris and witnessed the French Revolution in July 1789.

He returned to Ireland and found employment as a French tutor at Jones' Academy in Gorey, Co. Wexford, a profession which saw him highly respected across north Wexford. When the 1798 Rebellion broke out in Wexford, MacSheehy, who was a serving yeoman, switched allegiances and turned out with the insurgents. After the failure of the Rebellion, MacSheehy fled to his family connections based in France, upon which he was detained as an enemy alien. His cousin, Adjutant-General Bernard MacSheehy, who had been appointed as the first commanding officer of the Irish Legion, secured his release and influenced that a lieutenancy be bestowed on his cousin to serve in the newly formed Irish Legion. MacSheehy, like other Legion officers, became bored of the idle nature of the inactive Legion, which had been grounded at Lesneven in Brittany. A dispute occurred with a local, Monsieur Carrandra, which escalated into an organised pistol duel. After a round of misfires, it was agreed honour had been restored, however, Carrandra mocked MacSheehy for not accepting a duel of swords. Lieutenant Augustin Osmond accepted the offer of a sword duel on MacSheehy's behalf and severely wounded Carrandra, resulting in local animosity. The affair caused the Legion to be moved further south to the Breton town of Quimper. MacSheehy was later found unfit for service and he retired on a pension into civilian life. It is unknown to the authors what became of Patrick MacSheehy. Many thanks to Nicholas Dunne-Lynch for supporting us with this individual.

MacSUIBHNE, Dáithí / SWEENY, David – David Sweeny, nicknamed *Daithi na Miodoige* (David of the Dagger) was a native of Ballycroy, Co. Mayo. He was proclaimed an outlaw and escaped to America with his brother and sister.

MAGRATH, John – John Magrath was an insurgent, of Presbyterian background, who was arrested by the Crown forces after his involvement in the Rebellion. Having escaped from custody, he fled to the United States, settling in Charleston, South Carolina, where he established himself as a merchant. Magrath died on 6 February 1856, aged 77 years and was interred at First Scots Presbyterian Church Cemetery in Charleston.

His son Andrew (1813-1893) excelled in education and studied law in Harvard University. He entered politics in 1840 and was elected to the state legislator and eventually became a State Governor. Having been a member of the Succession Convention of 1860, he would serve as Secretary of the State of South Carolina (1860-61) and became Judge of the

Confederate District Court for South Carolina during the majority of the American Civil War, before briefly serving as the Confederate Governor of South Carolina. As a result of his political association with the Confederacy Magrath was imprisoned at Fort Pulaski in Georgia. Upon release, Magrath resumed private practice in Charleston until his death in 1893. His brother, William Joy Magrath (1817-1902), whose name honoured Henry Joy McCracken, would become the President of the South Carolina Railroad Company (1862-1878).

MAHON, John – John Mahon was a carpenter from Co. Clare, a county that only saw major disturbances in the Ennistymon area in January 1799. Mahon emigrated to the United States in 1800. Having stayed for a short period in New York City, he then relocated to Norfolk in Virginia, where he became employed in the Naval yards. His son, Denis Mahan and grandson Alfred Thayer Mahan would forge legacies for themselves in these same yards. (*See above*)

MAHON, Mary – Mary Mahon was the wife of John Mahon of Co. Clare, mentioned above. They had a notable son Denis Mahan and notable grandson Alfred Thayer Mahan.

Denis (*pictured*) was born in 1802 in New York and moved to the ship yards of Norfolk. Mahan graduated from West Point in 1824, first in his class. Such was his acumen that in his third year he was appointed acting assistant professor of mathematics and became a full-time professor. Professor Mahan's lectured and wrote about military fortifications and strategy were instrumental in the conduct of the Civil War by the officers on both sides. Most of the Civil War commanders, whether Union or Confederate, learned about entrenchment, fortifications, and how to conduct warfare in the classes that he taught at West Point, and from his pre-Civil War writings. Fort Mahan was one of the Civil War Defences of Washington. On 16 September 1871, after the West Point Board of Visitors recommended, he be forced to retire from teaching, Mahan committed suicide by leaping into the paddlewheel of a steamboat on the Hudson River.

Fort
Mahan
Earthworks of Fort Mahan are visible; follow path to the top of the hill.
Civil War Defenses of Washington
1861-1865

Alfred became a United States Naval Officer and historian. He was a graduate of the United States Naval Academy at Annapolis, Maryland and he served as a Union officer during the Civil War. He is perhaps best known as the author of the 1890 book "*The Influence of Sea Power Upon History, 1660-1783*," which advocated a navy of overwhelming force and is widely considered the most influential work on naval strategy ever written. Mahan would also serve as president of the Naval War College in Newport, Rhode Island from 1886 to 1889 and again from 1892 to 1893. He retired as rear admiral in 1896, but returned to the navy during the Spanish-American War to serve on the Naval War board.

Mahan Hall at the U.S. Naval Academy and the Naval War College were named after Alfred Thayer Mahan. Mahan's name became a household word in the German navy after Kaiser Wilhelm II ordered his officers to read Mahan, and Admiral Alfred von Tirpitz (1849–1930) used Mahan's reputation to finance a powerful surface fleet. He died in 1914 and is buried in Suffolk County in New York.

MAHON, John — John Mahon was an insurgent who fought in the Battle of Prosperous in the early hours of 24 May 1798, alongside his brother-in-law, Thomas Wylde. In early 1803, Mahon and Wylde were tasked by Michael Quigley to gauge the desire for further Rebellion in Kildare. They reported back that there was an enthusiastic desire. On 23 July 1803, when few Kildare men came to Dublin, Emmet was accused by the leadership for deception. When the insurrection failed, Mahon fled to Butterfield House with Wylde, Emmet, the Parrott Brothers, Michael Quigley and other conspirators. He fled into hiding for several months. On 12 December 1803, whilst hiding in a windmill near Philipstown, King's County (Tullamore, Co. Offaly), Mahon and Wylde were surrounded and upon being nearly caught, they fatally wounded Captain Charles Dodgson of the Fourth Dragoons. Knowing certain execution awaited them, they organised a boat passage to the United States and they fled from Ireland. In September 1820, the newspaper, the *Manufacturers and Farmer Journal* (Rhode Island), contained an obituary for John Mahon, who died on 28 August 1820 in Savannah, Georgia. Mahon left a wife and five small children in New York.

"In Savannah, on the 28ᵗʰ ult. Mr. John Mahon, a native of the city of Dublin, aged about 50 years. The deceased was one of those worthy Patriots who fought for their country during the Irish rebellion, in the year 1798, and again under the ever to be regretted Emmet, in 1803. Such an active part he took in the disturbances of the times, that a reward of 500 pounds sterling was offered for his

apprehension. He however eluded his pursuers, and arrived in the country in 1804, where he has since resided, and has been considered a worthy citizen."

MARKEY, Thomas – On 2 July 1798, Thomas Markey of Ardee was tried by general court-martial in Drogheda, Co. Louth, by order of Lieutenant-General Grey on charges of being a leading United Irishman in the Ardee district of Co. Louth. The Court-Martial was presided over by Major Oliver Fairclough, Captains Brough, Smith, Jones, Pepper, Brabazon and Lieutenant Galbraith. The Judge Advocate was Peter Van Hornrigh. Markey was also charged for administering illegal oaths, all of which he pleaded not guilty and defended himself. Two Ardee based witnesses testified against Markey; a grain merchant named Hand and Dan Kelly, a turned United Irishman who had testified against Michael Boylan of Blakestown House, who had been tried and executed opposite Drogheda's Tholsel on 22 June 1798. Kelly admitted membership of the organisation and having served on the committee with Markey, who is described as having held the position of a Chairman. Both witnesses did state that Markey never spoke of or promoted rebellion or disloyalty and only advocated the production of pikes to defend themselves against Orange attacks. Markey encouraged the Court to ignore the accusations that he had faced and that if he were to be transported or sentenced to serve His Majesty's Forces, then he would seek to make up by loyal and good conduct for any indiscretion that he had been guilty of. Markey was found guilty and sentenced to death

"*in such manner, time and place as Lieutenant-General Craig may think proper.***"**

However, he was not executed and instead was conveyed to the *Brunskill* prison tender in Dublin Bay. A historian who wrote in detail about this individual, Patrick Markey, claims that this change of sentence may have been influenced by John Foster of Collon, near Ardee, who was the conservative Speaker of the Irish House of Commons. This influence was recorded on a letter to Foster from Thomas Markey, dated **23** October 1798, who described himself as "the man whose life you saved." Within the letter, Markey urges Foster to help him flee to America or at least use his influence to get him off the *Brunskill*, and have him conveyed to Newgate Gaol (Dublin) at least, as he notes that the prison tender is causing him ill-health and much dissatisfaction due to the damp and overcrowded conditions. His plea was ignored and he remained aboard the *Brunskill* for the remainder of 1798. In a petition to Lord Cornwallis dated 4 December 1798, Markey thanked the Viceroy for mitigating his sentence and begged for permission to self-exile to America or any country not at war with Britain. We are unsure what the outcome of this petition was, but we know he was transferred to Newgate Gaol in Dublin during 1799.

On 5 August 1799, Markey wrote to Edward Cooke, the Under-Secretary at Dublin Castle, indicating that many Catholics in Co. Louth would be in favour of the plans for coalescing the Dublin and London governments into one United Kingdom Parliament. Clearly, this tact was to woo Cooke and to show loyalty. He asked to be released so he could muster such support from Louth's Catholics for such a Parliamentary Union. The outcome we are unsure of but Markey was eventually released on 20 March 1800 on the discharge orders of Hon. Judge Downs on giving £1000 security to appear in the Court of the King's Bench when required. Upon release, Markey returned to the "Wee County" of Louth on condition that his visit was short. Van Homrigh, the Judge Advocate who had originally sentenced Markey, noted his presence quite often in Drogheda and requested Major Henry Charles Sirr to travel from Dublin and attest him. By late July 1800, Markey was being held in Dundalk Gaol. He immediately petitioned Lord Castlereagh to be released seeing as he had been formally discharged by Judge Downs. Markey further wrote to Cornwallis stating that he was a victim of a conspiracy. Here there is a lapse of information. Miles Byrne wrote about Markey in his memoirs:

"Thomas Markey - Lieutenant at the formation of the Irish Legion the 7th of December 1803. Captain in April 1804. Captain aide-de-camp to the Minister of War, the Duke of Feltre, 1810. Chef de bataillon, aide-de-camp, 1812. Gros Major or Lieutenant-Colonel commanding then depot of a French Regiment at Brest in 1814. Put on half pay, 1815; re-employed in 1823, and again on half pay after the Spanish Campaign till 1833, when he obtained the maximum, full pension of retreat. Decorated with the cross of chevalier of the Legion of Honour, and with the Cross of Saint Louis. Markey retired to Fontainebleau, where he ended his days peacefully on the 6th of April 1854 at the advanced age of 84 years. Few Irish patriots suffered more than Thomas Markey. At Drogheda in 1798 he was tried by Court Martial and condemned to death; he was on the point of being executed, when a respite came, and his punishment was then commuted to transportation for life. He was bound with chains, thrown on board the convict ship in Howth Harbour, where he suffered all kinds of indignities for several months; he was removed to Kilmainham Gaol (possibly mistaken by Byrne for Newgate), and became the fellow prisoner of Emmet (Thomas Addis Emmet), Arthur O'Connor, MacNeven, Hugh Ware, etc. At the Peace of Amiens in 1802, he was allowed expatriate himself forever. He went to Bordeaux, where he met General Napper Tandy, with whom he would form many schemes for the independence of Ireland. - Tandy died in 1803 and bequeathed to Markey his sword of honour, which the latter prized as the greatest gift that could be bestowed on him. Markey was handsome and graceful, middle-sized; he was witty in conversation, with the manners of a highly well-bred man in society. He was extremely hospitable, and did the honours of his table like a true Irishman."

The Chief Secretary's Papers in the National Archives of Ireland highlight that on 2 May 1822, John Foster, by then Baron Oriel, wrote to the Chief-Secretary's Office in Dublin Castle requesting clemency for Markey (a linen dealer from Ardee, Co. Louth), who it seems was residing on the Continent. A pencilled note

165

from Richard Wellesley, the 1st Marquis Wellesley and Viceroy of Ireland states, *"I do not see grounds for granting this request."* On 6 November 1822, Eliza Markey of Drogheda, niece of Thomas Markey, petitioned William Meade Smyth, MP for Drogheda, requesting his assistance to obtain permission for her uncle to return to Ireland from Portugal due to ill health.

MARTIN, Christopher –

Martin was born in 1775 to James Martin and Marie Leasseye. A native of Dunboyne, Co. Meath, Martin held an influential role in the Meath United Irishmen. On 12 March 1798, he was one of the County Delegates who was arrested at Oliver Bond's residence in Bridgefoot Street. He was incarcerated in Kilmainham Gaol on 9 May 1798 for treasonable practices. His record at Kilmainham shows that he was discharged in April 1801 and 'transported' although evidence shows he fled to France. At the formation of the Irish Legion in late 1803, Martin became a sub-lieutenant. Miles Byrne claimed that Lieutenant Martin died of wounds received during the Walcheren Campaign of 1809. This was an error on Byrne's behalf as Martin, upon healing from wounds received, was later promoted but eventually left the Legion in 1812.

MASON, Patrick –

Patrick Mason was imprisoned in July 1798 for participation in a robbery. Having been court-martialled on 24 July 1798, he was sentenced to transportation, however this was reduced to exile to America. It's unknown if Mason had been a United Irishman, however, his sentence was commuted to voluntary banishment.

MATHEWS, Patrick –

Mathews was a Dublin based United Irishman who fled Ireland after participating in the 1798 Rebellion. He established himself at Albany in New York (*pictured*). On 20 August 1811, Patrick Mathews died, aged thirty-two years. *The Shamrock* published a worthy and detailed obituary to Mathews on 14 September 1811:

"The deceased was a native of Dublin, and at an early period the fire of that indignant spirit which may be crushed, but never extirpated, broke forth. He left his friends and his home to assist in recovering the independence of his oppressed and unhappy country; he fought in several battles and skirmishes; after three or four months incessant fatigue and danger, he returned to Dublin, but not thinking himself safe in his native city, when at that time scarcely no one could walk its streets, but an

CHURCH AND MARKET STS., ALBANY, 1805.

informer on the minions of murder and rapine, he sailed for America, with his wife, to whom he had been a short time before married, and arrived at New York where he commenced business, and where his wife died in the bloom of youth, of the fatal endemic which prevailed here. He came shortly after this city (Albany). He had for some time past laboured under a disease of the lungs, and the late extremely warm weather, combined with the exertions he made to attend his company in their military exercises at Guilderland on Monday last, accelerated his death. He possessed all the characteristic nationality of temper and feeling which is peculiar to an Irishman; quick in resenting an insult as forgiving, when acknowledged; honest, brave and generous, warm and zealous in his friendship, obliging as a neighbour, and affectionate as a parent, his patriotism and love for his adopted country, as a soldier and a citizen were ardent and sincere; he was President of the St. Patrick Society of Albany and Ensign of the Republican Green Company. He lived respected and esteemed, and died beloved and lamented by every class of citizens; he has left an orphan daughter, and an affectionate sister, to deplore his loss – his remains were interred in the Catholic cemetery."

MATHEWS, Thomas – The

Mathews family came, as 1798 exiles, firstly to Mercer County in Pennsylvania before relocating to Trumbull County in Ohio. In the *History of Mercer County*, it states that Mathews had been a personal friend of Robert Emmet and a United Irishman during the 1798 Rebellion. After the failure of the Rebellion, the family fled Ireland. Mathews left a large family in Ohio, dying on 11 December 1850 and was buried at the Old North Cemetery in Hubbard, Ohio.

McADAMS, Thomas – Thomas McAdams was with the Rev. Gibson when they left Ballymena, Co. Antrim, for New York, as exiles. McAdams settled in Philadelphia, where he became a teacher. He was involved in the short-lived U.S. Society of United Irishmen, which was based in Philadelphia.

McALLISTER – In a short biographical extract dedicated to Alexander F. McAllister (1840-1909), there contains some information that his paternal grandfather had taken part in the 1798 Rebellion alongside brothers, John and Henry Joy McCracken. The detail continues that the McAllister family who fled to America were relatives of President McKinley, whose distant relation, Francis McKinley was executed for his leadership role in north Antrim and Coleraine. McAllister's grandfather served with Winfield Scott in the War of 1812 and at the Battle of Lundy's Lane and throughout the campaigns along the Canadian

frontier. Alexander's father served as a captain on the old U.S. sloop-of-war, *Cyane*, at the capture of Vera Cruz.

McCABE, William Putnam –

William Putnam McCabe was born in Belfast in 1776 to watchmaker, Thomas McCabe and Jean Woolsey. He grew up in an exceptionally liberal household, as his father was a noted abolitionist, whose politics leaned heavily towards radical reform. W.P. McCabe became an apprentice in the textiles industry, learning the trade in Glasgow, Manchester and across the north of Ireland. Upon becoming a United Irishman, W.P. McCabe would use his network of contacts to help construct and solidify the society across much of Ireland, including south Ulster, northern Connacht and south-east Leinster, using his renowned technique of mimicry and disguises. Referred to as an emerald

pimpernel, McCabe's cool and collect acting helped him escape arrest on numerous occasions, including in one such case of masquerading as a Scottish merchant, when he was accosted by Dunbarton Fencibles in May 1798.

McCabe was somewhat involved in the insurrections in Kildare and in Connacht, but in a low-key role. He fled Ireland in December 1798 and travelled to Hamburg on a forged American passport, where he was greeted by Lady Pamela Fitzgerald, before travelling to Paris. Upon travelling to Scotland, under the alias of Lee, to communicate with the United Irish prisoners held at Fort George, he married Elizabeth Lockhart MacNeill. They settled at Rouen in France and McCabe immediately invested in establishing what would become a successful cotton mill. Still politically involved, McCabe was, by 1800, a high-ranking member of the reconstructed United Irish Directory. He was a chief organiser in the early stages of Robert Emmet's plans for a renewed insurrection and financed Michael Quigley to return to Ireland to assist Emmet. After the failure of the Emmet uprising in July 1803, McCabe became disillusioned with France and radical politics. It is known that he corresponded with Arthur Wellesley, Lord Castlereagh and William Pitt, which resulted in some relaxing of his banishment in Britain, but not Ireland. In 1817, he travelled to Ireland to settle some affairs in Belfast. His step-mother, who desired to keep McCabe out of his ailing father's will, reported him to the authorities and he was arrested and held in Kilmainham Gaol for eighteen months. His health started to fail due to the damp and cold conditions. He was released upon the influences of William Tennant and he returned to France, dying there on 6 January 1821. William Putnam McCabe was buried at Vaugirard Cemetery.

McCALLA, Samuel

McCALLA, Samuel – Samuel McCalla took part in the Rising in Co. Down in June 1798. Upon capture, he was sentenced to serve in His Majesty's forces abroad and was sent to the West Indies. Like others, McCalla focused on escaping from the misery of military discipline and tropical diseases of the West Indies to reach the United States. Successful in his escape, McCalla settled in South Carolina and worked as a mason and bricklayer. In 1817, he was reunited with his wife Mary and their son, Robert McCalla (*photographed*), who both emigrated from Ireland to join him in the United States. The family settled at Cannon Creek, Newberry County, and Samuel became an elder of the Associate Reformed Presbyterian Church in Cannon Creek. He also became a Justice of the Peace and  in 1823 he was appointed one of the Election managers of the district. Afflicted with fevers, Samuel McCalla died on 6 September 1824, aged 51 years, and was buried at Cannon's Creek Mission Church Graveyard in Newberry County, South Carolina.

McCAMBRIDGE- family lore from the Ballymena area of County Antrim tells a story of a McCambridge United Irishman. In 1800 when the Archer gang were at their height one of the gang members entered a Catholic Chapel in Ballymeana to warn McCambridge that Government troops were coming for him. Lore states that he quickly took heed and made his escape to New Orleans- with thanks to Paul McHugh.

However, this also could be another man named James McCambridge from Ballymena who was arrested in the crackdown after the affair in Ballymena and was sent to serve the King of Prussia. Only this McCambridge was cited as being a subject of mistaken identity and was actually a government loyalist. When this was realised, he was sent for but it was too late and he was never found. Could this be the same man?.

McCANN, Anthony – McCann, a Protestant landowner from Corderry, Co. Louth, was the first Chairman of the United Irishmen in that county. In the summer of 1797, informers reported on the activities of the Louth leadership, causing McCann to flee to Paris with Thomas Burgess, Patrick & John Byrne, Bartholomew Teeling, leaving Valentine Derry, Anthony Marmion, John Hoey, Bartholomew Callan and Edward O'Hare to take over the leadership. McCann joined

ny. "And absen-tce: replied Cobden.

A free pardon, it is said, is to be granted to M'Kan, one of the individuals who was compelled to exile himself from these dominions in consequence of his participation in the Irish Rebellion of 1798 Mr M'Kan has for many years been residing in Germany.

Napper Tandy on the failed expedition which landed on Donegal's Rutland Island on 16 September 1798. On 3 November 1798, after an arduous journey from Norway's port of Bergen, McCann arrived at Hamburg with Thomas Burgess and William Corbett. They applied to the French ambassador, Marragon, for passports, but were turned down. Interestingly, a famous Irish exile poem was composed by Thomas Campbell in 1800, called 'The Exile of Erin.' Campbell later described the origins of the poem:

"While tarrying at Hamburg I made acquaintance with some of the refugee Irishmen, who had been concerned in the Rebellion of 1798. Among these was Anthony McCann – an honest, excellent man – who is, still I believe alive – at least I left him in prosperous circumstances at Altona a few years ago. When I first met him, he was in a situation much the reverse; but Anthony commanded respect whether he was rich or poor. It was in consequence of meeting him one evening on the banks of the Elbe, lonely and pensive at the thoughts of his situation, that I wrote, 'Exile of Erin.'"

Upon the release of the State Prisoners from Fort George in 1802, McCann accommodated Samuel Nielson and travelled with him to Ireland aboard the 'Providence' on 6 August 1802, from the port of Cuxhaven. Whilst Neilson settled his affairs before travelling to America, McCann's story becomes somewhat lost to time. Historian, Paul Weber claims McCann joined Thomas Ridgeway, the proprietor of the 'Providence,' in a smuggling venture between the British and Irish Isles and the continent. When this venture collapsed in 1803, McCann, who was financially struggling, appears to have become an informer for the British authorities, however, we do not know for how long or how effective. In 1818, McCann requested that his name be removed from the proscribed fugitive list stating that he wished to return home to visit his aged father. In the letter, McCann admitted his membership of the United Irishmen but stated that he fled when his associates had been arrested. He was allowed to return for a period of three months, courtesy of the influence of John Leslie Foster M.P. In 1834, newspaper reports stated that a free pardon had been granted to McCann, who was still resident in Germany. In Madden's 'Literary Remains', Charles Tolme stated that McCann had married a German native named Flugge and had become a wealthy corn merchant.

McCANN, Patrick – McCann was a chemist from Co. Down, who was implicated in the 1798 Rebellion and sent to Kilmainham Gaol, where he was held until 1802. Upon release, he was able to flee to France and joined the Irish Legion. McCann was commissioned as Lieutenant in the Legion in December 1803, rising to Captain on 22 March 1804. McCann was wounded at the Battle of Flushing in August 1809. The wound resulted in McCann having his arm amputated at a hospital in Ghent. His wife, who was present at his bedside was overwhelmed with grief when McCann failed to improve, resulting in his death. She died within a month of the death of Patrick McCann, leaving a ten-year old orphan. McCann left a lasting legacy at Kilmainham Gaol with an etching carved into the wall a piece of graffiti which can be viewed today. Many thanks to Ailbhe Rogers for supplying us with a photograph of the carving.

McCARTHY, Denis – Denis McCarthy was recorded on an article in the *Irish American* (21 March 1857) detailing his participation in the 1798 Rebellion. Having fought in the Rebellion, he returned to his homestead near Baltinglass, Co. Wicklow and found that his brother James had been fatally wounded and the farmstead ruined. The story continues that he fled to Hamburg and met Thomas Campbell, the reputed author of '*An Exile of Erin*' before returning home and fighting with Michael Dwyer and Robert Emmet. He would have four sons, whom he honourably attached the names of Emmet, Wolfe Tone, Grattan and Edward (after Lord Edward Fitzgerald).

McCAULEY, Bridget, *née McCanna* – Bridget McCanna was the wife of James McCauley, from Co. Antrim, who emigrated to the U.S. after the 1798 Rebellion.

McCAULEY, James – McCauley was born in Co. Antrim ca.1771. After the 1798 Rebellion, he fled to the United States. His brother, Peter McCauley and his wife had also decided to self-exile. Peter's initial plan was to purchase a farm outside Philadelphia. Susan Lynch *née* McAuley, sister of James and Peter, joined in the voyage with her daughter, Kitty Lynch. Six weeks after James' arrival in Philadelphia, he rode out to inspect a farm that he had just purchased. He became overwhelmed from heat exhaustion and he fell dead from his horse.

McCAULEY, Peter – It is not fully known if Peter McCauley, a glazier by profession, exiled as a result of the 1798 Rebellion, having followed his brother, James McCauley to America, and settled in Pennsylvania.

McCLINTOCK, William - In

1797, the Crown authorities clamped down on the Derry United Irishmen, arresting Robert Moore of Molenan, and William McClintock, the city's leading haberdasher. Both were men of the highest respectability who had been involved in regional politics for over a generation and had been high ranking members of the Volunteers. McClintock and Moore were charged with treason and lodged within the City Gaol (photographed). Two months later, the renowned United Irish attorney, John Philpot Curran secured their freedom. McClintock quickly fled to America and into anonymity. By mid-1798 the insurgency across Co. Derry was in tatters. On 2 November 1798, the Corporation of Londonderry ordered that Henry Grattan, the Patriot MP, *"be disenfranchised from all the privileges of this city"* as he had been wrongly blamed as a major cause to the Rebellion. On the same grounds, the meeting also disenfranchised Robert Moore, William McClintock, Joseph Orr and Christopher Hardy. The act was pointless as most of these names had already fled from Ireland.

McCLURE, John – In October 1798, McClure was recorded as a prisoner in Carrickfergus Gaol, incarcerated for his part in the 1798 Rebellion. He was given permission to emigrate to America.

McCLURE, Elizabeth, *née Findley* – Elizabeth Findley was the wife of Theophilus McClure, a low rank insurgent officer during the Down Rebellion in June 1798. The family settled in Ryegate, Vermont, where Elizabeth died in 1846.

McCLURE, Theophilus – McClure was born in Co. Down in 1751. He joined the United Irishmen and fought with the insurgency during the 1798 Rebellion, in which he was styled as a captain and gave orders, on account of his experience with the Volunteers during the early 1780s. McClure was apprehended and acted as a Crown witness in the court-martial of John

Wightman, in which the accused received a sentence of flogging. McClure's own court-martial was held at Lisburn on 24 July 1798. He was sentenced to be transported for fourteen years to New South Wales, which was remitted to voluntary banishment. McClure and his family emigrated to the United States and settled in Ryegate, Vermont, where he died in 1838.
+

The McCLURG FAMILY *of*, *Limavady County L Derry*

McCLURG, Joseph — Joseph McClurg, a Presbyterian native of North Derry was patriarch of a family that prospered throughout the nineteenth century in the United States. Joseph McClurg, born in 1763, had participated in the 1798 Rebellion and had fled to the United States, seeking asylum from punishment in Ireland. It is stated that McClurg managed to escape to America by hiding himself within the hold of a ship. His wife, Ann Caldwell McClurg and their family sailed to join him afterwards, leaving Ann at the family farm in Bovevagh outside Newtown-Limavady for a few years. It is further mentioned within a short biography that Joseph was a proud Scotch-Irishman, who deeply adored his native land and the concept of liberty, thus naming his homestead, *Liberty Hall*. With the yellow fever gripping U.S. coastal cities like Philadelphia, the McClurg's relocated to Pittsburgh and with his son, old Joseph would establish the first iron mill in the growing city. Joseph McClurg died in Pittsburgh in 1825.

McCLURG, Alexander - Alexander McClurg, born in Bovevagh Limavady c.1786 to Joseph McClurg and Ann Caldwell. The young Caldwell would prosper in Pittsburgh, Pennsylvania. In 1817, he married Sarah Trevor and upon her premature death in 1839, he married again to Margaret Caskey. Having the means, he invested into Fort Pitt foundry in Pittsburgh, which would furnish every

battlefield of the American Civil War and every Union Dock with cannon; a business that made the family extremely wealthy. He not only carried forward and enlarged his iron industries at Pittsburgh, but established branches of his

173

Philadelphian dry-goods house at, Pittsburgh, Cincinnati, and Louisville. As the controlling partner in such concerns as *McClurg, Denniston & Company, McClurg, Trevor & Company, McClurg, Wade & Company*, and *McClurg, Darlington & Company*, and in other firms scarcely less important, he was notably enterprising and progressive, and until he was overtaken by the financial crisis of 1837, he was one of the most successful businessmen in the United States. Alexander McClurg died on 6 April 1873 and was interred at Allegheny Cemetery in Pittsburgh. His son, Alexander Caldwell McClurg Jr (1832-1901) (*pictured*), having studied at Miami University in Ohio, read law in the office of Chief-Justice Lowry before distinguishing himself during the American Civil War, reaching the rank of Lieutenant-Colonel and Brevet Brigadier-General. After the war, McClurg held a successful career as a publisher and bookseller.

McCLURG, James –

James McClurg, a son of Joseph McClurg and Ann Caldwell was born in Newtown-Limavady c.1785. In 1807, James McClurg, having helped his family establish their iron foundries in Pittsburgh, settled in Four Corners (now Westfield), New York, and would remain

James McClurg.

there until the War of 1812. He returned with his bride, Martha Eason, to Pittsburgh, where he utilized his knowledge of the iron business and the McClurg furnaces, in the casting of cannon, for the U.S. Government. James McClurg died on 26 May 1872 and was interred at Westfield Cemetery, Chautauqua County, New York. His son, Alexander McClurg (1820-1877) would become one of the Presidents of the Mississippi Railroad Company.

McCONAGHY, John –

A letter composed in 1896 gave descriptions of how John McConaghy, his wife and two sons, **Daniel** and **Hugh**, fled to the United States from their native Co. Derry. The book, *Exiles of '98*, states that the letter highlights Ardmore, Drumachose (Limavady) as their possible home townland, however we have not been able to verify this.

"John McConaghy, our Great Uncle, had two sons, Daniel and Hugh. He, with his two sons, had to flee from the County of his birth, having been a United Irishman and leader in the Enterprise. He would have been executed if he had

174

been arrested. At the age of 65 years, in 1798, he made his escape with his wife and two sons to this country."

McCORMACK – Andrew McCormack was born c.1800 in Nashville, Tennessee to a Dublin born father and a northern native mother, whose maiden name was McFarren. They had been a Protestant couple who had left during the 1798 Rebellion, marrying upon arrival in America. After the birth of Andrew, the family moved from Nashville to Fleming County in Kentucky, where old McCormack died in 1815. Andrew McCormack continued in his studies, learning by night and working by day. He removed the family to Sangamon County in Illinois. The family are well represented in the Calvary Cemetery.

McCORMICK, Richard – McCormick was a poplin trader, based at 9 Mark's Alley in Dublin and was a noted progressive liberal, having participated deeply in the Volunteer Movement of the early 1780s. At one stage of his career, McCormick employed over 200 workers. McCormick had served as Secretary on the Catholic Committee, which eventually led him to work with an aspiring lawyer, Theobald Wolfe Tone. Their relationship prospered and Tone privately nicknamed McCormick, '*Magog*' after a large statue of a Greek god at London's Guildhall. McCormick was involved in the United Irishman from its earliest infancy and became one of Tone's trusted confidants. By 1796, with the United movement being driven underground and Tone having fled to America, McCormick aligned with the militancy of Lord Edward Fitzgerald and Arthur O'Connor and eventually become a high-ranking member of the National Executive. In November 1796, French officer and Killarney native, Bernard McSheehy, who later became the first commanding officer of the Irish Legion, was sent to Ireland by the French Directory to engage with McCormick, on advice from Tone, who was in France preparing for what would become the Bantry Bay Expedition. After the failure of the Expedition, McCormick, unknowingly being watched by Dublin Castle informers, began to distrust Fitzgerald and O'Connor's motives. Suffering from pressures, he fled Ireland on 20 February 1798 for France. After the failures and losses brought on by the 1798 Rebellion, McCormick grew tired and disillusioned of reactionary politics and was eventually allowed to return to Ireland and in 1814, he moved to England, acting as guardian to the daughter of John Tennant, who had been killed in 1813 during the Saxon Campaign. On 26 May 1827, McCormick died.

McCRACKEN, Francis –

Francis McCracken, the brother of Henry Joy, John and Mary Ann, was born on June 4th 1762, to John McCracken and Ann Joy. Having supported his younger brother during the 1798 Rebellion and the Battle of Antrim, Francis McCracken was tried and charged with seditious and clandestine activities in July 1798. He managed to avoid penalties and was allowed to emigrate from Ireland, eventually establishing himself in Charleston, South Carolina, where he managed warehouses. McCracken resided in Charleston for two years and returned to Ireland in October 1800, residing with Mary Ann. He unsuccessfully attempted to dissuade Thomas Russell from participating in Robert Emmet's failed uprising.

In 1812, Francis, his maternal uncle, Henry Joy and friend, Robert Boyd Holmes were signatories to a petition in favour of Catholic Emancipation. During this period, the Presbyterian Church was hardening its stance towards emancipation and were morphing from being liberal republicans to conservative pro-unionists. Interestingly, many Ulster Presbyterians, who had been United Irishmen in 1798, had become Orangemen by the 1820s. Francis McCracken died in Belfast on 22 December 1842.

In the Common Pleas.

William Simms,
vs.   Case on Attachment.
Francis M'Cracken.

WHEREAS the Plaintiff in this action, did on the twenty-seventh day of July instant, file his declaration in the Office of the Clerk of this Honourable Court, against the Defendant, who is absent from and without the limits of this State, and hath neither Wife nor Attorney known within the same, upon whom a copy of the said Declaration with a rule to plead thereto within a year and a day, might be served :—It is therefore ordered, in pursuance of the Act of the General Assembly of the said state, in such case made and provided, that the said Defendant do appear and plead to the said Declaration, on or before the twenty-eighth day of July, which will be in the year of our Lord one thousand eight hundred and twelve ; otherwise final and absolute judgment will then be given and awarded against him the said Defendant.

W. S. Smith, C. C. P,

Office of Common Pleas, Charleston
District, 27th July, 1811

THE LATE FRANCIS M'CRACKEN, ESQ.—In our obituary this day will be found a notice of the death of Francis M'Cracken, Esq. ; but we feel that his memory is entitled to more than the formality usual on similar occasions. He was the last survivor of the first Belfast Volunteer Company, enrolled on the 26th of March, 1778, and, during a period of more than sixty years, he carried on business as a highly respectable merchant in this town, with the universal esteem of all classes of the community. His maternal grandfather was Francis Joy, who, in the year 1737, established the Belfast *News-Letter*, at that time the third, now the *first* newspaper in Ireland, and, consequently, the memory of Mr. M'Cracken is, at our hands, entitled to special consideration. We may add, that, at the period of his decease, this worthy old citizen was the eighty-first year of his age.

McCRACKEN, George

"In the churchyard at Mount Hope several generations of the old families of Aston are interred. Conspicuous among that number was George McCracken, who died only a few months before he had attained his hundredth year of life. George McCracken died on his estate on West Branch of Chester Creek in 1873. He was born in Ireland in 1773, and shortly after he came to this country (early in the century) settled in Aston, and continued to reside there until his death. Although his career was not marked with remarkable incidents outside of the usual happenings of rural life, he was a good citizen, who left an unblemished name to his numerous descendants. Four years before his death, on May 1, 1869, while a number of the family and friends had assembled at Mr. McCracken's house to attend a funeral there, the upper floor or the porch, on which about thirty persons were standing at the time, gave way, and fortunately, although several persons were hurt, no serious injury was sustained by anyone."

☞ George M'Cracken, within four months of 100 years old, died in Delaware county last week. Accompanied by his wife he emmigrated from Ireland in 1803 and spent nearly seventy years on the banks of Chester creek. He had been a soldier in his native country during the rebellion of 1798, and but a few weeks before he died he was able to recount the doings of his earlier days and the exploits of himself and comrades on board the Mohawk, the vessel which brought him across the ocean.

McCREERY, John – John McCreery was a mason from Ballymanister, near Bangor, Co. Down. Having took part in the 1798 Rebellion, McCreery was subsequently court-martialled at Newtownards on 21 July 1798, on charges of having acted as *"a traitor and rebel"*, reportedly citing to a neighbour *"Liberty or Death"*. McCreery was found guilty and was originally sentenced to transportation to New South Wales. However, mercy was granted to his plight and consideration was given in regards his wife had no support for their eleven children. McCreery was given leave to transport himself to the United States.

McCREERY, John – The first prominent historian of the United Irishmen, R.R. Madden, recorded that McCreery, a native of Donegal, settled in Petersburg, Virginia in late 1797, where he spent a lifetime constructing poems about his native land. McCreery died in 1825.

McDANIEL, Miles – McDaniel hailed from Enniscorthy, Co. Wexford. He was a nephew of Mogue Doyle, also recorded as an exile. McDaniel left Ireland in the early 1800s, having supposedly participated in the 1798 Rebellion, and settled at Port Hood, Cape Breton in Nova Scotia, where he was employed by Edward Hayes, a merchant. Around 1811-1813, McDaniel settled in the Margaree area of Nova Scotia. Many thanks to his great-great-great granddaughter, Eileen Coady of Margaree Forks, Inverness County (Nova Scotia), for supplying us with this information.

McDERMOTT, Bryan – Bryan McDermott hailed from a middle-class Catholic farming background in Hodgestown, near Clane, Co. Kildare. He was one of the leading Kildare insurgent leaders who surrendered at Odlum's Mills, near Sallins, Co. Kildare, on 21 July 1798. McDermott was placed into Kilmainham Gaol on 22 September 1798 and would remain there until 9 April 1802. Upon his release, McDermott left for France. Little is known of his time in France. In February 1803, he was requested by William Putnam McCabe to join Hugh Ware and Michael Quigley to return to Ireland and assist Robert Emmet in his plans for a renewed insurrection. Ware and McDermott would remain in France.

McDONALD, Alexander – McDonald was born c.1770 at Greyabbey, Co. Down. Having participated in the 1798 Rebellion, he fled to the United States with his wife, Alice Baille and their young children. The family settled at Steubenville in Jefferson County Ohio.

McDONALD, Issac – Issac McDonald was born in Co. Down in 1795 to Alexander McDonald and Alice Baille. McDonald would serve as Sherriff of Jefferson County (OH) and marry twice during his lifetime. McDonald died on 14 December 1872 and was interred at Bellefontaine Cemetery in St. Louis, Missouri. His son, Colonel Emmett McDonald (*pictured*), whose forename clearly honoured the fallen Robert Emmet, would serve in the Confederate Army during the American Civil War. He was killed by artillery at Hartville in Wright County, Missouri, on 11 January 1863.

McDONALD – McDonald was a brewer from Carlow Town, who faced ruin as a result of his participation or support for the United Irishmen. Upon wanting to sell his business, he was challenged in prices but local Protestant community rallied to McDonald's side and supported that he would receive a full and worthy price for the sale. Their rallying to his side was for his support and protection to many of Carlow's Protestants during the Rebellion. McDonald emigrated to the United States with a healthy fortune.

McDOUGAL, Alex – It is unknown precisely when this individual emigrated to Canada. His obituary, recorded in the *Watertown Republican* (3 August 1881) highlights that McDougal, who died aged 101 years, was a yeoman during the 1798 Rebellion, and was only eighteen years of age during the period. Upon emigrating to Canada, McDougal settled in Argenteuil County in Quebec, Canada.

McFATE, Samuel – Samuel McFate (1754-1842) was the son of Robert and Elizabeth McFate from Drumharriff on the county border Donegal and Fermanagh, near Pettigo. He participated in some capacity in the Rebellion and had to quickly flee to America as a result. He did not remain in America for long as he returned home to Co. Donegal, where he died in May 1842.

McGINNIS, Rev. Fr. Bernard – Fr. Bernard McGinnis was a Catholic Priest from south Co. Down and a United Irish Colonel, who was imprisoned after the Rebellion was crushed. He was still incarcerated in July 1799. McGinnis was subject to the Banishment Act however it is unknown to the authors what became of him.

McGLAHERTY, James – James McGlaherty had participated in the Battle of Antrim on 7 June 1798. He manged to flee from Ireland and ended his days aboard a ship on his way to the coast of Guinea to round up locals, possibly to feed the slave market of the southern states of America.

McGREGOR, John – In the *History of Clinton County*, there is biographical details of John McGregor. A native of Scotland, he was resident for some time in Co. Derry, where he worked as a weaver. He came to America with his six brothers as a result of their participation in the Rebellion. He settled in Frederick County in Virginia where he established an entertainment house. In 1802, he relocated to Ohio with his wife and children and later moved to Wilmington, where he opened a tavern. In 1813, McGregor ruptured a blood vessel whilst carrying a barrel of whiskey and died soon afterwards.

McILVAINE, Rev. Alexander – Alexander McIlvaine was a probationer from Letterkenny in Co. Donegal. He left Ireland in early 1798 and settled in Pennsylvania. He was brought before the Western Pennsylvania Presbyterian Presbytery and they accepted that he was of good standing, certifying him to preach in 1799. On 7 October 1800, McIlvaine married Catharine Canan.

McKEE, George –

George McKee was born around 1776. He began his career as a farmer at Magheraconluce which is situated between Ballynahinch and Lisburn in Co. Down. Folklore indicates that he was an officer in the United Irishmen and fought with distinction at the Battle of Ballynahinch on 13 June 1798. He managed to escape to Scotland for short period before he made it to the United States, alongside his brother Joseph, where their brother, David McKee had owned property in Newville

Pennsylvania. They arrived at Newville on 1 November 1798 and spent the winter at David's property, where George's wife, Margaret Ball McKee, gave birth to a child. In 1799, George moved to western Pennsylvania and settled at Fayette Township, in Allegheny County, where he purchased 400 acres on 7 March 1800. He spent the rest of his life as a farmer on 400 acres. The McKee family were members of the Reformed or Covenantor Presbyterian Church in Co. Down. George went onto become an elder in "Union" associate Reformed church in Fayette Township. His second wife was the granddaughter of his first cousin John McKee of the Prices Arms in Saintfield, who had originally lived about a mile from Saintfield on the Belfast Road. Deborah McKee came to Pennsylvania in 1812 with her father James McKee and family. George McKee died on 9 October 1839.

McKEE, Joseph –

McKee's participation as an insurgent in the 1798 Rebellion was so significant that he had to remain hidden for a period of time from the authorities and on one occasion he had to hide within a pile of timber, until he found an opportunity to flee to America. Whilst hiding, McKee was kept focused with a copy of the *Psalms*, and he occupied his time by committing them to memory. It is understood that he never needed the use of the *Psalms* book whilst participating in the Choir. It is also stated that his bitterness towards the British never softened after what he had experienced during the 1798 Rebellion. Joseph

McKee died on 9 November 1840, aged 75 years and was buried at Newville Cemetery in Cumberland County, Pennsylvania. McKee was a man of considerable influence, strict faith and perhaps the most intelligent church member in the vicinity. He is mentioned as having been a brilliant singer and for many years the clerk of the church choir. In fact, he left such an impression that the leadership of the choir was passed through his family until it became almost hereditary.

McKEEVER, Billy *alias* William Campbell – McKeever was from Upperlands, outside Maghera in Co. Derry. He was an active United Irish organiser across much of south Derry and north Tyrone. McKeever was implicated in the trial of William Orr in October 1797. For his part in the 1798 Rebellion, he fled like so many in the Maghera area to the United States.

McKENNA, Bernard & James– Bernard McKenna was a native of Aughnacloy in Co. Tyrone, who had been connected to the Defenders and the United Irishmen. Whilst Ulster suffered heavily during the 1797 crackdown, McKenna fled to Moville in Donegal, alongside his brother, James McKenna, successfully seeking passage to America. Whilst on the voyage they were briefly detained by a French warship, but were approved to carry on to Delaware. Bernard walked from Delaware to Long Island, New York whilst James settled elsewhere. Bernard began to teach in a respectable academy and upon realising he was unfit for the role he set about improving his situation by educating himself during his spare time to meet the standard. Such perseverance proved successful for McKenna and he was awarded a role in a higher-level school, earning $300 annually. His situation further improved when his new wife inherited a large fortune, which they invested into a farm. She also gave birth to two daughters. Tragedy struck when his wife died in 1808 and McKenna was dismissed from his teaching role. visited Bernard in New York. Bernard died in 1814 at the age of 60 years, leaving his young children in the care of the Catholic Church. In 1810, James became a sub-Sheriff of Chester County in Pennsylvania.

McKINLEY – In 1896, an article was published in which the author highlighted that his mother's maiden name was McKinley who apparently had to leave their family farm on the border of Counties Antrim and Derry as a result of the 1798 Rebellion. Upon arriving in the United States, the family resided in Pennsylvania and Ohio respectively. The author continued by stating that his maternal grandmother had died at the age of

107 years in Coleraine, and mentioned that she had maintained a steady communication with the family in America. The article was published in the *Abilene Weekly*, in response to the nomination of the future President of the United States, William McKinley, saying that he should be described as of Irish origin rather than Scots-Irish origin which was being put forward. The article does not mention the family association with the future President thus highlighting that family connections may have been lost throughout the century.

Francis McKinley of Connagher, born in 1756, was hanged in Coleraine for his prominent role in the north Derry and Ballymoney United Irish movement in June 1798. His wife fled from the family home in Connagher, near Dervock, Co. Antrim, and settled in Coleraine afterwards. Uncles of Francis McKinley are recorded as having fled to America. President McKinley's great-grandfather, John McKinley had emigrated from Connagher c.1740, with his wife, Esther Wilson.

McKINNEY, Rev. James - James McKinney, born on 16 November 1759, hailed from Cookstown, Co. Tyrone. He attended the University of Glasgow, graduating in 1778, but continued his studies in medicine. In 1781, he was licenced by the Reformed Presbytery in 1783. After a few months McKinney was ordained at Kirkhills and started to preach in north Antrim to the covenanting community. An entry extract from the diary of Samuel Barr shows how he was held in high esteem by not only his parishioners but further afield.

"June 6, 1790, I went to hear Mr. McKenny preach, and to take my farewell of him in Ireland, for I do not expect to hear him preach again. The men of this sect are the best preachers in the land and they are the best practical Christians. They speak the truth in seacon and out of season."

McKinney married **Mary Mitchell** in 1784 and together they had eight children. In 1792, the Covenanting ministers, William Stavely, William Gamble and William Gibson re-established the Reformed Presbytery. Tradition states that after a rousing speech called the *"Rights of God"* at Balinaboob, McKinney gained the attention of the authorities, who viewed him with suspicion. In 1793, he was forced to emigrate via Ballykelly on the back of a follower to stay dry. With his family to the United States and travelled throughout the U.S. eastern states preaching the Gospel and antislavery. He was responsible for the re-organising of the Reformed Church in

America, when Rev. Gibson was forced to emigrate in 1797, he had a solid alley in his mission. He was also a noted abolitionist. In 1798, McKinney settled in Duanesburgh and Galway, New York, accepting their ministerial call. He died in Rocky Creek in South Carolina on 16 September 1803.

McKITTRICK, James – (1773 –
1848) McKittrick, a United Irishman from Gillnahirk Parish, Newtownards in Co. Down, was tried and sentenced to fourteen years transportation, however this was commuted to self-exile to America. He briefly settled in New York with relations by marriage, David and Andrew Bryson. McKittrick would return to Co. Down, establishing a drapery. He died in 1848 and is remembered at Bangor Abbey Graveyard.

McLELLAND, William – McLelland, the son of a wealthy farmer, led the contingent of United Irishmen from the Islandmagee area in south-east Antrim. He mustered his men at a place called Knowehead Brea and made his way to the village of Ballycarry, where he mustered his men behind James Orr's column of insurgents. Folklore states that they arrived too late for battle and only seen the heights of Donegore Hill, after Antrim was retaken. In the days succeeding the Antrim Rebellion, McLelland fled to the United States, but returned to Ireland within a decade, becoming a yeoman and a successful smuggler.

McMAHON, Bernard – McMahon was born in 1775. Details of his Irish background are quite scarce. It is recorded that he left Ireland due to the

political turmoil in 1796, and settled in Philadelphia, where he was briefly employed by William Duane at the pro-Jeffersonian *Aurora* newspaper. A gardener by profession, McMahon would establish himself by importing various seeds not already embraced by the Americans. In 1802, he published the *"Catalogue of Garden Grass, Herb, Flower, Tree and Shrub Seeds & Flower seeds etc,"* of the various herbage that he dealt with. McMahon became employed as a horticulturalist advisor to President Thomas Jefferson and was influential in the garden designs at Jefferson's Monticello estate. Jefferson entrusted McMahon to carefully nurse the seeds brought back from the Lewis and Clark expedition. McMahon died on 18 September 1816. In his honour, a west-coast broadleaf evergreen was formally granted the name *Mahonia* in recognition of McMahon's botanical skills.

McNEILLY, John & Family – John McNeilly (1739-1832) was a patriarch of a large Covenanter family from Rathfriland, Co. Down. During the Rebellion, his eldest son, Robert, served with the Down insurgency and attempted to escape to America but was captured. His family, believing Robert to be safe in America emigrated to join him, not knowing he was incarcerated in an Irish prison. The family settled in Bucks County, Pennsylvania, where John became postmaster of Plumstead in 1805. John McNeilly died on 18 March 1832 and was interred in the Old Covenantor Churchyard in Locust Grove, Philadelphia. His remains were later removed to Philadelphia's Woodlands Cemetery.

McNEILLY, Robert – Robert McNeilly was son of John McNeilly and Rachel Bingham. When the Rebellion was crushed Robert attempted to escape from Ireland by stowing aboard an American bound vessel, but was caught and suffered three years imprisonment, with no contact from his parents. Three years later, Robert returned to Rathfriland to find his family had all emigrated. He then travelled to America to join them.

McNISH, Rev. John – John McNish, also recorded as McNiece, was born in Belfast in 1772. Having graduated in theology from Glasgow University, McNish returned home in the mid-1790s and was sent on ministerial trials to Templepatrick Presbyterian Church and later at Clough in Co. Antrim. It appears that some sections of the community disagreed with McNish's sermons, however he was eventually ordained as minister of Clough. McNish clearly had joined the United Irishmen, as he led a column of insurgents from Clough to Ballymena on 7 June 1798. It's unclear if he was arrested immediately after the collapse of Rebellion or if he was court-martialled, but it seems he was aboard the *Peggy* in May 1799, destined to reside in America as an exile. Upon settling in America, McNish immediately started to preach. He led a ministry around a number of churches and in 1815 he was released of his ministry duties to be a full-time teacher at North Salem Academy. He died in 1839 and was interred at Colonial Cemetery, Fulton County (NY). Thanks to Gareth McCullough.

McNUTT, James – James McNutt is mentioned in a biography of his son, J.M. McNutt, who was a lumber dealer based in Hustonville, Illinois. J.M. was born in York County, Pennsylvania in July 1798, the son of James and Nancy *née* Yates, who had fled Ireland as exiles.

McNUTT, James – McNutt, born in 1771, emigrated from Ireland in July 1798, arriving in the United States in September. He settled in Indiana County, Pennsylvania, where he married Sarah Armitage. Together, they had a large family, who they reared on their farm. McNutt died in 1841 and was interred at a family plot in Brush Valley, Indiana County.

McPOLIN, Daniel & Hugh – The McPolin brothers, Daniel and Hugh, were masons, who hailed from Rostrevor, Co. Down. Having participated as insurgents during the 1798 Rebellion, they were tried at Newry, Co. Down, on 10 July 1798 and sentenced to be transported for life, however, they were allowed to settle their affairs and emigrate to the United States.

McWILLIAMS, Daniel – McWilliams, a native of Ballynascreen Co. Derry, was involved in the 1798 Rebellion, fleeing to Philadelphia where he established a store.

MERRICK, Dominick – Merrick was born in 1790 at Ballindine, Co. Mayo. His family had connections to the United Irish Rebellion and as a result of their involvement had their property confiscated ultimately meaning they had to flee to America. The family settled in Little York, Canada.

MILES, "Rev". John – John Miles was a probationer at the Presbyterian Church of Moneyrea in Co. Down. It seems that he was only months away from becoming a bonified Presbyterian minister until the Rebellion took hold. He was a Colonel-Commander in the United Irishmen and was arrested after the Battle of Ballynahinch and held prisoner for a period before being granted permission to exile to the United States. On 3 May 1799, Rev. Miles sailed aboard the *Peggy*, but it seems Miles had hoped to go to France to continue the struggle and was unimpressed with John Caldwell, who ordered that the ship remain on course for America. The Presbyterian Synod of June 1799 would prevent Miles from preaching. It is unknown at present what happened to John in America. It is certainly possible like many he became a minister in his own right.

MILLIKEN, Israel – Milliken, a Belfast Presbyterian bookseller and a United Irishman, was conveyed to Kilmainham Gaol on 1 May 1797 on charges of treasonable practices (*Kilmainham Gaol record pictured*). He was not released until January 1801. During his incarceration, an acquaintance of Milliken, Sampson Clarke, petitioned the Lord Lieutenant on his behalf, citing that Milliken was hoping to sail to America. It is unknown if he actually sailed to America as evidence highlights that Milliken founded the Belfast City Baths in 1805. In 1834, he co-financed a watch-tower that was constructed over the Burial Ground in Shankill, which prevented body-snatchers from carrying out their vile acts. When the United Irish historian, R.R. Madden was compiling the biographical details of northern United Irishmen, he was graciously assisted by Milliken. Having established a large wealth through various business ventures, Milliken would die at his Peter's Hill residence on 9 January 1857, aged eighty-six years. He was interred at Shankill Burial Ground, Belfast.

MOFFETT, Francis – Within the publication, *"The History of Montana,"* there mentions within a short biography of pioneer, Mary Bedford, that her Irish parents had fled to the United States, because of her father's participation in the Rebellion of 1798. The Moffett family, who were Protestant in their faith, settled in Ohio where they spent the rest of their lives farming.

MOLYNEAUX, Samuel - Samuel Molyneaux (1759-1823) emigrated from Killead, Co. Antrim to Mountpleasant in Kentucky. It is unknown if he was an active participant during the Rebellion and the only evidence that we have to substantiate a possibility of him being an exile is the year in which he left and his obituary, which stated that Molyneaux had been an *"enthusiastic friend of freedom"*. The Molyneaux family continued to reside at Killead and one of its noted descendants was James Henry Molyneaux (*pictured*), Baron Molyneaux of Killead, KBE, PC, who was leader of the Ulster Unionist Party (1979-1995).

186

MONKS, Thomas – Thomas Monks, a note forger, is said to have been deeply concerned in the United Irish movement who, when circumstances made it convenient, became a spy and an informer. His evidence resulted in the transportation of former associates. Living under threat from retribution, Monks escaped aboard a privateer ship as a deckhand.

MONTGOMERY, Moses – Having participated in the Rebellion, Montgomery fled to the United States, settling in Columbia in Lancaster County, Pennsylvania, where he built a tavern on the north side of Locust Street. At the outbreak of the War of 1812, Montgomery raised a company of volunteers.

MONTGOMERY, William – William Montgomery, a native of Aughnacloy, Co. Tyrone, was born into a Presbyterian farming background in 1776. Having participated in the 1798 Rebellion, he fled to America. Montgomery is recorded in the publication, *"Montgomery's of Hardin County Kentucky"*, which supplies detail about him residing in Baltimore, Maryland, for two years, before relocating to the frontier state of Kentucky, entering into merchandising in Hardin County. In July 1807, he married Virginian native, Elizabeth Withers. William Montgomery died on 4 March 1831 and was buried at Fort Knox in Kentucky.

A grandson, U.S. Congressman, Alexander Brooks Montgomery, *(pictured)* graduated from Georgetown College in 1859; from Louisville Law School in 1861 and engaged in agricultural pursuits in Hardin County, Kentucky, (1861-70). Montgomery was admitted to bar in 1870, and practiced law in Elizabethtown, Kentucky, before becoming judge of Hardin County (1870-74). Between 1877 and 1881, Montgomery served as a member of the Kentucky State Senate. In 1887, he was elected as a Democrat to the Fiftieth Congress and to the next three succeeding Congresses, serving until 1895. An unsuccessful candidate for re-election, he was appointed a member of the Dawes Indian Commission to reach a treaty with the Five Civilized Tribes (1895-98).

His brother, Judge James Montgomery (1840-1919) of Elizabethtown, Kentucky. In late 1862, he entered the Confederate Army, joining the command of General John H.

Morgan and remained in the army until the close of the war. Having followed the fortunes and misfortunes of the Southern Confederacy to the end, Mr. Montgomery returned home and in 1865 was admitted to the bar and began the practice of law at Elizabethtown. He was appointed to fill a vacancy in the office of County Attorney of Hardin county, and in 1867 was elected to a four-year term in that office. For approximately half a century he was a prominent lawyer of the local bar and became attorney for the Louisville and Nashville Railroad Company, which he also served at one time as a director. He left behind a large military family and his children filling some of the most prominent rolls within the military.

MOORE, John – John Moore, from Limavady, Co. Derry, was implicated in the 1798 Rebellion and was imprisoned in Belfast. It is unknown exactly where he operated with the insurgency. His parents, Thomas and Mary Moore, petitioned the government via their landlord, Lord and Lady Connolly, to have his sentence of transportation to New South Wales reduced to perpetual banishment to America. It is unknown where exactly Moore ended up. There is no record of him being sent to New South Wales although a possible relation, Tristram Moore (1767-1839) of Carrowreagh, near Limavady, was sent there aboard the *Atlas II* in 1802.

MOORE, Robert – In 1797, the Crown authorities moved against the the United Irish leaders that remained in the City of Londonderry, arresting Robert Moore of Molenan, a wealthy ironmonger. Moore was of the highest respectability who had been involved in regional politics for over a generation and had been a Volunteer officer in the 1780s; a founding member of the chamber of commerce and a governor of the city poor house and infirmary. He had also represented his congregation of First Derry at the Presbyterian Synod a number of times. Moore was charged with treason and lodged at the City Gaol. Two months later the renowned United Irish barrister, John Philpot Curran, succeeded in gaining his freedom. By mid-1798, the rebel movement across Derry was in tatters. On 2 November 1798, Derry Corporation ordered that Henry Grattan, the Patriot Party M.P. "*be disenfranchised from all the privileges of this city*" as he had been "*concerned in bringing about the Rebellion*". On the same grounds, the meeting also disenfranchised Robert Moore, William McClintock, Joseph Orr and Christopher Hardy. Most of these men had already exiled from Ireland. In September 1798, Moore had already left for America, having settled in Baltimore, Maryland, and became involved in the *Benevolent Hibernian Society of Baltimore*, alongside Dr. John White Campbell. Moore died in Baltimore in June 1807, at the age of 55 years.

MOORE, Thomas – Thomas Moore was a merchant from Coleraine, Co. Derry, who left Ireland prior to the 1798 Rebellion due to his membership of the United Irishmen, settling in Philadelphia.

MORRES, Hervey – Morres was born on
7 March 1767 to Matthew Montmorency Morres and Margaret Magan, at Rathailean Castle, in Co. Tipperary. His background was prestigious, but Morres was born into a low middle-class Catholic family. In 1782, Morres enlisted as a cadet in the Liégeois regiment of Vierzet in the Austrian army, where he distinguished himself at the Siege of Belgrade in 1788. Having served in Lacy's Regiment, Morres would become an officer in Count Kavanagh's regiment of cuirassiers and fought under Prince Hohenlohe and General Wurmser in the wars against the infant French Republic. Noted as a courageous officer, Morres was promoted to aide-de-camp to Prince Charles

of Fürstenberg. In September 1795, Morres married Louise de Helmstadt, and decided to return to Ireland.

Upon settling at Knockalton in Co. Tipperary, Morres corresponded with the Viceroy, Earl Camden, regarding the state of the country and advising how to combat invasion from France. In 1796, he was commissioned as aide-de-camp to General Ralph Dundas, however, he resigned by the time of the Bantry Bay episode. Morres became a member of the United Irishmen and was given rank as commander of the Tipperary United Irishmen before rising to Adjutant-

General of Munster. When the United Irish leadership were rounded up, Morres fled to the midlands, where it is not known what participation he played at the time of the Humbert expedition. Fearing arrest, Morres fled to Hamburg, arriving there on 7 November 1798. He was referred to meet Lady Pamela Fitzgerald, who used her influence to procure a passport into France for Morres, however, it failed. When Napper Tandy and William Corbett arrived in Hamburg after their failed expedition to Ireland, they were arrested alongside Morres. Held in dire conditions, Morres' morale declined. His wife died whilst he was in German custody, and he was eager to be reunited with a lock of her hair that he kept within his waistcoat, taken by the authorities during his arrest. In September 1799, Morres was extradited back to Britain and further to Ireland to stand trial. This trial collapsed on many errors relating to his arrest and he was bailed on 10 December 1801. Morres travelled to France and thanked

Napoleon Bonaparte for his influence in securing his release. A freeman, Morres would return to Ireland and settle in Malahide, Dublin. He played no known role in the Emmet uprising of 1803, however, the authorities did watch his movements. Morres married Helen Esmonde, the widow of Dr. John Esmonde of Osbertstown, the United Irish leader who was executed during the 1798 Rebellion. In 1811, he was invited by France to take a commission in the French Army, an invitation he accepted. Morres bid his final farewells to Ireland and emigrated to France, where he received a colonelcy and a staff role under General Augereau. After the defeat of Napoleon, Morres unsuccessfully attempted to win a commission in the British Army, however, he was awarded French citizenship. On 25 June 1817, he was awarded a Knighthood of St. Louis and retired on half-pay in France, where he researched his renowned genealogy and published the first antiquarian research of round towers of Ireland. Hervey Morres died on 9 May 1839 at Saint-Germain-en-Laye.

MORRISON, John – Morrison is simply recorded as having fled to the United States *"in company with a brother of the martyred Emmett."* This clearly refers to Thomas Addis Emmet, however Emmet emigrated to America from France in late 1804, having not resided at liberty in Ireland since the Spring of 1798. Morrison might have been residing in France before he chose to emigrate to the United States. The *Boston Semi-Weekly Advertiser* stated in his obituary that Morrison had acquired a vast fortune enterprising dry goods in his partnership merchant firm, *Kelly & Morrison*. He retired in the late 1820s and delved into prayer and devotion at Dr. Phillip's Church on Wall Street. He died after a long illness on 24 June 1843, aged 67 years. He was interred close to the Emmet family vault at Marble Cemetery in Manhattan. His daughter married Dr. Abraham Thew Hunter, a notable New York physician.

MORRISON, Robert- 1782-1863

Morrison was the great-great grandfather of Marion Morrison or John Wayne, the Hollywood star. It has been the subject of dispute if Robert Morrison was in fact a United Irishman, who at only 16 years of age and with his father deceased, he may have not been in a position to have taken part in the insurrection. Randalstown claim him as one of their own and local legend says the family belonged to Connor Presbyterian Church congregation. Morrison emigrated to New York between 1799 and 1800, with his mother. One such  folk story claims that a warrant had been issued for Robert's arrest due to his participation with the insurgency; however, this has been unsubstantiated. John

Wayne famously referred to himself as *"just a Scotch Irish boy"*. *Photo John Wayne (The Longest Day, 1962) & Connor CoI*

MULHALL, Michael, Rev. - Mulhall was a Dominican priest, based at Dublin's Denmark Street seminary, who was involved in the Society of United Irishmen. He eventually fled to New York.

MUNNELLY, Rev Fr. Tom – Fr. Tom Munnelly was a parish priest who got caught up in the 1798 rebellion. He fled to America. Munnelly was administrator of the Parish of the Backs in Co. Mayo. He supported the French captain, Truc, during the Franco-Irish occupation of Killala, in north Mayo. He went on the run after the suppression of the rebellion and was captured in November 1799. He was then sent to New Geneva where he faced transportation but escaped to the United States.

MURPHY, Andrew – Andrew Murphy was born at Kilmartin, Co. Wexford in 1780. His 1843 obituary in the *Pittsfield Sun* supplies us with much detail given towards his part in the horrors of 1798. When the conflict was at an end he fled to the United States. However, upon approaching the American coastline at Sandy Hook, his ship was boarded by a British frigate and Andrew, being a subject of the Crown, was taken prisoner and impressed into the Royal Navy. These maritime incursions by the Royal Navy occurred quite often until the War of 1812. In June 1806, upon seeing an opportunity to escape from his ship, Murphy jumped overboard during a storm and swam the short distance to the coast of Canada. Here, he found refuge for a short period at Halifax in Nova Scotia before eventually made his way to the United States. He settled in Allegheny County on a farm in Lower St. Clair Township. In 1813, he married Sarah Seymour Mead and together they had a number of children, including James Redmond Murphy. Murphy was described in his obituary as one of the most industrious, energetic and honest citizens in the country. Andrew Murphy

died on 22 May 1843 and was buried in St Phillip's Roman Catholic Cemetery in Crafton, Pennsylvania.

MURPHY, James – James Murphy was a native of Co. Wexford and is believed to have played a significant role in the United Irish uprising at St. John's in Newfoundland in April 1800. Murphy was described by Colonel John Skerrett, the commander of the St. John's garrison and veteran of the Durham Fencibles defence during the Battle of Arklow, as *"the wretch James Murphy, a villain and an artful bigot."* Murphy, it seems, was to blame for the converting of many Newfoundland Militia to become United Irishmen. Murphy's brother, Dennis Murphy, emigrated to Port Hood in Nova Scotia in 1802, and was joined by his agitating brother in 1804. *The History of Inverness County*, claims that Murphy had been *"a soldier in the Irish Rebellion of 1798, and was also on a warship for several years following that time,"* which signifies that he possibly had been impressed into the Royal Navy and then demobbed after the Treaty of Amiens in 1802. James Murphy married Catherine MacDonald and together they had a large family in Nova Scotia, in which their descendants are still evident today, and well represented at the Holy Cross Cemetery. Murphy died by drowning on 16 September 1816.

MURPHY, John '*Captain Murphy*' – A native of Co. Louth, John Murphy was a seafarer. On 22 August 1798, when General Jean Humbert's force anchored at Kilcummin Strand in Killala Bay, Co. Mayo, he ordered a despatch to be sent to the Directory in Paris, exclaiming that he had landed in Ireland. John Murphy accepted the task and sailed immediately to France. Miles Byrne described Murphy within his memoirs:

"On landing, Murphy instantly posted to Paris to present General Humbert's despatches to the French Government, and the reception he met with the gracious and flattering indeed to an Irish heart. The Directory instantly presented him with pistols of honour…Captain Murphy was then put at the disposition of the Minister of the Marine."

Murphy remained in France and was eventually posted as Grand Pilot at the port of Brest, holding a rank of captain. After the fall of Napoleon and the re-establishment of the Bourbon regime, Murphy was put on half pay, with a meagre pension of 800 francs per year. Miles Byrne's memoirs gives us more insight into Murphy's background, claiming he had a wife and six children in Rush in north Co. Dublin, who were dependent of Murphy's success in France. He was obliged to seek employment from merchants at Nantes. This new employment saw Murphy commanding merchant ships between France and Patagonia in South America. Byrne further recalled seeing Murphy at the port of Nantes in 1835, describing him as quite broken down; a sad comparison compared to when he first became acquainted with Murphy in 1803, in which he recalled Murphy, then aged fifty, being athletic and well proportioned.

MURPHY, Matthew – It is recorded in *Erin's Sons: Irish Arrivals in Atlantic Canada, 1761-1853*, that on 4 January 1861, Matthew Murphy, who had reputedly fled Ireland after his participation at the battles of Ross and Vinegar Hill, died at St. John's, Newfoundland, aged 94 years. Murphy had been employed as a storekeeper by Pat Morris for over thirty years.

MURPHY, William – Murphy was obliged to leave Dublin in 1798, and became a resident of New York City for several years. He later returned to Ireland and prospered in business.

MURRAY, James – Murray, a butcher from Warrenpoint, Co. Down, was tried by court-martial at Newry on 26 July 1798, on charges of having participated as an insurgent during the 1798 Rebellion. It was agreed that he would enter into recognisances to sail to America.

MURRAY, Paul – Murray was born at Kilmurry, near Newtownmountkennedy, Co. Wicklow, in 1768 to Thomas Murray and Mary McCarthy. Miles Byrne described Murray in an episode of the 1798 Rebellion in his memoirs:

*"**Mr. Paul Murray, from near the town of Wicklow arrived here** (The insurgent camp at Baravore in Glenmalure, Co. Wicklow) one night accompanied by a number of men from his neighbourhood. I had to wait on him in the morning respecting prisoners who were escorted to the glen by his party. I found him at Pierce Harney's; he was lying on a bed in his clothes, well dressed, with new topped boots, etc, all which formed a singular contrast with our tattered, worn out coats, but poor fellow, he was just escaping from his hiding place, to take the field for the first time. I never saw Paul Murray before this morning. I little thought that we should become afterwards so well acquainted in a foreign land. One day in 1803 coming out of the London Coffee House, Rue Jacob, at Paris, I saw a man dressed in a snuff-coloured coat and top boots; on coming near, I said to the person who was with me how like that man is to poor Paul Murray whom I met in the Wicklow Mountains in '98. But Murray was arrested in Dublin by Major Sirr, and of course was transported, so it cannot be him. But it was the very same P. Murray and we soon recognised each other and spoke of our adventures in the Wicklow Mountains. I introduced him next day to Mr. Thomas Addis Emmet who obtained a commission for*

him in the Irish Legion at its formation, and we made several campaigns in Spain and Portugal in the same battalions. He retired afterwards on a pension and died at Dunkirk at an advanced age. There never was a truer or better friend and comrade than Paul Murray of Kilmurry, near Wicklow."

O'Hara's Pedigree's records that Murray reached the rank of Captain in the Irish Legion by 1809. Murray died at the French port town of Dunkerque in 1853.

NEILSON, Samuel – *The Jacobin*

Samuel Neilson, one of the founding fathers of Irish Republicanism, was born on 17 September 1762 at Ballyrogan, Co. Down, to Rev. Alexander Neilson and Agnes Carson. After Neilson completed his basic education, he travelled to Belfast, where he served an apprenticeship under his brother, John Neilson, a successful woollen-draper. In September 1785, Neilson married Nancy Bryson, daughter of a wealthy Belfast merchant, and established his own business, the Belfast Woollen Warehouse in High Street, which, within five years, was one of the most successful warehouses in Belfast, supplying the Neilson Family with great financial comforts. Having an interest in politics, Neilson would publicly support the liberal, Robert Stewart, later Lord Castlereagh, during his campaign to be Member of Parliament for Co. Down. Neilson most probably later regretted his campaigning and support for Castlereagh, considering he would become ruthless during the crackdown upon the United Irishmen in the late 1790s, during his tenure as Chief Secretary of Ireland. Neilson had become a member of the liberal Northern Whig Club and the 1st Belfast Volunteer Company. In late 1789, Neilson became fascinated with the events taking place in France. The idea of the Third Estate holding the reins of power enthused him.

Being a frequent attendee of the Third Presbyterian Church on Belfast's Rosemary Street, Neilson became close with Belfast businessman, Henry Joy McCracken and the Simms Brothers, William and Robert, noting that they shared his enlightened political views. In October 1791, the inaugural meeting of the Belfast Society of United Irishmen was held, with some of Belfast's liberals in attendance, including William Drennan, Thomas Russell and Theobald Wolfe Tone, who was so encapsulated by the meeting that he returned to Dublin and formed a branch of the organisation there. The society welcomed all shades of liberalism, including radical elements and parliamentary progressives. They viewed the newly published and highly controversial '*Rights of Man*' by Thomas

Paine as their society's fundamental political theories. Neilson's zealous liberal outlook and his Francophilia earned him the nickname, '*The Jacobin*,' from Wolfe Tone. With Neilson editing and financing the initiative, the *Northern Star* was officially inaugurated on 4 January 1792, causing much excitement in Belfast. His passion towards the initiative, which grew to a subscription of nearly 4000 readers, overwhelmed the fact that it nearly bankrupted him. The paper contained not only foreign and domestic news from a liberal viewpoint but was the organ of the United Irishmen. The government set about quashing the newspaper and rounded up the various shareholders, including Neilson with libel charges, placing financial pressure on Neilson. Although acquitted, he pressed on. In June 1795, with the Society of United Irishmen already declared illegal, Neilson, Thomas Russell, Wolfe Tone and Henry Joy McCracken ascended to McArt's Fort on the summit of Belfast's Cave Hill and swore

"never to desist in our efforts until we had subverted the authority of England over our country, and asserted our independence."

In the autumn of 1796, with habeas corpus suspended, the authorities focused on bringing down Neilson and his newspaper. On 16 September 1796, Neilson was arrested and brought to the newly constructed Kilmainham Gaol in Dublin. He would remain there until early 1798, without trial. During his incarceration, the *Northern Star* was targeted during the Castle's crackdown on the United Irishmen in Ulster. In May 1797, the offices and printing press were intentionally smashed by the Monaghan Militia, effectively ending the *Northern Star*. Upon his release, Neilson's health started to falter; his wealth was nearly diminished and he had turned to alcohol, relying on fellow United man, John Sweetman, for financial subsistence. Neilson would become a militant United Irishman alongside Lord Edward Fitzgerald and was deeply involved in organising the insurrection.

On 19 May 1798, Fitzgerald was arrested in Dublin, however, Samuel Neilson was for a long time, blamed for the arrest. He was later accused by some of his contemporaries as having informed the Castle of Fitzgerald's whereabouts, whilst some historians effectively blamed the drunk Neilson for foolishly leaving the door of the safehouse open, having visited Fitzgerald only an hour beforehand. The arrest of Lord Edward Fitzgerald was indeed the result of informers, but not the fault of Samuel Neilson. With the Leinster Directory and the main instigators of the planned insurrection detained, Samuel Neilson was the last prominent leader still active.

On the evening of 23 May 1798, Neilson, having given his orders to the local Dublin leaders to take up their positions, made his way to the barley fields of Smithfield to join a party of insurgents close to Newgate Gaol, with the mission to break out Fitzgerald. Again, history attacks the legacy of Neilson. Accounts claim him to have approached Newgate whilst heavily inebriated, allowing himself to be recognised and arrested. On 25 June 1798, Neilson and the other remaining United Irish leaders were brought before a Special Commission. Neilson, who was financially broke, was represented for free by John Philpot Curran. He helped broker a deal, known as the Kilmainham Treaty, between the Government and the United Irish State Prisoners, which would see all of the State Prisoners banished from Ireland if they supplied all information about the mechanisms of the United Irish movement. The Government did not fulfil their part of the agreement and the State Prisoners remained in confinement. On 19 March 1799, they were sent to Fort George in Scotland, where they would remain until July 1802, after Britain and France had ceased hostilities. Upon release, Neilson, whose health was suffering, sailed to Hamburg. Whilst the remaining United Irishmen aimed to spend their time on the continent, Neilson yearned to see his family and start a new life in the United States. On 6 August 1802, Neilson illegally sailed for Ireland aboard the *Providence*, with fellow exile, Anthony McCann. He remained in Ireland until December 1802, organising his affairs, before sailing to New York. Hoping

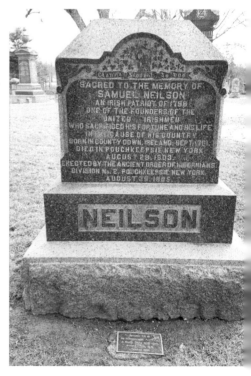

to re-establish the *Northern Star* and bring his family to America, Neilson settled himself in New York City. On 28 August 1803, whilst boating on the Hudson River, Neilson fell ill. On the following day, Samuel Neilson died suddenly as a result of yellow fever and was interred at Poughkeepsie Rural Burial Ground.

✦

The NEILSON BROTHERS *of Ballycarry, Co. Antrim*

NEILSON, Samuel – The story of the Neilson brothers of Ballycarry, Co. Antrim (often referred to as Nelson) include some of the most harrowing descriptions to befall upon any family during the 1798 Rebellion. The night following the Battle of Antrim, two Neilson brothers, Samuel and John, were arrested and taken to Carrickfergus to be tried by court-martial. They were sentenced to be transported abroad to the West Indies to serve in His Majesty's forces. Their younger brother, William Neilson, or Willie Nelson of Ballycarry, a lad of sixteen years, was caught in possession of a stolen horse and was hanged close to the homestead. Their mother, a widow, had basically lost three of her sons as a result of the insurrection, which resulted in her becoming deranged.

Whilst sailing to the West Indies, Samuel Neilson died from the fever. Today, the Neilson/Nelson family are remembered in Ballycarry, with the naming of a close. Many thanks to David Hume for the photograph.

NEILSON, John – John Neilson was born c.1770 at Ballycarry, Co. Antrim. He served an apprenticeship in Belfast as an architect but his

involvement as a United Irishman in the 1798 Rebellion would have bittersweet results that would affect both his family and his profession. His involvement in the Antrim Rebellion resulted in his court-martial sentence to serve His Majesty's forces in the inhospitable West Indies, which led to an estrangement from his wife. His brother, Samuel, also received the same fate but unfortunately died on the voyage to Martinique. His youngest brother, William, would be executed close to the family homestead, leaving only a young sister to care for their mother who mentally suffered as a result. John Neilson managed to escape from the West Indies to Philadelphia, becoming a naturalised citizen in September 1804. Having relocated to Virginia, Neilson would become employed by President Thomas Jefferson as one of his chief-architects for the Monticello, a unique mansion that is chiefly associated with the legacy of Jefferson, and is printed on the rear of an American nickel coin. Neilson also participated in the design of the University of Virginia and President James Madison's Montpelier mansion. Neilson died at Refuge, near Keene, Virginia, on 24 June 1827 and was interred in Maplewood Cemetery in Charlottesburg, where a recently erected memorial recognises not only American achievements but his membership of the United Irishmen. Interestingly, Neilson had desired in his will that his library collection be left to Mary Ann McCracken of Belfast.

NEVIN, John-

John Nevin of Kilmoyle was a member of the Secessionist Presbyterian Church at Ballywatt, near Coleraine, Co. Derry. He was a local Captain of the Ballyrashane United Irishmen, and at a meeting he was betrayed by an informer, Nathaniel Chesnutt, and was imprisoned at Carrickfergus Gaol. Nevin was released before June 1798 and took a leading role in the 1798 Rebellion with Peter Lyle. He manged to escape Ballymena with Lyle and sought refuge at the Moore household. In the middle of the night, both fugitives awakened to find Moore had fled and the doors bolted shut. In a panic they escaped out a window to safety. From there

some narratives change. One of the popular stories is that Nevin was smuggled in a barrel to Moville, Co. Donegal, to a ship bound for Charleston. In America, Nevin settled in Knoxville, Tennessee, where he opened a dry goods store which allowed him to trade with the Indians. He died in Knoxville on 19 May 1806. A Nevin relative commissioned a set of beautiful, earthenware jugs with the following inscription:

"To the memory of John Nevin of Killmoyle, who was by the foes of Reform Banish'd from his Native home in June 1798. He lived in the state of Exile 7 years, 11 months, 8 days & departed this life in Knoxfield (sic), Tennisee ye 19th of May 1806. Much lamented by his Friends Acquaintances & Friends to their Country".

These two Nevin commemorative jugs are on permanent display at Ballymoney Museum, Co. Antrim.

NEVIN, Robert – Robert Nevin was court-martial' Co. Down and was permitted to transport himself to America.

NIXON, Jacob, Dr. - On 15 August 1801, the following letter composed by Cavan native, Jacob Nixon to the newly elected U.S. President, Thomas Jefferson.

"Sir,
As a total stranger to you an apology is necessary, for intruding with this letter, this I hope you will excuse when I mention I am an Irish Exile. Henry Jackson who probably has the happiness of your acquaintance, formerly of Dublin is my freind, & formerly in Coercisien with me.—
I have been bred a Surgeon, If you will, so as its not disagreeable to you, to allow me, either, in Army, or Navy, the same situation I will not do less than render much service
It wd. be wrong to say anything without trial.—I am with very good wish. Yr. truly Obt Servant
Jacob Nixon"

Jacob Nixon, a native of Cootehill, Co. Cavan, moved to Dublin to study chemistry. He later established an apothecary in Lisburn before removing to Belfast. Nixon became a valued member of the United Irishmen and was arrested in 1797 and sent to Kilmainham Gaol. After the Rebellion, he like many fled to the United States and settled in Norfolk Virginia. Jacob Nixon passed away in 1826 and was buried at Fairfax Cemetery, Loudoun County, Virginia.

O'BRIEN, Daniel – The *Democratic Advocate* (29 January 1881) recorded the death of Daniel O'Brien, at an advanced age: **"Daniel O'Brien, familiarly known at Scranton, Pennsylvania, died in the poorhouse there on Saturday (22 January 1881), at the age of 111. He had a remarkable memory, and told of his personal experiences in the Irish Rebellion of 1798. He was one of the pioneer settlers of Scranton, and until 1870 was a hard worker as a drayman."**

O'BRIEN, William – William O'Brien was born in 1768 into the O'Brien family, the Earls of Inchiquin and direct descendants of Brian Boru. It

.blished that O'Brien emigrated to the United States as a result of the 1798 rebellion, with his lands and titles confiscated from him by the British and reputedly handed over to the Protestant branch of the O'Brien family. O'Brien travelled to the U.S. aboard a ship, commanded by Captain John Stevens. He would later marry Stevens' half-sister, Eliza West, in New York's St. Peter's Church in 1810. At the time of this marriage Eliza was only fifteen years old and O'Brien at forty-two years. Despite the vast age difference, they are reported to have had a very good life together. He plied his trade as a merchant and became successful in the ship broker and insurance business based in New York. His obituary stated that no Irishman of any importance ever passed through the port of New York without passing through the residence of O'Brien's Broome Street residence. William O'Brien died on 31 August 1846 and was buried in the old St Patricks Cemetery at Mott & Prince Street, later moved to Calvary Cemetery in Brooklyn. O'Brien was survived by his two sons, William and John O'Brien. Both were engaged for many years in the Mechanics Bank, one as a book keeper and the other as a teller. They eventually left the bank and formed *W & J O'Brien* brokerage which was based at New York's Wall Street.

O'CONNOR, Arthur

O'CONNOR, Arthur - Arthur O'Connor was born at Connerville, near Bandon, Co. Cork, on 4 July 1763 to Roger Conner, a wealthy Protestant landowner, and Ann Longfield, a sister of Lord Longueville. The Conner Family had gained their status from generations of merchants, correct investments and marriages within the Protestant Ascendency. They appear to have been arrogant in the belief that they were the direct descendants of Ruairí Ua Conchobhar, the last High King of Ireland and this idea was certainly embraced by Arthur's eccentric brother and fellow United Irishman, Roger O'Connor. This idea encouraged both brothers to transition their surname from Conner to O'Connor, to legitimise their arrogant claim.

O'Connor was educated at Trinity College in Dublin, receiving his BA in 1782. He travelled to Britain and across the continent, where he embraced egalitarianism. Having become a lawyer, O'Connor returned to Ireland to practice, however, he immediately became immersed in politics. Influenced by many liberal relatives and friends, O'Connor was presented by Lord Longueville with a purchased common seat in the Irish House of Commons, representing the borough of Philipstown, King's County (Tullamore, Co. Offaly). O'Connor became noted for radical and outlandish speeches. He expressed his support to the French Revolution and in retaliation of Britain declaring war on France in 1793, he composed, '*The Measures*

ARTHUR O'CONNOR Esqr
Drawn from the Life in Maidston Jail

of Ministry to prevent a revolution are the certain means of bringing it on.' On 4 May 1795, O'Connor lost the support of his uncle when he publicly announced in the Commons that Roman Catholics should be granted the right to sit amongst them and denounced the parliamentary corruption gripped by the Protestant Ascendency. His politics saw him become a member of the United Irishmen in 1795. Along with Lord Edward Fitzgerald, O'Connor encouraged a more radical outline within the movement, which led to clashes with constitutional reformers like Thomas Addis Emmet, who disagreed with O'Connor's encouragement of open revolt and to instead wait for French assistance. O'Connor and Fitzgerald travelled to France in May 1796 to encourage such assistance.

His arrogant attitudes, claiming himself to be somewhat of an Irish General Washington, did not charm the French Directory, who continued to support Wolfe Tone. In February 1798, O'Connor was arrested at the English port town of Margate, whilst preparing an illegal journey to France. He was tried at Maidstone in what became a national sensation, with Westminster's Leader of the Opposition, Charles James Fox, openly defending O'Connor. Although acquitted, O'Connor would spend much of 1798 held within various prisons, disallowing him from supporting the insurgency. In 1799, he was sent with the other State Prisoners to Fort George in Scotland, where his arrogance once again set about antagonism with Thomas Addis Emmet, which nearly concluded in a duel. In 1802, the prisoners were released and the sour relationship was slightly mediated by fellow United Irishmen, who were successful in cancelling the duel.

O'Connor travelled to France, battling with Emmet for the position as the United Irishmen's sole representative with the Paris authorities. Bonaparte awarded O'Connor as a General within his Imperial Army. In 1807, having immersed himself into French society and the Napoleonic nobility, O'Connor married Eliza, the daughter of the Marquis of Condorcet. Arrogantly, O'Connor altered his surname to Condorcet-O'Connor.

Financially struggling and with little support from the O'Connor family, he borrowed large sums from another Irish exile in France, William Putnam McCabe. These repayments to McCabe eventually led to a law suit. O'Connor purchased a chateau at Le Bignon, in Loiret (*illustrated*). After the fall of Bonaparte and his ostracising by the restored Bourbon, O'Connor retired to a peaceful life at Le Bignon, where he wrote several political pamphlets and his unpublished memoirs. Arthur O'Connor died on 25 April 1852 and was interred within the family tomb on his estate.

O'CONOR, Charles –

Charles O'Conor was born in 1736 at Bellanagare, Co. Roscommon, to the antiquarian, Charles O'Conor and Catherine O'Hagan. The family held vast lands in Roscommon and were the direct descendants of the O'Conor royal clan, who had ruled Connacht during the medieval era. O'Conor, inherited the Mount Allen farm and eventually married Mary Dillon, who gave birth to two sons, Thomas and Denis O'Conor. Politically, O'Conor was a liberal and served in the Catholic Committee, which advocated for reform of the penal code against Roman Catholics. O'Conor would befriend the renowned Thomas Russell and Theobald Wolfe Tone. Whilst visiting Connacht in early 1792, Tone swore young Thomas O'Conor into the United Irishmen. It is unknown if Denis participated in such radical politics, but when the United Irishmen was driven underground, old O'Conor appears to have stepped back from politics. After the 1798 Rebellion, Thomas O'Conor fled to the United States with old Charles O'Conor following not long afterwards. In 1808, Charles O'Conor died at his son's large farm in rural New York.

O'CONOR, Thomas -
Thomas O'Conor was born on 1 September 1770 in Dublin to Charles O'Conor of Mount Allen and Mary Dillon. O'Conor was grandson of Charles O'Conor, a renowned antiquarian and co-founder of the Catholic Committee. Unlike Arthur O'Connor, this O'Conor clan claimed actual legitimacy to the O' Conor Don title, meaning they were the direct descendants of the Gaelic O'Conor royal line of Connacht. On 13 January 1792, Thomas O'Conor was personally sworn into the United Irishmen by Theobald Wolfe Tone. The O'Conor's would become instrumental in the organising of the United Irishmen in Connacht, however, they played a minute role during the Rebellion. Knowing he was a marked man, Thomas fled to the United States, settling in New York City in 1801. He married Margaret O'Connor, who gave birth to two children: Charles O'Conor and Eliza Margaret O'Conor. Interestingly, Thomas O'Conor partnered with William Kernan, a fellow exile, in purchasing over 40,000 acres in New York's Steuben County with the aim of

settling new Irish immigrants there. By June 1814, the venture had failed and with rural life not appealing anymore, O'Conor had returned to New York City and bought a large share of the popular New York newspaper of the Irish emigres, *The Shamrock* or *Hibernian Chronicle*, later becoming its sole owner and editor. The paper was vehemently anti-British and anti-Federalist in its rhetoric and helped rally New York's Irish population to defend New York during the War of 1812. O'Conor used his newspaper to attack Rufus King, the former US ambassador to Britain, who refused to grant asylum to the United Irish State Prisoners in 1798. The paper started to dwindle by 1817, forcing O'Conor to establish, *The Globe* newspaper. In 1816, he co-founded the *Shamrock Friendly Association* alongside William J. MacNeven and Thomas A. Emmet and dedicated the use of his office as a base for newly arrived Irish to find employment and to help them settle in New York. O'Conor would dedicate himself to various organisations throughout his later life, including service to various committees of the *Irish Emigrant Society* and the *Society of Friendly Sons of St. Patrick*. Thomas O'Conor died at Sands Point in New York on 9 February 1855 and was interred at St. Patrick's Old Cathedral Cemetery.

His son, Charles O'Conor (1804-1884), became a successful attorney, but is mostly remembered for his conservative politics, including his stance on slavery. O'Conor was particularly vocal against abolitionists and against any progress of women in society. He was the unsuccessful Democratic candidate for Lieutenant Governor of New York in 1848 and he also became a member of the *Directory of the Friends of Ireland*, a society that was organized in anticipation of a Rising in Ireland. In 1852, O'Conor endorsed Franklin Pierce as U.S. President, who in turn later rewarded him as U.S. Attorney for the Southern District of New York (1854-1855). In 1854, O'Conor married Mrs. Cornelia Livingston McCracken, however, they would have no children. After the American Civil War, O'Conor was

the senior counsel for Jefferson Davis, the former President of the Confederacy, who was charged for treason and, as special deputy Attorney-General for the

State of New York, O'Conor played a prominent role in the prosecution of William M. "*Boss*" Tweed and members of the Tweed Ring. In 1872, Charles O'Conor was nominated for President by the Straight-Out Democratic Party with Charles Francis Adams, the son of John Quincy Adams, as his running-mate. What was unique was that Charles O'Conor would become the first Roman Catholic to be nominated for the U.S. Presidency. The election was won by incumbent President Ulysses S. Grant of the Republican Party.

O'DUFFY, Denis — A native of Maghera, near Spancil Hill, Co. Clare, the story of O'Duffy is unique. The Schools' Folklore Commission collected a story about O'Duffy from Ballycar National School in the 1930's.

"He was a member of the Society of United Irishmen, and held a high rank. He used to be drilling men in Tyredagh at nightime. This did not long continue unknown to the authorities. Brown, a Captain of the yeomanry in Newgrove was rather liberal in his ideas and told O'Duffy to desist from his military activities, as his actions were known to the powers that be. When the Rebellion of '98 broke

out in Wexford, O'Duffy led his men from Clare to take part in the insurrection. They had to pass Bunratty Castle, which was then held by the British Military. O'Duffy and his men were attacked and scattered. Most of them reassembled and reached Wexford to take part in some minor engagements as the Rebellion was mostly over, when they arrived."

When the Rebellion collapsed, O'Duffy, knowing he was a wanted man, fled to France and eventually joined the Irish Legion. Some sources claim that he was killed in battle on the continent during the Napoleonic Wars, however, the above folklore states that he returned home to Co. Clare.

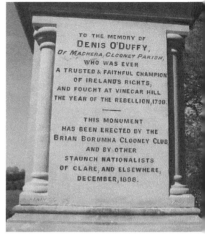

(Left) The Denis O'Duffy Memorial, Clooney, Co. Clare

O'FINN, Edmund –

O'Finn was born c.1767 in Co. Cork. In 1796, he joined the Cork Legion of Yeomanry, a guise used by many United Irishmen to learn and gain military experience. It has been speculated that O'Finn was a leading United Irishman and may have served on the Munster Directory. In January 1798, he fled from Ireland when a warrant of High Treason was issued against him. He was named on the Exile Bill, with the threat of execution if he returned to Ireland. O'Finn had travelled to London and became deeply involved in the relationship between the United Irishmen and their English ideological brethren, the London Corresponding Society. He was requested by Fr. Coigly to travel to France to interact with the United Irish leadership there. Whilst in France, O'Finn would support James Napper Tandy in his feud with Wolfe Tone and Edward Lewins, but he would not accompany Tandy on his expedition to Ireland in September 1798. O'Finn remained in France and financially struggle for several years. On December 29th 1801, whilst residing at No.1 rue de la Salpetrieres in Bordeaux, he composed a praising letter to Thomas Jefferson, the President of the United States:

"In the Number of those who unsuccesfully struggled for the Liberty of Ireland, my Name has the Honor of being enroled as a proscribed—& seeing our Hopes deferd, I have fixd here as a merchant in the general line of Comn. Business.

To my Countrymen, everywhere, your Character is well known as their Friend & Benefactor, and Citizen of the World. You will never be deceived in whatever favorable opinion you may entertain of us—

I am happy in the opportunity of forwarding some Papers to your Adress, as it procures me the means of offering my mite of respect and attachment.—

Any Command you may be disposed to send or commit to my Care, I shall receive as a particular Honor.— EDMD. O'FINN
formerly of Cork

O'Finn joined the French Army and became a colonel in the Lanciers de Bergh, serving in the Peninsular War. On September 25th 1811, whilst leading a reconnaissance party along the banks of the Azava River, near Ciudad Rodrigo, they were surrounded by a unit of British cavalry. O'Finn, deciding to cover his soldier's retreat was surrounded and killed. One of the British officers, a native of Cork, recognised the remains of O'Finn as those of an acquaintance of his youth and ordered that he buried with dignity.

O'HARA, Kean

— We found conflict of facts in the story of the O'Hara's of Coolaney, Co. Sligo, who settled in Kentucky. The *Irish Pioneers in Kentucky* highlights in some detail that Kean O'Hara emigrated to the United States with his brother, James O'Hara, and his father, as a result of the 1798 Rebellion however his headstone at Saint Francis Cemetery in Scott County (KY) records the following: *"Kean O'Hara, born in Ireland Nov 24. 1768. Emigrated to America in 1793. A citizen of Kentucky in 1798. Married in 1800. Died in Franklin Co. Ky. Dec 23. 1851."* O'Hara would become a schoolteacher, serving the districts of Danville, Woodford and Franklin Counties throughout his long career. It is claimed in a short biography that one of O'Hara's most famous student was Zachary Taylor, who would become the 12th President of the U.S. The same biography also reiterates the fact that the O'Hara's were exiles of Ireland. He married Helen Sue Hardy of Maryland in 1800 and together they would have a large family. Their most well-known child was Theodore O'Hara (1820-1868), a distinguished Kentuckian poet, journalist and Confederate soldier, who authored, *"The Bivouac of the Dead."*

O'KELLY, Patrick

— Patrick O'Kelly is one of the few exiles to write a general history of the 1798 Rebellion. Born c.1781 at Kilcoo, near Athy, Co. Kildare, O'Kelly, was descended from the O'Kelly clansmen whose lands were absorbed by the duchy of Leinster in the Sixteenth Century. Only seventeen years of age at the time of the Rebellion, O'Kelly was elected to represent the southern Kildare insurgents who were camped on Knockaulin Hill on 28 May 1798. He was elected to negotiate terms of surrender with Major-General Ralph Dundas. O'Kelly found Dundas an honourable officer and did not trust the motives of General Gerard Lake, who demanded that the insurgents surrender on the grounds of Castlemartin demesne. O'Kelly refused this demand. Dundas accompanied by two dragoon officers, rode to Knockaulin and accepted the surrender of the 6000 insurgents, allowing them to return home upon surrendering their weapons. He also supplied O'Kelly with a generous pardon.

After the Rebellion, O'Kelly, who was residing at his father's farm of Kilcoo, decided to emigrate to the United States. After the death of his father, Sylvester Kelly in 1803, the lease of their lands was passed onto Patrick O'Kelly. O'Kelly emigrated to Baltimore, Maryland, leaving the lands of Kilcoo in the care of his brother, John Kelly. Whilst in Baltimore, O'Kelly became a respected teacher in a prestigious academy, however, upon hearing of the death of his brother, he had to return home to face the arrogance from the land agents of the Duke of Leinster. The lease for the lands of Kilcoo and Coolroe expired on 1 May 1825. Another brother, Thomas Kelly, attempted to amend the situation, however, he was told by land agent, Henry Hamilton, *"Don't send for the Colonel (O'Kelly's rank in the Rebellion), he shall never get a perch of the duke's estate."* O'Kelly returned from Baltimore but failed to regain his father's old lands. O'Kelly wrote: *"In consequence of not being able to obtain, either from the duke or his agents, the re-possession of those two extensive farms, where I was born and brought up, I was forced to emigrate with my family to France, where I continued for seven years. There I gained many friends of the highest order among the French, and procured for my children an education which has ushered them into notice and respectability in this city."*

GENERAL HISTORY

or

THE REBELLION OF 1798.

WITH MANY

INTERESTING OCCURRENCES OF THE TWO PRECEDING YEARS.

ALSO, A BRIEF ACCOUNT OF

THE INSURRECTION IN 1803,

WILL BE SUBJOINED.

BY P. O'KELLY, Esq.
Translator and Publisher of Abbe MacGeoghegan's History of Ireland.

DUBLIN:
PRINTED FOR THE AUTHOR BY J. DOWNES, 4, YORK-STREET.
MDCCCXLII.

Whilst in France, O'Kelly translated Abbé MacGeoghegan's History of Ireland, however, he returned to Ireland in 1831 and settled for a brief period at 20 Greville Street, close to Dublin's Mountjoy Square. In 1834, he also published a worthy book, *"Advice and Guide to Emigrants, going to the United States of America."* In 1842, Kelly published one of the first leading nationalist accounts of the 1798 Rebellion, *"A General History of the 1798 Rebellion"*. Patrick O'Kelly died at 3 Margaret Place on 11 July 1858 and was interred at Goldenbridge Cemetery in Dublin.

O'KEON, Henry – O'Keon, a native of Killala, Co. Mayo, had been a former priest who served in the French Army. He participated in the Humbert expedition, which landed at Killala in August 1798. After the collapse of that expedition, he was apparently convicted in Castlebar but reprieved upon the word of Bishop Stock. He travelled to France, having *"carried off from Dublin another man's wife."* O'Keon would serve in the French Army under Napoleon and was one of the first recipients of the *Legion d'honneur*. O'Keon died on 6 July 1817 at Rue Traversiere, Auxerre, France.

O'MALLEY, Austin (Augustine) – A native of Burrishoole, Co. Mayo, O'Malley was born in 1760 to Owen O'Malley and Margaret Blake, a middle-class Catholic landowning family, closely related to the principal clan. Upon learning of the French landing at Killala in late August 1798, O'Malley travelled to join them, bringing with him many of his tenants and employees. O'Malley was given a commission in the Franco-Irish forces and fought at the Battles of Castlebar (27 August 1798) and Ballinamuck (8 September 1798). After the Rebellion was quashed in Connacht, O'Malley fled to Achill Island and was smuggled to France aboard a yacht, stolen from Denis Bingham. Commissioned as Captain in the Irish Legion in March 1804. In August 1804, the Legion's Adjutant-Major, Alexis Couasnon had an argument with Captain O'Malley after he referred to O'Malley as stupid during a training session. Couasnon refused to apologise. Miles Byrne described the situation in his memoirs:

"Captain O'Meally (sic) then told him he was a coward, and unworthy to be admitted amongst gentlemen, etc. Though O'Meally (sic) might not be as expert as other officers in the manoeuvres, none could surpass him in his knowledge of the etiquette of duelling; his native land of Connaught never produced a cooler, nor a braver, nor an honourable antagonist than he was...He glorified in the part he had taken with General Humbert in Ireland in 1798; and the great sacrifices his family suffered and went through, in the loss of property of every kind was his pride."

The matter was taken to the Legion's commander, Adjutant-General Bernard MacSheehy, who insisted honour would be restored with a pistol duel. Couasnon was wounded and O'Malley was incarcerated for fifteen days at the Chateau in Brest, on orders of MacSheehy. O'Malley served with distinction in the Legion during the Walcheren Campaign and the Peninsular War. Having married a daughter of a French general, O'Malley yearned to return to the lands of his father in Mayo. His eyesight had begun to fail him by the end of the Napoleonic Wars and he formally retired from service with a pension. O'Malley returned to Ireland in 1836, an old war veteran and completely blind. His aim was to have his lands restored to him. His quest failed. Austin O'Malley died at Carrowkeel, Co. Mayo in May 1849. He was often referred to by his insurgent rank of Colonel O'Malley by locals instead of his French rank.

O'MALLY - Mentioned in the biography memoirs of Miles Byrne as having escaped to America after taken an active role in the rebellion on 1798. He may have travelled to France as an American citizen. No other information has been found.

O'NEILL, Dennis – O'Neill was a native of Co. Wexford, who fled to Hamburg in late 1798.

O'NEILL, John – John O'Neill fled Ireland to the United States in 1799. It is unclear if he was a United Irishman or if he left as a direct result of the 1798 Rebellion. During the War of 1812, a British Naval party landed on the coast of Maryland and were met by a number of local Militiamen. After an exchange of shots, the militiamen retreated apart from O'Neill, who was eventually captured. Fearing that a martyr would be made out of him if he was killed, he was released.

O'RAW, John – John O'Raw was born in Ballymena, Co. Antrim, in 1783. A Roman Catholic in his faith, he was fifteen years old when he fought alongside his Presbyterian neighbours at the Battle of Antrim on 7 June 1798. In *South Carolina Irish*, it records that O'Raw was, ***"sentenced to hang, he escaped and, through the intercession of his loyalist father, remained free until his immigration to America."*** In 1806, O'Raw arrived at Charleston, South Carolina, and was briefly employed by merchants, *C. & H. O'Hara*. After a period of financial struggle, he served in the U.S. Navy during the War of 1812. After the conflict, he returned to Charleston and established a grocery on Meeting Street, eventually owning two slaves. O'Raw returned to Ireland in 1829 and died in 1841.

O'REILLY, Terence – O'Reilly was apparently born in Dublin on 4 November 1783 and fought in the 1798 Rebellion in Co. Wicklow. Upon arrival in France, O'Reilly was promoted to Lieutenant in the Irish Legion on 11 January 1804. In 1809, he was decorated with France's elite medal, the *légion d'honneur*, alongside William Lawless, for having saved their regimental eagle during the Siege of Flushing and was promoted to Captain. O'Reilly commanded a company of voltigeurs at the Battles of Baudzen and Goldberg in August 1813, which saw much of his regiment obliterated to severe artillery bombardment. On 15 March 1814, during the revival of the Bourbon Monarchy, O'Reilly was promoted to Colonel or *chef de bataillon* in the 101st Regiment of the line, however, he showed allegiance to Napoleon upon his return from Elba. He was staff officer to General Loison at the Battles of Ligny, Qautre-Bras and Waterloo. O'Reilly retired on half-pay to the town of Evreux.

O'ROURKE, Edmond – Edmond O'Rourke was a native of Co. Wexford, who resided not far from the village of Kiltealy. On 15 August 1798, after having served as an insurgent during the 1798 Rebellion, O'Rourke married Mary Kearns, sister of Fr. Mogue Kearns, a Wexford insurgent leader, who was executed at Edenderry, King's County (Co. Offaly), on 21 July 1798. The newlyweds left Ireland and escaped to France, where Edmond served in the French cavalry during the Napoleonic Wars. After his apparent participation in the Battle of Waterloo, O'Rourke fled to the United States with Mary and their family. The family folklore continues to describe that upon arriving in New

York, Mary and four children succumbed to a fever epidemic, leaving Edmond with one son, with little prospects available to them but to migrate west. The author's late grandmother, whose family hailed from north Co. Wexford was known to have highlighted family links to Fr. Mogue Kearns.

O'TOOLE, James – James O'Toole was a native of Co. Donegal, who was born c.1730, thus making him nearly 70 years old at the time of the Rebellion. In his obituary, it stated that he was implicated in the Irish Rebellion in 1798 with Lord Edward Fitzgerald, this being most likely an exaggeration. He fled his native Ireland as an old man, travelling to the U.S. where he settled in St. Louis and established the first brewery there. Interestingly, in 1857, when he was 125 years old, O'Toole relocated to Kansas.

"One who lives on his claim, near the edge of this city, is, perhaps, the oldest man in America. If not, I will venture a small wager that he is the most active of his age. He is Mr. James O'Toole. He was born in the County of Donegal, in the North of Ireland, somewhere about the year 1730. He was an old man in the Irish rebellion in 1798, when, becoming implicated with Lord Fitzgerald, he fled his country, to seek freedom in our then young republic. His life has been chequered with many changes. He has been tossed about among various scenes and by many diverse circumstances. He moved to St. Louis thirty years ago, and established the first brewery there. He moved to the Platte Purchase in 1838, and lived in Buchanan County, near Bloomington, until two years ago, when he came to Kansas and made a pre-emption, and he can now walk eight or ten miles with ease, to visit his friends or attend to business affairs. He says his age is about one hundred and twenty-five years".

O'TOOLE, Mary – Mary O'Toole (1769-1874) was an exile to the United States, arriving in 1804. Apparently, she was a prominent member within the United Irish movement and saw action in several engagements during 1798. She was also a witness to the Dunlavin Green Massacre (*memorial pictured*), on 24 May 1798, when 36 prisoners, accused of being United Irishmen, were shot dead by the Saundersgrove Yeomanry, in the west Wicklow village. Having originally settled in Philadelphia, Mary married but had no children and she became a widow in 1836. She had played a part in the War of 1812 by assisting in equipping the men who went to the Pea Patch. She is reported to have died in

August 1874 at the advanced age of 105 years. It is unknown if O'Toole was her

maiden name or most likely her husband's surname. Mary O'Toole was interred at the Holy Sepulchre Cemetery in Essex County, New Jersey.

ORR, Joseph – Joseph Orr was an associate of the Derry United Irishman, Christopher Hardy. In 1797, fearing arrest for his deep associations with the United Irishmen and burned all the papers in his possession before fleeing to France. It's unknown what happened to Orr afterwards.

ORR, James - *The Bard of Ballycarry*

James Orr was born in 1770 in Ballycarry, Co. Antrim. Although educated at home, young Orr excelled at his studies and was a noted intellect. He became a weaver by profession and having liberal political views, he joined the Society of United Irishmen, which later resulted in him seeing action at the Battle of Antrim, led by Henry Joy McCracken. Orr fled to the United States immediately after the Rebellion, but finding it did not suit his tastes, returned to Ireland and resided in his native Ballycarry, where he composed much of his renowned poetry in his Ulster-Scots dialect, with one extract evident within the pages of passports of Irish citizens today. A heavy drinker, Orr died on 24 April 1816 and was interred at old Templecorran Graveyard, near Ballycarry.

JAMES ORR.

The United Irishman and poet, James Orr was born in the parish of Broad Island county of Antrim, in the year 1770. His father was a weaver, and held a few acres of land near Ballycarry. He followed his father's occupation, and on his father's death inherited the family homestead. When quite young he courted the muse, and, joining the United Irishmen in his youth, many of his best poems appeared in the Belfast paper called the *Northern Star*, the avowed organ of the society up to 1797, when it was suppressed.

Orr was known as the poet of Ballycarry and his effusions were popular through Ireland. On 7th June, 1798, he took an active part in the battle of Antrim, and on the occasion he is credited with saving many lives. After the conflict he escaped to America, where he wrote for the press. Returning to Ireland he published by subscription in 1804 in Belfast a collection of his poetry. His song, called "The Irishman," is a great favourite all over Ireland. Unfortunately he took to drink, and died in the prime of life on 24th April, 1816, at Ballycarry in Templecorran parish. In the parish churchyard there is over his grave a handsome monument raised by public subscription.

"While close-leagu`d crappies raised the hoards
O`pikes, pike-shafts, forks, firelock,
Some melted lead – some saw`d deal boards-
Some hade, like hens, in byre-neuks:
Wives baket bannocks for their men,
Wi` tears instead o`water,
An` lasses made cockades o`green
For chaps wha us`d to flatter
Their pride ilk day"

PARKS – Parks was recorded by Miles Byrne as an Irish exile, who having little good fortune in the United States, relocated to Paris, where they resided at a hotel on rue Vaugirard. Byrne's brief descriptions of the family gave details about them being accomplices of David Bailie Warden.

"A good Irish patriot…who had to go seek home in some of the cheap back settlements of the United States of America, where he had to live with his wife and two children, a son and a daughter, on very limited mean, for several years till a near relative bequeathed to him a large fortune. He then came with his family to live in Paris."

PARKS, Flora, *née Caldwell* – Flora Caldwell was born at Ballymoney, Co. Antrim, the daughter of John Caldwell and Elizabeth Calderwood. Flora travelled with her brother, John Caldwell Jr, aboard the *Peggy* in May 1799. She was married to John Parks of Ballymoney, who had already fled to the United States. Their family included: James Hamilton Parks (1797-1877), Elizabeth Jane Parks (1799-1813), Florence Parks (b.1803), Sarah Mary Parks (1804-1806), Mary Parks (b. 1806) and John Parks Jr (d.1816). Flora Parks died on 24 January 1814.

PARKS, James – James Parks, an attorney from Ballymoney, Co. Antrim, fled with the Caldwell family to the United States. In April 1805, he married Catherine Caldwell at his brother's New York residence. Parks died on 24 April 1813 at Newburgh, New York.

PARKS, John – John Parks, brother of the above-mentioned James Parks, was a husband of Flora Caldwell, a cousin of the Caldwell siblings of Harmony Hill. In 1799, Parks fled with the Caldwell's to New York. He died prematurely on 24 April 1813, at Newburgh, New York.

PARROTT, John – John Parrott was an older brother of Joseph and William Parrott of Rathcoffey, Co. Kildare, who were insurgents during the 1798 Rebellion. Son of William Parrott and Winifred Ware, Parrott, a glazier and a painter by profession, was a first cousin of north Kildare insurgent leader, Hugh Ware. Whilst his brother, Joseph Parrott, left Ireland for France in May 1802, John and William Parrott remained at Rathcoffey. During the preparations for the Emmet uprising of 1803, the Parrott brothers played significant roles in the Kildare insurgency who supported Emmet. He commissioned his brother-in-law, Thomas Colgan, to manufacture Emmet's renowned green uniform. On 23 July 1803, after the Emmet uprising failed, John and William Parrott fled with the bulk of the leadership to Butterfield Lane, before going into hiding with Michael Quigley at Rathcoffey Demesne and finally to Ardfry, Co. Galway, where it is reputed that their father was employed as a gardener. On 12 October 1803, Quigley, Nicholas Stafford, the Parrott Brothers and their associates were arrested and brought to Dublin Castle. Parrott was placed into Kilmainham Gaol on 23 October 1803 and was not discharged until 13 September 1805. Parrott left Ireland and settled in Philadelphia. When his brother, Joseph Parrott died in

France, it was recorded on his dossier that a brother in Philadelphia would get half of his estate.

PARROTT, Joseph – Joseph Parrott was born in 1781 in the
north Co. Kildare townland of Rathcoffey. His father, William Parrott, a gardener, hailed from Nottinghamshire in England whilst his mother was Winifred Ware, an aunt of Hugh Ware of Rathcoffey, who eventually commanded the Irish Legion during later period of the Napoleonic Wars. Parrott followed his first cousin into the United Irishmen and served under him and William Aylmer during the 1798 Rebellion. Parrott, most likely because of his age, held no significant rank and was not listed during the surrender of the Kildare and Wexford insurgent commanders on 21 July 1798. In April and May 1802, Hugh Ware was released from custody and given a period of time to organise his affairs before exiling himself from Ireland for life.

Upon bidding farewell to his native Rathcoffey, Ware was joined by his cousin, Joseph, who had escaped detention after the 1798 Rebellion. Irish Legion historian, Nicholas Dunne-Lynch has composed some reasons to why Parrott decided to leave Ireland, one being Parrott's desire to enjoy freedom for his religious and political opinions. Parrott left Ireland for France with Ware, Bryan McDermott of Timahoe, John Reilly of Kilcock and Michael Quigley of Rathcoffey. In December 1803, Parrott walked from Paris to Morlaix in Brittany to receive his commission as Lieutenant in the newly created Irish Legion. Parrott is an intriguing character in the history of the Legion. By 1805, the Legion had suffered with some resignations of Irish officers, such as Thomas Addis Emmet, James Blackwell, Valentine Derry and William James MacNeven, who became frustrated by Napoleon's lack of interest in an Irish Expedition. Parrott tendered his resignation but it was refused. He continued to serve in the Legion as an exemplary officer and his commendable actions were later noted by Colonel William Lawless, although it is ironic to note that Perrott unsuccessfully tendered more resignations whilst being such an exemplary soldier. Having served as second-in-command of the Carabineer company in the Second Battalion, under his cousin, Hugh Ware, Parrott had been promoted to Adjutant-Major of the Third Battalion and received a promotion to Captain in 1810. Feeling side-stepped in further advancement, Parrott once again tendered his resignation but to no avail. He served as Captain of the Legion's 2nd Chasseurs during the Saxon

Campaign of 1813. On 19 August 1813, the regiment suffered tremendous casualties at the Battle of Goldberg, in which Parrott received a wound. Continuing to serve on the front, he witnessed the horrific Battle of Löwenburg in Silesia, which saw the regiment practically depleted along the banks of the River Bober. Out of 1600 who marched out in April 1813, only 24 officers and 94 other ranks survived by early October.

Parrott would earn the *Legion d'honneur* in 1813 and was promoted to command the Carabineer Company of a newly constructed Second Battalion in late 1813, and served well during the siege of Antwerp. After the final fall of Bonaparte in June 1815, the Irish Legion was completely disbanded in September 1815. Parrott settled in the town of Abbeville in the Somme region of France. In 1817, he retired completely from the army and decided to initiate a new business venture of importing British cotton-spinning machines. Nicholas Dunne-Lynch gives detail that Parrott may have financially suffered as he petitioned the French *Dauphin* to be recalled to the army in 1827 but to no avail. After the July Revolution of 1830, Parrott again petitioned the government, this time with success. He was appointed commander of the Fort de Pierre Chatel, a remote medieval fort in the French Alps (*pictured*). Captain Parrott died on 25 May 1834.

Fort de Pierre-Chatel.

The PATTERSON Family *of Cappagh, County Tyrone*

PATTERSON, Ann *neé Graham* – Ann Patterson, *neé* Graham, was the wife of Francis Patterson, fleeing to the United States with him and their family after the 1798 Rebellion. They had arrived in Delaware County in Pennsylvania by April 1799, in time for the birth of their son, James Patterson (1799-1889). They eventually moved west to Tennessee. According to her headstone in the Irish Cemetery in Tazewell, Tennessee, she was born on 12 January 1772 and died on 2 May 1857.

PATTERSON, Francis –

Francis Patterson, the patriarch of the Patterson family, was born at Cappagh, Co. Tyrone c. 1764. He was married to Ann Graham. He is cited in the *First Families of America* as having participated in the Rebellion in 1798. He escaped death and emigrated with his family to Delaware County, Pennsylvania. After several years in Pennsylvania, the family moved west to Tennessee. Patterson died on 2 January 1845 and was interred at the Irish Cemetery, Tazewell, in Claiborne County, Tennessee.

PATTERSON, Robert – (1792-1881)

Robert Patterson was the oldest son of Francis Patterson and Ann Graham, being six years old at the time of the 1798 Rebellion. After arriving in the United States, the Patterson family settled in Delaware County Pennsylvania. The young Robert started his career as a successful businessman in Philadelphia, however, he would serve in the War of 1812 and would become an officer in the 2nd Pennsylvania Militia and eventually the Regular Army. In 1817, he married Sarah Ann Engle and they would Patterson would lead a successful career in the

Army, particularly during the Mexican-American War (1846-48) gaining promotion to Major-General and gaining victories at Veracruz. In the interim period between 1848 and the start of the American Civil War, Patterson prospered in the cotton trade, owning over thirty mills, and becoming one of the United States' largest cotton mill owners.

In 1861, Patterson was recalled into service as Major-General of the Pennsylvania Volunteers and the Army of the Shenandoah. He is today remembered for his victory over Stonewall Jackson but his paramount failure to prevent Confederate General Joseph Johnston's forces joining with those of General Beauregard, which resulted in the historic Union defeat at the First Battle of Bull Run would stain his legacy and he was forced out of the Army not long afterwards. An interesting piece of fact and tribute to his Irish roots is that Robert Patterson named his son, Robert Emmet Patterson, after the United Irish leader. Another son, Frances Engle Patterson, became a Brigadier-General in the Pennsylvania Volunteers. He was tragically killed when his pistol accidentally discharged at

Fairfax Courthouse. Robert Patterson died on 7 August 1881 and was interred at Laurel Hill Cemetery, Philadelphia.

The PATTISON Brothers – The six

Pattison brothers, originated from Co. Cavan. After having participated as United Irishmen or involved themselves in the 1798 Rebellion, they fled to the United States. Noted as:

"all youngsters of bad stock".

The brothers are recorded as having all prospered in their new adopted country. The youngest brother, Dr. John Pattison (1792-1858) was but a child of six years during the period of turmoil in his native land, when he was brought to the United States by his brother. He graduated from Pennsylvania Medical College. Having married Sarah Oakley, the couple settled in Fairfield County in Connecticut and reared four sons: Frances, Nelson, William (*photographed*) and John W. Dr. John Pattison died on 30 December 1858 and was interred at Aspetuck Cemetery in Fairfield County.

His son, John Wesley Pattison (*pictured*), was born in Fairfield County in 1830. His father had hoped that his namesake would study divinity or engage in medicine. John Pattison Jr instead became a noted correspondent for the *New York Herald*, who died in 1878 at Jefferson City in Missouri, whilst holding a principal clerkship in the Secretary of State's office. He had married Henrietta Redinour in 1856 at Dodge County in Kansas and became a Captain in the U.S. Militia.

PLUNKETT, John - Plunkett was apprehended for having participated

in the Wexford Rebellion and was subsequently sent to New Geneva, a transit camp in Passage East, Co. Waterford. It was stated that he had wished to go to America and offered security never to return. His Special Prisoner Petition is viewable in the National Archives of Ireland (SPP 258).

PORTER, Alexander – (1785-1844)

Alexander Porter was the son of Rev. James Porter and Anna Knox. His father, Rev. Porter, a zealous United Irishman, was tried at Newtownards, Co. Down, after the crushing of the Down Rebellion and was executed on 2 July 1798. Alexander Porter, only a teenager, was apparently a standard bearer for the insurgents at the Battle of Ballynahinch and was forced to hide for several weeks as a result. He made his way to Ballindrait, near Lifford, Co. Donegal, and hid with a distant relation, Andrew Stilley. Having been recognised, young Porter was cared for by Donald McGinley of Guystown. In 1801, his uncle, Alexander Porter, arrived from the United States, having emigrated there in 1793, to visit family. He returned to the U.S. taking young Alexander and James Porter with him and settling in Nashville, Tennessee. Young Alexander received a limited schooling; studied law; was admitted to the bar in 1807 and with recommendation from General Andrew Jackson, he moved south to Louisiana and commenced practicing in the Attakapas region of the Territory of Orleans. He became the delegate to the

convention which framed the first State constitution in 1812; member, lower branch of the Louisiana State legislature 1816-1818; judge of the State supreme court 1821-1833; elected as a Whig to the United States Senate to fill the vacancy caused by the death of Josiah S. Johnson and served from 19 December 1833, until 5 January 1837, when he resigned due to ill health. He constructed Oaklawn Manor in 1837, a plantation house, near Franklin, Louisiana. He was again elected to the United States Senate in March 1843, but did not take his seat due to ill-health. Alexander Porter died in Attakapas, Louisiana on 13 January 1844. His Oaklawn sugar cane plantation and its associated slaves were inherited by his brother, James. Former President, John Quincy Adams, stated: ***"He was a man of fine talents, amiable disposition, pleasant temper, benevolent heart, elegant taste and classical acquirements. His death is a grievous loss to the country,"***

PORTER, James – James Porter, born in May 1793, was the son of Rev. James Porter and Anna Knox. In 1801, he was brought, along with his brother to the United States by his uncle, Alexander Porter, who had already established himself there. Having resided in Nashville, Tennessee, the Porter brothers were encouraged by General Andrew Jackson to move to Louisiana to forge their careers. James Porter would excel at the State bar. After the death of his brother, Porter inherited the Oaklawn plantation and its slaves, an estate valued at $250,000. Having spent his final years in reclusive privacy, Porter died at Oaklawn on 24 March 1849. He was interred close to his brother at Nashville City Cemetery in Tennessee.

POTTS, Rev. Charles – Charles Potts was born in Clontibret, Co. Monaghan, in 1775. His family had encouraged Charles for the ministry from an early age. He was educated in theology at Glasgow University, before he returned to Ireland. He was licenced by the Presbytery of Monaghan to preach the gospel. It was at the same time the United Irishmen were on the rise and he joined the society in 1795. The society soon found use for a young enthusiastic minister and he was sent to Paris to open communication with the French National Convention. When away he travelled around France and Switzerland. In July 1797, whilst under fear of arrest or death from the authorities, Potts left for the United States, but he did not cease in corresponding with United Irish leaders. After his death, his widow found a trunk with various letters, including some from the United Irish leader, Archibald Hamilton Rowan, thus highlighting this link. Rev. Potts preached for a time in some vacant churches across Pennsylvania, before settling in Philadelphia, where there was a radical Presbyterian society. He soon decided to organise the southern part of the city into a congrgation and establish a new Church.

POTTS, Rev. George C. – George Potts was licenced to preach to the Monaghan preceptory, after he had graduated from Glasgow University. In 1795, he joined the United Irishmen and immersed himself in liberal politics, including visiting Paris in 1796. In 1797, when Monaghan suffered during the Dragooning of Ulster, Potts decided to leave Ireland and establish himself in the United States. He preached in Delaware County, Pennsylvania,

before settling in Philadelphia, where he organised and set up the Fourth Congregation. He was ordained here in 1800 as their pastor. Potts married Mary Engles and together they had four children. He died on 23 September 1838 in Philadelphia and was interred at Mount Moriah Cemetery.

"Early in the year 1800 a call was extended to Mr. George Potts, then a licentiate of the Presbytery of New Castle, and he was ordained and installed on May 22, 1800..... Mr. Potts was born in the County of Monaghan, Ireland, educated at the University of Glasgow, and licensed by the Presbytery of Monaghan. He came to the United States in 1797."

Rev. Pott's son, Dr. Thomas Reed Potts (1810-1874, *pictured*) became a famous physician, civic leader, and was the first Mayor of St. Paul, Minnesota. He was also elected the first president of the Town Board. Interestingly, he practiced in areas associated with some Irish exiles of 1798, Natchez in Mississippi and Galena in Illinois, before later settling in St. Paul, Minnesota. His personality was described as fun, humorous and social, and his practice was termed "*kind-hearted*". Thomas' son, Henry S. Potts, worked as a surveyor in Ramsey County, Minnesota, and led a party up to the Klondike Gold Rush.

POWERS, Michael – Michael Powers was born
in 1769 in Co. Wexford into a farming background. He had been a veteran insurgent of the 1798 Rebellion in Wexford. Having escaped to England immediately after the insurrection, Powers made plans to emigrate to Boston in 1802 where he found ample employment as a labourer and actually returned to briefly visit Ireland in 1817. He returned to Boston with his second cousins, Michael and John McDonald and Timothy Kennedy. To ease their period of settling in Boston, Powers kindly had lent £23. 7s to Michael McDonald, £20 to John McDonald and £91. 5s to Kennedy however they refused to pay him back, resulting in Powers using legal avenues to secure his money. Due to no recording of the lending, Powers could not prove his case to the court. On March 2nd 1820, Timothy Kennedy was murdered, resulting in Powers being arrested. Powers was tried for the murder of Kennedy and even though there was no witness to the murder, Powers was found guilty and was subsequently executed on May 25th 1820. He never denied or confirmed that he had killed his second cousin, Timothy Kennedy. Powers settled his will, leaving several guineas to his relations in Ireland and donated $50 to the poor of Boston.

PRINGLE, Rev. Francis

PRINGLE, Rev. Francis – Born in Scotland in 1747, Francis Pringle was ordained as minister of the Associate Presbytery of Belfast in 1772. During his time in Belfast, he increased the size of his ministry and invested to improve the meeting house to decent standards. Interestingly, during the 1790s, many of his congregation had joined the United Irishmen, however he was initially against the concept. A group of men approached him looking for his gun, in which Pringle stated that he did not have one and those present were subject to a lesson on why what they were doing was wrong. This objecting to the oaths of the United Irishmen would be preached in his church which caused a rift. Deciding that he could not continue with his divided ministry of twenty-six years he dissolved the congregation and resolved to emigrate to America. He left for a brief stay to his native home of Kirkaldy, where he preached for a year before leaving for the United States. With his wife **Margaret *née* Black**, and his dependant family, they arrived in New York City, where he was received to the local Associate Presbytery of New York. In May 1800, Pringle was called to the Associate Presbytery in Pennsylvania and in 1802 he was installed at the minister of Carlisle where he remained until 1832, he died in New York in 1833 at his son's residence. Attached is a clipping from the *Belfast Newsletter* (17 January 1834) regarding Pringle's death in America.

At New York, on the 2d of Nov. 1833, the Rev. Francis Pringle, in the 85th year of his age, and the 61st of his Ministry. He was a native of Fifeshire, Scotland, and was ordained Minister of the Presbyterian Secession Congregation of Gilnahirk, near Belfast, in year 1772. In the year 1798 he removed to Scotland, and shortly after to America; and was settled at Carlile, where he exercised his Ministry, in connexion with the Secession Church, for upwards of 30 years. Owing to the infirmities of age, he resigned his pastoral charge in 1832, and from that time resided with his eldest and only surviving son, Toomas Pringle, Esq. New York, where he finished his earthly course. During an illness of several weeks, a murmur was never heard from his lips. He meekly bowed to the divine will, and manifested an unshaken trust in that Redeemer whom he loved and served during his protracted life. As an evidence of the estimation in which he was held as an eminent and influential Minister, by his brethren on both sides of the Atlantic, it is proper to mention, that he was appointed to the office of Clerk to the Synod both in Ireland and in America.

On the 5th inst. in the 23d year of her age, Elizabeth Anderson, daughter to Mr. Samuel Anderson, Gilnahirk, and grandaughter to the late Rev. Francis Pringle. She was an eminently dutiful daughter and affectionate sister. She was for a number of years a zealous Sabbath school teacher in the Gilnahirk Sabbath school. During life she exemplied the power and purity of true religion, and felt its consolations at her departure.

PURSE, Jonathan

PURSE, Jonathan – Jonathan Purce was captured after the 1798 Rebellion and charged, alongside his brother, William Purse, as an officer of the United Irishmen in Maghera, Co. Derry. The Rebellion Papers (NAI *620/3/19/2*) give some detail to Purse's trial in late June 1798, in which he was sentenced to receive 1000 lashes, followed by transportation for life however this was commuted to self-exile to America. The Purce family settled in Philadelphia.

QUEERY, John – It is thought that John Queery of Belfast participated in the Battle of Antrim, under Henry Joy McCracken. His brother, Thomas Queery had been imprisoned in May 1798 for attempting to seduce a soldier to desert. After the failure of the Antrim Rebellion, Queery remained by Henry Joy McCracken's side at their hideout in the Belfast Hills. He was also present when McCracken was arrested at Carrickfergus, attempting to board a ship. Queery was also arrested and brought before a court-martial, in which he pleaded guilty and was sentenced to transportation for life. This was later remitted to voluntary banishment to America.

QUIGLEY, Edward – Died in 1855 in Newfoundland, Canada. Inscribed on his headstone at Saint Joseph's Roman Catholic Cemetery, at Avalon Peninsula, is:

*"**Erected by his wife Anastasia Quigley. In memory of her beloved husband EDWARD QUIGLEY. A native of Co. Wexford, fought in the Irish Rebellion of 1798. May he rest in peace.**"*

Interestingly, the inscription exclaiming his association with the 1798 Rebellion appears to have weathered or been tampered with.

Photo obtained online with thanks to Shawn Power.

QUINLAN, Mary, *née Ryan* – Mary Ryan was a native of Co. Tipperary, who married Michael Quinlan. As a result of the political upheaval in Ireland, they emigrated to Charleston, South Carolina. Mary Quinlan died on 22 February 1836 and was interred beside her husband at St. Mary of the Annunciation Cemetery in Charleston.

QUINLAN, Michael – Quinlan was a native of Co. Kerry, who emigrated to the United States in 1800, with his wife, Mary Ryan Quinlan and their young family. The Quinlan's settled in Charleston, South Carolina, and became established merchants. Quinlan's headstone directs us to the fact that he was an emigre of 1798. It contains the following: *"Having emigrated to this City in 1800 on account of the political troubles which then agitated his country."* Quinlan died on 20 July 1828, aged 73 years. He was interred at St. Mary of the Annunciation Cemetery in Charleston (SC).

QUINN, John – John Quinn, a native of Newtownards, Co. Down, was imprisoned aboard the *Postlethwaite* in Belfast Lough, after his participation in the 1798 Rebellion. Having being sentenced to transportation, the sentence was reduced to voluntary banishment to the United States.

RABB, John – John Rabb had been an early member of the Belfast Society of United Irishmen and had also previously been secretary in the Irish Volunteers. Rabb was a printer by trade and participated in the printing of the *Northern Star*. In 1794 he was tried on charges of seditious printing with the other owners of the *Northern Star* and decided to flee the country as a result. He settled in Philadelphia.

RATTIGAN, Edward – Edward Rattigan was one of the chief United Irish insurgent commanders in Dublin in May 1798. was implicated in the 1798 Rebellion for the United Irishmen and had to make a swift journey into exile. He went to France, joined the French Army and died at the Battle of Marengo on 14 June 1800.

REDFERN, Robert - Robert Redfern, was born c.1769. His background is somewhat clouded as we are unsure of his native place. In July 1795, Redfern established his own leatherworking business on Belfast's Castle Street. Having strong links to the United Irishhmen, Redfern was arrested in Belfast and was

conveyed to Kilmainham Gaol in 1 May 1797. Whilst incarcerated, Redfern composed multiple letters to the Dublin authorities urging them to allow him to emigrate to the United States. His Special Prisoner Petition, held in the National Archives of Ireland (*NAI*, SPP 261) contains a letter, dated 13 October 1798, stating: *"I was informed by Mr. Mazden, (sic) that the prisoners are at liberty to go to America as soon as they pleased. It is my wish to leave this country but I must inform your Lordship, that is entirely out of my power, from my confinement which is seventeen monthsto pay my passage…I entrust your Lordship to take my distressed situation into your consideration, and I expect Government will be so humane as to send myself and my family to America at their expense."* During this period, his brother who resided in England, William Redfern, had been sentenced to transportation for his involvement in a naval mutiny. He would become '*Father of Australian Medicine*' and the district of Redfern in Sydney is called in his honour. By December 1798, correspondence with Dublin Castle shows Robert's willingness to go to Hamburg, stating that his property and his wealth had been squandered by his imprisonment. On 22 April 1801, Robert Redfern was bailed with the intention of him being transported, most possibly to a country not at war with Great Britain. His destination remains unknown. It remains possible that he went to Portugal before settling in the United States. By 1817, Redfern was residing in Philadelphia, working as a saddler. He would remain there for several years. In 1824, Redfern was in correspondence with his brother in New South Wales, who had established himself there as a leading surgeon. Robert Redfern and his son, William Redfern (1809-1895) sailed aboard, the *Phoenix*, bound for Sydney, as free settlers. Redfern received a land grant for 2000 acres at Campbell's Creek near Bathurst, NSW. Robert Redfern died on 3 September 1853 and was interred at Bathurst Cemetery.

> ROBERT REDFERN, SADDLER,
>
> BEGS leave to inform his friends and the public, that he has commenced business in Castle-street, in the shop lately occupied by Mr. James Martin, and has laid in a large assortment of all kinds of materials in the Saddling, Coach, Car, and Car Harness line ─ And hopes by his carefulness and attention to business, to give general satisfaction to those who pleases to favour him with their commands.
>
> N. B. Horses measured and neatly fitted. A Journeyman and an Apprentice wanted.
>
> I believe from the above Redfern's practice in England and Dublin, that he is very capable of the business.
>
> JAMES MARTIN.

REED, Thomas ─ Thomas Reed was born in 1768 at Drogheda, Co.
Louth to Denis Reed and Mary Heiny. Miles Byrne briefly recorded this individual in his memoirs: **"*Reed took an active part in the politics in the North of Ireland, for which he had to abandon his home and escape to France in 1798. Fortunately for him, he brought with him a small sum of money, the interest of which sufficed for his frugal habits of living ─ he was more than fifty years of age.*"** Reed had been promoted to Lieutenant in the Irish Legion in December 1803. He retired from the military in 1806.

REILLY, Rev. John ─ John Reilly was born c.1770, at Ballybay, Co.
Monaghan. In October 1797, the authorities enforced a crackdown against the United Irishmen in Co. Monaghan, which had one of the strongest United Irish communities outside of the north-east. Reilly initially settled in Philadelphia, where he became a teacher but later studied theology, under Rev. Dr. Wylie, an exile. He was licenced by the middle Presbytery in 1809 and ordained in 1813. He preached in South Carolina and married Jane Weir however his life and ministry were cut short when he died on 25 August 1820, at Beaver Dam. Rev. Reilly was interred at the Covenanter Cemetery in Chester County (SC).

REILLY, John – John Reilly of Kilcock, Co. Kildare, was one of the principal leaders of the northern Kildare insurgency during the 1798 Rebellion. A shoemaker by profession, he would join the insurgents who were commanded by William Aylmer and Hugh Ware. On 21 July 1798, the collective of Kildare's remaining leaders surrendered at Sallins, Co. Kildare. On 22 September 1798, Reilly was incarcerated in Kilmainham Gaol, remaining there until April 1802. Upon his release, Reilly fled to France. With support from Nicholas Dunne Lynch, we have been able to piece together Reilly's life. On 3 February 1808, he married Jeanne Marie Manach at Landerneau in Brittany. Reilly remarried on 7 January 1817 to Marie Renee Poisson. On 28 March 1850, Reilly died at his residence in Sizun, Brittany.

REYNOLDS, Dr. James – Born c.1765, in Clonoe, Co. Tyrone to miller, James McReynolds and Margaret Cornwall. Reynolds was educated at the University of Edinburgh and graduated in medicine. Upon arriving back in Ireland, Reynolds briefly practised in his mother's hometown of Stewartstown, Co. Tyrone. Reynolds was purportedly the brother-in-law of Theobald Wolfe Tone. Having been a member of lodge no. 758, he would become president of Tyrone's Freemasons in the early 1780s. Reynolds was not only involved in the Volunteer Movement but he played an important role in the formation of the United Irishmen and when the organisation was proscribed and he was implicated in the Rev. Jackson trial, Reynolds fled from Ireland. In May 1794, he sailed aboard the *Swift*, from Belfast to Philadelphia. Upon sailing from Ireland, he toasted to the death of King George III. Upon arrival in America, he attached himself to other radicals including United Irish exile, John Daly Burk and John Beckley, a clerk in the U.S. House of Representatives. Reynolds became an outspoken supporter of Thomas Jefferson. Reynolds' politics would become not only ultra-radical but temperamental. He would publicly denounce George Washington and challenged a newspaper editor to a duel in 1799. A close confident of the Tone Family, he was entrusted with Tone's money and journals during the latter's journey to France in 1796. Reynolds returned to medicine during the Yellow Fever epidemic, which had gripped the seaboard cities of the United States and was employed at the Philadelphia General Hospital. When Matilda Tone and her family returned to the United States, they found that Wolfe Tone's possessions and money were lost. Reynolds was a noted alcoholic and died on 25 May 1808.

REYNOLDS, Michael – Reynolds was a United Irish Colonel who led the failed attack at Naas, Co. Kildare during the 1798 Rebellion. With the authorities searching for him, Reynolds hid in the Wicklow Mountains. On 25 June 1798, he and his party of fugitives joined the Wicklow and Wexford insurgents in an attack in what was to become the Second Battle of Hacketstown, on the Carlow and Wicklow border. Reynolds suffered a horrific wound during the attack but his undaunted bravery during the attack on the defended houses is well noted. Reynolds is reputed to have died from his wounds several days after the attack and this is generally accepted by some 1798 historians, however, one source states that he fled to London and then into obscurity abroad.

REYNOLDS, Thomas –

Reynolds was born at 9 West Park Street in Dublin on 12 March 1771 to Andrew Reynolds and Rose Fitzgerald, a distant relation to the Duke of Leinster and Lord Edward Fitzgerald. He was tutored in London and by Catholic priests at Liege. In his youth Reynolds was influenced by men like Simon Butler, who would become the first Chairman of the Dublin United Irishmen, thus highlighting liberal sympathies. In 1789, whilst travelling across the continent, Reynolds would witness the attack on the Bastille in Paris on 14 July 1789. Upon returning to Ireland, he became involved in the Catholic Committee and would become a close associate with Richard McCormick and Theobald Wolfe
Tone. In March 1794, Reynolds married Harriet Witherington, youngest sister of Matilda Witherington, wife of Wolfe Tone. In 1797, he completed a full purchase of Kilkea Castle, near Athy, Co. Kildare. At this point, Reynolds had become a leading member of the United Irishmen in Co. Kildare and served on the Leinster Directory. Upon learning details of the insurrection plans cast by

Lord Edward Fitzgerald and knowing of an upcoming meeting of County Delegates, Reynolds, who was starting to suffer financially, decided to inform on the United Irishmen to Dublin Castle. The organisation was badly rocked on 12 March 1798, when Reynolds' information launched an arresting raid upon the Leinster Directory, who were meeting at Oliver Bond's residence on Bridge Street. Soon afterwards, Reynolds, under threat
of assassination by the United Irishmen was forced to reside within the confines of Dublin Castle. His Kilkea homestead had been severely raided by Crown Forces, who believed that Lord Edward Fitzgerald was hiding there. The damage was so pronounced that the residence was not renovated and repaired for thirty years.

Reynolds would become the chief prosecution witness in the trials of leading United Irishmen, John McCann, Oliver Bond and William Michael Byrne. For his role in informing on his former associates, Reynolds was awarded the Freedom of the City of Dublin and a healthy annual pension. Fearing retribution, Reynolds left Ireland with his family and settled in Monmouthshire in Britain before moving to London. He would later be appointed Postmaster-General of Lisbon during the Peninsular War. In 1817, he would be promoted British Counsul to Iceland. After his retirement, Reynolds resided in Paris for the remainder of his day, dying on 18 August 1836. His remains lie at Welton Churchyard, near Brough, Yorkshire. Having brought down the bulk of the United Irish leadership in Leinster, Reynolds' legacy still remains firmly as the most effectively dangerous informer in Irish history.

RIDDLE, Hugh – Hugh Riddle, a Methodist native of Co. Down, fled to the United States as a result of his participation in the 1798 Rebellion. Having married Rebecca Lee, they resided at Cherry Tree in Clearfield County, Pennsylvania. Hugh Riddle died on 21 March 1856, aged 77 years, and was interred at Mount Zion Independent Church Cemetery, in Mahaffey, Pennsylvania.

RODGERS, Peter – A native of Cork City, Rodgers was an artisan who fled from Ireland at the age of seventy, for his support of the United Irishmen. Rodgers resided in Washington D.C. where he had the following slogan above his store:

"*Peter Rodgers, Saddler, from the Green Fields of Erin and tyranny, to the Greens streets of Washington and Liberty.*"

RODGERS, William – Companion of Rev John Black to America. See BLACK Rev John.

ROGERS, Patrick Kerr –

Rogers was a Presbyterian from Omagh, Co. Tyrone. It is stated that he had published seditious articles in the Dublin newspapers during the turbulent period of 1798, which resulted in him fleeing to Philadelphia in August 1798. Whilst there, Rogers attended medical college, graduated in 1802 and proceeded to practice in both Philadelphia and Baltimore. He later became a lecturer in natural philosophy and chemistry at William and Mary College from 1819 to 1828. With his wife, Margaret Blythe, they would have three sons who went on to do great work for progressing American science. One son, William Barton Rodgers (*pictured*) was an esteemed geologist and physicist who founded MIT (Massachusetts Institute of Technology). James Blythe Rogers taught in Baltimore and practiced medicine. Robert Empie Rogers was a chemist and doctor.

ROSE, James -

Rose was a calico-printer from Windy Arbour who was deeply implicated in the Dublin United Irish movement. He was ordered to banishment and was residing in Manchester, England, in the years succeeding the Rebellion.

ROWAN, Archibald Hamilton –

Archibald Hamilton was born on 12 May 1751 in Rathbone Place, London, to Gawen Hamilton and Jane Rowan. His maternal grandfather, William Rowan took an influential role in young Archibald's future. On condition that he would receive a strict education; not to visit Ireland for 25 years, and to adopt the Rowan surname predominantly over his natural name, he would be awarded a vast fortune. Young Archibald would lean more in his father's politics, which were liberal and often radical. Having graduated from Westminster Academy, he attended Queen's College in Cambridge, but his unruly manner, including the tossing of his lecturer into a river, saw him suspended. He would complete his education at Warrington and a further spell in Cambridge before deciding to emigrate to France. Here, he resided predominantly in Rouen. His friendship with Lord Charles Montagu would see him accept an officer commission in the Portuguese Army, a role he held only briefly. Upon returning to Paris, he became acquainted with Benjamin

Franklin, who inspired Rowan, an English Militia officer, to support the colonials in their war against Great Britain. In October 1781, he married Sarah Anne Dawson, a strict and somewhat controlling figure in Rowan's life.

In 1784, Rowan relocated to Ireland, settling at a comfortable farm estate in Rathcoffey in north Co. Kildare. He became active in the Volunteer movement throughout the mid-1780s, joining his father's Killyleagh Company in Co. Down however, the movement was in decline, having peaked in 1782. Befriending William Drennan, Rowan's path in entering radical Irish politics was set. Rowan would become one of the earliest members of the Dublin Society of United Irishmen, often chairing principal meetings, including exclaiming toasts of congratulations to the French in their military exploits. His inflammatory nature saw him become a target for Dublin Castle. His enthusiasm eventually saw many of his Rathcoffey tenants become United Irishmen, including Hugh Ware. In December 1792, he was arrested for distributing seditious pamphlets and held on remand for a year. In January 1794, whilst represented by John Philpott Curran, Rowan was fined £500 and sentenced to two years imprisonment at Newgate Gaol, in which he received comforts befitting his status. Having interacted with Rev.

ARCHIBALD HAMILTON ROWAN F
Late President of the Society of
United Irishmen at Dublin

William Jackson, Rowan was again watched by Dublin Castle's informers. On May 1st 1794, using bribes and a detailed plan, he escaped quite easily from Newgate in what would become an embarrassing affair to the Irish authorities. A bounty of £2000 was issued for the apprehension of Rowan but it was too late. He had sailed to France. There he interacted with Thomas Paine and Robespierre and witnessed the mass guillotining of members of the Paris Commune, which did not diminish his respect for French republicanism. Rowan was introduced by Paine to the U.S. Ambassador, James Munroe, the future President, who supported Rowan's choice to settle in America. Travelling under the alias of James Thomson, Rowan sailed to America aboard the *Columbus*, arriving in Philadelphia in September 1795. There he would reside close to Wolfe Tone and Tandy, choosing to remain in the United States when the others opted to relocate to France the following year. Receiving scant support from Ireland, he attempted calico printing whilst residing in Wilmington, Delaware, but this venture failed.

After the failure of the Rebellion in Ireland, Rowan was eager to return home. Having corresponded with Lord Castlereagh, shown support towards the Union Bill and encouraging his eldest son to join the Crown Forces in a show of loyalty, Rowan was allowed to sail to Europe in mid-1800. There he joined his family at

Altona, where many Irish refugees were residing. It would take three years for Whitehall to pardon Rowan, allowing him to visit London. On 27 July 1806, Rowan was officially allowed to return to Ireland and resided at his ancestral homestead, Killyleagh Castle in Co. Down (*pictured*). He would remain a liberal throughout the remainder of his life and openly supported Daniel O'Connell and the new Catholic Association. Rowan died in Dublin on 1 November 1834 and was interred within the vaults of St. Mary's Church.

RUSSELL – Russell was an Antrim born yarn-merchant who was deeply implicated in the Society of United Irishmen. Having been arrested and tried at the Clonmel Assizes in early 1798, he was unsuccessfully represented by Thomas Addis Emmet. He was sentenced to transportation for life however, this was mitigated to service to His Majesty abroad. Russell was sent to serve in a Crown regiment in the West Indies, but managed to escape to the United States. On travelling to France in early 1803 on terms of business, Russell encountered Addis Emmet, who in turn introduced him to Arthur O'Connor and Dr. MacNeven. Russell was sent to Ireland to interact with the United Irish Executive, who were engaged in the planning of what would become Emmet's uprising of 1803. Russell sailed back to the United States before the events unfolded.

RYAN, Connar – Ryan was born in 1780 and got caught up in the 1798 Rebellion. A news article in 1893 states that he participated in the engagements in Cappawhit, Cullohill and Monasterevan. Judging from the place names Cullohill and Monasterevan it appears he came from what was then the Queen's County (Laois). Ryan eventually left Ireland and settled in Canada. He lived to the age of 106 years and every Sunday without fail would walk a mile and half to mass. His wife died a day before Ryan, aged two months before her 100th birthday.

SAMPSON, William - Sampson was born into a Church of Ireland family in the City of Londonderry on 17 January 1764 to Rev. Arthur Sampson & Mary Spaight. Having grown up in a conservatively religious home, young Sampson, during his early education, embraced the Volunteer Movement of the early 1780s and eventually opened his mind towards "***embracing the cause of***

the people." A note of interest is that Sampson was earlier assisted by Robert Stewart, who then expressed liberal ideals. Stewart, would later politically transform into a deep-rooted Irish conservative upon becoming Marquess of Londonderry & Lord Castlereagh, whose support in the late 1790s of the ultimate destruction of radicalism in Ireland is well recorded. Educated in law at Trinity College in Dublin without graduating, Sampson left Ireland for several years to tour North Carolina whilst visiting his uncle.

In 1790 he married Grace Clarke of Castle Street, Belfast and together they would build a family; William Sampson Jr, John Philpot Sampson and Catherine Anne Sampson, whilst residing on High Street. After succeeding his terms at Lincoln's Inn, he was fully admitted to the Irish bar in 1792. His legal experience saw him joining the counsel of John Philpot Curran, and together they would represent the defence counsel for many tried United Irishmen across Ireland's judicial circuit. Being disturbed by the grievances of Ireland's Catholics, Sampson's conscience led him to join the Society of United Irishmen. Sampson's position in the Society of the United Irishmen strengthened with time. With many of the moderate liberals leaving the society, post-1794, due to the political transition from active constitutionalism to militant radicalism; the opportunities arose for Sampson to progress his talents and become influential. An example of Sampson's boisterous personality included his heckling at the Irish ascendancy in the Irish House of Commons, upon their discussions of the Insurrection Acts, in which upon someone called "*That the Speaker do leave the Chair*," Sampson shouted from the populated upper-gallery, "*Aye, and let the greatest rascal amongst you take it.*"

Sampson set about to obtain redress for those being attacked and forced from their properties in the sectarian outrages in Armagh and Tyrone, which in a sense, made him a marked man. He contributed to the United Irish newspapers, *The Northern Star*, and *The Press*, under the pseudonym, '*Fortescue.*' His writings attacked government policies, corruption and the treatment of Irish Catholics. One of his famous satirical writings was **"A Faithful Report of the Trial of Hurdy-Gurdy at the Bar of the Court of the King's Bench."** Continuing his support for the United Irishmen's chief barrister, John Philpot Curran, Sampson participated on the defence team for William Orr, who was tried in late 1797 for administering an illegal oath, which had since been classified as an act of high treason under the recently passed Insurrection Act. On 12 February 1798, Sampson was called to support John Stockdale, a Dublin printer, whose premises were raided by the military, for having printed "*The Press*," a short-lived Dublin based United Irish broadsheet. Upon visiting the house, Sampson was surrounded and threatened at bayonet point. Having been arrested, a blunder would see him immediately released. However, the authorities focused on bringing down Sampson. Raids were ordered in places that he often frequented or resided in. Knowing his chances of practicing unhindered were diminished. Frustrated, Sampson sent correspondence to the Lord Lieutenant, Lord Camden and to the Attorney-General, Arthur Wolfe, claiming that he would surrender himself if he was offered a fair trial.

"No answer being given, I remained in Dublin until the 16th of April, when the terror became so atrocious that humanity could no longer endure it. In every quarter of the metropolis, the shrieks and groans of the tortured were to be heard."

Having been offered shelter by Lord Moira, Sampson sailed for Whitehaven in England, where he was immediately arrested for refusing to give his name upon landing and conveyed to Carlisle Prison. Whilst there, he penned a letter to the Secretary of State, the Duke of Portland, requesting a fair trial. Again, his letters were ignored. He was sent back to Dublin on 5 May 1798 where he was held under guard at the Castle Tavern. Here, Sampson learned of the excessive brutalities being forced upon the Irish people. A North Cork sentinel told him of the horrific actions that were carried out in Kildare.

"They had their will of the men's wives and daughters. I asked him if the officers permitted that; and he answered by a story of one who had ordered a farmer...to bring him his daughter in four-and-twenty hours, under pain of having his house burned. The young girl had been removed to a neighbouring parish. The father would not be the instrument of his daughter's pollution. And this young soldier assured me he had been one who, by his officer's command, had burned the house of the father. And this was called loyalty to the King and the British constitution; and now this crime, with a million of others, is indemnified by law."

On 7 May, Sampson was conveyed to the Bridewell where he was held for the duration of the summer of 1798, whilst Ireland descended into gruesome chaos. Whilst in prison, and hearing that he would be allowed to self-exile, Sampson was informed that the American ambassador, Rufus King, had publicly denied entrance to the USA for United

Irish exiles. His health began to fail whilst incarcerated and he was encouraged to plead to the authorities for his allowance to go to Portugal. Mr. Montgomery, the MP for Sampson's native county and friend of Lord Cornwallis, took leniency on Sampson's position and petitioned for Sampson to be allowed to sail for Portugal. On 6 October 1798, Sampson's old acquaintance, Lord Castlereagh, signed the passport for Sampson to sail to Portugal. Upon being released from the Bridewell Prison, Sampson was acquainted with his faithful servant, John Russell. As they walked along Abbey Street, they faced the sneers and jibes of loyalists who mocked their cropped hairstyles. A shot was fired but Sampson continued his journey, ignoring the spectators. Upon reaching the dock, to board the **Lovely Peggy**, Sampson noticed that Russell had been wounded by a gunshot wound to the shoulder but had remained defiant in keeping it quiet until they were away from the mob. On 24 November 1798, Sampson left Ireland for good. Several days later, his ship was badly damaged off the coast of Pwllheli in Wales, where he remained until the Spring of 1799.

Sampson reached Oporto in Portugal in early March 1799. However, this trip was cut short on 22 March, when the authorities arrested him on the orders of

an English official, who claimed that Sampson had seditious writings on his person. After a short trial and his health failing, he was expelled from Portugal and eventually reached the residence of André Cusac in the Dordogne region of France. He was eventually reunited with his family in Paris and together they settled in Montmorency. In 1805, upon attempting to travel to England, via Hamburg, he was rearrested. After some diplomatic pressures, he was informed he was fully banned from entering his native island for life, however, he was allowed to sail for America. On 4 July 1806, the Sampson Family arrived in New York City, USA. William Sampson strived to promote the United Irish principles of political reform and religious toleration as a distinguished attorney and legal reformer. His daughter, Catherine, married William Tone, son of Theobald Wolfe Tone, who also resided in New York, with his mother, Matilda Tone. In 1813, he published, "The Catholic Question in America," where he successfully defended the right of a Catholic priest's confessional privilege not to be manipulated and used as evidence during a court case. This was the first case of its kind in the USA. William Sampson died in New York on 28 December 1836, aged 72 years and was originally interred close to William James MacNeven at Riker Farm Cemetery in Queens but his remains were moved to Green Wood Cemetery in Brooklyn, close to the Tone Family plot.

"Being of the favoured cast, and far from having any personal griefs, the road to advancement on the contrary very open to me, I could have no motive but that of

compassion for my country. I was never inclined to political contention; and it required strong conviction to move me to sedition...the griefs of Irishmen are undeniable" - William Sampson.

SCALLAN, John – Scallan had been a seafarer, who at the time of the Fall of Wexford on 30 May 1798, played a significant role in capturing Lord Kingsborough from sailing away from Wexford. As a reward for the capture, Scallan was promoted as an Admiral in the Wexford Navy, a role that was more

symbolic than practical considering the insurgents were only equipped with small fishing boats. He was also instrumental in securing three barrels of gunpowder from a Guinea cutter which had sailed close to the Wexford coast. After the Wexford Rebellion, Scallan fled. Wexford 1798 historian, Brian Cleary, states that Scallan became a captain on a West Indies freighter, and died at sea in 1835.

SCOTT, Matthew – Scott, a merchant, originated from Carrick-on-Suir, Co. Waterford. During the 1798 Rebellion, Scott was barbarously flogged on the orders of the notorious magistrate, Thomas Judkin '*Flogging*' Fitzgerald, and was imprisoned. After the Rebellion, Scott fled to the United States, however, he never mentally healed from the harsh experiences. After several years in America, Scott returned to Ireland, where it is claimed he lost his sanity and committed suicide.

SCOTT, James – Scott, from Ballymaconnell in Co. Down, was a United Irish commander of the Bangor insurgents during the 1798 Rebellion. Historian, Michael, indicates that Scott was given clearance to leave Ireland for the United States after the Rebellion.

SCOTT – The father of the legendary daredevil, Samuel Gilbert Scott, was a carpenter who originated from Newtownbarry (now Bunclody) in Co. Wexford. Having been involved in the 1798 Rebellion, he emigrated to America. In 1813, Samuel G. Scott was born in Philadelphia. Nothing is known about the father, bar his participation in the Rebellion, but his son left a lasting showman legacy behind. Sam Gilbert became famous America and Britain for his daring act of high diving and other stunts that he had learned during his service in the U.S. Navy, having adapted in scaling masts and rigging. Having been discharged, Scott made a living in daring stunts, including one which saw him dive from the precipice of Niagara Falls. In December 1837 he visited Britain, where he entertained thousands in Liverpool. He then went on to dive and jump from the Menai Bridge in North Wales; the Chain Pier, Brighton; a cliff in Cornwall; a chimney in Bury into a shallow canal; and from ships docked in Manchester, Plymouth, Portsmouth and London. During this tour, he promoted the risks by suspending himself

AWFUL DEATH OF SAM SCOTT.
THE GREAT AMERICAN DIVER.

with a rope around his neck. His final show was on 11 January 1841, at London's Waterloo Bridge, in which his stunt failed and his rope slipped, causing him to accidentally hang himself.

The SERVICE Family (Thomas, Mary & William) –

Thomas Service, a Belfast Presbyterian, is cited as having being taken prisoner in 1798 as an insurgent and managed to escape to the United States. His son, William Service was born in Belfast on 27 September 1798. In the *History of Mercer County*, it notes William Service had emigrated in 1800 to the United States with his mother. They travelled to Huntington County in Pennsylvania, joining Thomas Service, who had preceded them. The family relocated to Cool Spring Township in Mercer County (PA). William Service died on 9 June 1868

and was buried at Jackson Centre Presbyterian Burial Ground in Mercer County.

SERVICE, John – John Service was recorded as a prisoner aboard the prison tender, the *Postlethwaite*, in Belfast Lough immediately after the 1798

234

Rebellion. He was discharged on the grounds that he would settle his affairs and exile himself to the United States.

SHANKS, John – John Shanks was born in 1775, in Poyntzpass, a village on the border of Counties Armagh and Down. Shanks was born into a Presbyterian family on the Co. Down side, in an area called 'The Fourtowns'. John Shanks joined the United Irishmen when he was working in Newry in the mid-1790s. When he returned home to Poyntzpass, he set up his own branch, known as '*The Fourtowns Boys*,' commissioning a local blacksmith, named Kerr, to produce their pikes. In 1797, during the Dragooning of Ulster, the Ancient Briton Fencibles, who were responsible for the Ballyholland Massacre, were garrisoned in the area and became a nuisance for Shanks to operate. The Ancient Britons burnt the homesteads of many Fourtown locals, irrespective of political belief. During the atrocity, Shanks was taken prisoner. Wanting to make an example of him, they decided not to kill him immediately, but instead to take him to Newry so they could execute this ringleader publicly. The soldiers made it as far as the Sheepbridge Inn, a short distance to the north of Newry, before they decided to stop for the night. Shanks made good this lapse in their vigilance, and escaped. After a period, he took ship for America, arriving in Baltimore, Maryland. He returned to Poyntzpass, in 1807. In 1810, he married a local girl, named Ringland, and found work as a weaver with William Dinsmore of Loughadian. Shanks died in 1825, and was buried by the Fourtowns Presbyterian Church, known then as the '*Rock Meeting House*'. With thanks to Robb Morrow.

SHAW, John – John Shaw was the son of innkeeper, Jonas Shaw, from Lisburn, Co. Antrim. The family hailed from the Quaker community in Lisburn. Shaw, showing some ambition, aimed to build a factor to compliment the flourishing linen trade. Shaw was recorded by the authorities as being present in Co. Tyrone and was known as an agitator, particularly in the Cootehill area. In 1796 he was confronted at a market fair by Robert Carlisle, who claimed that Shaw had threatened him into taking the treasonable United Irish oath. John Shaw was arrested and sent to Newgate Gaol in Dublin. William Sampson, a leading United Irish barrister, was called to represent Shaw which resulted in him being released on bail. Soon afterwards, he was again issued with a warrant for his arrest. In response, he emigrated to New York. Whilst there, he suffered financial difficulties and soon sank into severe debt. It unknown what became of John Shaw in the United States.

The SHAW Family of Co. Antrim – John Shaw, a native of New York, was born c.1756 to William Shaw and Jane Wood. Having briefly served as a colonial loyalist during the American Revolution, he emigrated to Ireland and married **Isabella Tennant**, a native of Ballymoney, Co. Antrim, on 7 May 1777. Shaw became involved in the United Irish movement and fought in the

Antrim Rebellion. He fled with his family to America in 1799, settling in Cayuga County, New York. The family who joined him and Isabella in the United States included: **Eliza Shaw** (1780-1852), **Robert Tennant Shaw** (1783-1824), **Daniel John Shaw** (1785-1873), **Ann Shaw** (1786-1844), **Margaret Shaw** (1791-1811), **Isabella Shaw** (1793-1794) and **William Tennant Shaw** (1796-1870). John Shaw died on 29 March 1840. His wife, Isabella Tennant Shaw died on 24 February 1828. They are interred at the Shaw Vault in Aurelius, Cayuga County (NY).

SHAW, William – William Shaw, a native of Saintfield, Co. Down, was arrested after having participated in the 1798 Rebellion. He was sentenced to transportation to New South Wales however this was remitted to voluntary banishment to the United States.

SHERRARD, James – James Sherrard was born in 1757 to William Sherrard (1720-1771) and Margaret Johnston, in Newton Limavady, Co. Derry. His siblings included John, Elizabeth and Margaret. The family had been involved in the shipping, insurance and farming industries since their arrival after the Williamite Wars. James Sherrard is reported in the publication, "*The Sherrard Family of Steubenville*" to have participated in the 1798 Rebellion and subsequently fled to America with the aid of good friends on both sides of the conflict, to reach Philadelphia. His brother, John Sherrard, had emigrated to America in the early 1770s and fought in the American War of Independence. He had originally settled in the Appalachian Mountain region in Pennsylvania and purchased a farm. John had invited his widowed mother and brother to join him in the New World. They answered his call and both arrived in Philadelphia, however soon after their mother got homesick. James decided to return to Limavady with his mother with the intention of coming straight back. They had previously sold their farm in Limavady and actually managed to gain it back. After the Rebellion, James Sherrard fled to the United States but did not return to his brother's farm and the story of his escape to America was passed to John's family by their cousins, the Johnston's of Brownsville. John Sherrard relocated to Jefferson County in Ohio and died in April 1809.

SHIELDS, Daniel – Family folklore from the Ballymena area mentions the Shields family, who hailed from Ahoghill, Co. Antrim, as participants in the Battle for Ballymena. Daniel Shields became a wanted man and fled to America and briefly settled in New York for several years before he returned to Ireland. Shields died in 1826.

SIBBET, John – John Sibbet hailed from Killinchy, Co. Down. Having participated in the Rebellion, he was subsequently tried for stealing horses and sentenced to serve His Majesty's forces abroad for life. Sibbet was sent to the West Indies, where he befriended Andrew Bryson. Sibbet escaped and made his was to Philadelphia.

SIMPSON, Rev. James – Rev. Simpson was the Minister of the First Newtownards Presbyterian Church. Having being a United Irishman, he was arrested during the 1798 Rebellion and conveyed to the Belfast prison tender, the *Postlethwaite*. He was sentenced at court-martial to transportation for life, however this was commuted to banishment to the United States and left on the *Peggy* in May 1799. In America, Simpson travelled to Huntingdon, Pennsylvania,

> Belfast Presb. report, That the Rev⁴ Tho* L. Birch & the Rev⁴ ꞏ Ja* Simson, being charged with Seditious Practices, were permitted by Government to leave the Kingdom. That the Presb. declared the

where he started to minister with the permission of the Presbytery. His services were in high demand Between 1800 and 1803, charges were brought against Simpson and he was expelled from the presbytery in 1803. It's unknown what happened to Simpson after this.

SIMPSON, William – Rev. Mullin, in his book, *Limavady and the Roe Valley*, mentioned a letter from Rev. Tennant of Roseyard to his son John Tennant, a United Irishman who fled to France. The letter –

"It seems to be certain William Simpson, Ballycrum, your uncle's brother-in-law, with a great number of respectable inhabitants about Newtown-Limavady, are sent to Belfast for transportation (and were rescued from death by Lord H. Murray). We wish to hear more about them as well as of William and all friends."

William Simpson was a captain in the Limavady United Irishmen. After being imprisoned in Belfast after the 1798 Rebellion, he was bailed to settle his affairs before sailing to the United States.

SINCLAIR, Rev. William – William Sinclair was born in 1775 at Tobermore in Co. Derry, and studied at the University of Glasgow. By 1786, he was preaching in Newtownards, Co. Down, and later joined the United Irishmen. In October 1791, Sinclair would become a founding member of the Belfast Society of United Irishmen at Drew's Tavern. In July 1792, Sinclair partook in the Belfast celebrations of Bastille Day and participated in a debate calling for Catholic Emancipation. In November 1796, whilst maintaining a public show of loyalty, he assisted Lord Castlereagh in the administering of an oath of allegiance to 300 of his tenants. In 1798, Sinclair was promoted to the position of Adjutant-General of the United Irishmen in

Co. Down, after the arrest of Rev. Steel Dickson. His role at the Battle of Ballynahinch is unclear however, he was arrested soon afterwards and was incarcerated into the prison tender, the *Postlethwaite* in Belfast Lough. His participation in the United Irishmen led to his manse being burned by the Crown soldiers. He petitioned Lord Castlereagh, hoping to receive leniency, however, his pleas were ignored. Sinclair was banished to the United States and in 1799, he sailed to New York aboard the *Peggy*, alongside other '98 exiles. He was accepted by the Presbyterian Church in Baltimore, Maryland and rebuilt a career at preaching. In 1808, he established the Baltimore Academy. To his pupils he was noted as a friend and a guide. Along with fellow exile, Dr. Campbell White, Sinclair continued to be a radical voice in Baltimore and served on the committee of the *Baltimore Hibernian Benevolent Society*. Rev. William Sinclair died after a short illness on 9 November 1830.

SLOAN, Dr. John — Sloan, born c.1760, was a Tyrone native who studied

in Dublin's Royal College of Surgeons and practiced for ten years prior to leaving for Europe. Sloan participated in the 1798 Rebellion and was arrested, tried for treason and sentenced to death. Fortunately, his friends intervened and the sentence was communed to 1000 lashes. After receiving half of the sentence, he was released and fled Ireland for America. He settled in Chambersburg, Pennsylvania and practiced medicine until his death in 1831.

SMITH, Charles — Smith was a grocer from St. Mary's Abbey in Dublin,

who had joined the United Irishmen in 1792. In 1800, facing trouble for illegally producing alcoholic spirits, he fled to the United States and settled in New York City.

SMITH, James — Smith was a calico-printer, based at

Ryevale, near Leixlip, Co. Kildare. Having been a United Irishman, Smith was deeply involved in the 1798 Rebellion in Kildare, serving under William Aylmer and Hugh Ware. When the insurgent leaders surrendered at Odlum's Mills, near Osberstown, Co. Kildare, on 21 July 1798, Smith was incarcerated as a State Prisoner at Kilmainham Gaol in Dublin. After the Treaty of Amiens, these State Prisoners who were held in Ireland, were allowed to sort their affairs before exile. Smith sold his business and married Julianne Marie Burke on 16 July 1802 at St. Andrew's Church in Dublin. They travelled to France via London and established themselves in Rouen, where they invested in the cotton industry. The Smith's had several children: Marguerite (born 1803), Edmond Julian (born 1805), Marie Catherine (born 1806), Jean Thomas (born 1807), Adelaide (born 1808), the twins, Désirée and Julie (born 1810), Jacques (born 1810) and William Henry

(born 1813). Most of the children would not reach adulthood. With the war causing industrial recession in Rouen, Smith applied to the Duke of Feltre, who directed Smith to the Irish Legion. Smith was commissioned as Lieutenant on 11 November 1812 however, he would not experience the Saxon Campaign, which resulted in the Irish Legion facing near obliteration. After the Napoleonic Wars, Smith was placed on half-pay and the family continued to struggle financially. He was awarded French citizenship by King Louis XVIII in 1817. He served again in the French Army and was awarded promotion to Captain in the Corsican Legion. In September 1833, he was awarded a *Légion d'honneur*, and later died in France, having fulfilled a comfortable military career.

SMITH, James – (1769-1840) James Smith was born in Newtownards, Co. Down c.1769. Having been a United Irishman, Smith fought in the 1798 Rebellion and upon its failure he managed to flee to Scotland where he was

apprehended. Smith was returned to Ireland, court-martialled and ordered to be banished to America. Smith settled in Ryegate, Vermont, a location that welcomed many Ulster Presbyterian exiles of 1798, with his wife and together they raised a large family. James Smith died at Ryegate in 1840.

SMITH, Stewart – Within the *History of Delaware County and Ohio*, there contains a brief note that Stewart Smith had fled Ireland, having participated in the 1798 Rebellion. In August 1808, he settled at Boke's Creek in Delaware County, Ohio. He died on 7 April 1827, aged 64 years, and was interred at Boke's Creek Cemetery.

SMITH, Rev. Thomas – In 1799, Rev. Smith, the minister of Second Randalstown Presbyterian Church, emigrated to America for his involvement in the 1798 Rebellion, leaving his Co. Antrim church without a minister for five years. Regarding his background, Thomas Smith was born on 20 March 1755. He had been ordained on 12 October 1780. On 8 September 1783, Smith married Jane Weir and in 1785, he was given responsibility to oversee the construction of a meeting house in Randalstown, separate to the old Congregation. Smith settled in Pennsylvania and began to

preach as pastor of the Associate Reformed Synod. Rev. Thomas Smith died on 12 February 1832 at Tuscarora Township, Juniata County, Pennsylvania and is interred at McCoysville Cemetery.

SPARROW, Samuel – Sparrow, born c.1769, was a native of Gorey, Co. Wexford and son of William Sparrow and Susan Harrison. His family were notable Protestant farmers and merchants. Being liberal in his politics, Sparrow joined the United Irish movement in Co. Wexford but there is no record of any participation during the violent insurrection. He clearly was arrested as he petitioned Dublin Castle for clemency in August 1798, claiming his membership of the United Irishmen had been a foolish mistake and that he did not take up arms against the King. Having been given a chance, he emigrated the following year to the United States with his new bride, Mary Roe of Ballinclare. They settled in Charlestown, Massachusetts, for six years, before they returned to Gorey to care for old William Sparrow. The family returned to America in 1817, settling briefly in Utica, New York, for several years before establishing themselves in Huron County, Ohio. Samuel Sparrow died on 1 October 1838 and was interred at Kenyon College Cemetery in Knox County (OH).

The SPENCE Family *of Belfast/Kilkeel, County Down*

SPENCE, James – The patriarch of the Spence Family, whom we believe originated from Kilkeel, Co. Down. Spence fled to the United States after having participated in the 1798 Rebellion, taking his wife, Mary Matteson Spence and their family with him. They settled in Onondaga County, New York.

SPENCE, Mary *née Matteson* – Mary Matteson Spence, wife of James Spence and matriarch of the Spence family, emigrated to the United States after the failure of the Rebellion. Mrs. Spence died on 11 September 1827, aged 60 years, and was interred at Cardiff Cemetery in Onondaga County (NY).

SPENCE, Mary Ann – Mary Ann Spence (1787-1876) was the mother of Major J.S. van Patten (1822-1914), who served in the Union Army during the American Civil War. Her father, James Spence, is said to have been an insurgent officer during the Irish Rebellion of 1798. Due to his participation and strong political principles, he and family had to exile to America. Mary Ann arrived in America as a youth from her "*native Belfast*" in either 1798 or 1799. The family settled as farmers in upstate New York. In February 1809, Mary Ann married Ryer van Patten, and together they would have a large family. Her sister's memorial claims they were possibly native to Kilkeel, Co. Down.

MARY VAN PATTEN

Mary Ann Spence van Patten died on 24 September 1879 and was buried at Elmwood Cemetery in Cortland County (NY).

SPENCE, Nancy – Nancy Spence was born in Co. Down in 1798, to James Spence and Mary Matteson. She died on the 4th February 1809.

SPENCE, Robert – Robert Spence was born on 11 February 1782 to James Spence and Mary Matteson, being only sixteen years old when he fought during the Rebellion, alongside his father. When the family settled in outback New York, Spence moved to Tully in Onondaga County, New York, and married Anna Savage. After her sudden death in 1817, Spence married Jane McKee, having a large family. Robert Spence died on 4 August 1853 and was buried at Cardiff Cemetery in Onondaga County.

SPENCE, Sarah '*Sally*' – Sarah Spence was born on 4 July 1784 in Co. Down to James Spence and Mary Matteson. After the family settled in Onondaga County in upstate New York, she married Dr. James McNish, son of Alexander McNish, a Revolutionary War hero. Sarah Spence McNish died on 12 July 1866 and was interred at Maple Hill Cemetery, Munson, Ohio.

SPENCE, Ann – Ann Spence was born on 7 April 1792 to James Spence and Mary Matteson. Whilst residing at Onondaga County, Ann married Irish born, Thomas Bittles and settled at Newbury, Geauga County, New York, where she died on 4 July 1876.

STEELE, Rev. Robert –

Steele was born c.1767 in Ballykelly, Co. Derry. Having been educated in the Limavady area, he attended the University of Glasgow for three years, earning a theology degree. Steele returned to his native county and was licenced to preach on 29 July 1788 and was eventually ordained at Scriggan Presbyterian Church in Dungiven on 7 March 1790. On 24 June 1791, he married Isabella Hazlett Steele, a liberal, became a strong supporter of the United Irishmen movement and was an organiser in the Dungiven area. After the Rebellion, Steele was arrested and conveyed to the prison ship, anchored in Belfast Lough, the **Postlethwaite**. He pleaded guilty to treason and rebellion before a court-martial. He was  sentenced to banishment and in 1799, he sailed to America with his wife and the youngest of their three children. As a result of the court-martial and his plea, his name was erased from the Ulster Presbytery of Ministers.

That the Rev⁴ Robert Steel, having pleaded Guilty to a charge of Treason & Rebellion before a Court Martial his name was erased from the List of the Presbytery. That John Pinkerton & Ruben Rogers,

Steele settled in Pittsburgh, Pennsylvania, where his brother was a merchant. He applied to join the Presbytery but the processing would take some time to administer. He was granted permission to go on probation and eventually became a minister of the First Pittsburgh Presbyterian Church in October 1802. Rev. Robert Steele died on 22 March 1810 as result of a tragic accident, in which a fire had taken hold in Pittsburgh and Steele went to help quell the flames. He helped transport water from a frozen hole in the Allegheny River and afterwards travelled around the town gathering funds to aid those who lost their homes. The extreme temperature changes took their toll and Steele eventually succumbed to a fever.

STEVENSON, James & Martha

STEVENSON, James & Martha – Born in 1772, James Stevenson, a native of Co. Derry, would become deeply implicated in the United Irishmen and would suffer arrest and imprisonment in Londonderry Gaol. In August 1797, George Hill M.P. secured Stevenson's release on the condition that he immediately emigrate to America. In the publication, *"Portrait and biography of Seneca and Schuyler Counties"*, James and his wife, **Martha Lowther**, came to America as political refugees, settling in Albany before relocating to Tyre in Seneca County, New York c. 1812 and became dedicated worshipers at the United Presbyterian Church. They held a farm of 72 acres at Tyre. James Stevenson died on 8 September 1850 and was interred at Maple Grove Cemetery

in Seneca County with '*An Irish Exile. Fled to America in 1798*,' etched on his headstone. Martha died on 17 July 1858, aged 82 years. They are interred together at Maple Grove Cemetery in Seneca County. Their son, **Gawin Stevenson** was born in Co. Derry in 1796 and was only a small child when taken to the United States. He remained farming at Tyre and died there in July 1871. Another son, Robert L. Stevenson was born in 1807 at Albany, before the family firmly settled in Seneca County. In addition to running his farm in Tyre, Robert was also very involved in local politics holding positions such as town supervisor and also serving as a representative in the state legislature.

STOREY, Thomas - Thomas Storey, a Belfast based printer, hailed from a notable Presbyterian family of Islandbawn, Co. Antrim. His brother, John Storey, who was a leader of the Kells United Irishmen at the Battle of Antrim on 7 June 1798, was like his brother, a printer for the *Northern Star*. In 1796, Thomas Storey was arrested for his United Irish membership but escaped from custody within a barrel and escaped to America. Storey would remain in the United States until 1812. His brother, John Storey, was tried and acquitted in April 1798 for administering the United Irish oath to a Monaghan Militiaman, however, he was executed later that summer for his role in the Battle of Antrim. Upon returning to Ireland, having been granted permission by the authorities, Storey became a successful businessman. He died in 1827 and is interred at his family's burial plot in Antrim, where his executed brother's remains also lie.

The STUBBS Family of Dublin

William Stubbs was born at Whitewood, Co. Meath, in 1757. On 20 May 1781, he married **Margaret Reade** at St. Paul's Church on Dublin's Arran Quay. Their children were: **Edward Joseph Stubbs** (1785-1864), **Catherine Stubbs** (b.1790), **Michael Peter Stubbs** (1792-1880), **Richard Stubbs** (b.1793), **William Stubbs** (1795-1857), **Laurence Stubbs** (b.1797) and **Mary Ann Stubbs** (b. 1800). Within a decade, Stubbs became a wealthy clothier merchant based at Inn's Quay. On 12 March 1798, he harboured Dr. William James MacNeven, before his eventual arrest. In 1805, the Stubbs Family emigrated to the United States and settled at Wayne in Steuben County, New York. Margaret Reade Stubbs died in May 1813 at their New York farm. William Stubbs died in Washington D.C. on 19 December 1831. The Stubbs family lineage is intertwined with other emigres of 1798. Roseanna Marie Stubbs married William Kernan, an exile of the 1798 Rebellion and their son, Francis Kernan married Hannah Devereux, a daughter of Nicholas Devereux, who hailed from Enniscorthy, Co. Wexford, and who witnessed the horrors of the insurrection of 1798.

SWAIL, Valentine – After the battle of Ballynahinch, Swail, a native of Loughkeelan, near Ballycuttler, Co. Down, hid from the authorities in the Montalto demesne in Co. Down. He had served in the insurgency as was one of Monro's adjutants during the battle, and had tried and failed to offer advice to persuade Monroe to attack the drunken Monaghan Militia, who were stationed in the burning village of Ballynahinch on the night of 12 June 1798. Swail hid from the authorities for two weeks, being supplied with food by his servant Shelah Durnin. After negotiations, he was eventually allowed to emigrate to America with his family.

SWAN, Robert – A native of Ulster, Swan, who had fled to the United States was noted to fall upon financial difficulty whilst in America. John Caldwell hired Swan to paint his New York residence but made a poor job of it. A victim of poverty, Swan gained the attention of the Irish community in New York who thought of raising a subscription for his passage back to Ireland.

SWANTON, Robert – Swanton was born on 5 September 1774 to William Swanton and Sarah Denis. The Swanton's hailed from Ballydehob, Dunmanway, Co. Cork. Having been deeply connected with the United Irishmen, Robert Swanton, was imprisoned in Cork Gaol. The information regarding his release or escape is non-existent, however he decided to flee to France. Irish Legion historian, Nicholas Dunne Lynch, adds that Swanton held the rank of sub-lieutenant in the Legion from 1804 to 1806. In June 1806, he tendered his resignation and officially left the Legion in August 1806, stating that he wished to emigrate to the United States, as his father and brother had settled there. Upon arriving in New York City, Swanton was actively supporting Jeffersonian politics and eventually became a city alderman. On 28 July 1814, he married Anne Long. In 1815, at a time when he was highly involved in supporting newly arrived Irish immigrants, along with Thomas Addis Emmet, William J. MacNeven, William Sampson and David Bryson, Swanton was resident at 98 Cherry Street in Manhattan. He was the author of *'The Manifesto to the People of Ireland,'* and was later promoted to become Judge of the Marine Court in New York City, a position he would hold for sixteen years, acquiring much wealth and a respected social standing. Swanton was an avid supporter of his friend, Martin van Buren, during his campaign for the Presidency. In 1836, having retired, Swanton returned to west Cork and died at Ballydehob on 15 February 1840. He is interred at Abbeymahon Graveyard, Dunmanway, Co. Cork (*pictured*).

SWANTON, William – William Swanton was father of the above listed Robert Swanton. When Robert resigned from the Irish Legion in 1806, he claimed he wished to join his father and brother in the United States.

SWEETMAN, John – John Sweetman was born c.1752 in Dublin to master brewer, John Sweetman and his wife, Mary (*nee* Sweetman). Throughout his early life, Sweetman flourished in business as a brewer alongside his brother, Patrick Sweetman, gaining considerable wealth. His wealth brought much

flamboyance. He was known to adore artworks and held within his collection, several paintings from renowned European artists, including Peter Paul Rubens' **'*Orpheus and Eurydice*'** (*pictured*). In 1784, he married Mary Atkinson. Involved in politics, especially the Catholic Committee, it was inevitable that Sweetman would eventually join the Society of United Irishman, in which a near relation, Valentine Lawless of the Baronet of Cloncurry, was also heavily involved in. Sweetman's politics radicalised throughout the 1790s and he became a leading personality in the United Irishmen. He was a member of the Leinster Delegation of United

Irishmen, which met at Oliver Bond's house on 12 March 1798. Sweetman was arrested and held at Kilmainham Gaol, becoming a State Prisoner. To cover his expenses, Sweetman had to auction his prized and beloved art collection. On 19 March 1799, Sweetman was sent to Fort George in Scotland and would remain there in relative comfort until the cessation of hostilities between Great Britain and France. Upon arriving on the continent in the summer of 1802, Sweetman travelled to Lyons in France before settling in Paris, where he was noted by Miles Byrne as within the collective of prominent exiles such as Thomas Addis Emmet and Hampden Evans. By 1820, Sweetman grew tired of Parisian life and with  allowance from the Government, was allowed to return to Dublin. John Sweetman died on 5 May 1826 and was interred in Swords, Co. Dublin.

SWINEY, John – John Swiney was born on August 7th 1773 in Cork City to Daniel Swiney and Eleanora Anglin. An acquaintance of John and Henry Sheares, Swiney became a United Irishman. He was a woollen draper by trade, with his shop, which became the provisional headquarters of the Cork City United Irishmen, situated near the junction of Shandon Street and Blarney Street. To gain military experience, Swiney joined the Loyal Cork Legion under Lord Donoughmore, a tactic used by many subversive United Irishmen across Ireland, however, his actions and agitations against the church tithe payments and informers had marked Swiney as a wanted man to the Government. On 28 March 1798, whilst visiting Roger O'Connor in prison, Swiney was arrested and immediately sent to Dublin. Swiney was imprisoned throughout the 1798 Rebellion and was eventually sent to Scotland's Fort George as a State  Prisoner, where he lived in reasonable comfort until the Treaty of Amiens ended hostilities between Britain and France. In August 1802, Swiney travelled to the continent with Thomas Addis Emmet, Joseph Cormick and Hugh Wilson, who settled in Brussels for several months. In the summer of 1803, Swiney travelled back to Cork City from Le Harve to participate in Robert Emmet's uprising, however, he learned that his native Cork had a poor United Irish structure and had no appetite for revolt. Swiney eventually sailed back to France in an open boat, carrying the news of the failed rebellion and the execution of Robert Emmet.

Swiney received a lieutenancy in the Irish Legion, followed by a captaincy in the March 1804 promotions, however, he played a role in one of the darkest episodes of the Legion's earliest days; the infamous duel with fellow Corkman, Thomas Corbett. The Legion was formed by decree of Napoleon Bonaparte with the aim of sending an expedition to Ireland, however, it was formed in a divided state. The United Irish emigrés were divided into several camps; the Emmetites and the O'Connorites. Swiney was a hardline supporter of Thomas Addis Emmet whilst the Corbett brothers, Thomas and William, were followers of Arthur O'Connor. On 3 June 1804, Thomas Corbett refused to sign a document which confirmed that the entire regiment had sworn allegiance to Bonaparte, claiming that Swiney, had not done so.

The next day, Swiney struck Corbett on the Legion's parade ground of Morlaix and a fight ensued. After a period of detention, the quarrel was far from over. After his release, Corbett challenged Swiney to a duel of pistols. On 20 September 1804, Corbet and Swiney met at Lesneven and attempted the duel was attempted several times dues to misfires and Corbett receiving wounds, which did not deter him from surrendering. The paces were decreased from ten to six and Swiney's sixth bullet ended the duel. Thomas Corbett suffered from multiple wounds and succumbed that evening. The feud caused much consternation within the Legion, resulted in several resignations and damaged its honour with France during the period. The

dishonour of the duel effectively ended Swiney's time with the Legion. With Napoleon not honouring any interest towards an expedition to Ireland, many of Swiney's allies in the Emmet faction resigned their commissions and went to the United States. Swiney followed suit. After his resignation, he married a local woman, Marie Victoire Pezron, and settled in Morlaix (*pictured*), where he established himself as a successful wool and cloth merchant. Being a dedicated United Irishman, Swiney's support for abolition of slavery extended to him naming his son, Gustave Emmanuel Toussaint Swiney (1808-1888), after the black Haitien hero, Toussaint Louverture. Gustave Swiney (*pictured*) would become councillor of the Morlaix and Lanmeur cantons between 1848 and 1852 and also held the title of Mayor of Plouégat-Guerrand His oldest son, Jean Francois Edmond Swiney (1806-1858) would be father to General Michel

Edmond Swiney, who became Military Governor of Corsica in 1889. John Swiney died at Morlaix on 19 October 1844 and was interred at Saint Martin's Cemetery within the town.

TANDY, James Napper - James Napper Tandy, the son of James Tandy & Maria Della Jenkins, hailed from an influential and wealthy Protestant Dublin family. Some history claims his year of birth as 1740 but the entrance of '*James Naper Tandy*,' on St. Audoen's baptismal records proves that he was in fact born in February 1738, thus making him sixty years of age at the time of the Rebellion. James Napper Tandy was educated at a Quaker boarding school in the southern Kildare village of Ballitore, graduating several years after Ireland's most noted liberal Whig, Sir Edmund Burke. During the same year he married Ann Jones and later had one child, James Tandy. Tandy, because of his affluent family background, entered the maritime and merchant business quite early in his life, earning him a lifetime of contacts across Ireland, Britain and some

European ports. Known for his agitation in corporation politics, he distinguished himself in a multitude of movements across Dublin and became very popular, especially amongst his associates in the Trade Guild. In the 1770s, he became influenced by the news of the liberal and patriotic reformers agitating in America, particularly in regards the trade aspect. When Britain tightened its own economic belt during the American Revolution, it led to harsh tariffs upon the Irish market, thus angering Irish merchants. In 1779, Tandy was publicly vocal about preventing English manufactured goods being used to Ireland and cried out for Free Trade. He played a relatively leading role in the Volunteer Movement of the late 1770s, which resulted in the 1782 Parliament. He had been an artillery officer in the Dublin Volunteer Corps, with one of his cannon cast with "*Free Trade or ...?...*" upon its breech cascable.

The period of the Volunteer Movement & Grattan's Parliament was indeed a positive stepping stone for Tandy's interests but not wholesome for him to appreciate. Ireland was racked with major social and political issues that needed reforming. Due to the Ascendency's vetoing power over crucial issues, the changes had not been as radical as Tandy had hoped and this was proven by their disregard for the calls of Catholic Emancipation. He would spend the 1780s in a state of enriching his principles and intensifying his support for progressive reforms through the Irish Whig network. Tandy was seen as an unconstitutional radical to many of the moderate Irish liberals and an eccentric, especially when he vocally supported the occurrences across France during their revolutionary period. His popularity amongst the wider Guild circle never waned due to his assertive moral obligations. One occasion saw him leading a mob that were designed to destroy the construction works at Dublin's new Customs House because they feared the new building would injure the trade of merchants and tradesmen who resided close to the Old Customs House on Essex Quay and was costing phenomenal costs whilst at the same time, he co-led the closing stages of developing the Grand Canal in opening Dublin trade to the south of the country.

In October 1791, Theobald Wolfe Tone returned from Belfast with news of the new radical organisation that had been established there; the Society of United Irishmen. Tone set about establishing a similar grouping in Dublin and invited Napper Tandy to the inaugural meeting. On 9 November 1791, at the Eagle Tavern in Dublin's Temple Bar, the Dublin Society of United Irishmen was formed. Simon Butler chaired the event with Napper Tandy being honourably elected as its first secretary. Tandy would play an intrinsic role in the proceedings of the society throughout late 1791 and early 1792 and helped build it into a solid political movement. His influence and militancy also saw Tandy sworn into the predominantly Catholic secret society; the Defenders. Links like this would start a working and beneficial coalescence between the Defenders and United Irishmen when both organisations were heavily proscribed by the government post-1794. Wolfe Tone later wrote of Tandy's instant interest in establishing a Dublin Society of the United Irishmen:

"It is but justice to an honest man, who has been persecuted for his firm adherence to his principles, to observe here, that Tandy in coming forward on this occasion, well knew that he was putting in the most extreme hazard, his popularity among the corporations in the City of Dublin, with whom he had **enjoyed the most unbounded influence for near twenty years: and, in fact, in the event, this popularity was sacrificed. This did not prevent his taking his part decidedly."**

His son, James Tandy, a former officer in the East India Company and Dublin based wine merchant, joined the growing organisation in 1792 but resigned from the Society along with "forty respectable gentlemen" over the issue of universal suffrage, which resulted in a strained relationship with Napper Tandy for much the remainder of his father's life. On 18 April 1792, Tandy was arrested at his house on Chancery Lane on the orders of the Irish House of Commons and brought to Newgate Gaol on charges of offering out the Solicitor-General & MP for Gorey, John Toler (Lord Norbury), to a duel, after Toler apparently mocked Tandy's looks. On his liberation, at the close of the Session, Tandy, who was not only slighted but infuriated, published a statement in the public papers, expressing his views on Toler. He called Toler, **"a calumniator and liar," "a** *pander,*" and "*an imperious and impertinent upstart whose peevish petulance he would not submit to.*" An inquiry was called to investigate the issue for any dishonourable conduct and the matter was resolved to Toler's success. Tandy sued the Viceroy, Lord Westmorland, who in turn brought proceedings against Tandy. The proceedings were grounded on the alleged illegality of a proclamation, offering a reward for Tandy's arrest when in fact it was illegal to arrest a person on a charge of a breach of privilege without summoning the party to the bar of the House of Commons and Tandy also stressed that there was no functionary for any Viceroy, legally appointed, to call for such an arrest when in fact the position was filled by a letter of patent, under an English seal, which was not recognised in the Irish legal system. It was clear that Tandy's past and his politics disgusted the establishment.

In February 1793, Tandy faced a collective of legal proceedings against him. The first being his distributing of the of Thomas Paine's "*Common Sense*"; the second being his membership of the Defender Movement at Castlebellingham, Co. Louth and thirdly for embodying severe structures against the affluent Beresford Family. Knowing that the authorities were amassing a strength for his demise, Tandy accepted the worrying predictions of his attorney, Matthew Dowling, and fled to England, where he would remain hidden until 1795.

Corresponding with another Irish exile, Archibald Hamilton Rowan, Tandy decided to flee to the security of the United States of America. Tandy settled at Wilmington in Delaware for several years, amongst Archibald Hamilton Rowan and Theobald Wolfe Tone, who had fled Ireland upon fear of arrest. In March 1797, he sailed, on invitation from the French Ambassador of the United States, for France. Having briefly stayed in Hamburg, he made his way to Paris and immediately became enlisted in an official role within the French military. Within months of having impressed the French Directory, he obtained the rank of General of a division and was to play a leading role in the French expeditions to Ireland. In early September 1798, Tandy, joined by several Irish exiles and a French force of 3,000, sailed from Dunkirk aboard the *Anacreon*, and landed on the rugged Rutland Island, off Donegal's wild western coastline. The date was 16 September 1798. Upon disembarking upon the desolated island with its wind battered post office, Tandy learned from the postmaster, Harry McNelis, of the failed Humbert expedition that had collapsed at Ballinamuck only the week previously. It is often claimed that Tandy and his associates decided to get drunk to a point that Tandy had to be carried back to the ship, having decided to sail back to France, however, it seems he only posted several proclamations before setting sail again. The proclamation had called upon Irishmen:

"*to strike from their blood-cemented thrones the murderers of your friends*" and to "*wage a war of extermination against your oppressors.*"

In order to avoid the Royal Navy, the *Anacreon* sailed north and around the Shetland Islands before docking at Bergen (Norway) in the Kingdom of Denmark for replenishment. When the British blockaded the port, Tandy and the other Irish officers decided to make their way overland to Hamburg in order to re-enter France. Having reached Hamburg, this group of Irishmen which consisted of Tandy, William Corbett and James Blackwell, stayed at the **"American Arms,"** hoping to make their way to Paris the following day. In the early hours, the hotel was surrounded by the Hamburg Guard and the men were apprehended and held in brutal conditions in a Hamburg prison. The reason being that the British Government had issued a peremptory demand to detain these men. Conditions were that horrific that Corbett

later described being chained for over a month in a dungeon, where the water reached his knees and where many prisoners froze to death throughout the harsh winter months. The French Directory were infuriated and demanded their immediate release, classifying them as "naturalized Frenchmen and belonging to the service of the Republic." However French relations with Hamburg were not particularly strong and the prisoners would remain within these conditions until they were banished to England on 29 September 1799 and from there back to Dublin's Kilmainham Gaol to face charges. On 12 February 1800, Tandy was placed on trial in Dublin and acquitted by the lenient Lord Kilwarden, however he was conveyed to Lifford Gaol in Donegal for the Rutland Island affair. Here he would languish until April 1801 and faced trial once again. Pleading guilty to treason, James Napper Tandy was sentenced to death by hanging, beheading and quartering. It did not end there for him as the political atmosphere in Europe was progressing towards peace between France and Britain after nearly a decade of war. It is believed that Napoleon Bonaparte would not entertain the Treaty of Amiens of 1802 as long as Napper Tandy was awaiting a death sentence. With this, Tandy was instantly released. This release was seen as an important diplomatic success for Paris and he was received with distinction in France in March 1802. James Napper Tandy died on 24 August 1803, aged 65 years. He received a large military funeral fit for any Napoleonic General in Bordeaux. It is presumed that his remains were later exhumed and brought back to Ireland and buried within the family crypt at St. Mary's Churchyard in Julienstown, Co. Meath.

Jonah Barrington would later write this of Napper Tandy:

"His person was ungracious; his language neither eloquent nor argumentative; his address neither graceful nor impressive; but he was sincere and persevering, and though in many instances erroneous and violent, he was considered to be honest. His private character furnished no ground to doubt the integrity of his public one; and, like many of those persons who occasionally spring up in revolutionary periods, he acquired celebrity without being able to account for it, and possessed influence, without rank or capacity."

TENNANT, John –
Tennant was born on 11 October 1772 to Rev. John Tennant and Anne Patton at Roseyards, Ballymoney, Co. Antrim. Tennant was raised in the faith of Presbyterianism and was educated by his father and then served an apprenticeship under Samuel Givan, a grocer from Coleraine, Co. Derry. Here, Tennant learned the value of hard work and respect towards his Presbyterian principles. In the 1790s, his older brother, William Tennant had become a high-ranking United Irishman. The younger Tennant was involved in the organisation but not to the same extent. During the crackdown of the United Irishmen in Ulster in April and May 1797, Tennant fled Ireland for France, via London, Hamburg and The Hague.

In 1799, he joined the French Army and held a temporary rank of Major during French conflicts with Britain. When the Irish Legion was established in late 1803 by a decree from Napoleon, Tennant was given a captaincy. On 2 December 1804, each regiment in the services of France was ordered to send two officer representatives to the coronation of Napoleon at Notre Dame, Paris. Tennant and William Corbett represented the Irish Legion during his event, which saw Napoleon place the Crown on his own head in confident and symbolic arrogance. He was also honourably presented with the Irish Legion's own regimental eagle by Bonaparte. On 9 November 1809, Tennant was promoted *chef de bataillon* of the Legion's fourth battalion. He would eventually command the first battalion when it was merged into a full fighting battalion. In 1813, for his services to France, the Emperor, Napoleon Bonaparte, presented Tennant with the *Légion d'honneur*. On 19 August 1813, Tennant, led his regiment into battle at Löwenberg against the Russians. Severe casualties would be inflicted upon the Irish Legion, including its commander, John Tennant.

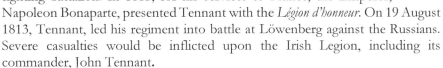

"Poor Tennant was giving orders to have the ranks closed and the gaps filled, which had been opened by the artillery, when he fell. He was cut completely in two; the cannon ball striking a belt in which he carried his money served as a knife to separate his body. The soldiers dug his grave with their bayonets, and when burying him found several pieces of gold that fell out of his entrails and part of his gold watch."

Le Sacre de Napoléon by Jacques-Louis David

THOMPSON, Dominick

THOMPSON, Dominick – Dominick Thompson, a native of Co. Derry and a well-known contractor, had to flee to America for his involvement in the 1798 Rebellion. Thompson became one of the contractors who helped construct the Market Street Bridge in Philadelphia, under Timothy Palmer. The

bridge's two side spans were 150 feet each. Supposedly, this was the first permanent bridge over a major American river, as well as the world's first bridge with regular masonry piers in deep water. It was completed in 1805. It is worth noting that Thompson's two older brothers, William and John Thompson had emigrated some years beforehand and had taken part in the American War of Independence.

THOMPSON, William – William Thompson was an Englishman, who was employed by Henry Joy McCracken c.1790, and brought to work in Belfast. At the time of the 1798 Rebellion, Thompson was working as a calico printer and still closely connected to the McCracken Family, although it is unknown if

he participated in the insurrection. After the arrest of Henry Joy McCracken, Thompson was brutally flogged for refusing to give evidence against his former employer. Not long afterwards, Thompson emigrated, leaving a letter to Mary Ann McCracken, a memento that she kept all of her life. It read: *"Miss Mary. Excuse the manner I take, to return my thanks for the goodness and care, you took in my late little mischances, for to you I may say I owe my health; I would have returned my warmest thanks verbally; only a crisis like this; When you have lost a Brother, mankind a true friend; and myself the only man on Earth I ever had a true or sincere regard for, or perhaps ever will; as I shall quit this country in a few hours, never to return, any trinket sent to me, that ever belong'd to him, I would look upon it as the instrumental part, of my religion, and learn from its philanthropic owner to live and die."*

TICKLAR – Ticklar was a United Irishman who, in 1797, was ordered to travel to Scotland under the alias of Donaldson, disguised as a piper. His mission was to spread United Irish principles across Scotland. Upon arriving at Donaghadee, Co. Down, he became distressed when the principal United Irish leaders did not show up. Panicked, Ticklar fled to the United States.

TIERNAN, James - Having played a principal role all commander of the Clane insurgents in Co. Kildare during the 1798 Rebellion, Tiernan surrendered and was imprisoned at Kilmainham Gaol on 22 September 1798. He was released in February 1800. In his notes it states that he was willing to go to America if he was allowed to prepare. Tiernan returned to Dublin to assist in the Emmet uprising of July 1803, however, he was not trusted by many of the Kildare men as he had reputedly fled from his commanding role during the 1798 Rebellion.

TONE, Martha 'Matilda' *née Witherington* – Martha Witherington was born at 69 Grafton Street in Dublin on 17 June 1769 to William, Witherington and Catherine Fanning. Having been introduced to Theobald Wolfe Tone, they quickly eloped and married on 21 July 1785 in Dublin's St. Anne's Church. The Tone family would include: Richard Tone (died in infancy), William Tone, Maria Tone and Francis Tone. In support of her husband, Matilda, as he adoringly called her, went into exile with him, firstly to Wilmington, Pennsylvania and then to Paris, France. In 1804, having spent several years in financial duress, she received her long-awaited pension of 1,200 francs from the French authorities. She moved to an apartment in the Latin Quarter, at 51 rue St.

Jacques, to be close to her son, William, who was studying at Lycée Imperial. Matilda would suffer the horrors of losing both Maria and Francis to tuberculosis.

On 12 April 1811, the Emperor, Napoleon Bonaparte, was hunting in the forests outside of Paris. Whilst sitting in his carriage, Matilda Tone abruptly broke protocol and approached Bonaparte and explained herself and her reasons to approach him in such a manner. She reminded Bonaparte of her late husband and the plight in which her family had suffered since his death. Bonaparte recalled his respect for Wolfe Tone and would award William Tone privileged status and citizenship. Whilst the young Tone progressed in his military academy and eventually rose to become a war hero, Matilda continued to reside with a meagre existence in Paris. On 19 August 1816, Matilda married Thomas Wilson, an old friend of her husband, who often supported her. She now styled herself Matilda Tone Wilson.

DEATH OF THE FORMER MRS. WOLFE TONE.— The District papers chronicle the death, at her residence, in Georgetown, on Sunday, the 18th, in the 81st year of her age, Matilda, relict of the late Thomas Wilson, Esq., of Scotland. This estimable lady, born in Ireland, on the 17th of June, 1768, was first married to the illustrious patriot, Theobald Wolfe Tone, well known in Irish history as the friend and companion of the *martyred* Emmett.— Mrs Tone resided in France at the time of her husband's death. The estimation in which she was held —and her own moral and literary worth—had gained her many powerful friends. The most elegant encomium ever pronounced on woman, was that which Lucien Bonaparte bestowed upon her, in recommending her case, and that of her children, to the attention of the French Chambers; the effect of which was manifested by the *unanimous* grant of an annual pension She preserved, in her eighty-first year the energy of intellect that made her the companion of her husband, and the warmth of heart that even her cruel sorrows could not chill.

Her funeral took place at Georgetown, yesterday attended, generally, by the natives and friends of Ireland, the country for which Wolfe Tone died, and which possessed her heart to the last.

The new couple set sail for the United States in 1817, settling outside Washington D.C. in 1819. Feeling that the time was right for publication, Matilda immersed herself into the task of releasing her late husband's entire literary works, which she had cared for since 1798. It was officially edited by William Tone and it would become a bestseller. After the death of her last remaining child in 1828, Matilda descended into a very private life, spending her later years defending Wolfe Tone's legacy and focusing on erecting a stone over his Bodenstown grave. Matilda Tone Wilson died on 18 March 1849. Today, her remains lie next to her son at Greenwood Cemetery in Brooklyn, New York.

TONE, William Theobald

William Tone (1791-1828) was the son of Theobald Wolfe Tone and Matilda Witherington. He was born in Dublin on 29 April 1791. Tone was only three years old when his parents fled into exile, firstly to Pennsylvania and then to Paris. After the death of Wolfe Tone, Matilda remained in Paris, caring for the children, enrolling William Tone at the Lycée Imperial. In 1807, whilst suffering from tuberculosis, the disease which claimed the lives of his siblings, William travelled to the United States with his mother, hoping the sea voyage would cure his ailments. After settling some of the affairs of Theobald Wolfe Tone, they returned to Paris.

In late 1810, Tone enrolled at the École de Cavalerie at St-Germain-en-Laye, where he studied cavalry warfare and composed various enlightening essays. After Matilda brazingly approached Napoleon Bonaparte, whilst he was on a hunting excursion, she reminded him of Wolfe Tone, whom Bonaparte had respected during their various meetings in 1797-98 and humbly consented to help the Tone family. William Tone was given official recognition and French citizenship. In early 1813, upon completion of his studies, Tone was promoted as cornot in the 8th regiment of chasseurs and was placed at the front. He received various lance wounds during the Battle of Leipzig, however his bravery was well renowned. He was known by his fellow officers as *Petit Loup* (Little Wolf) and he would receive promotion and awarded the *legion d'honneur* by the end of the year. After the abdication of Bonaparte, Tone gave his allegiance to the restored Bourbon order and even personally addressed King Louis XVIII on military matters, however, when Napoleon returned from Elba, Tone quickly rejoined his old Emperor. Tone saw action in the Lowlands Campaign, but faced a dilemma when Napoleon lost the Battle of Waterloo.

WILLIAM THEOBALD WOLFE TONE

In October 1816, Tone arrived in New York City. He followed his father's footsteps by studying law and was guided by his father's old friend, William Sampson. Whilst studying law, Tone casually composed an essay focused on military improvement, which came to the attention of John Calhoun, the Secretary of War. Calhoun embraced Tone's abilities and experiences and offered him a rank and a place on the Board of Fortification. Tone married Catherine Sampson, the daughter of William Sampson, who would give birth to a daughter, Grace Georgiana Tone (1825-1900). After editing his father's journals into a complete memoirs, William Tone, having suffered much physically throughout his life, eventually died on 10 October 1828, at Washington D.C. Both William and Catherine were initially buried at Riker-Lent in Queens, New York, but were later re-interred at Greenwood Cemetery in Brooklyn, along with Matilda Wolfe Tone.

TOWNSEND, "Rev". James — James Townsend, often referred to as Townsley, was a Presbyterian probationer from Greyabbey, Co. Down. His participation in the Down Rebellion of 9-13 June 1798, resulted in him being able to escape to the United States of America. Under the King's Pardon Act, a bounty of £50 was offered for his capture, thus becoming what was then known

as '*A Fifty Pounder*,' thus signifying he held some influence within the United Irish movement. He was noted as Munro's second-in-command during the Battle of Ballynahinch and was often referred to '*Citizen Townsend*.' Townsend would descend to an unfortunate end when he took his own life in 1805 at his residence in Savannah, Georgia.

TRENOR, Thomas – Trenor, a native of Co. Monaghan, was born on 17 March 1761 and educated at Trinity College, Dublin. He was a noted athlete and he held a record of 21 feet in the sport of long-jumping. Commerce appealed to the young Trenor, who, upon completion at Trinity, took on a role with wine merchants, Conway, McAuley and Hughes. Trenor's abilities and loyalty to business saw him buy a large share in the business within five years. Upon the death of Conway, the family left his share to Trenor, whom they regarded highly, thus making him the sole owner of the business and financially wealthy. Upon meeting Catherine Eustace at a banquet, the couple soon married against the wishes of her family, who hailed from the ascendency and Trenor, who hailed from the common class. The couple disregarded the wishes of the Eustace Family and married at Lazor's Hill Chapel of Ease, with Rev. Dr. Lyman

THOMAS TRENOR

presiding over the ceremony. Trenor escalated in the United Irishmen, holding the rank of Treasurer and was present at a delegation meeting at Oliver Bond's residence on 12 March 1798, which was raided by Major Henry Charles Sirr. Trenor was conveyed to Dublin Castle and held in the Birmingham Tower (*pictured*) with John McCann and William Michael Byrne, who were both executed in July 1798. Trenor utilised a plan from simply looking at his means. He wore a roquelaure cloak and requested hair powder from the sentinel guards. Whilst leaving the toilet, Trenor disguised himself as best as he could and simply walked out through the Castle gates and crossed the moat unnoticed. Upon escaping from Dublin, Trenor travelled to Kilkea Castle in Co. Kildare, the residence of Thomas Reynolds, a United Irish informer. He eventually escaped from Ireland aboard one of his merchant ships and sailed for Norway, where he made his way through Zealand, Hanover and into France.

Upon hearing of the expedition to Ireland (Humbert), Trenor travelled to the Free City of Hamburg. Whilst there he disguised himself as a seaman and sailed to Liverpool, where he observed the disembarking of French prisoners who surrendered at Ballinamuck. Hiding at an acquaintance's residence in Cumberland for several months, Trenor learned of the United Irish leadership having entered into conditional terms of banishment, an idea upon which Trenor believed would end his plight as a fugitive. Upon arriving in Dublin to plead his case, he was immediately arrested, placed in Kilmainham Gaol and held for nearly three years, forcing him to sell much of his business to procure funds. Whilst in Kilmainham Gaol, he shared a cell with William Corbett, who had been arrested in Hamburg after Tandy's expedition to Rutland Island. Noticing Corbett's health was seriously deteriorating, Trenor's wife, who resided with her husband in the cell, tended and cared for the young Corbett. Trenor organised an escape for Corbett. He requested his brother to visit him, however, he asked him to wrap his body in a silken ladder before entering the prison. The escape was a success. After the Treaty of Amiens, Trenor was released on condition of banishment and secured leave to travel to Portugal to sell his remaining assets. Trenor had lost his entire livelihood, a value of £120,000, in which he blamed the conservative US ambassador to Britain, Rufus King. Upon sailing to America, his ship was overrun by pirates, who added to Trenor's misfortune by robbing him of what wealth he had in his possession.

The Trenor Family eventually arrived in the United States and settled at Bennington in Vermont, where he established an iron-works, which employed one hundred and fifty men. Tariff legislation by Congress prevented Trenor from gaining the wealth he was once acquainted with. One story from Bennington states that a man named Ayres composed a poem mocking Trenor's thick brogue and the fact he kept goats. Trenor was eventually fined $50 for physically assaulting Ayres in consequence. Upon selling his business in 1815, the family moved to Cooperstown in New York, where they attempted farming. This also did not fill Trenor's appetite for success and he eventually established a mercantile business in Lansingburgh. Trenor retired in comfort and was a leading figure in the Irish community in New York alongside Thomas Addis Emmet, William J. MacNeven and William Sampson. In 1832, Trenor was granted a three month visit to Ireland, where he dined with Daniel O'Connell and shook hands with the man who arrested him at Oliver Bond's residence, Major Sirr. Thomas Trenor died on 6 September 1848.

TYRELL – Miles Byrne recorded this individual in his memoirs: **"*Captain. 7ᵗʰ December 1803. Never joined the Legion because of the bad state of his health. He was one of the Irish exiles much considered by all his acquaintance.*"**

VANCE, John – Vance is cited as having fled Ireland during the 1798 Rebellion. He died on 16 June 1849, aged 76 years, and was interred at Newville Cemetery in Cumberland County, Pennsylvania. It is unknown exactly where Vance hailed from in Ireland but we believe it may have been the Antrim area, considering that an extended Vance family resided at Antrim and had taken part on both sides during the Battle of Antrim on 7 June 1798.

WALKER, Abraham – Abraham Walker fled Ireland towards the end of May 1797. He was a merchant from Newry, Co. Down and an active member of the United Irishmen. He would often use their newspaper the *Northern Star* for advertising.

NOTICE OF PARTNERSHIP.

ABRAHAM, JOHN and ISAAC WALKER, fons of the late John Walker, of Newry, merchant, beg leave to info rm their friends and correspondents, that they have entered into a joint partnerfhip, under the firm of

ABRAHAM WALKER & CO.

and intend carrying on and continuing the bufinefs of their late father; and hope by their attention to fuch orders as they may receive, to merit the attention of their employers.

N. B. They are impowered by their father's Executors, to fettle and account with his creditors and debtors.

Newry, September 9, 1795.

WALLACE "Rev." Charles – Charles Wallace, the son of Hugh Wallace of the Parish of Kilcronaghan, Co. Derry, was educated at University of Glasgow and upon returning to Ireland was licenced to preach by the Tyrone Presbytery. Having led a party of insurgents to Maghera, Co. Derry, he was arrested and sentenced to receive 800 lashes and to be transported abroad, however this was reduced to self-exile to America. He joined the Caldwell family of Ballymoney aboard the *Peggy,* which set sail for New York on 3 May 1799. He relocated to Chester County in Pennsylvania, where in 1802 he gained his Naturalisation

Mr Charles Wallace, being charged with Treason & Sedition, got leave to transport himself to America, & is not now under the care of the Presbytery.

WALLACE, James – After participating in the 1798 Rebellion, Wallace was placed in the prison ship, the *Postlethwaite,* for his involvement. After providing securities, he was released to exile to the United States. It is unknown what happened him in the United States.

WALLACE, William - William Wallace had fled Ireland to the United States after the 1798 Rebellion but had returned in 1803 to assist in the Emmet uprising. He was arrested and placed in Carrickfergus Gaol.

WALSH, Thomas – Thomas Walsh, who fled to Newfoundland after the 1798 Rebellion, died in 1879. His obituary stated that *"he fought manfully for his country in 1798."*

WALTERS, John – An obituary from the Monaghan newspaper, *The People's Advocate* (March 1887) records the story of the exile, John Walters, who was born in Co. Monaghan on 17 March 1779. Walters died in Detroit, Michigan, on 2 March 1887.

"John Walters, a survivor of the Irish Rebellion of 1798, and said to be the oldest resident of Detroit, Michigan, died in that city on March 1st while being carried in an ambulance from the home of his son to St. Mary's hospital. Had he lived until the 17th of the present month he would have been 108 years old. About a year ago, he fell while dressing for Church, and fractured his right thigh, which injury was the ultimate cause of his death. Mr. Walters was born in County Monaghan, Ireland. He took an active part in the national affairs immediately preceding the Irish insurrection in the closing years of the century, and when the rebellion was crushed, he was obliged to flee the country, a reward of £100 having been proclaimed for his head. With three companions he put to sea from Dundalk Bay in an open boat, and after drifting about for four days, was picked up by a French vessel bound for America. The four patriots landed at Boston in December 1798. Mr. Walter's subsequently settled in Buck County, Pennsylvania, and engaged in farming. He was one of the contractors for the construction of the Pennsylvania Canal from Easton to Bristol, and accumulated a large property, most of which he lost in his old age. His wife died in 1858. Since 1873, he lived in Detroit with his son, G.W. Walters, the only surviving member of his family. His faculties were wonderfully well preserved up to a few months ago, and he was able to read an ordinary newspaper print without glasses. He was an inveterate smoker nearly all his life, and used liquor in moderate quantities. His politics were the old-fashioned Democratic sort. He was a serious practical Catholic and a regular attendant at St. Aloysius Church up to the time of his accident. May he rest in peace."

WARDEN, "Rev." David Bailie – David Bailie

Warden was born in 1772, at Ballycastle, Co. Down, to Robert Warden and Elizabeth Bailie. Warden, under the wishes of his parents, went to study at Glasgow University, where he excelled at theology, medicine and the arts. Having being awarded a BA, he accepted a probational license to preach in the Presbytery of Bangor, under the Rev. James Porter of Greyabbey. Like Porter, Warden also became a United Irishman, making him a target for the authorities.

On 7 June 1798, Warden self-appointed himself as a local commander to replace Rev. Steel Dickson, after the lack of action in the district. On the morning of 7 June he climbed Scrabo hill, only to find no rallying of the local United Irishmen. Warden attempted to rally the United Irishmen into action. On 9 June 1798, following the Battle of Saintfield, he led 300 rebels to attack Newtownards and established a Committee of Public Health. Warden became aide-de-camp to Henry Monro during the Battle of Ballynahinch. For his part in the insurrection, he was arrested and held in the dark confounds of the prison tender, *Postlethwaite*, in Belfast Lough, along with Rev. William Steel Dickson. Dickson later commented: "*Had it not been for the lively, rational, and entertaining conversation of Mr. David B. Warden…a poor probationer…whose father was a tenant to the Earl of Londonderry.*" After six weeks of such suffering, Warden agreed to self-exile to the United States and escaped the fate of Rev. Porter. However, the Presbytery of Bangor refused to supply Warden with his probationer credentials, thus making it hard for him to preach in the Presbyterian Church in America.

> Bangor Presb. report, That Mess.ᵗˢ Jaˢ Hull, John Miles & David Warden, lately Licentiates of their Presbytery, having been charged with being concerned in the Insurrection of June 1798 & not having stood their Tryals, but as they understand having sailed for America, are not to be considered as Probationers under their care. They farther

Upon settling in New York, Warden gave up preaching and became a teacher, becoming a principal at Columbia Academy in Kinderhook. In 1801, he became head tutor at Kingston Academy in Ulster County, New York. Warden tutored many children from some of America's leading families. In 1806, he accepted an appointment as Secretary of the American Legation in Paris, an offer sanctioned by President Thomas Jefferson and General Armstrong, the Minister Plenipotentiary of the U.S.A. In August 1811, Warden returned to Paris as Consul and represented U.S. trade interests. In December 1812, the U.S. Ambassador, Joel Barlow died. Warden arrogantly claimed the position onto himself, which provoked much anger in Washington D.C. On 10 June 1814, Warden was dismissed from office. Warden remained in Paris. He continued with academia and became a prolific author of political theories, and was awarded as a Member of the Academie des Sciences in Paris. Living a life on borderline poverty in Paris, Warden eventually passed away on 9 October 1845.

WARE, Hugh – Born on 19 January 1776, into a Catholic middle-class farming family that descended from Sir James Ware, Hugh Ware was native of Rathcoffey, Co. Kildare and held a high rank in the Kildare United Irishmen during the 1798 Rebellion. He was the son of land surveyor, Patrick Ware and Catherine O'Farrell. Throughout June and early July 1798, Ware was attached to the insurgents under his childhood friend, William Aylmer of Painstown, who established their camp on the boglands of Timahoe, Co. Kildare, striking at the northern Kildare towns of Maynooth and Kilcock to maintain supplies and to hamper local loyalist units. After the end of the Rebellion in Leinster by mid-July 1798, Ware surrendered on condition to Dublin Castle with the remaining leadership of the Kildare, Wicklow and Wexford insurgents and therefore became a State Prisoner. On 9 April 1802, Ware was released from Kilmainham Gaol on conditions of perpetual banishment and chose to reside in France, which was no longer at war with Britain, following the Treaty of Amiens.

Having spent several months preparing for his departure, Ware spent May of 1802 at Rathcoffey. He eventually sailed for France, disembarking at Dieppe in June 1802. Having arrived at Paris, Ware settled at 309, rue de Buci, Faubourg, St-Germain, near Paris. Ware would receive a lieutenancy in the Irish Legion and with his new friend and fellow exile, Miles Byrne of Monaseed, they turned down a carriage so they would walk from Paris to the regimental depot at Morlaix in Brittany, in order to physically prepare themselves. Ware would show tremendous valour throughout the various campaigns, particularly during the Peninsular War as captain of a company of grenadiers (1809-1813). For bravery at Astorga and Ciudad Rodrigo, he was promoted to *chef de bataillon*. Ware would succeed a badly wounded William Lawless to command the second battalion of the Irish Legion in August 1813, an intense period for the Irish Legion, as it became close to total obliteration. Ware would also receive a grapeshot wound to his head and his horse killed from below him, but would continue to fight. With the Irish Legion numerically shattered, Ware would lead the remnants during a 900km march back to Bois-le-Duc, constantly threatened by enemy Cossacks. For his gallantry, Ware was awarded with an honourary *Chevalier de Légion d'honneur*. Ware would

continue to serve Bonaparte's crumbling empire and on 14 January 1814, Ware led a successful sortie on British soldiers during the defence of Antwerp. When Napoleon was exiled to Elba, Colonel Ware retired from active service and settled at the city of Tours. After the July Revolution of 1830, he regained a colonelcy and formally retired on 5 November 1833, with a comfortable pension of 3725 francs per year. He returned to Tours and died on 5 March 1846.

WARNOCK, George – Warnock was a soap-boiler from Belfast and a United Irishman. After the Battle of Antrim, Warnock was arrested and questioned by John Pollock in which he revealed some information to the authorities but only enough to secure him from execution or transportation. He revealed that the two six-pounder brass cannons of the Belfast Blue Volunteer Company, that had been used by the Antrim insurgents, had originally been hidden in his cow-house, but he refused to disclose any names of his associates. Warnock was given permission to emigrate.

WARREN, Elizabeth & Family – In 1798, Elizabeth Warren was 11 years old. It's stated that Elizabeth was imprisoned twice in 1798 and was due to due to be burned by the insurgents however, she was saved by British soldiers. She and family eventually emigrated to Canada however, it is not known if they emigrated as a result of the rebellion.

WATT, Gawin – Watt had been a leading Belfast United Irishman. After the failure of the Antrim Rebellion, he met Mary Ann McCracken who was searching for her brother, Henry Joy McCracken, when he was in hiding in the Belfast hills. Watt took Mary Ann to Henry Joy's hiding place. In early July 1798, he was arrested at Carrickfergus and after his trial in April 1799, he placed in the hold of the prison ship the '*Postlethwaite*' in Belfast Lough, awaiting to be sent to New Geneva, in Co. Waterford.

TUESDAY, APRIL 16.

Courts-Martial commence fitting to-morrow the trial of such persons as may be brought before them.

The following persons were this day sent from Provot prison on board the Postlethwaite, and are be sent to Pruslia with the other Prisoners, now Duncannon Fort, viz. James Hunter, Gawn W James M'Caw, Alexander Finlay, Henry Flemi John Moffat, Hugh Devlin, David Bell, Benja Crockat, Thomas Dobson, and William Ellison Robert Robertson, also a prisoner, made his esc from the prison during the night.

Having originally been sentenced to serve the King of Prussia, Watt's sentence was reduced to voluntary banishment. He went like many to the United States.

WEIR, John – Weir was born in Co. Donegal on 4 May 1777. As a result of his involvement in the 1798 Rebellion, Weir fled Ireland and settled in Wilmington, Delaware, where he worked in a powder factory for fourteen years. In 1812, he married Jane Roney and volunteered for service in the U.S. Army during the War of 1812, in which he distinguished himself and reached the rank of captain. The Weir family moved to the rural area of Freeport in Armstrong County, Pennsylvania. Weir died on 28 February 1869.

WHITE, Dr. John Campbell – White was born at Templepatrick, Co. Antrim in 1757 to Lancashire native, Rev. Robert White and Jane Thompson. In his youth, White studied medicine in the University of Glasgow.

Having returned to Ireland, White became an apothecary in Belfast, and became noted by Martha McTier as a second level of physicians who *"may pick up a little money and no fame among the poorer sort."* Around 1801, White, who had played a role in the United Irishmen, fled to Baltimore, in Maryland, with his wife, Elizabeth Getty White and children. The White family who emigrated to the United

States included: Robert White (1780-1847), William James White (1784-1809), Thomas Brown White (1827-1825), Patrick Campbell White (1787-1859), Ann White (1789-1810), Joseph White (1791-1867), John White (1792-1862), Henry White (1794-1882), Stevenson White (1797-1826) and Decimus White (1800-1826). In 1803, he founded and became first President of the Baltimore Benevolent Hibernian Society and a founder and trustee of Baltimore College. Having trading experience from his time in Belfast, White also established a mercantile house, '*John White Campbell & Sons*' and also established a distillery. On 13 August 1816, he gifted Thomas Jefferson with melon seeds, which originated from Persia, that his sons had procured from Sir Gore Ousley. Having fulfilled a successful medical and business career, White died in Baltimore on 16 July 1847.

White's grandson, William Pickney Whyte (1824-1908, *pictured right*), a Democrat Senator, would become Attorney-General of Baltimore (1887-1891). Another descendent, Henry White (*pictured left*) would become U.S. Ambassador to France and a signatory of the Treaty of Versailles in 1919. He was deemed by Presidents, Theodore Roosevelt and Woodrow Wilson as one of the most effective foreign diplomats in U.S. history. The family also married into the family of Marcus McCausland who had settled in Baltimore and was from a large land owing family in Limavady.

WILSON, Hugh –
Wilson was born on 10 July 1772 into a financially comfortable family in Belfast. He was educated in the classics but refused to follow his father into the medical profession. Instead, he found employment at the mercantile house in Dublin before settling with a banking clerk role with the National Bank of Ireland. In 1797, having already joined the United Irishmen, Wilson moved to Cork to work at the banking house of Messrs. Thomas Roberts & Co; a role which supplied Wilson with a decent income. Whilst in Cork, he maintained correspondence with his United Irish friends in Dublin, including Oliver Bond. When Bond's house was raided on 12 March 1798, the authorities found this correspondence, thus marking Wilson as an associate. Having been arrested, Wilson was conveyed to Dublin Castle for questioning, upon which he refused to surrender any knowledge to the interrogation from a childhood acquaintance, the Chief-Secretary, Lord Castlereagh. It was within the Castle that Wilson was incarcerated for most of the hot summer of 1798, during which he sometimes received cruel treatment from the guards. Wilson was sent to the comforts of Fort George in Scotland and would remain there until 1802. After the Treaty of Amiens, he was sent to the continent and travelled with Thomas Addis Emmet to Hamburg. The party travelled to Amsterdam, where they met Robert Emmet. Low on funds, Wilson and the youngest Emmet travelled by foot to Paris. Fearing being destitute,

Wilson continued on foot across France to Bordeaux, where he found employment in the mercantile house of McCarthy Freres. He left France for the USA in 1805 and sailed to Charleston, South Carolina, and immediately established himself as a merchant between New Orleans (*pictured*) and the Caribbean ports of Havana, San Domingo and Martinique. His business flourished immensely and he often revisited Europe on such business trips. In September 1815, he married Ann Colbiornssen, whilst trading in Copenhagen. Having gained much wealth, Wilson and his wife settled on the Virgin Island of St. Croix and continued to trade with the United States. On 14 July 1829, whilst on business, Wilson died at his residence at New Haven, Connecticut. His obituary in the *Connecticut Herald* (21 July 1829) stated:

"*DIED: in this city, on Tuesday last, Mr. Hugh Wilson, aged 59, a native of Ireland, and for many years past a resident of the island of St. Croix.*"

WILSON, Thomas, Dr. –

Thomas Wilson of Ballyclare, Co. Down, studied medicine at the University of Edinburgh and upon completing his studies, he returned home to live in Newtownards, Co. Down. He became Secretary of the Ards Reform Club, a member of the Belfast Reading Society and member of the Committee of Public Safety which was set up in the midst of the Rebellion. Wilson was arrested and sentenced by court-martial to transportation, however this was reduced to banishment to the United States. In 1802, Wilson and his wife were permitted to return to Ireland on the account of his research before the rebellion and settled at Magherafelt, Co. Derry.

WITHERSPOON, James –

Witherspoon was born in 1755 in Belfast. His family were members of the Knockbracken Reformed Presbyterian Church. Witherspoon, a weaver by trade also served the church as a clerk. Like many of the Knockbracken congregation he had joined the United Irishmen and participated at the Battle of Ballynahinch. It is unknown what happened to James immediately after crackdown on the Down insurgency but it seems he evaded the authorities. In the summer of 1803, Witherspoon played a minor role in the Emmet uprising and was to interact with Thomas Russell and James Hope in encouraging another insurrection in Down. This would not materialise. After the failure of Emmet's uprising, Witherspoon was arrested and spent periods of incarceration in Dublin and Downpatrick Gaol. Having given assurances, Witherspoon and his sons, **John Witherspoon** and **James Witherspoon Jr**, gave assurances that they would leave Ireland forever and sail to the United States, arriving in New York City in 1804. James Witherspoon died at his residence, 212 Bowery Lane, on 19 February 1812 and was buried at Green–Wood Cemetery in Brooklyn.

WOODS, William – Woods and his brother (unnamed) emigrated to the United States in 1798, settling in Westmoreland County, Pennsylvania. He married Eizabeth Davidson and relocated to North Beaver Township in Lawrence County (PA).

WRIGHT, Joseph – Joseph Wright was a resident of Dublin City when he became involved in some capacity in the 1798 Rebellion. He fled to Baltimore, Maryland, with his young family, with some of his children later settling in Ohio.

WYLDE, Thomas – Wylde was the English born son of cotton manufacturer, Henry Wylde, who had established a factory in the village of Prosperous, Co. Kildare, in the 1780s. Henry Wylde had smuggled arms to America during the War of Independence (1775-1783) and had been acquainted with Dr. Benjamin Franklin. The village of Prosperous suffered economically in the mid-1790s, thus producing an agitated local population. This anger was unleased at 2am on the morning of 24 May 1798, when the insurgents destroyed a garrison of Cork City Militia, under the ruthless pitch-capper Captain Swayne and a detachment of Ancient Briton fencibles. Along with John Esmonde of Osberststown, Thomas Wylde was one of the principal leaders of this attack. In October 1798, Wylde was arrested and tried for the murder of Swayne. Having

experienced nearly two years imprisonment before being tried, Wylde was eventually acquitted and joined his father at his new cotton enterprise in Dublin's Cork Street. During Robert Emmet's plans for insurrection, Wylde and his brother-in-law's, Michael Quigley and John Mahon, were tasked with gauging the appetite towards insurrection from their old compatriots in Co. Kildare. On the eve of Emmet's uprising, Wylde and Mahon further stressed their observations claiming the county was ripe for revolution. On 23 July 1803, when few Kildare men came to Dublin, Emmet was accused by the leadership for deception. When the insurrection failed, Wylde fled to Butterfield House with Emmet, the Parrott Brothers, Michael Quigley and other conspirators. He fled into hiding for several months. On 12 December 1803, whilst hiding in a windmill near Philipstown, King's County (Tullamore, Co. Offaly), Wylde and Mahon were surrounded and upon being nearly caught, they fatally wounded Captain Charles Dodgson of the Fourth Dragoons.

Knowing certain execution awaited them, Wylde and Mahon organised a boat passage to the United States and fled from Ireland. After Wylde arrived at New York, he settled back into cotton manufacturing and resided at the corner of Cross Street and Mulberry Street in Manhattan. He died on Tuesday, 19 January 1813, aged 38 years.

WYLIE, Rev Samuel Brown – (1773-1852)

Samuel Brown Wylie was born in Co. Antrim, on 21 May 1773. He was educated at the University of Glasgow, where he distinguished himself as a scholar, and graduated with a Master of Arts in 1797.

Having begun teaching in Ballymena, Wylie was compelled to flee from his native land in consequence of his connection with the efforts in favour of Irish independence. He emigrated to America, in October, 1797, settling in Philadelphia. In 1798, he was appointed a Tutor in the University of Pennsylvania and studied theology privately, and under the direction of the Rev. William Gibson, becoming licensed by the Reformed Presbytery, at Coldenham, New York on 24 June 1799. He was ordained *sine titulo* by the Reformed Presbytery, at Ryegate, Vermont on 25 June 1800, and was the first Covenanter minister ordained in America. A sincere abolitionist, Wylie accompanied the Rev. James McKinney on a mission throughout the Southern States to abolish slavery from the pale of the Covenanter Church. At Rocky Creek in South Carolina, they succeeded in influencing Covenanters to voluntarily free their slaves to the value of 3000 guineas.

> **WYLIE, SAMUEL BROWN,** M.A. 1797.
>   Teacher in (1) Ballymena, Ireland, (2) Cheltenham, Pa., 1797-98; Tutor in University of Pennsylvania, 1798; subsequently established a Private Academy; Pastor of the First Reformed Presbyterian Church of Philadelphia, 1802-52; Professor in the Theological Seminary of the R.P. Church, 1809-51; Professor of Languages in University of Philadelphia, 1828-45; Vice-Provost thereof, 1838-45; D.D. (Dickinson) 1816; born at Moylarg, Co. Antrim, 21st May, 1773; died at Philadelphia, 14th October, 1852.

Wylie preached for some time in newly organized societies of Philadelphia and Baltimore. In November 1803, he was installed pastor of the Philadelphia congregation. At the organisation of the Theological Seminary in Philadelphia, he was appointed as a professor, and remained in the role from 1810 until his resignation in 1817. He was re-elected, and served from 1823 until he resigned in 1828. His most noted publication, *"The Two Sons of Oil,"* first published in 1803, was lauded as the best presentation of the position of the Covenanter

Church in America. Additionally, his sermon on the "Obligation of Covenants," sets forth in clearest terms the old doctrine of the Covenanters. Rev. Wylie died, at his residence in Philadelphia on 13 October 1852.

FINIS

APPENDIX 1 – Understanding that not all exiles have been collected, we have still decided to highlight the breakdown of county percentages as shown.

COUNTY PERCENTAGES %

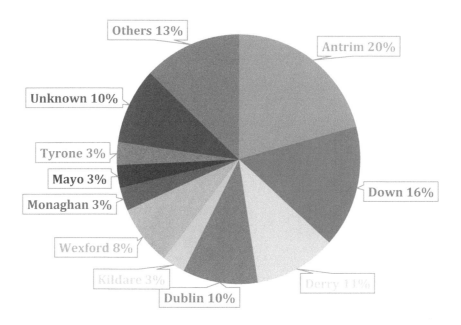

APPENDIX 2 – The complete list of those included in the Fugitive Bill, and Banishment Act, alphabetically arranged.

BANISHMENT ACT

Thomas Andoe,
Alexander Astley
William Aylmer
Edward Boyle
Thomas Brady
James Bushe
Patrick Byrne
Patrick Byrne
Garrett Byrne
Henry Banks
Peter Bannon

John Barrett
Denis Carthy
John Castles
John Chambers
John Comyn
Joseph Cormick
Peter Corcoran
Farrell Cuffe
George Cummings
Joseph Cuthbert
Richard Daly

Joseph Davis
Richard Dillon
Patrick Devine
John Dorney
Matthew Dowling
Michael Doyle
Thomas Dry
Thomas Addis Emmet
Hampden Evans
Andrew Farrell
Denis Farrell
Edward Fitzgerald
Michael Flood
James Geraghty
Robert Goodman
Rowland Goodman
John Greene
Laurence Griffin
James Haffey
Patrick Hanlon
John Harrison
William Houston
Edward Hudson
Peter Ivers
Henry Jackson
Morgan Kavanagh
Edward Cruikshank Keane
John Keenan
Lawrence Kelly
John Kennedy
John Gorman Kennedy
John Kinkead
John Kinselagh
John Lacey

George Lube
John Lynch
Patrick Lynch
William Putnam McCabe
Bryan McDermott
William James MacNeven
Patrick McCann
Christopher Martin
Patrick Madden
Francis Meagher
Israel Milliken
Patrick Mowney
Michael Mulhall
Samuel Neilson
Robert Neilson
Arthur O'Connor
Richard O'Reilly
Michael Quigley
Robert Redfern
John Reily
Thomas Reynolds
James Rose
Thomas Russell
John Sweetman
James Smith
William Sampson
Henry Speers
John Swing
James Ternan
Daniel Tolan
Hugh Ware
Hugh Wilson
John Young

FUGITIVE BILL

Rev. ? Adair, Comber, Down
Thomas Gunning Bashford Jr, Belfast
William Burke, Nenagh
James Burke, Co. Tipperary
Andrew Bryson, Newtownards
William Campbell *alias* McKeever
Patrick Cooke, Harmanstown, Dublin.
John Cormick, Dublin
William Cullen, Co. Wicklow
Michael Delaney, Co. Kildare

Valentine Derry, Dundalk
Thomas Dixon, Co. Wexford
Duckett, Killarney, Kerry
Miles Duignan, Grafton St, Dublin
Cornelius Egan, Carneybeg, Tipperary
Michael Fitzpatrick, Kilquade, Wicklow
Joseph Holt, Co. Wicklow
Dr. Thomas Houston, Belfast
James Hull, Bangor, Down
John Jackson, Dublin

Dr. James Jackson, Newtownards
James Kelly, Haggardstown, Louth
Matthew Kenna, Burtown, Co. Kildare
Bryan Keogh, Drummin, Co. Wicklow
Edward J. Lewins, Dublin
William Lawless, Dublin
Alexander Lowry, Co. Down
Anthony McCann, Co. Louth
Richard M'Cormick, Dublin
John M'Guire, Kilmullin, Wicklow
Arthur M'Mahon, Hollywood, Down
Rev. Mathew Miles, Moneymore, Derry
Harvey Morres, Co. Tipperary
Joseph Mouritz, Dundalk
James Neale, Newcastle, Co. Wicklow
John Nevin, Kilmoyle, Antrim
John O'Brien, Co. Tipperary
Edmund O'Finn, Cork
Joseph Orr, Derry
Robert Orr, Belfast
James Plunkett, Roscommon
Michael Reynolds, Naas, Kildare
Dean Swift, Dublin
John Scully, Newcastle, Wicklow
Miles Short, Co. Wicklow
Owen Short, Co. Wicklow
James Napper Tandy, Dublin
Bartholomew Teeling, Co. Armagh
Theobald Wolfe Tone, Dublin
Rev. James Townsend, Greyabbey
Samuel Turner

REFERENCES

NEWSPAPERS

(Robert Adrain) *Daily Herald*, 14 August 1843 (CT)

(Edward Barret) *The Gazette of the United States*, 5 August 1800 (PA).

(Blennerhasset) 'The Blennerhassets', *The Jeffersonian Democrat*, 11 January 1861 (OH)

(Blennerhasset) 'Mr. Burr's; United Irishman,' *Federal Gazette*, 12 January 1807 (MD)

(John Boyle) 'An Irish Exile Dead,' *Boston Evening Transcript*, 30 March 1849, (MA).

(Mary Harman Byrne) *The Bedford Gazette*, 13 July 1860 (PA).

(Patrick Byrne) *New York Gazette and General Advertiser*, 25 February 1814 (NY).

(Patrick Byrne) *Boston Pilot*, 21 July 1866 (MA).

(Patrick Byrne) *Boston Pilot*, 4 August 1866 (MA).

(William Byrne) *American and Commercial Daily Advertiser*, 21 December 1805 (MD)

(John Caldwell) *Irish American*, 2 August 1851 (NY)

(Cannon) *The American Citizen*, 30 November 1864 (PA).

(John Cormick) *The Daily Crescent*, 21 March 1851 (LA).

(Dr. John Cox) *The Southern Clarion*, 21 October 1831 (MS).

(John Cronly) *New York Freeman's Journal and Catholic Register*, 20 August 1842 (NY).

(John B. Cumming) *Charleston Courier*, 25 July 1842 (SC).

(Hans Denniston) *Evening Post*, 17 June 1837 (NY).

(John Devereux) *Alexandria Herald*, 16 March 1812 (VA).

(George Dobbin) *The Shamrock*, 7 December 1811 (NY).

(James Douglas) *Alexandria Gazette*, 18 February 1895

(John Driscoll) *The Shamrock*, 25 January 1817 (NY).

(Innes Duncan) *The Evening Bulletin*, 11 June 1892 (KY).

(James Finlay) *The Shamrock*, 30 November 1811 (NY).

(Jeremiah Fitzhenry) *The National Gazette and Literary Register*, 28 July 1829 (PA)

(Bernard Gallagher) *Seattle Post-Intelligence*, 29 June 1894 (WA).

(Guager Gregg) Washington Review and Examiner, 30 August 1823 (D.C.)

(Nicholas Harper) *Newark Daily Advertiser*, 31 January 1843 (NJ).

(George Hore) *New England Palladium*, 3 September 1819 (MA).

(Edward Hudson) *Boston Pilot*, 4 August 1866 (MA).

(Thomas Keegan) *'Death of an Aged Irishman,'* Sacramento Daily Record-Union, 29 March 1889.

(Edward Lennon) *The Maryville Times*, 4 March 1891 (TN).

(Thomas Logan) *The Columbian*, 7 July 1812 (NY).

(John Mahon) *Manufacturers' and Farmers' Journal*, 4 September 1820 (Rhode Island).

(Denis McCarthy) *The Irish American*, 21 March 1857 (NY).

(Alex McDougal) *The Watertown Republican*, 3 August 1881.

(McKinley) *Abilene Weekly Reflector*, 16 July 1896 (KA).

(Thomas Monks) 'United Irishman,' *The Gazette of the United States*, 28 June 1800 (PA).

(John Morrison) *Boston Semi-Weekly Advertiser*, 28 June 1843, (MA)

(Andrew Murphy) *The Pittsfield Sun*, 29 June 1843 (MA

(William Murphy) 'Irish Millionaires,' *New York Freeman's Journal and Catholic Register*, 27 October 1849 (NY).

(Daniel O'Brien) *The Democratic Advocate*, 29 January 1881 (MD)
(James O'Toole) 'The Oldest Man,' *White Cloud Kansas Chief*, 10 September 1857 (KA)
(Mary O'Toole) 'Death of an Aged Woman,' *The Democratic Advocate*, 29 August 1874 (MD)
(Michael Powers) 'Execution of Powers,' *Hillsboro' Telegraph*, 3 June 1820 (NH).
(Michael Powers) 'Michael Powers,' *Berks and Schuylkill Journal*, 3 June 1820 (PA).
(Thomas Reynolds) *The Shamrock*, 26 October 1811 (NY).
(Connar Ryan) *The Agassiz Record*, 25 March 1893 (British Columbia)
(Scott) 'Scott the Diver,' *The Commercial Advertiser*, 13 March 1841 (NY).
(Matthew Scott) *The Shamrock*, 15 August 1812 (NY).
(Hugh Ware) *Boston Pilot*, 25 April 1846 (MA).
(Hugh Wilson) *The Connecticut Herald*, 21 July 1829 (CT).
(Thomas Wylde) *The Shamrock*, 23 January 1813 (NY).

PRINTED PRIMARY SOURCES

Binns, J., *Recollections of the Life of John Binns*, Philadelphia, 1854.
Mrs. Byrne (ed.), *Memoirs of Miles Byrne*, Paris, 1863.
Cloney, T., *A Personal Narrative of those Transactions in the County Wexford in which the Author was engaged, during the awful period of 1798*, Dublin, 1832.
Cullen, L. *Wexford and Wicklow Insurgents of 1798*, Enniscorthy, 1959.
MacNeven, W.J., *"Pieces of Irish History…*, New York, 1807.
O'Kelly, P., *General History of the Rebellion of 1798…*, Dublin, 1842.
Sampson, W., *Memoirs of William Sampson, an Irish Exile*, London, 1832.

BIBLIOGRAPHY

Adams, A.N., *A History of the town of Fair Haven, Vermont: in three parts*, Fair Haven, 1870.

Atwater, S., *History of the City of Minneapolis, Minnesota, New York*, Munsell, 1893.

Barrett, W., *The old Merchants of New York City*, New York, 1866.

Barrows, F.I., *History of Fayette County, Indiana: her People, Industries and Institutions*, Indianapolis, 1917.

Baskin, O.L., et.al, *History of Delaware County and Ohio*, Chicago, 1880.

Beiner, G., *Remembering the Year of the French: Irish Folk History and Social Memory*, Madison, 2009.

Beiner, G., *Forgetful Remembrance: Social Forgetting and Vernacular Historiography of a Rebellion in Ulster*, Oxford, 2018.

The Biographical Encyclopedia of Ohio, Cincinnati, 1876.

Biographical, Genealogical and descriptive History of the First Congressional District of New Jersey, New York, 1900.

Biographical Record of Ogle County, Illinois, Chicago, 1899.

Biographical Sketches of the Leading Men of Chicago, Chicago, 1868.

Book of Biographies: The Volume contains Biographical Sketches of Leading Citizens of Lawrence County, Pennsylvania, Buffalo, 1897.

Barrows, F.I., *History of Fayette County, Indiana: Her People, Industries and Institutions*, Indianapolis, 1917.

Boyd, S.L. and Gottschalk, K.C., *The Parrish Family, including the allied families of Belt, Boyd, Cole and Malone, Clokey, Garrett, Merryman, Parsons, Price, Tipton…*Santa Barbara, 1935.

Brink, W.R & Co., *History of Madison County, Illinois…*, Edwardsville, 1882.

Bruce, P.A, et.al., *History of Virginia*, New York, 1924.

Chambers, L., *Rebellion in Kildare 1790-1803*, Dublin, 1998.

Conard, H.L., *Encyclopedia of the History of Missouri*, New York, 1901.

Connor, R.D.W, et al., *History of North Carolina*, Chicago, 1919.

Cook, A.M.G., *History of Baldwin County, Georgia*, Anderson, 1925.

Coughlan, R.J., *Napper Tandy*, Dublin, 1977.

Courtney, R., *Dissenting Voices: Rediscovering the Irish Progressive Presbyterian Tradition*, Belfast, 2014.

Cullen, S, et.al. *Fugitive Warfare: 1798 in North Kildare*, Clane, 1998.

Cutter, W.R., *Genealogical and Family History of Southern New York and the Hudson River Valley*, New York, 1913.

Dawson, K.L., *The Belfast Jacobin: Samuel Neilson and the United Irishmen*, Dublin, 2017.

Dickson, C., *Revolt in the North, Antrim and Down in 1798*, 2nd edn, London, 1997.

Douglas, D. *The Only Safe Place: The Irish State Prisoners at Fort George*, Perth, n.d.

Doyle, D.N., *Ireland, Irishmen and Revolutionary America 1760-1820*, Dublin, 1981.

Du Bois, W.E., *A Record of the families of Robert Patterson (the Elder), emigrant from Ireland to America; 1774; Thomas Ewing, from Ireland, 1718; and Louis Du Bois, from France, 1660*, Philadelphia, 1847.

Dupuy, C.M., *A Genealogical History of the Dupuy Family*, Salt Lake City, 1984.

Durant, S.W., *History of Lawrence County, Pennsylvania*, Philadelphia, 1877.

Durant, S.W., *History of Oneida County, New York*, Philadelphia, 1878.

Durey. M., *Transatlantic Radicals and the Early American Republic,* Kansas, 1997.

Durey, M (ed.), *Andrew Bryson's Ordeal. An Epilogue to the 1798 Rebellion*, Cork, 1998.

Dwight, B.W., *The History of the Descendants of John Dwight, of Dedham, Massachusetts*, New York, 1874.

Elliott, M., *Partners in Revolution: The United Irishmen and France*, New Haven, 1990.

Ellis, F. and Evans, S., *History of Lancaster County, Pennsylvania: with biographical sketches of many of its pioneers and prominent men*, Philadelphia, 1883.

Fanning, T., *Paisanos: The Irish and the Liberation of Latin America*, Gill Books, 2016.

Gahan, D., *The People's Rising: Wexford 1798*, Dublin, 1995.

Gahan, D., *Rebellion! Ireland in 1798*, Dublin, 1997.

Gallaher, J.G., *Napoleon's Irish Legion*, Southern Illinois University Press, 1993.

Gilmore, P., Parkhill, T., and Roulston, W., *Exiles of '98: Ulster Presbyterians and the United States*, Belfast, 2018.

Gilmore, P., *Irish Presbyterians and the Shaping of Western Pennsylvania, 1770-1830*, University of Pittsburgh Press, 2018.

Gleeson, D.T., *The Irish in the South, 1815-1877*, Chapel Hill, 2002.

Gleeson, D.T., *The Green and the Gray: The Irish in the Confederate States of America*, Chapel Hill, 2013.

Gowdy, M.M., *A Family History comprising the surnames of Gade, Gadie, Gaudie, Gawdie, Gawdy, Gowdy, Goudy, Goudey, Gowdey…* Lewiston, 1919.

Gresham, J.M. (ed.), *Biographical and Historical Souvenir for the Counties of Clark, Crawford, Harrison, Floyd, Jefferson, Jennings, Scott, and Washington, Indiana*, Chicago, 1889.

Griffin, W.D., *The Irish Americans*, New York, 2006.

Gurley, A.E., *The History and Genealogy of the Gurley Family*, Hartford, 1897.

Gurley, L.B. *Memoir of Rev. William Gurley*, Cincinnati, 1854.

Hall, T.J., *The Hall Family of West River and Kindred Families*, Denton, 1941.

Hames, J.H., *Arthur O'Connor, United Irishman*, Cork, 2001.

Harvey, C.B., *Genealogical History of Hudson and Bergen Counties, New Jersey*, New York, 1900.

Haycraft, S., *A History of Elizabethtown, Kentucky, and its surroundings*, Elizabethtown, 1921.

Hayes, R., *The Last Invasion of Ireland: When Connacht Rose*, 2nd edn, Dublin, 1939.

Hill, M., Turner, B., and Dawson, K. (eds.), *1798 Rebellion in County Down*, Newtownards, 1998.

History of Butler County, Pennsylvania, Chicago, 1895.

History of Tennessee from the Earliest Time to the Present…, Nashville, 1886.

Hunter, C.L., *Sketches of Western North Carolina, Historical and Biographical*, Raleigh, 1877.

Hyde, W. and Conrad, H.L., *Encyclopedia of the History of St. Louis*, New York, 1899.

4

Jordan, J.W., *Colonial and Revolutionary Families of Pennsylvania: Genealogical and Personal Memoirs*,

Jordan, J.W. and Hadden, J., *Genealogical and Personal History of Fayette County, Pennsylvania*, New York, 1912.

Jordan, J.W., *A History of Delaware County, Pennsylvania, and its people*, New York, 1914.

Jordan, J.W. (ed.), *Genealogical and Personal History of Beaver County, Pennsylvania*, New York, 1914.

Jordan, J.W., *Genealogical and Personal History of Western Pennsylvania*, New York, 1915.

Keogh, D. and Furlong, N. (ed.), *The Mighty Wave: The 1798 Rebellion in Wexford*, Dublin, 1996.

Latimer, W.T. "David Bailie Warden, Patriot 1798," *Ulster Journal of Archaeology*, vol 23, 1907, pp. 29-38.

Macdougall, J.L., *History of Inverness County, Nova Scotia*, Ontario, 1972.

MacSuibhne, P., *Kildare in '98*, Naas, 1978.

McAllister, A.H.T., 'The Romantic Life of Thomas Trenor: Treasurer of the Society of United Irishmen,' *Overland Monthly and Out West Magazine*, vol 32, issue 188, 1898, pp.130-136.
McCracken, S., *The Presbyterians of Magilligan: Heritage Guide 1600-1900*, Antrim, 2019.

McCracken, S., *The Battle of Antrim: The Story of 1798*, Antrim, 2020.

McGarry, S., *Irish Brigades Abroad: From the Wild Geese to the Napoleonic Wars*, Dublin, 2014.

McNeill, M., *The Life and Times of Mary Ann McCracken, 1770-1866: A Belfast Panorama*, 2nd edn, Newbridge, 2019.

Madden, R.R., *The United Irishmen: Their Lives and Times*. 2nd edn. 4 vols. Dublin, 1858,

Meagher, T.J., *The Columbia Guide to Irish American History*, New York, 2005.

Memorial Record of the Counties of Delaware, Union and Morrow, Ohio, Salem, 1895.

Memoirs of Georgia, Atlanta, 1895.

Mercer, J.K. *Representative Men of Ohio 1896-97*, Columbus, 1896.

Miller, E. and Wells, F.P., *History of Ryegate, Vermont*, Salem, 1987.

Miller, K.A., *Emigrants and Exiles: Ireland and the Irish Exodus to North America*, New York, 1988.

Miller, K.A. et al., *Irish Immigrants in the Land of Canaan: Letters and Memoirs from Colonial and Revolutionary America 1675-1815*, New York, 2003.

Mitchell, A., *South Carolina Irish*, Charleston, 2011.

Montgomery, D.B., *A Genealogical History of the Montgomerys and their descendants*, Owensville, 1903.

Montgomery, J., *Medical Society of Franklin County: its history and sketches of early practitioners of the County*, Chambersburg, 1892.

Mullin, T.H., *Coleraine in Georgian Times*, Coleraine, 1977.

Mulloy, S, (ed.) *Victory or Glorious Defeat: Biographies of Participants in the Mayo Rebellion of 1798*, Dublin, 2010.

Newsinger, N. (ed.) *United Irishman: The Autobiography of James Hope*, London, 2001.

O'Brien, M.J., *Irish Pioneers in Kentucky: A series of articles published in the Gaelic American*, Louisville, 1916.

O'Donnell, R., *The Rebellion in Wicklow, 1798*, Dublin, 1998.

O'Donnell, R., *Aftermath: Post-Rebellion Insurgency in Wicklow 1799-1803*, Dublin, 2000.

O'Donnell, R., *Robert Emmet and the 1798 Rebellion*, Dublin, 2003.

O'Donnell, R., *Robert Emmet and the Rising of 1803*, Dublin, 2003.

O'Grady, B., *Exiles and Islanders: The Irish Settlers of Prince Edward Island*, Montreal, 2004.

Old Ballymena: from 'Walks about Ballymena,' in the Ballymena Observer, Ballymena, 1998.

Packenham, T., *The Year of Liberty*, London, 1972.

Patten, J.M., *History of the Somonauk United Presbyterian Church near Sandwich, De Kalb County, Illinois*, Chicago, 1928.

Perrin, W.H., *History of Crawford and Clark Counties, Illinois*, Chicago, 1883.

Pictorial and Genealogical Record of Greene County, Missouri, Chicago, 1893.

Portrait and Biographical album of DeKalb County, Illinois, Chicago, 1885.

Portrait and Biographical Record of Seneca and Schuyler Counties, New York, Chicago, 1895.

Powell, W.H., *Officers of the Army and Navy (volunteer) who served in the Civil War*, Philadelphia, 1893.

Power, J.C. and Power, S.A., *History of the Early Settlers of Sangamon County, Illinois*, Berwyn Heights, 1876.

Punch, T., *Erin's Sons: Irish Arrivals in Atlantic Canada, 1761-1853*, Baltimore, 2008.

Records of the General Synod of Ulster, from 1691 to 1820, Belfast, 1890-98.

Robinson, K., *North Down and Ards in 1798*, Bangor, 1998.

Rowland, E., *Varina Howell: Wife of Jefferson Davis*, Gretna, 1998.

Ruttenber, E.M., *City of Newburgh: A Centennial Historical Sketch*, Newburgh, 1876.

Ruttenber, E.M, and Clark, L.H., *History of Orange County, New York*, Philadelphia, 1881.

Schenck, J.S. (ed.), *History of Warren County, Pennsylvania*, Syracuse, 1887.

Shepherd, H.E., *History of Baltimore, Maryland, from its current founding as a town to the current year, 1729-1898*, Uniontown, 1898.

Sherrard, R.A., *The Sherrard Family of Steubenville*, Philadelphia, 1890.

Stewart, A.T.Q., *Summer Soldiers: The 1798 Rebellion in Antrim and Down*, Belfast, 1995.

Stewart, D., *The Seceders in Ireland, with Annals of Their Congregations*, Belfast, 1950.

Stout, T., *Montana: Its Story and Biography*, Chicago, 1921.

Swoope, R.D., *Twentieth Century History of Clearfield County, Pennsylvania and Representative Citizens*, Chicago, 1911.

Swope, G.E., *History of the Big Spring Presbyterian Church, Newville, Pa., 1737-1898*, Westminster, 2008.

Sylvester, N.B., *History of Saratoga County, New York*, Philadelphia, 1878.

Taylor, A., *The Civil War of 1812: American Citizens, British Subjects, Irish Rebels & Indian Allies*, New York, 2010.

Tenney, W.J., *The Military and Naval History of the Rebellion in the United States. With Biographical Sketches of Deceased Officers*, New York, 1865.

The Past and Present of Rock Island County, Illinois, Chicago, 1877.

The Patterson & Pattison Family Association: A contribution of various Patterson & Pattison Family Records, Minneapolis, 1963-67.

The United States Biographical Dictionary and Portrait Gallery of Eminent and Self-Made Men, New York, 1878.

Tillyard, S.L., *Citizen Lord: The Life of Edward Fitzgerald, Irish Revolutionary*, New York, 1999.

Waddell, J.A., *Annals of Augusta County, Virginia, from 1726 to 1871*, Staunton, 1902.

Warner, A (ed.), *History of Beaver County, Pennsylvania, Philadelphia*, 1888.

Weber, P., *On the Road to Rebellion: United Irishmen and Hamburg 1796-1803*, Dublin, 1997.

Wells, F.P., *History of Barnet, Vermont*, Burlington, 1923.

Whelan, F., *God Provoking Democrat – The Remarkable Life of Archibald Hamilton Rowan*, Dublin, 2015.

Whelan, F., *May Tyrants Tremble: The Life of William Drennan, 1754-1820*, Dublin, 2020.

White, J.G., *A Twentieth-Century History of Mercer County, Pennsylvania*, Chicago, 1909.

Whitney, W.A., *History and Biographical Record of Lenawee County, Michigan*, Michigan, 1879.

Whittemore, H., *History of Montclair Township, State of New Jersey*, New York, 1894.

Williams, T.J.C., *The History of Washington County, Maryland*, Chambersburg, 1906.

Wilson, D.S., *United Irishmen, United States: Immigrant Radicals in Early Republic*, 2011.

Young, A.W., *History of Chautauqua County, New York*, Buffalo, 1875.

Young, R.M., *Ulster in '98: Episodes & Anecdotes*, n.d.

ELECTRONIC JOURNALS

Bric, M.J. "The American Society of United Irishmen." *Irish Journal of American Studies*, vol. 7, 1998, pp. 163–177. *JSTOR*, www.jstor.org/stable/30002412. Accessed 28 Dec. 2020.

Brown, Lindsay T. "The Presbyterian Dilemma: A Survey of the Presbyterians and Politics In Counties Cavan and Monaghan over Three Hundred Years: Part II of a Series on The Monaghan Presbyterians." *Clogher Record*, vol. 15, no. 2, 1995, pp. 30–68. JSTOR, www.jstor.org/stable/27699389. Accessed 18 Dec. 2020.

Brundage, D. "Matilda Tone in America: Exile, Gender, and Memory in the Making of Irish Republican Nationalism." *New Hibernia Review / Iris Éireannach Nua*, vol. 14, no. 1, 2010, pp. 96–111. *JSTOR*, www.jstor.org/stable/25660948. Accessed 27 Feb. 2021.

Byrne, C.J. "The United Irish Rising of 1798 and the Fencibles' Mutiny in St. John's, 1800." *An Nasc*, vol.11, no.4, 1998, pp.15-23.

Coolidge, J. L. "Robert Adrain and the Beginnings of American Mathematics." *The American Mathematical Monthly*, vol. 33, no. 2, 1926, pp. 61–76. *JSTOR*, www.jstor.org/stable/2300067. Accessed 19 Dec. 2020.

Davidson, M.A., and Murphy, H. "Samuel Sparrow's Repentance for His Rebel Role in '98." *The Past: The Organ of the Uí Cinsealaigh Historical Society*, no. 28, 2007, pp. 78–86. *JSTOR*, www.jstor.org/stable/25520135. Accessed 19 Mar. 2021.

Dunne-Lynch, N. "Joseph Parrott (1781-1834): A Kildare '98 Rebel in the Service of France." *Journal of the County Kildare Archaeological Society and Surrounding Districts*, vol. 20, no. 4, 2014-15, pp. 118-147. *Academia*, www.academia.edu/22330012. Accessed 29 Dec. 2020.

Farrell, W. E. "Andrew Jackson 7th President of the United States and the Jacksons Of Ballybay 1803-1824." *Clogher Record*, vol. 19, no. 2/3, 2007, pp. 202–238. *JSTOR*, www.jstor.org/stable/27699566. Accessed 01 Mar. 2021.

Ingham, G. R. "IRISH REBEL, AMERICAN PATRIOT: WILLIAM JAMES MacNEVEN." *History Ireland*, vol. 23, no. 5, 2015, pp. 16–18. *JSTOR*, www.jstor.org/stable/43556414. Accessed 12 Feb. 2021.

Kavanagh, M., "Fr. Mogue Kearns, A Rebel Priest in 1798." *Carloviana -Journal of the Old Carlow Society*, no.45, 1997, pp. 38-41. www.carlowhistorical.com.

Kelly, J. "OFFICIAL LIST OF RADICAL ACTIVISTS AND SUSPECTED ACTIVISTS INVOLVED IN EMMET'S REBELLION, 1803." *Analecta Hibernica*, no. 43, 2012, pp. 129–200. *JSTOR*, www.jstor.org/stable/23317181. Accessed 19 Mar. 2021.

Lambert, E. "Irish Soldiers in South America, 1818-30." *Studies: An Irish Quarterly Review*, vol.58, no.232, 1969, pp. 376-195. JSTOR, www.jstor.org/stable/30087890. Accessed 24 Dec 2020.

Landy, C. A. "Society of United Irishmen Revolutionary and New-York Manumission Society Lawyer: Thomas Addis Emmet and the Irish Contributions to the Antislavery Movement in New York." *New York History*, vol. 95, no. 2, 2014, pp. 193–222. *JSTOR*, www.jstor.org/stable/newyorkhist.95.2.193. Accessed 22 Dec. 2020.

Maher, M. "Oliver Bond." *Dublin Historical Record*, vol. 11, no. 4, 1950, pp. 97–115. *JSTOR*, www.jstor.org/stable/30080082. Accessed 04 Feb. 2021.

Manning, C. "Hervey Morres and the Montmorency Imposture.'" *History Ireland*, vol. 28, no. 2, 2020, pp. 22–25. *JSTOR*, www.jstor.org/stable/26915177. Accessed 02 Mar. 2021.

Markey, P. "Thomas Markey, United Irishman." *Journal of the County Louth Archaeological and Historical Society*, vol. 26, no. 4, 2008, pp. 595–598. *JSTOR*, www.jstor.org/stable/27730024. Accessed 17 Dec. 2020.

McEvoy, B. "The United Irishmen in Co. Tyrone." *Seanchas Ardmhacha: Journal of the Armagh Diocesan Historical Society*, vol. 3, no. 2, 1959, pp. 283–314. *JSTOR*, www.jstor.org/stable/29740693. Accessed 02 Jan. 2021.

McGarry, S. "NAPOLEON'S IRISH LEGION: THE LIFTING OF THE THREE-MONTH SIEGE OF ANTWERP IN MAY 1814 MARKED THE END OF A 125-YEAR-OLD TRADITION OF IRISH MILITARY SERVICE IN FRANCE." *History Ireland*, vol. 22, no. 5, 2014, pp. 24–27. *JSTOR*, www.jstor.org/stable/23850521. Accessed 21 Dec. 2020.

O'Grady, B. *Exiles and Islanders: The Irish Settlers of Prince Edward Island*. McGill-Queen's University Press, 2004. *JSTOR*, www.jstor.org/stable/j.ctt7ztq9. Accessed 22 Dec. 2020.

O'Hara, A. "'The Entire Island Is United: The Attempted United Irish Rising in Newfoundland, 1800." *History Ireland*, vol. 8, no. 1, 2000, pp. 18–21. *JSTOR*, www.jstor.org/stable/27724740. Accessed 31 Dec. 2020.

O'Sullivan, H. "The Background to and the Events of the Insurrection of 1798 in Dundalk and North Louth." *Journal of the County Louth Archaeological and Historical Society*, vol. 24, no. 2, 1998, pp. 165–195. *JSTOR*, www.jstor.org/stable/27729828. Accessed 18 Dec. 2020.

Parkhill, T. "The Wild Geese of 1798: Emigrés of the Rebellion." *Seanchas Ardmhacha: Journal of the Armagh Diocesan Historical Society*, vol. 19, no. 2, 2003, pp. 118–135. *JSTOR*, www.jstor.org/stable/25746923. Accessed 18 Dec. 2020.

Patterson, J. G. "Republicanism, Agrarianism and Banditry in the West of Ireland, 1798-1803." *Irish Historical Studies*, vol. 35, no. 137, 2006, pp. 17–39. *JSTOR*, www.jstor.org/stable/20547408. Accessed 26 Dec. 2020.
Johnston, J.S. "Sketch of Theodore O'Hara." *Register of Kentucky State Historical Society*, vol. 11, no. 33, 1913, pp. 65–72. *JSTOR*, www.jstor.org/stable/23367250. Accessed 06 Jan. 2021.

Quinn, James. "'The Dog That Didn't Bark': The North And 1803." *History Ireland*, vol. 11, no. 3, 2003, pp. 14–16. *JSTOR*, www.jstor.org/stable/27725035. Accessed 03 Feb. 2021.

Weber, P. "The United Irishmen & Hamburg." *History Ireland*, vol. 5, no. 3, 1997, pp. 26–30. *JSTOR*, www.jstor.org/stable/27724481. Accessed 28 Dec. 2020.

Woods, C. J. "Samuel Turner's Information on the United Irishmen, 1797-8." *Analecta Hibernica*, no. 42, 2011, pp. 181–227. *JSTOR*, www.jstor.org/stable/23317233. Accessed 20 Dec. 2020.

"John Glendy, of Maghera, Co. Derry, Presbyterian Minister and Patriot, 1798." *Ulster Journal of Archaeology*, vol. 13, no. 3, 1907, pp. 101–105. *JSTOR*, www.jstor.org/stable/20608633. Accessed 23 Dec. 2020.

WEBSITES

Déjardin, C. and Dunne-Lynch, N., 'James Smith of Leixlip: calico printer, United Irishman and veteran of Napoleon's Army' *David Skinner* [web blog], 30 June 2020, http://www.skinnerwallpaper.com/wordpress/?m=202006 (Accessed 11 January 2021).

Olsen, K. J., 'Aunt Flora Remembers the Irish Rebellion of 1798' *Journal of the American Revolution*, 27 September 2018, https://allthingsliberty.com/2018/09/aunt-flora-remembers-the-irish-rebellion-of-1798/

www.emmetry.org

www.humbertsfootsteps.wordpress.com

www.slideshare.net/magomick/in-humberts-footsteps

www.irishmeninparis.org (Accessed 17 January 2021)

www.mannioncollection.ca (Accessed 30 December 2020)

www.lompochistory.org/wp-content/uploads/2017/02/legacy-43.pdf (Accessed 29 December 2020) – *Notes related to Theophilus McClure*.

The Irish-Australian Transportation Database (www.nationalarchives.ie).

The Irish Prison Registers 1796-1924 (www.findmypast.ie)

We found correspondence from various Irish exiles to President Jefferson and President Madison on the following source: https://founders.archive.gov

To support us on many of the biographies throughout the project, we used *Find A Grave*, *Ancestry*, *Irish Newspaper Archive*, *GenealogyBank* and *Findmypast*, which were all very helpful.

DICTIONARY OF IRISH BIOGRAPHY

Andrews, H. "Edward Hudson," *DIB*
Geoghegan, P.M. "Valentine Derry," *DIB*
Geoghegan, P.M, "Matthew 'Mat' Dowling (1756-1805)," *DIB*
Geoghegan, P.M. "John Glendy," *DIB*
Geoghegan, P.M. "Hervey Montmorency Morres," *DIB*
Geoghegan, P.M. "David Bailie Warden," *DIB*
Geoghegan, P.M. "Samuel Brown Wylie (1773-1852)," *DIB*
Hourican, B. "Alexander Porter," *DIB*
Kelly, J. "Arthur O'Connor," *DIB*
Long, P. "Edward Fitzgerald (c1770-1807)," *DIB*
Lunney, L. "Robert Adrain (1775-1843)," *DIB*
Maguire, W.A, and McCabe, J. "William Putnam McCabe," *DIB*
Maguire, W.A. "John Tennent," *DIB*
McCabe, D. "George Lube (Looby)," *DIB*
McCabe, D. "John Swiney," *DIB*

Murphy, D. "William Lawless (c1764-1824)," *DIB*

Murphy, D, and Kleinman, S. "Edmund O'Finn." *DIB*

Murphy, M. "Nicholas Devereux," *DIB*

O'Brien, G. "Samuel Neilson," *DIB*

O'Donnell, R, "Garret Byrne," *DIB*

O'Donnell, R, and Kleinman, S. "Miles Byrne (1780-1862)", *DIB*

Thuente, M.H. "William Sampson," *DIB*

Quinn, J. "John Binns (1772-1860)," *DIB*

Quinn, J. "Thomas Ledlie Birch," *DIB*

Quinn, J. "Thomas Corbet," *DIB*

Quinn, J. "William Corbet," *DIB*

Quinn, J. "John Devereux (1778?-1860)," *DIB*

Quinn, J. "William Dowdall," *DIB*

Richey, R. "Thomas Wylde," *DIB*

Quinn, J. "Thomas Addis Emmet," *DIB*

Whelan, K. "Lord Edward Fitzgerald (1763-1798)," *DIB*

Woods, C.J. "William Aylmer," *DIB*

Woods, C.J. "Patrick Byrne (1740/41-1814)," *DIB*

Woods, C.J. "James Joseph MacDonnell," *DIB*

Woods, C.J. "William James MacNeven (MacNevin)," *DIB*

Woods, C.J. "Richard McCormick," *DIB*

Woods, C.J. "Arthur McMahon (McMechan)," *DIB*

Woods, C.J. "Austin O'Malley," *DIB*

Woods, C.J. "James Reynolds (c.1765-1808)," *DIB*

Woods, C.J. "Archibald Hamilton Rowan," *DIB*

Woods, C.J. "John Sweetman (1751/2-1826)," *DIB*

Woods, C.J. "James Napper Tandy", *DIB*

Woods, C.J. "Matilda (Martha) Tone," *DIB*

Woods, C.J. "William Theobald Wolfe Tone (1791-1828)," *DIB*

Woods, C.J. "Hugh Ware," *DIB*

St. Paul's Church in Lower Manhattan, NYC. The church entrance is adorned with an obelisk on the south side, dedicated to Thomas Addis Emmet and a ornate column on its northern side, dedicated to W.J. MacNeven. The influence of the United Irishmen in early 19th Century America would clearly solidify a deep relationship between Ireland and the United States of America.

L - #0029 - 050722 - C286 - 229/152/16 - PB - DID3339140